To: Professor Slade

From: William

05/09/2011

Corporate Governance and the Global Financial Crisis

Over the last two decades there has been a notable increase in the number of corporate governance codes and principles, as well as a range of improvements in structures and mechanisms. Despite this, corporate governance failed to prevent a widespread default of fiduciary duties of corporate boards and managerial responsibilities in the finance industry, which contributed to the 2007–2010 global financial crisis. This book brings together leading scholars from North America, Europe, Asia-Pacific and the Middle East to provide fresh and critical analytical insights on the systemic failures of corporate governance linked to the global financial crisis. Contributors draw from a range of disciplines to demonstrate the severe limitations of the dominant corporate governance framework and its associated market-oriented approach. They provide suggestions on how the governance problems could be tackled to prevent or mitigate any future financial crisis and explore new directions for post-crisis corporate governance research and reforms.

WILLIAM SUN is Leader of the Corporate Governance and Sustainability Research Group (CGSRG) at Leeds Metropolitan University.

JIM STEWART is Running Stream Professor in Leadership and HRD and Director of the Human Resource Development and Leadership Research Unit at Leeds Metropolitan University.

DAVID POLLARD is Reader in Enterprise and Knowledge Management at Leeds Metropolitan University.

Corporate Governance and the Global Financial Crisis

International Perspectives

Edited by

WILLIAM SUN, JIM STEWART AND
DAVID POLLARD

CAMBRIDGE
UNIVERSITY PRESS

CAMBRIDGE UNIVERSITY PRESS
Cambridge, New York, Melbourne, Madrid, Cape Town,
Singapore, São Paulo, Delhi, Tokyo, Mexico City

Cambridge University Press
The Edinburgh Building, Cambridge CB2 8RU, UK

Published in the United States of America by
Cambridge University Press, New York

www.cambridge.org
Information on this title: www.cambridge.org/9781107001879

© Cambridge University Press 2011

First published 2011

Printed in the United Kingdom at the University Press, Cambridge

A catalogue record for this publication is available from the British Library

Library of Congress Cataloging-in-Publication Data

Corporate governance and the global financial crisis: international perspectives / edited
by William Sun, Jim Stewart, David Pollard.
   p. cm.
  ISBN 978-1-107-00187-9 (Hardback)
  1. Corporate governance. 2. Global financial crisis, 2008–2009.
I. Sun, William, 1962– II. Stewart, Jim, 1952– III. Pollard, David, 1946–
IV. Title.
  HD2741.C7793 2011
  338.6–dc22

                   2011001067

ISBN 978-1-107-00187-9 Hardback

Contents

Figures

Tables

Contributors

ROGER BARKER is Head of Corporate Governance at the Institute of Directors, UK.

BLANAID CLARKE is Associate Professor of Corporate Law and Director of Research in the Law School at University College Dublin. She was one of the founding members of the Centre for Corporate Governance at University College Dublin and has been involved both at a national and international level in regulating takeovers.

THOMAS CLARKE is Professor of Management and Director of the Research Centre for Corporate Governance at the University of Technology, Sydney.

CHUNYAN LIU is a PhD programme student at the Graduate School of Economics, Kyushu University, Japan.

JIANLEI LIU is a PhD programme student at the Graduate School of Economics, Kyushu University, Japan.

JAY W. LORSCH is the Louis Kirstein Professor of Human Relations at the Harvard Business School, Harvard University, and currently Chairman of the Harvard Business School Global Corporate Governance Initiative and Faculty Chairman of the Executive Education Corporate Governance Series.

ROBERT A. G. MONKS is a pioneering shareholder activist and corporate governance adviser and an expert on retirement and pension plans. He is the author of *Corporate Governance* (WITH NELL MINOW), *Watching the Watchers*, *The New Global Investors* and *Corpocracy*, and was a founder of Institutional Shareholder Services, Lens Governance Advisers and The Corporate Library.

FLORIAN MÖSLEIN is Assistant Professor of Law at the University of St Gallen, Switzerland. He is also Senior Research Fellow at the Faculty of Law, Humboldt University of Berlin, Germany.

ROLAND PÉREZ is Professor Emeritus in Economics and Management at Université Montpellier I, France, and Chairman of the Scientific Committee of French Review for Corporate Governance (RFGE). He was Chairman of the International Research Network on Organizations and Sustainable Development (RIODD) (2007–9), and Chairman of the French Academy of Management (SFM) (2006).

DAVID POLLARD is Reader in Enterprise and Knowledge Management at Leeds Business School, Leeds Metropolitan University. He has held visiting professorships in China and is frequently invited to lecture or to provide research seminars for various universities abroad.

NASSER SAIDI is Executive Director of the Hawkamah Institute for Corporate Governance and Chief Economist of the Dubai International Finance Centre Authority. He has been a member of the IMF's MENA Regional Advisory Group since 2009 and Co-chair of the MENA Regional Corporate Governance Forum since 2004.

STEVEN L. SCHWARCZ is the Stanley A. Star Professor of Law and Business at Duke University and Founding Director of the Duke University Global Capital Markets Center. He has testified before committees of both the Senate and House of Representatives and has been an advisor to the United Nations on international receivables financing. He is currently the Leverhulme Visiting Professor at Oxford University.

JAMES SHINN is Lecturer at Princeton University and serves on the boards of several technology firms and non-profits, including the Yale Center for Corporate Governance.

JIM STEWART is Running Stream Professor in Leadership and Human Resource Development, Director of the HRD and Leadership Research Unit and Director of the Doctorate in Business

Administration Programme at the Faculty of Business and Law, Leeds Metropolitan University.

WILLIAM SUN is Leader of the Corporate Governance and Sustainability Research Group (CGSRG) and Independent Chair for PhD Viva Voce Examinations at the Faculty of Business and Law, Leeds Metropolitan University. He is Visiting Professor of Management at Harbin Engineering University and Harbin University of Commerce. He is editor of the series *Critical Studies on Corporate Responsibility, Governance and Sustainability*.

ROMAN TOMASIC is Professor of Law and Chair in Company Law at Durham Law School, Durham University, UK.

VIJAYA THYIL is Senior Lecturer in Finance at Deakin Business School, Deakin University, Australia.

KONARI UCHIDA is Associate Professor of Finance at the Faculty of Economics, Kyushu University, Japan.

CHRISTOPH VAN DER ELST is Professor of Business Law and Economics at the Faculty of Law, Tilburg University, the Netherlands. He is also Professor of Commercial Law and Corporate Governance at the Law School of Ghent University, the Netherlands, and a visiting professor at the College of Europe, Belgium and at the University of Torino (CLEI), Italy.

SUZANNE YOUNG is Associate Professor and Director of Corporate Responsibility and Global Citizenship at the Graduate School of Management, La Trobe University, Australia.

PEER ZUMBANSEN is Professor of Law and Canada Research Chair in Transnational Economic Governance and Legal Theory at Osgoode Hall Law School, York University, Canada.

Acknowledgements

This edited volume is the result of a collective effort of scholars and experts across ten countries. We wish to thank all the contributors for their intellectual contributions, collaborations and support of this work.

For their academic engagement, we wish to thank Professor Fuxiu Jiang, Renmin University of China; Banu Kring, İzmir University of Economics; Pradeep Ray, University of New South Wales; Sangeeta Ray, University of Sydney; Zahid Riaz, University of New South Wales. Special thanks are due to James McRitchie, publisher of CorpGov.net, for his great support to the volume editorial process. A special thanks also to the volume editorial assistant Maggie Meng.

This work was supported by the Faculty of Business and Law, Leeds Metropolitan University. We particularly thank Professor Ian Sanderson, the Faculty Director of Research, and Lawrence Bellamy, Leader of the Strategy and Business Analysis Subject Group, for their kind support throughout the research process.

At Cambridge University Press, special thanks are due to Paula Parish, Philip Good, Carolyn Fox, Jo Breeze and Karen Oakes. They have done a great job with the processes leading to the volume publication. Thanks also to the Press's anonymous reviewers who provided us with insightful and generous feedback.

We wish to thank the following scholars who participated in the review process of the volume chapters and their contributions to the volume are specially acknowledged: Mathew Appleyard, Leeds Metropolitan University, UK; Gabriel Eweje, Massey University, New Zealand; Guler Manisali-Darman, Corporate Governance and Sustainability Center, Turkey; James McRitchie, publisher of CorpGov.net, USA; Paul Manning, Leeds Metropolitan University, UK; Neil Richardson, Leeds Metropolitan University, UK; David Russell, De Montfort University, UK; Roman Tomasic, Durham University, UK; Christoph Van der Elst, Tilburg University, the Netherlands; Suzanne Young, La Trobe University, Australia.

1 Introduction: rethinking corporate governance – lessons from the global financial crisis

WILLIAM SUN, JIM STEWART AND DAVID POLLARD

Since the 1980s, worldwide corporate governance issues have attracted much media attention. Issues like corporate fraud, corporate failure and collapse, abuse of management power, excess of executive remuneration, and corporate social and environmental irresponsibility have all been topical in media reports, public forums, academic debates, governmental policy and regulatory agendas. Nevertheless, many of these corporate governance issues would not have been so prominent and exposed, had it not been for the global financial crisis of 2007–10. Many scholars, policy analysts and corporate practitioners have linked the severity and increasingly circular nature of the financial and economic crisis to corporate governance failures, whether systemic, functional or technical (see details in the following sections). Various corporate governance reforms have taken place in Europe and the United States among other countries (several chapters in this volume mention those reforms).

Yet, until now, there has been little research concentrating on an in-depth understanding of what exactly went wrong with corporate governance, how corporate governance failures contributed to the current financial crisis, and how we may reform and improve corporate governance to prevent its future institutional, systemic and moral failures. This volume brings together leading scholars from North America, Europe, Asia-Pacific and the Middle East to explore the systemic failings of corporate governance in relation to the global financial crisis and their underlying theses and approaches, and suggests ways forward for future corporate governance. The volume addresses three general themes that cover the theoretical foundations and dominant approaches of corporate governance, the complex roles of institutional shareholders and boards, and the search for new directions for post-crisis corporate governance research and reforms.

Generally, this volume takes a critical perspective on corporate governance, aiming at reflecting on corporate governance failures, rethinking what we have believed, accepted or taken for granted in terms of corporate governance perspectives, paradigms, approaches and methodologies, and learning corporate governance lessons from the global financial crisis. The core issues of corporate governance are examined internationally in different societal contexts, yet the international insights are often cross-referencing and reach some similar conclusions, since the current financial crisis is on a global scale and the dominant corporate governance model, like shareholder primacy, has been influential worldwide over decades. This volume is a multidisciplinary research collection contributed by scholars from the disciplinary backgrounds of business and management, economics, law and political science. The contributions are based on multiple methodologies, including conceptual exploration and development, critical review, case study and empirical analysis.

The global financial crisis of 2007–2010

The global financial crisis began with the US subprime mortgage crisis in 2007, triggered by the bursting of a housing bubble in the United States in late 2006. The subprime mortgage crisis was both a real estate and financial crisis, marked by a sharp rise in mortgage delinquencies and foreclosures, dramatic decline in the market value of subprime mortgage backed securities, and a large drop in the capital and liquidity of many banks and financial institutions, as well as widespread tightening credit. In a domino effect, the financial crisis originated in the credit crunch in the United States, spread over quickly to other sectors and countries and caused a series of financial and economic crises such as the collapse of US and European housing markets, collapse of the global stock markets, collapse of the global financial systems, financial markets, and many large banks and financial institutions, the greatest recession of the global economy since the Great Depression and the European sovereign debt crisis. The cost and negative consequences of the financial crisis are immense.

In August 2009 the International Monetary Fund (IMF) calculated that the total cost of the global financial crisis reached $11.9 trillion, including cash injections into banks, and the cost of purchasing toxic assets, guarantees over debt and liquidity support from central banks. That was equivalent to one-fifth of the entire world's annual economic output (Conway, 2009). The Pew Charitable Trusts issued a report stating that between 2008 and 2009 the United States suffered massive losses of income, jobs, wages and wealth, the cost including $650 billion of GDP income, 5.5 million jobs, $360 billion in wages, $3.4 trillion of real estate wealth (July 2008–March 2009), $7.4 trillion stock wealth (July 2008–March 2009) and $230 billion fiscal rescue cost. The total cost is equivalent to an average household loss of $188,250 in the United States alone (Swagel, 2009).

Causes of the global financial crisis were rather complex. On 15 November 2008, leaders of the G20 declared that the financial crisis was caused by (1) 'market participants [seeking] higher yields without an adequate appreciation of the risks and fail[ing] to exercise proper due diligence'; (2) 'weak underwriting standards, unsound risk management practices, increasingly complex and opaque financial products, and consequent excessive leverage combin[ing] to create vulnerabilities in the system'; and (3) 'policy-makers, regulators and supervisors, in some advanced countries, not adequately appreciating and addressing the risks building up in financial markets, keeping pace with financial innovation, or considering the systemic ramifications of domestic regulatory actions'.[1] The core theme in the G20 leaders' declaration of the root causes is particularly linked to financial risks, risks tied up with innovative financial products through 'securitization' processes (product risk), vulnerable financial systems (system risk), uncertain and unstable financial markets (market risk), and inadequate policy-making and regulation that might create risks or failed to address risks (policy risk).

The role of corporate governance in the financial crisis: the debate

When a number of large and influential banks and financial institutions and other publicly held companies collapsed or were bailed out during the financial crisis, there was a real concern about the appropriate governance of those corporations. Did those collapsed or nearly collapsed corporations in particular, and all corporations in general, have proper corporate governance practices in the United States and other countries before and during the financial crisis? As many banks and financial institutions were the makers of innovative, yet highly risky, financial products (and derivatives) and/or investors and traders of those financial products, they were either risk-creators

and -distributors or risk-takers. They were at the centre of the financial crisis with questionable governance practices. However, the question of whether and to what extent corporate governance played a
significant role in the financial crisis cannot be answered without a
debate. Basically there have been three different views and positions in
the debate.

The first view is that the financial crisis was unrelated or little
related to corporate governance. Scholars have shown that since the
1970s corporate governance in the United States and other developed
countries has improved significantly (e.g., Adams, 2009; Cheffins,
2009). For example, in many companies independent directors were
introduced, board chairmen and CEOs were separated, corporate
audit and risk committees were established, executive pay was
increased and incentive-driven to deliver value for shareholders,
minority shareholders' rights were protected, and institutional shareholders and hedge funds became more active in monitoring and disciplining corporations.

Since the 1990s, corporate governance codes in many countries,
corporate governance principles and guidelines provided by the
Organisation for Economic Co-operation and Development (OECD),
the World Bank and the IMF, and corporate governance reforms and
regulations had intensively channelled corporate behaviours and
actions towards accountability and responsibility. The Sarbanes-
Oxley Act of 2002, in particular, is believed to have strengthened
corporate governance by making mandatory many best practices of
corporate governance, such as board independence and audit procedures, with severe penalties for any breach of the legislation. Thus, in
2006 Christopher Cox, Chairman of the Securities and Exchange
Commission (SEC), optimistically reported to the US Congress that
'We have come a long way since 2002. Investor confidence has
recovered. There is greater corporate accountability. Financial
reporting is more reliable and transparent. Auditor oversight is significantly improved' (quoted in Rezaee, 2007, p. 38).

Hence, the logical conclusion is that publicly held corporations
were, in general, governed satisfactorily before and during the financial crisis (Cheffins, 2009), with no significant correlation between
corporate governance and the financial crisis. Cheffins suggests that
the sharp decline of stock markets in 2008 was not necessarily related
to corporate governance performance. Based on his empirical study of

thirty-seven firms removed from the S&P 500 index during 2008, Cheffins concludes that corporate governance in those firms functioned tolerably well and did not fail in the financial crisis. A further empirical study by Adams (2009), using a large sample of data on financial and non-financial firms from 1996 to 2007, shows that the governance of financial firms was on average not worse than that of non-financial firms. She also indicates that boards of banks receiving bailout money were more independent than the boards of other banks, and bank directors received far less compensation than directors in non-financial firms.

The second view in the debate is that the financial crisis was closely associated with the insufficient implementation of corporate governance codes and principles while current corporate governance frameworks are not wrong in general. This position is presented by the OECD. In June 2009, the OECD Steering Group on Corporate Governance issued a report stating that there are four weak areas in corporate governance contributing to the financial crisis, including executive remuneration, risk management, board practices and the exercise of shareholder rights. It asserted that the principles of corporate governance, as agreed standards among the OECD countries many years before the financial crisis, had adequately addressed those key governance concerns and the 'major failures among policy makers and corporations appear to be due to lack of implementation' of the principles (OECD, p. 55).

Thus, for the OECD, an ineffective implementation of existing corporate governance arrangements and principles is the key issue. The OECD is sceptical of the effectiveness of legislation and regulation in implementing corporate governance principles, and emphasizes the role of voluntary codes and corporate initiatives for better implementation. The UK has made a similar claim that there were no major problems with corporate governance codes prior to the financial crisis and the only problem remained with the implementation of the codes. It is believed that 'complying with the Code in itself constitutes good governance' (Financial Reporting Council, 2010, p. 2).

The third view in the debate is that the financial crisis was at least in part caused by a systemic failure of corporate governance. Perhaps few people would disagree with the OECD's identification of the areas of corporate governance failure, however many people have started to think that the failure of corporate governance may not be purely an implementation issue, but more a fundamental systemic failure of institutional arrangements underpinned by several increasingly popular paradoxical assumptions, such as shareholder primacy, profit maximization, effective incentive system, rational self-interest human behaviour, universal agency problems, efficient market for corporate control, etc. As Heineman Jr posits, 'These board failures [in the financial crisis] represent, in turn, a signal failure of the broad governance movement that gained momentum at the beginning of this decade' (Heineman Jr, 2008). Using the similar words of Julian Birkinshaw, co-founder of the London Business School's Management Labs, Caulkin (2009) highlights that the financial crisis is both a failure of the invisible hand of market and a failure of the visible hand of management (including boards and management teams). As the crisis was created by people, the management of financial firms is spotlighted at centre stage. Yet Caulkin makes it clear that 'management was hijacked by ideology'.

The origins of today's events can be traced back to the 1970s and the backlash against the cosy corporatism of the 1960s, which would become 'Reagonomics'. The concern then was that after two decades of post-war easy pickings, the Western economies had gone soft. Faced with formidable competition from Japan and newly emerging Asian economies, bloated Anglo-American conglomerates needed cutting down to size, with managers obliged to focus on shareholders' rather than their own concerns. (Caulkin, 2009)

The corporate governance framework since the 1980s has largely been shaped by 'Reagonomics' – a version of market fundamentalism influenced by neoclassical economics. Caulkin vividly describes such a corporate governance framework:

The company's job was to make money for shareholders; the individual's job was to pursue self-interest, allowing the invisible hand to work its magic; and the job of governance was to align 'agents' (managers) with 'principals' (shareholders) by incentives and sanctions. The carrot was pay linked to stock price, often in the form of stock options. The stick: high levels of debt and a vigorous market for corporate control, which ensured that underperforming assets could readily pass into the hands of sharper managers at hungrier companies. (Caulkin, 2009)

Ultimately, it is the Anglo-American corporate governance paradigm and underlying assumptions that have troubled the finance industry and the whole economy. For example, Visser (2010) argues that we have been facing multifacets of greed permitted or encouraged by governmental policies, institutional arrangements, ideologies and cultures. Self-interest and incentive systems led to executive greed, leveraging and risk transfer led to banking greed, deregulation and speculation led to financial market greed, self-regulation and short-term profit maximization led to corporate greed, and shareholder capitalism led to capitalist greed. Clarke (2009) further criticizes the Anglo-American model of corporate governance and states that this model, in its US manifestation, has enabled, permitted or tolerated excess power and wealth at the hands of CEOs, and incentivized investment bank executives to pursue vast securitization and high leveraging to enrich themselves greedily at the severe cost of shareholders, investors and other stakeholders. While the Anglo-American model of capitalism had been paradigmatically promoted to the rest of the world, it evidently induced the collapse of the financial institutions worldwide.

Generally, we take the third view in the above debate. We may agree that corporate governance reforms in developed countries in recent years have generated some fruitful outcomes, such as independent boards, shareholder activism and widely accepted codes and principles as best practices. However, if we also agree that corporate governance not only failed to prevent the financial crisis, but actually encouraged and permitted corporations to create and take excessive financial and business risks for short-term profit maximization, we may see that the problem with corporate governance is not just some technical or implementation issues. The problem is systemic and fundamental, involving models, paradigms, approaches and the orientation of corporate governance systems. Now that the Anglo-American corporate governance model has gained momentum globally since the 1990s through the globalization movement and global capital flows, the unprecedented and greatest global financial crisis since the Great Depression has taught us to rethink whether the failure of corporate governance resides in the model and paradigm itself, in its underlying theses and associated approaches.

The systemic failure of corporate governance

To understand the systemic issues of corporate governance, we should return to the basic question: what is corporate governance? Both the Cadbury Code and the OECD provided the same definition of corporate governance: 'Corporate governance is the system by which business corporations are directed and controlled' (Cadbury, 1992, p. 15; OECD, 1999). However, as Monks and Minow (2001) and Clarke (2007) among others note, the common understanding of corporate governance is often narrowly confined to the structure and functioning of the board or the rights of shareholders in corporate decision-making. For example, in the UK Corporate Governance Code corporate governance is defined as being 'about what the board of a company does and how it sets the values of the company' (Financial Reporting Council, 2010). Yet, Margaret Blair takes a much broader view of corporate governance and refers corporate governance to 'the whole set of legal, cultural, and institutional arrangements that determine what publicly traded corporations can do, who controls them, how that control is exercised, and how the risks and returns from the activities they undertake are allocated (Blair, 1995, p. 19).

Further to Blair's definition, we think that corporate governance mainly involves four-level legal, cultural and institutional arrangements, including regulatory governance, market governance, stakeholder governance and internal (or shareholder) governance. Thus in a broad sense, 'corporate governance system' refers to the whole set of regulatory, market, stakeholder and internal governance. Regulatory governance means the public order and control over corporations by state statutes, governmental and professional bodies' regulations, and government policies. Market governance is the use of various market mechanisms (such as supply and demand, price signal, free competition, market entrance and exit, market contract and market bid) to control and discipline corporate behaviour and action. Stakeholder governance is the direct and indirect control or influence over corporate business, decision-making and corporate behaviour by key stakeholder groups who have direct or indirect interests in the corporation. Typical stakeholders may include investors, banks, suppliers, customers, employees, government and local communities. Internal corporate governance is the institutional arrangement of checks and balances among the shareholder general meeting, the board of directors and management within the corporation, prescribed by corporate laws.[2] While the board may be at the centre stage of internal governance, as many people believe, the shareholder general meeting and management are equally important in the checks and balances.

However, many people tend to neglect the close triple relationship in internal governance and mistakenly regard shareholders and their representatives on the board as 'outsiders' rather than 'insiders' in the internal corporate governance structure.[3] Indeed, it is contradictory to see shareholders as 'owners' and members, yet 'outsiders', of the corporation.

What does a systemic failure of corporate governance mean for the financial crisis? First of all, there was a regulatory failure in governing financial companies before the financial crisis, manifested in substantial deregulation and lack of regulation in the finance industry. In this volume, Thomas Clarke (Chapter 2), Roman Tomasic (Chapter 3) and Roland Pérez (Chapter 6) address the regulatory problems (deregulation, regulatory gap and self-regulation) as a key source of the weak corporate governance system that contributed to the financial crisis. In 1933, in his inaugural address, the US President Franklin D. Roosevelt declared that 'There must be a strict supervision of all banking and credits and investments; there must be an end to speculation with other people's money' (Rosenman, 1938, p. 14). However, the strict supervisory rules over the finance industry in response to the Great Depression had been gradually abandoned from the 1980s onwards when neo-liberal ideology became prevalent and dominant all over the world.

The typical example is the Gramm-Leach-Bliley Act passed in the US Congress in 1999, which repealed the Glass-Steagall Act of 1933 separating commercial banks from investment banks. While commercial banks were allowed to use ordinary people's savings to speculate in financial markets with excessive risks taken, this new enactment symbolized 'The Death of Gentlemanly Capitalism' (Augar, 2001) and the new era of 'Casino Capitalism' (Strange, 1997). In 2000, the US Congress passed the Commodity Futures Modernization Act, which allowed the self-regulation of futures and derivatives, declaring that all attempts to regulate the derivatives market are illegal (Mason, 2009). Derivatives, what Warren Buffet referred to as 'financial weapons of mass destruction' in 2003, were then astonishingly traded. In 2007, the world GDP was around $65 trillion in total, the total value of the companies listed in the world stock markets was at its all time peak of $63 trillion, but the total value of derivatives was $596 trillion – more than eight times the size of the real economy (Mason, 2009).

Other significant regulatory failures may include the permission of investment banks to substantially increase their debt level and leverage; the permission of depository banks to move massive amounts of assets and liabilities off balance sheets into structured investment vehicles and conduits to hide their debts, insufficient capital and high risks taken; and the lack of regulation over the shadow banking system, consisting of non-depository bank financial institutions to lend businesses money or invest in 'toxic assets' (such as subprime mortgage backed securities) with a significant high level of financial leverage.

The advocacy of deregulation and self-regulation came with the idea that the market is the most efficient and rational way of allocating resources, monitoring corporations and disciplining corporate underperformance and misbehaviour. For neoclassical economists, pressure from the market for corporate control, the capital market and the managerial labour market are the most powerful force to align the interests of managers with the interests of shareholders. Market governance is seen as the best alternative to institutional deficiencies and hierarchical governance failures (for more details and references, see Sun, 2009, pp. 21–6). However, the key assumption of market efficiency and rationality has long been criticized as too simplistic and counter-experiencing (e.g., Rescher, 1988; Fligstein, 1990; Hampden-Turner and Trompenaars, 1994; Roy, 1997), as the assumption is based on purely calculative and deterministic economic conditions outside social interactive and interrelated processes and individually multiple and complex experiences, which are not simply and straightforwardly rational and efficient. The efficient market hypothesis depends on an even flow of information through to the market. Hence, disclosure and transparency are prerequisites for market efficiency.

However, Steven L. Schwarcz (Chapter 5) points out that although most of the risks were disclosed in the financial market as required by the US federal regulations, the disclosure was still ineffective. Apart from the problem of information asymmetry, there is a problem of information failure inherently embedded in a 'complex system' of financial markets where price volatility and liquidity were nonlinear functions of patterns arising from the interactive behaviour of many independent and constantly adapting market participants. Not only can this produce cognizant complexity (i.e., too complex to understand), but it can also produce a 'tight coupling' within credit markets where events tend to move rapidly into a crisis mode with little time or opportunity to intervene. Schwarcz's argument echoes the view of Joseph E. Stiglitz, Nobel laureate in economics, who believes that 'when information is imperfect, markets do not often work well – and information imperfections are central in finance' (Stiglitz, 2009, p. 9).

Blanaid Clarke (Chapter 4) further analyses that while share price in the stock market is supposed to be the objective standard of managerial efficiency (Manne, 1965), in practice the share prices of the banks did not reflect the inefficiencies which subsequently proved so costly to the global market. While the market for corporate control is supposed to be the optimal way of governing, in practice there were no opportunities to cheaply acquire the banks and even if there had been, it is unclear whether there would have been support for a change in risk management structures either at board or at investor level. Thus, the fundamental prerequisites for the operation of market disciplinary force were not in place. Both Schwarcz and Clarke, among others, suggest that the market-discipline approach to financial markets, financial institutions and corporate governance has failed.

Stakeholder governance is typically seen in German and Japanese corporations where banks, employees, suppliers and major customers exert significant influence on corporate decision-making through specific institutional arrangements. For example, the German codetermination system and the Japanese lifetime employment guarantee traditionally safeguard the interest of labour in corporations. Banks have long-standing close relationships with corporations. Suppliers and major customers may become involved in corporate governance through interlocking shareholdings and cross-directorships (Charkham, 1994; Keasey *et al.*, 1997; Clarke, 2007). Although stakeholder theory has gained popularity over the last two decades and stakeholder interests have been considered by many companies in the Anglo-American business environment, there is no formal stakeholder governance system and structure established in the Anglo-American model. Thus, for stakeholder theorists, the reason why the Anglo-American corporate governance system failed is because of the absence of stakeholder involvement in corporate governance. The institutional arrangements failed to represent stakeholder interests (e.g., Blair, 1995; Hutton, 1995).

In the Anglo-American corporate governance model, regulatory governance, market governance and stakeholder governance are seen as governing forces external to the corporation.[4] The internal governance system prescribed by corporate laws has a formal hierarchical governance structure consisting of the shareholder general meeting, the board of directors and management (represented by the CEO). As discussed intensively over the last two decades, the systemic failures of internal corporate governance are marked by shareholders' reluctance to monitor corporations and passivity in attending shareholder general meetings, boards' incompetence and lack of independence, and CEOs' dominance and abuse of power (for details and references, see Sun, 2009, pp. 51–64). In this volume, Robert A. G. Monks (Chapter 7) emphasizes that a key problem with Anglo-American corporate governance is that shareholders, both institutional and individual, do not behave like owners.

Even though a small number of institutional shareholders may be considered real owners, their responsible activist ownership is inhibited by encouraging conflict of interest. Roger Barker (Chapter 8) further indicates that institutional investors did not provide an effective governance counterweight to the poor decision-making of bank boards and other financial companies prior to the financial crisis, either by being too passive or insufficiently engaged, or by even encouraging adoption of high risk business strategies.

In regard to the malfunctioning of the board, Jay W. Lorsch (Chapter 9) recognizes that board failure in the 2008 financial crisis was different from that in 2002 when boards failed to identify and stop management malfeasance and fraud. The more recent board failures were primarily attributable to the growing complexity of companies operating multiple businesses. In those companies, assuring an adequate and accurate flow of information from the lower level to the upper is a significant challenge. While board members are largely dependent on management for an accurate and transparent flow of information, it is questionable whether boards could receive adequate information to understand the performance issues and risks their companies face.

Themes of the volume

This volume aims to critically examine the fundamental failings of current corporate governance systems and understand how corporate governance failures contributed to the global financial crisis, exploring how corporate governance problems may be addressed effectively to help prevent or mitigate any similar financial crisis in the future.

There are three general themes/perspectives in this volume. The first theme is that the market-oriented approach typically associated with the Anglo-American corporate governance model is behind corporate governance failures, which largely contributed to the global financial crisis. The market-oriented approach (or the market discipline approach, or simply, the market approach) to corporate governance to which we refer here is in a broad sense characterized by deregulation, self-regulation, the market for corporate control and other market discipline mechanisms, with governing activities driven by financial-dominant incentives such as pure shareholder value, short-term profit maximization and managerial compensation.

The first part of this volume concentrates on examining what is wrong with the market-oriented approach to corporate governance and how it was linked to the financial crisis. The five chapters in Part I contribute to the understanding of corporate governance causes of the global financial crisis that are believed to originate in the worldwide deregulation of financial institutions and markets (Thomas Clarke), the ideological belief in the inherent superiority of self-regulation (Roman Tomasic), the overconfidence in the disciplining mechanism of the market for corporate control promoted by finance economics (Blanaid Clarke), the insufficient and ineffective disclosure due to information failure inherently embedded in a complex system of financial markets (Steven L. Schwarcz), and the excessively financialized corporate governance and instrumented management with a focus exclusively on shareholder value and short-term profit gain (Roland Pérez).

The second theme of this volume is that the failure of internal governance systems in relation to unchecked corporate decision-making, poor risk management, inadequate remuneration policies and managerial misbehaviour in the financial crisis is caused directly by the breakdown of the triple relationship between shareholders, the boardroom and management. Thus, shareholder engagement, effective board functioning, and proper board–management and shareholder–corporation relationships are essential for good corporate governance. The often conflicting role of institutional shareholders and a complex shareholder–corporation relationship are examined by Robert A. G. Monks and Roger Barker.

While the fiduciary duty of board directors is frequently emphasized in the literature, many people tend to neglect the fiduciary responsibility of institutional shareholders. The commitment to ownership-based governance is often diluted by the lack of responsibility of shareholders – shares loaned, shares sold short, shares whose vote is contracted away from the economic beneficiary (Robert A. G. Monks) and by the diversified portfolio strategy of most institutional fund managers (Roger Barker). For Monks, regulation rather than self-regulation is the only workable solution to ensure shareholder responsibility for stewardship in the fiduciary chain. Yet Barker argues that while the restrictive approach to corporate governance may be justifiable for the finance sector, it would be undesirable for the rest of the economy because of the very possibility of regulatory failure.

Board effectiveness is addressed by two empirical studies based on the US and Japanese business environments. Jay W. Lorsch's chapter focuses on the boardroom–management relationship. Drawing from the experiences of directors of many complex companies, Lorsch finds that board effectiveness rests not on pure legislative prescriptions, but on what transpires within individual boards. The most challenging task for boards is to maintain a delicate balance in their relationship with management. Boards must be challenging and critical on the one hand and supportive on the other. They must sustain an open and candid flow of communication in both directions and seek sources of understanding outside management without offending management.

In Japan, where the market for corporate control is less active, internal governance mechanisms become more important for monitoring and disciplining management. Empirical research by Chunyan Liu, Jianlei Liu and Konari Uchida demonstrates that independent directors played a positive role in disciplining management against their performances (through management turnover) and protecting shareholder wealth (via maintaining dividend policy) during the financial crisis. Their research supports the view that well-designed corporate governance structures serve an important role during crisis times when agency conflict becomes severe.

While a basic regulatory framework is essential for internal control and risk management, Christoph Van der Elst's chapter reviews regulatory practices across Western Europe over the last decade and during the financial crisis. Van der Elst notes that significant progress towards integrated regulations on risk management in Europe has been made in recent years, with a shift from risk management being considered as a financial and operational issue to being a pivotal element of good corporate governance. Regulatory provisions have been particularly strengthened after the financial crisis. Still, the regulatory integration of risk management and internal control in the corporate legal framework is fragmented and incomplete. His empirical research on the real estate investment industry also raises important issues regarding the tension created between compliance with a referential framework and the state of the art of the risk management system, and the difficult process of balancing entrepreneurship and risk management.

The third theme of this volume is that a disembedded and 'value-free' economic approach to understanding corporate governance is inappropriate, and the propriety and effectiveness of corporate governance frameworks in a society is better addressed by multidisciplinary studies, holistic thinking and contextual understandings. It is arguable that a good corporate governance system in a free market economy is a systemic integration of regulatory governance, market governance, stakeholder governance and internal governance, with sufficient flexibility for dynamic variations of governing modes and mechanisms in different times and contexts. It is obvious that a basic legal and regulatory framework is needed for maintaining the order of free market competition and good governance. The financial crisis tells us that stricter regulations are particularly needed in the finance industry. Yet we also need to be aware of the regulation limits, as regulations are often reactive rather than proactive to corporate activities, and inappropriate regulations may also lead to corporate governance failure or business failure. Hence, a balance between regulatory governance and other governance modes and mechanisms should be carefully considered.

Continuing from the critical studies of corporate governance failures in Parts I and II, the five chapters in Part III point to some new directions for corporate governance research and reforms as a post-crisis agenda. Peer Zumbansen's chapter points out the shortcomings of a functional, ahistorical and disembedded approach in corporate law and governance research over the past three decades, which is more interested in exploring and designing regulatory responses to the quick 'fixing' of the system failures than fundamentally understanding the changing, evolving and increasingly complex nature of the business corporation and its regulatory environment.

Rapid developments of globalization of markets, information technology, knowledge economy and the 'financialization' of the corporation have opened up regulatory spaces and transformed formal rule creation in politically embedded state legal systems towards an emerging system of decentralized and specialized transnational regulatory regimes unfolding in a web of hard and soft laws, blurring the regulatory boundaries between national and international, public and private, formal and informal. Zumbansen's chapter implies that corporate governance research and reforms must examine and understand the new emerging context of the increasingly de-territorialized corporate governance regimes re-embedded in the new global business environment.

Florian Möslein's chapter recognizes the limitation of the narrow understanding of corporate governance defined by corporate internal hierarchical governance and argues that the financial crisis was much more related to wider contractual relationships in the financial markets. Using the term 'contract governance', Möslein highlights the importance of the coordinating or steering effects of the whole contractual network of markets where corporations are embedded and the impact of legal, social, cultural and mutually agreed conditions and institutional frameworks of contractual relations on the 'contract for control'.

James Shinn's empirical research examines the effects of the financial crisis on the mechanisms of change in corporate governance. Shinn finds that the financial crisis has brought about more pressures for corporate governance reforms from investors, stakeholders and public voters through the public ordering mechanisms (via regulatory change), and has attenuated some of the 'private ordering' mechanisms through good governance bargains struck between firms and investors. His research illustrates the dynamic changes of corporate governance modes and mechanisms in different times and contexts, showing a current trend towards more regulatory changes demanded by the public.

Nasser Saidi's chapter finds that Islamic financial institutions have displayed more resilience (though not risk immune) amid the global financial crisis because of stricter rules imposed on lending and investment by Islamic law. His finding supports the argument that sound corporate governance could be both principle-based and rule-based, being embedded in different social and cultural environments. Saidi further suggests that the way out of the crisis is through *intelligent regulation*; regulation that does not pre-empt or hinder market-driven adjustments, but supports and strengthens financial innovation and the market, doing so through creating and maintaining a culture of transparency and accountability.

Finally, Suzanne Young's and Vijaya Thyil's chapter calls for a holistic, multiple-disciplinary approach, integrating multiple lenses and perspectives in understanding corporate governance practices as a post-crisis research direction. Young and Thyil argue that the conventional dominance of economic or legal approaches to corporate governance is limited, excluding wider and crucial variables that collectively impact upon effective governance. While every variable in the governance system should be considered to ensure effectiveness, some variables are more important than others, depending on the situation and environment, thus pointing to a contingency approach. In the current post-crisis time, a balance between compliance and behavioural approaches is important – regulation to ensure timely and valid disclosure and good structures, alongside a focus on ethics, culture, leadership, power and human resource practices to ensure organizational objectives are met in an ethical manner.

Conclusions

Since the global financial crisis, there has been a puzzle in many people's minds: Why could not the increasingly improved corporate governance codes, principles, structures and mechanisms in the advanced countries in the last two decades constrain commercial pressures and greed and prevent a widespread default of fundamental director and CEO responsibilities in the financial industry (Heineman Jr, 2008)? This volume may solve this puzzle by arguing that the financial crisis was largely contributed to by the failures of corporate governance, despite some technical improvements in recent years. There has been a systemic failure of corporate governance; not just the failure of some elements, parts, or simply implementation issues. While claiming this, we define corporate governance broadly as a systemic set of legal, cultural and institutional arrangements, which determine how the corporation is governed, for what purpose and for whose interests. Thus, the failure of the corporate governance system refers widely to the failures of regulatory governance, market governance, stakeholder governance and internal (or shareholder) governance, all of which are involved in the corporate governance system as a whole.

What we intend to explore is not just how corporate governance failed in preventing the financial crisis, but also why it failed. Contributions in this volume help to understand the wide contextual backgrounds and developments of the economy, politics, financial institutions and social cultures over the last three decades or beyond, where corporations were embedded, corporate governance frameworks were reset and developed, and corporate control was truly exercised. Contributors in this volume highlight the severe limitations of the dominant corporate governance framework (mainly in the Anglo-American environment, but also more or less worldwide) and its associated market-oriented approach to corporate governance, explain how those linked to the financial crisis, examine the problems with its internal (or shareholder) governance structures and mechanisms and suggest how the governance problems could be resolved. Contributions are also made in regard to how the future corporate governance research and reforms could be redirected.

One of the important lessons we may learn from the financial crisis and corporate failures is that in relation to the narrow definition of corporate governance mentioned above, many people tend to examine corporate governance issues narrowly in terms of rules, institutions, positions, actors, behaviours and activities within a particular corporate governance framework, what Sun terms as 'the structure-action view of corporate governance' (Sun, 2009, pp. 174–6), rather than reflexively understanding what lies behind the appearance of structure and action constructed by certain beliefs, values, cultures, ideologies and social conventions, and why and how the structure and action have been formed in the first place. Thus, although some technical issues might have been addressed and corporate governance improved the fundamental problems indiscernible by traditional static and mechanistic modes of thinking are still there and little touched.

By exploring the causes of corporate governance failures and the ways of overcoming them, this volume begins to address this key philosophical/methodological issue in corporate governance thinking and to move beyond the constraints of traditional modes of thinking. Further research along this path is certainly needed. Ultimately, corporate governance is a fundamental concern with the purpose of the corporation and for whose interest it would be legitimized, justifiable, and how the corporation could be better governed to serve the public good, the whole economy and society, apart from making profits for shareholders. As Adrian Cadbury made clear:

In its broadest sense, corporate governance is concerned with holding the balance between economic and social goals and between individual and communal goals. The governance framework is there to encourage the efficient use of resources and equally to require accountability for the stewardship of those resources. The aim is to align as nearly as possible the interests of individuals, of corporations, and of society. (Cadbury, 2003)

Perhaps how to balance the different goals and interests is the most fundamental and difficult issue in corporate governance. Sun (2009, pp. 233–4) notes that there are three dilemmas in contemporary capitalism: the conflicts between private interest and public interest, between economic interest and social interest, and between share-holder interest and managerial interest (a version of self-interest vs. others' interest). Current corporate governance problems are embed-ded in the larger problems of governance in Western democratic societies. Yet, as capitalism is always extremely efficient at responding to and adapting to changes in the general values of its context (Jackson and Carter, 1995, p. 883), corporate governance will surely be self-adjusted and self-developed further, flexibly and dynamically, to not just help prevent or mitigate any financial crisis in future, but also to help make a better society.

Notes

1 'Declaration of the Summit on Financial Markets and the World Econ-omy', issued by The White House, *The Washington Times*, 15 November 2008.
2 Traditionally, internal governance is actually 'shareholder governance', as in corporate law theory board directors are representatives (trustees) of shareholders, and management are agents, hired by the board. The intro-duction of independent directors since the 1970s may dilute the theoret-ical dominance of shareholder governance. However, with the prevalence of shareholder primacy since the 1980s, independent directors also have fiduciary duties to serve shareholder interests, which are indifferent from the duties of other directors.
3 Independent directors who represent outside stakeholders rather than shareholders may be regarded as 'outsiders'.

4 Employees are working within the corporation, yet they are excluded from the internal governance system in the Anglo-American model. Thus, if employees participate in stakeholder governance in order to have some influence on corporate decision-making, their activities may be viewed as external to the internal governance system.

References

Adams, R. 2009. 'Governance and the financial crisis', ECGI Working Paper Series in Finance, available at http://ssrn.com/abstract_id=1398583, last accessed 2 July 2010.

Augar, P. 2001. *The Death of Gentlemanly Capitalism: The Rise and Fall of London's Investment Banks*. London: Penguin Books.

Blair, M. 1995. *Ownership and Control: Rethinking Corporate Governance for the Twenty-First Century*. Washington, DC: Brookings Institution Press.

Cadbury, A. 1992. *Report of the Committee on the Financial Aspects of Corporate Governance*. London: Gee and Co.

  2003. 'Foreword', in Claessens, Stijn, *Corporate Governance and Development*. Washington, DC: Global Corporate Governance Forum, Focus 1.

Caulkin, S. 2009. 'Corporate apocalypse', *Management Today*, 1 January.

Charkham, J. 1994. *Keeping Good Company: A Study of Corporate Governance in Five Countries*. Oxford: Clarendon.

Cheffins, B. R. 2009. 'Did corporate governance "fail" during the 2008 stock market meltdown? The case of the S&P 500', ECGI Working Paper Series in Law, available at http://ssrn.com/abstract=1396126, last accessed 20 March 2010.

Clarke, T. 2007. *International Corporate Governance: A Comparative Approach*. London: Routledge.

  2009. 'A critique of the Anglo-American model of corporate governance', CLPE Research Paper 15/2009, 5 (3), available at http://ssrn.com/abstract=1440853, last accessed 16 June 2010.

Conway, E. 2009. 'IMF puts total cost of crisis at £7.1 trillion', *The Telegraph*, 8 August.

Financial Reporting Council, 2010. *The UK Corporate Governance Code*, 28 May 2010, available at www.frc.org.uk/corporate/reviewCombined.cfm, last accessed 2 June 2010.

Fligstein, N. *The Transformation of Corporate Control*. Harvard University Press.

Hampden-Turner, C. and Trompenaars, F. 1994. *The Seven Cultures of Capitalism*. New York: Doubleday.

Heineman, Jr, B. W. 2008. 'Boards fail – again', *BusinessWeek*, 26 September.

Hutton, W. 1995. *The State We're In*. London: Jonathan Cape.

Jackson, N. and Carter, P. 1995. 'Organisational chiaroscuro: throwing light on the concept of corporate governance', *Human Relations* 48 (8): 875–89.

Keasey, K., Thompson, S. and Wright, M. 1997. 'Introduction: the corporate governance problem – competing diagnoses and solutions', in Keasey, K., Thompson, S. and Wright, M. (eds.), *Corporate Governance: Economic and Financial Issues*. Oxford University Press: 1–17.

Manne, H. G. 1965. 'Mergers and the market for corporate control', *Journal of Political Economy* 75: 110–26.

Mason, P. 2009. *Meltdown: The End of the Age of Greed*. London: Verso.

Monks, R. and Minow, N. 2001. *Corporate Governance*. Oxford: Blackwell Publishing.

OECD 1999. *Principles of Corporate Governance*. Paris: OECD.

    2009. 'Corporate governance and the financial crisis: key findings and main messages', June, available at www.oecd.org/dataoecd/3/10/43056196.pdf, last accessed 16 July 2009.

Rescher, N. 1988. *Rationality: A Philosophical Inquiry into the Nature and the Rationale of Reason*. New York: Oxford University Press.

Rezaee, Z. 2007. *Corporate Governance Post-Sarbanes-Oxley*. Hoboken, NJ: John Wiley & Sons.

Rosenman, S. (ed.). 1938. *The Public Papers of Franklin D. Roosevelt, Volume Two: The Years of Crisis, 1933*. New York: Random House.

Roy, W. G. 1997. *Socializing Capital*. Princeton University Press.

Stiglitz, J. E. 2009. 'Harsh lessons we may need to learn again', *China Daily*, 31 December, p. 9.

Strange, S. 1997. *Casino Capitalism*. Manchester University Press.

Sun, W. 2009. *How to Govern Corporations So They Serve the Public Good: A Theory of Corporate Governance Emergence*. New York: Edwin Mellen Press.

Swagel, P. 2009. 'The cost of the financial crisis: the impact of the September 2008 economic collapse', PEW Financial Reform Project Briefing Paper#18, available at http://www.pewfr.org/admin/project_reports/files/Cost-of-the-Crisis-final.pdf, last accessed 18 June 2010.

Visser, W. 2010. 'CSR 2.0: from the age of greed to the age of responsibility', in Sun, W., Stewart, J. and Pollard, D. (eds.), *Reframing Corporate Social Responsibility: Lessons from the Global Financial Crisis*. Bingley: Emerald Group Publishing.

The failure of the market approach to corporate governance

Introduction to Part I

The five chapters in Part I explore the failures of corporate governance that contributed to the global financial crisis, with a focus on examining the limitations of the market-oriented approach to corporate governance, which in a broad sense is characterized by deregulation, self-regulation, the market for corporate control and other market discipline mechanisms. Thomas Clarke begins by examining the specifically corporate governance causes of the global financial crisis. He identifies the origins of the crisis in the enthusiasm for deregulation of financial institutions and markets, resulting in the rapid growth of securitization. The huge explosion of global derivatives set the context in which risk management and corporate governance were abandoned by major financial institutions. The rating agencies and executive incentives played roles in encouraging rather than managing risk. He suggests that international efforts to coordinate a regulatory response to the crisis should be considered.

Examining the failure of British banks during the global financial crisis, Roman Tomasic finds that this failure has been attributable in part to an uncritical adherence to market self-regulation, a widely held assumption that soft law codes of corporate governance were more effective than legislation or government regulatory action. He argues that although formal legal rules and government regulation alone have limitations in being able to ensure corporate accountability, the simple pursuit of self-regulatory or soft law mechanisms is not adequate, either. The failure of British banking regulation during the financial crisis calls for a more thoroughgoing review of existing corporate governance mechanisms, and also calls for more effective external monitoring and control of corporate governance failures.

The market for corporate control theory originated in financial economics and has dominated the corporate governance landscape worldwide since the 1960s. Blanaid Clarke notes that the disciplinary functioning of the market for corporate control through takeovers did not operate to control inefficient management in the run-up to the banking crisis. She finds that the failure of market discipline is because the fundamental prerequisites for the operation of this disciplinary force were not in place. The share prices of the banks did not reflect the inefficiencies that subsequently proved so costly to the global market. There were no opportunities to acquire the banks cheaply, and even if there had been, it is not clear that there would have been support for a change in risk management structures either at the board or the investor level. She suggests that not only will regulation be required to resolve corporate governance problems that the market for corporate control cannot control, but it also may be required to deal with the very mechanics of the market processes that underlie the operation of the market for corporate control.

The functioning of market disciplines requires transparency and accuracy of information, and thus full disclosure of information has been a key to regulation of the financial markets. However, Steven L. Schwarcz shows that although most, if not all, of the risks giving rise to the collapse of the market for structured securities backed by subprime mortgages were disclosed, the disclosure was ineffective. He argues that disclosure failed because of the complexity of those securities and transactions. Information failure was inherently embedded in a 'complex system' of financial markets in which price volatility and liquidity were nonlinear functions of patterns arising from the interactive behaviour of many independent and constantly adapting market participants. Not only can this produce cognizant complexity (i.e., too complex to understand), but it can also produce a 'tight coupling' within credit markets, where events tend to move rapidly into a crisis mode with little time or opportunity to intervene. He also points out that information failure (e.g., lost, diverged, hidden, deceived) also derived from the human nature of market participants, including the inherent self-interest of human behaviour. This behaviour created externalities (e.g., system risks) in the financial crisis for the protection of individuals themselves, not the financial system as a whole. He concludes that information failure implies that the market-discipline approach to financial markets and financial institutions has failed. There could be some solutions to address the market complexity issues and information failure. However, viable solutions appear to be second best.

Concerned with purely financial objectives of corporations, Roland Pérez develops a key argument that finance, instead of keeping to its 'serving' position, has become dominant, even 'arrogant' in corporations and has ruled management through its governance regime. The progression from finance seized with hubris to excessively financialized governance and finally instrumented management has led to the breakdown of the finance industry and the economy in successive waves since September 2007. This breakdown reflected 'failing regulations' or the end of the myth of self-regulation either by the markets themselves or via professional bodies. He suggests a new framework that is built on a new paradigm of finance considered as a social science rather than a physical one, a corporate governance system less shareholder- and more stakeholder-oriented, and management vision broadened and more responsible.

2 | Corporate governance causes of the global financial crisis

THOMAS CLARKE

This chapter seeks to penetrate the catastrophe of the global financial crisis to examine its specifically corporate governance causes. The origins of the crisis in the enthusiasm for deregulation of financial institutions and markets, and the rapid growth of securitization, are explored. The huge explosion of global derivatives is considered as the context in which risk management and corporate governance were abandoned by major financial institutions. The role of the rating agencies and of executive incentives in encouraging rather than managing risk is investigated. Finally, the international effort to coordinate a regulatory response to the crisis is considered.

The apparent ascendancy of Anglo-American markets and governance institutions was profoundly questioned by the scale and contagion of the 2008 global financial crisis. 'America's financial institutions have not managed risk; they have created it' (Stiglitz, 2008). The crisis was initiated by falling house prices and rising mortgage default rates in the highly inflated US housing market. A severe credit crisis developed through 2007 into 2008 as financial institutions became fearful of the potential scale of the subprime mortgages concealed in the securities they had bought. As a result, banks refused to lend to each other because of increased counterparty risk that other banks might default. A solvency crisis ensued as banks were slow to admit to the great holes in their accounts that the subprime mortgages had caused (partly because they were themselves unaware of the seriousness of the problem) and the difficulty in raising capital to restore their balance sheets. As an increasing number of financial institutions collapsed in the United States, the UK and Europe, successive government efforts to rescue individual institutions, and to offer general support for the financial system, did not succeed in restoring confidence as markets continued in free-fall, with stock exchanges across the world losing almost half their value (Figure 2.1).

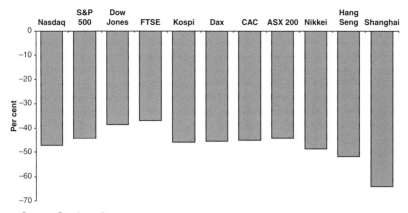

Source: Stock exchanges

Figure 2.1 Collapsing stock exchanges in 2008 global financial crisis (year to December 2008)

Financial insecurity rapidly became contagious internationally as fears of a global economic recession became widespread and stock markets around the world crashed. This financial crisis was larger in scale than any crisis since the 1930s Great Depression, involving bank losses conservatively estimated in October 2008 by the IMF (2008) as potentially $1,400 billion dollars, eclipsing earlier crises in Asia, Japan and the United States (Figure 2.2). Martin Wolf was quick to realize the implications of the crisis, as he put it in the *Financial Times* (5 September 2007):

We are living through the first crisis of the brave new world of securitised financial markets. It is too early to tell how economically important the upheaval will prove. But nobody can doubt its significance for the financial system. Its origins lie with credit expansion and financial innovations in the US itself. It cannot be blamed on 'crony capitalism' in peripheral economies, but rather on responsibility in the core of the world economy.

Origins of the crisis

In the cyclical way markets work, the origins of the 2008 financial crisis may be found in the solutions to the previous market crisis. The US Federal Reserve, under the sage Alan Greenspan, responded to the collapse of confidence caused by the dot-com disaster and Enron failures in 2001/2 by reducing US interest rates to 1 per cent, their

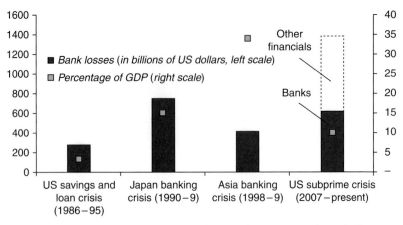

Note: US subprime costs represent staff estimates of losses on banks and other financial institutions. All costs are in real 2007 dollars. Asia includes Indonesia, Malaysia, Korea, the Philippines and Thailand.
Sources: World Bank; IMF staff estimates.

Figure 2.2 Comparison of international financial crises

lowest in forty-five years, flooding the market with cheap credit to jump-start the economy back into life. US business did recover faster than expected, but the cheap credit had washed into the financial services and housing sectors, producing the largest speculative bubbles ever witnessed in the American economy (Fleckenstein, 2008). The scene was set by the 1999 dismantling of the 1932 Glass-Steagall Act which had separated commercial banking from investment banking and insurance services, opening the way for a consolidation of the vastly expanding and increasingly competitive US financial services industry. Phillips (2008, p. 5) describes this as a 'burgeoning debt and credit complex': 'Vendors of credit cards, issuers of mortgages and bonds, architects of asset-backed securities and structured investment vehicles – occupied the leading edge. The behemoth financial conglomerates, Citigroup, JP Morgan Chase et al., were liberated in 1999 for the first time since the 1930s to marshal banking, insurance, securities, and real estate under a single, vaulting institutional roof.'

In this newly emboldened finance sector the name of the game was *leverage* – the capacity to access vast amounts of credit cheaply to take over businesses and to do deals. Wall Street investment banks and hedge funds flourished with their new-found access to cheap credit. Exotic financial instruments were devised and marketed internationally: futures, options and swaps evolved into collateralized debt obligations (CDOs), credit default swaps (CDSs) and many other acronyms, all of which packaged vast amounts of debt to be traded on the securities markets. Abandoning their traditional financial conservatism, banks looked beyond taking deposits and lending to the new businesses of wealth management, and eagerly adopted new instruments and business models. As the IMF put it:

> Banking systems in the major countries have gone through a process of disintermediation – that is, a greater share of financial intermediation is now taking place through tradable securities (rather than bank loans and deposits) . . . Banks have increasingly moved financial risks (especially credit risks) off their balance sheets and into securities markets – for example, by pooling and converting assets into tradable securities and entering into interest rate swaps and other derivatives transactions – in response both to regulatory incentives such as capital requirements and to internal incentives to improve risk-adjusted returns on capital for shareholders and to be more competitive . . . Securitization makes the pricing and allocation of capital more efficient because changes in financial risks are reflected much more quickly in asset prices and flows than on bank balance sheets. The downside is that markets have become more volatile, and this volatility could pose a threat to financial stability. (IMF, 2002, p. 3)

Global derivatives markets

As the new financial instruments were developed and marketed, the securities markets grew massively in the 2000s, dwarfing the growth of the real economy. For example, according to the Bank of International Settlements, the global derivatives markets grew at the rate of 32 per cent per annum from 1990, and the notional amount of derivatives reached $106 trillion by 2002, $477 trillion by 2006, and exceeded $531 trillion by 2008 (though gross market value is a small fraction of this) (McKinsey & Company, 2008, p. 20). The supposed purpose of this increasingly massive exercise was to hedge risk and add liquidity to the financial system. Derivatives allow financial institutions and corporations to take greater and more complex risks such as issuing more mortgages and corporate debt, because they may protect debt holders against losses. Since derivatives contracts are widely traded, risk may be further limited, though this increases the number of parties exposed if defaults occur.

Complex derivatives were at the heart of the credit market turmoil that
rippled through financial markets in 2007, raising concerns about the
financial players' abilities to manage risk as capital markets rapidly evolve.
Unlike equities, debt securities and bank deposits, which represent financial
claims against future earnings by households and companies, derivatives are
risk-shifting agreements among financial market participants. (McKinsey &
Company, 2008, p. 20)

Because of this fundamental difference and indeterminacy McKinsey
did not include derivatives in their calculation of the value of global
financial assets, an indication of the ephemeral quality of derivatives.
Yet derivatives certainly have their defenders who claim they make an
essential contribution to international liquidity. A riveting analysis of
the legacy of the former Chairman of the Federal Reserve in *The New
York Times*, detailed how Alan Greenspan defended derivatives
markets as an innovation helping to develop and stabilize the international financial system: 'Not only have individual financial institutions become less vulnerable to shocks from underlying risk factors,
but also the financial system as a whole has become more resilient.'
Others were less sanguine, and both George Soros and Warren Buffett
avoided investing in derivatives contracts because of their impenetrable complexity. Buffett described derivatives in 2003 as 'financial
weapons of mass destruction, carrying dangers that, while now latent,
are potentially lethal', and pointed out that collateralized debt obligation contracts could stretch to 750,000 pages of impenetrable (and
presumably unread) text (*The New York Times*, 8 October 2008).

  Greenspan was sceptical about successive legislative efforts to regulate
derivatives in the 1990s. Charles A. Bowsher, Head of the General
Accounting Office, commenting on a report to Congress identifying
significant weaknesses in the regulatory oversight of derivatives, said in
testimony to the House Sub-Committee on Telecommunications and
Finance in 1994: 'The sudden failure or abrupt withdrawal from trading
of any of these large U.S. dealers could cause liquidity problems in the
markets and could also pose risks to others, including federally insured
banks and the financial system as a whole. In some cases intervention has
and could result in a financial bailout paid for or guaranteed by taxpayers.' In his testimony at the time, Greenspan was reassuring: 'Risks in
financial markets, including derivatives markets, are being regulated by
private parties. There is nothing involved in federal regulation per se
which makes it superior to market regulation', though he did accept

derivatives could amplify crises because they connect together financial institutions: 'The very efficiency that is involved here means that if a crisis were to occur, that that crisis is transmitted at a far faster pace and with some greater virulence.' When the Commodity Futures Trading Commission, the federal agency which regulates options and futures trading examined derivatives regulation in 1997, the head of the Commission, Brooksley E. Born, said in testimony to Congress that such opaque trading might 'threaten our regulated markets or, indeed, our economy without any federal agency knowing about it', but she was chastised for taking steps that would lead to a financial crisis by Treasury officials (*The New York Times*, 8 October 2008). The explosive potential of derivatives was always present, as the implosion of the hedge fund Long Term Capital Management (LTCM) in 1998 revealed. With equity of $4.72 billion and debt of $124 billion LTCM had managed to secure off-balance sheet derivative positions of $1.29 trillion (mostly in interest rate swaps). The rescue of LTCM by a consortium of banks led by the Federal Reserve Bank of New York, in order to maintain the integrity of the financial system, was a harbinger of how a decade later on massive systemic financial risk-taking would be rescued by governments after the event, rather than regulated by governments before the event.

The corporate governance causes of the crisis

The explanation of why investment banks and other financial institutions took such spectacular risks with extremely leveraged positions on many securities and derivatives, and the risk management, governance and ethical environment that allowed such conduct to take place, is worth detailed analysis. Nobody imagined the scale of the tragedy that befell Wall Street's leading investment banks. 'Wall Street: RIP', pronounced *The New York Times* (28 September 2008). 'A world of big egos. A world where people love to roll the dice with borrowed money, of tightwire trading, propelled by computers . . . that world is largely coming to an end.' Replacing the triumphal past was disillusion and disorientation: 'Enthusiasm was gone from Wall Street yesterday, replaced by a febrile uncertainty and a foreboding that 2008 might turn into 1929' (*Times Online*, 1 October 2008). No one had imagined this all could happen this quickly, or could anticipate when it might end. Before the end of October 2008 more than half a trillion dollars had been lost in subprime investments by major international banks (Table 2.1).

Table 2.1 *Subprime losses by international banks October 2008*

	Company	Country	($US bn)
1	Citigroup	US	66.6
2	Merrill Lynch	US	54.6
3	Wachovia	US	52.7
4	Washington Mutual	US	45.6
5	UBS	Switzerland	44.2
6	HSBC	UK	27.4
7	Bank of America	US	21.2
8	JP Morgan Chase	US	18.8
9	Lehman Brothers	US	18.2
10	AIG	US	16.8
11	Royal Bank of Scotland	UK	16.5
12	Morgan Stanley	US	15.7
13	IKB Deutsche	Germany	14.7
14	Fannie Mae	US	12.7
15	Deutsche Bank	Germany	11.4
16	Ambac	US	10.3
17	Wells Fargo	US	10
18	MBIA Inc	US	9.4
19	Barclays	UK	9.2
20	Credit Agricole	France	8.6
21	Credit Suisse	Switzerland	8.1
22	HBOS	UK	7.5
23	Canadian Imperial Bank of Commerce	Canada	7.1
24	Fortis	Belgium/Netherlands	6.9
25	Bayerische Landesbank	Germany	6.7
26	Freddie Mac	US	6.7
27	ING	Netherlands	6.5
28	Société Générale	France	6.4
29	Mizuho Financial Group	Japan	6.2
30	Dresdner Bank	Germany	5
31	Bear Sterns	US	3.4
32	WestLB	Germany	3.1
33	BNP Paribas	France	2.7
34	UniCredit	Italy	2.7
35	Lloyds TSB	UK	2.6
36	Nomura Holdings	Japan	2.5
37	DZ Bank	Germany	2
38	Natixis	France	2
39	Swiss Re	Switzerland	1.8

Table 2.1 (*cont.*)

	Company	Country	($US bn)
40	HSH Nordbank	Germany	1.7
41	LBBW	Germany	1.7
42	Commerzbank	Germany	1.2
43	Mitsubishi UFJ	Japan	1.2
44	Sumitomo	Japan	1.2
45	AXA	France	1.1
	Total losses		582.60

Sources: Individual banks; central banks.

Masters of the Universe

Each financial boom is associated not only with reckless risk-taking and wildly inflated rewards, but an indulgent culture proclaiming the new Masters of the Universe. Tom Wolfe coined this phrase (based on a children's comic book) for financial *parvenus* in the middle of the 1987 boom in his book *The Bonfire of the Vanities*.[1] The hubris returned a decade later with the NASDAQ boom, and the posturing of the executives of Enron, Worldcom and other companies who, in strenuous self-promotion, declared they were leading the best companies in the world, before they ran out of funds and then ran out of hype as they faced the courts. With the recovery of US financial markets after the Enron debacle, the explosion of financial innovation gave the world a new breed of Masters of the Universe in the derivatives dealers and hedge fund managers who manipulated trillions of dollars, while charging immense fees. This long financial boom of recent years saw the culture of financial excess permeate through swathes of the rich industrial countries as people were encouraged to live on debt with escalating mortgages and multiplying credit cards.

Symptomatic of the humiliating fall from assumed greatness was the end of Lehman Brothers, a 158-year-old Wall Street institution forced into bankruptcy by an incapacity to face reality. Lehman's had failed before in 1984, selling itself to American Express at a discount price (Auletta, 1986). The Chairman at the time, Lewis L. Glucksman, said, 'We never made a culture where people were concerned with the firm and not just each other. We had a level of greed here and personal selfishness that was disgraceful' (*The New York Times*, 19 January 1986). Later Richard S. Fuld became Chief Executive, returning Lehman's back to being an independent bank in 1994. Lehman's was the fourth largest investment bank on Wall Street and was a self-proclaimed 'innovator in global finance'.

As the Wall Street investment banks stumbled, Fuld had dinner with Henry Paulson in April 2008 and came away thinking Lehman's had a 'huge brand' with the US Treasury. The announcement of a first quarter 2008 loss of $2.8 million and a larger second quarter loss of $3.9 billion exposed the weaknesses in Lehman's position. As Fuld cast about for a white knight to invest in the firm in the United States, Europe and among Asian sovereign wealth funds, Lehman's was publicly presenting a rosy view of its future. After the company collapsed, three separate federal investigations began into the conduct of Lehman's in the final months, and Fuld was hauled in front of the US Congress House of Representatives oversight committee. Democratic congressman John Sarbanes, referring to a June 2008 statement in which Fuld insisted the company's liquidity was strong, said, 'Either he has lost all perspective and is completely clueless or he is quite savvy and deceiving people' (*Financial Times*; *The New York Times*, 6 October 2008).

Deregulation

Financial institutions are critical to the operation of any economy, and traditionally subject to a framework of firm regulation, however as the financialization of the US and international economy proceeded, paradoxically the regulatory touch lightened considerably. In the words of one US finance expert in the years before the crisis:

> We were developing a system of very large, highly levered, undercapitalized financial institutions – including the investment banks, some large money centre banks, the insurance companies with large derivative books and the government-sponsored entities . . . Regulators believe that all of these are too big to fail and would bail them out if necessary. The owners, employees and creditors of these institutions are rewarded when they succeed, but it is all of us – the taxpayers – who are left on the hook if they fail. This is called private profits and socialized risk. Heads, I win. Tails, you lose. It is a reverse Robin Hood system. (Einhorn, 2008a, pp. 16–17)

The abolition of the Glass-Steagall Act in 1999 paved the way for a regulatory loosening of the US financial system, enhanced in 2004 by a new SEC rule intended to reduce regulatory costs for broker-dealers that were part of consolidated supervised entities. Essentially this involved large broker-dealers using their own risk-management practices for regulatory purposes, enabling a lowering of their capital requirements (the core capital which a bank is required to hold to support its risk-taking activities, which normally includes share capital, share premium and retained earnings). In addition the SEC amended the definition of net capital to include securities for which there was no ready market, and to include hybrid capital instruments and certain deferred tax assets, reducing the amount of capital required to engage in high risk activities. Finally the rule eased the calculations of counterparty risk, maximum potential exposures and margin lending, and allowed broker-dealers to assign their own credit ratings to unrated companies. Einhorn comments on this regulatory capitulation of the SEC: 'Large broker-dealers convinced the regulators that the dealers could better measure their own risks, and with fancy math, they attempted to show that they could support more risk with less capital. I suspect that the SEC took the point of view that these were all large, well-capitalized institutions, with smart, sophisticated risk managers who had no incentive to try to fail. Consequently, they gave the industry the benefit of the doubt' (2008a, p. 16).

Rating agencies

As international financial markets have expanded, the role of the credit rating agencies (CRAs) has proved critical. The International Organization of Securities Commissions (IOSCO) claims that

CRAs assess the credit risk of corporate or government borrowers and issuers of fixed-income securities. CRAs attempt to make sense of the vast amount of information available regarding an issuer or borrower, its market and its economic circumstances in order to give investors and lenders a better understanding of the risks they face when lending to a particular borrower or when purchasing an issuer's fixed-income securities. A credit rating, typically, is a CRA's opinion of how likely an issuer is to repay, in a timely fashion, a particular debt or financial obligation, or its debts generally. (2003, p. 1)

Yet the question asked by everybody when the financial crisis erupted was how could asset-backed securities containing subprime mortgages and other high risk debt possibly be given AA credit ratings by Standard and Poor's or Moody's?

The answer was again that financial innovation had outpaced regulatory prowess. The rating agencies, instead of monitoring rigorously the growth of financial markets and instruments, had become junior partners in this enterprise. Coffee (2006) in his critique of the failure of the gatekeeper professions in US corporate governance, including auditors, corporate lawyers and securities analysts, raises the following issues regarding rating agencies:

Concentration

Given the immense capacity of the rating agencies to influence the fortunes of financial institutions and instruments in terms of the public perception of risk, they have maintained a highly profitable duopoly with Standard and Poor's Ratings Services and Moody's Investor Services, only recently joined by Fitch Investor Services for specialised submarkets. The SEC has supported this entrenched market position, reinforced by a reputational capital only now being challenged.

Conflicts of interest

Traditionally the rating agencies rated thousands of clients in the corporate debt business with little chance of being captured by single clients. However, as the importance of the structured debt market grew, there were only a few investment banks active but the scale of the market grew exponentially. From the 1970s the rating agencies business changed from their revenue coming from subscribers for their ratings services, to their revenue coming from the issuers of debt products, creating a context for capture by clients' interests.

Complex financial products

Rating corporate debt utilizing corporate financial history and audited financial statements is less difficult than complex structured finance products issued by investment banks. Understanding the nature of the underlying assets and cash flows generated by these assets, and the risks involved over time, is a major undertaking. The rating agencies deny any obligation to do due diligence on the portfolio backing structured finance products.

Timing and relevance

Even if the rating agencies were close in their original rating, they do not review how a debt product may change over time in different market conditions, and rating agencies were slow to downgrade sub-prime asset backed securities (Coffee, 2006; Scott 2008, pp. 23–4).

The rating agencies believed in the investment banks of Wall Street, and in their risk controls, and assumed that 'everything was hedged'. Though the CRAs do have the power to review non-public information to assess the creditworthiness of institutions and securities, they did not have the inclination, manpower or skills to do this thoroughly in all cases, and they did not get paid until they gave a rating.

The market perceives the rating agencies to be doing much more than they actually do. The agencies themselves don't directly misinform the market, but they don't disabuse the market of misperceptions – often spread by the rated entities – that the agencies do more than they actually do. This creates a false sense of security, and in times of stress, this actually makes the problems worse. Had the credit rating agencies been doing a reasonable job of disciplining the investment banks – which unfortunately happen to bring the rating agencies lots of other business – then the banks may have been prevented from taking excess risk and the current crisis might have been averted. (Einhorn, 2008a, p. 13)

Risk management

Financial businesses' activities in rapidly changing markets are highly sensitive to variance, and it might be expected that as the financial services industries have grown inexorably and financial products have become more complex, the sophistication of risk management techniques will have developed in parallel. However the reality is that innovation in financial products has far exceeded the capacity of risk management measurement and monitoring tools to gauge risk. The most widely employed risk management tool is value-at-risk (VaR), which measures how much a portfolio stands to make or lose in 99 per cent of the days. But as Einhorn argues, this measure ignores what might happen at the moment of greatest risk:

A risk manager's job is to worry about whether the bank is putting itself at risk in the unusual times – or, in statistical terms, in the tails of distribution. Yet, VaR ignores what happens in the tails. It specifically cuts them off.

A 99 per cent VaR calculation does not evaluate what happens in the last 1 per cent. This, in my view, makes VaR relatively useless as a risk management tool and potentially catastrophic when its use creates a false sense of security among senior managers and watchdogs. This is like an airbag that works all the time, except when you have a car accident. By ignoring the tails, VaR creates an incentive to take excessive but remote risks. (Einhorn, 2008a, p. 11)

Yet VaR was the tool international finance industries relied upon in transactions involving billions of dollars. For example UBS was the European bank with the largest losses from the crisis, involving the Swiss government and central bank providing an aid package of $59.2 billion to take risky debt securities from its balance sheet. In a report to shareholders published in April 2008, UBS laid bare the risk management failings that had led to such immense losses (though wealthy clients continued to desert the bank in droves, withdrawing $58 billion in the third quarter of 2008). The report highlights in worrying detail the incomplete risk control methodologies, with market risk control (MRC) placing considerable reliance on VaR and stress limits to control the risks of the business, without implementing additional risk methodologies, or aggregating notional limits even when losses were made (2008a, p. 13):

(1) Mortgage portfolio trades were certified by the UBS investment bank's quantitative risk control: '[B]ut with the benefit of hindsight appears not to have been subject to sufficiently robust stress testing. Further, the collateralised debt obligation desk did not carry out sufficient fundamental analysis as market conditions deteriorated . . .' (2008a, p. 30).
(2) With regard to asset-backed securities trading, also, there were incomplete risk control methodologies. 'There was considerable reliance on AA/AAA ratings and sector concentration limits which did not take into account the fact that more than 95 per cent of the asset backed securities trading portfolio was referencing US underlying assets (i.e. mortgage loans, auto loans, credit card debt etc)' (2008a, p. 32).
(3) In fixed income there was a growth orientation: 'The investment bank was focused on the maximisation of revenue. There appears to have been a lack of challenge on the risk and reward to business area plans within the investment bank at a senior level. UBS's

review suggests an asymmetric focus in the investment bank senior management meetings on revenue and profit and loss, especially when compared to discussion of risk issues. Business-peer challenge was not a routine practice in those meetings . . . Inappropriate risk metrics were used in strategic planning and assessment. Investment Bank planning relied on VaR, which appears as the key risk parameter in the planning process. When the market dislocation unfolded, it became apparent that this risk measure methodology had not appropriately captured the risk inherent in the business having subprime exposures' (2008, p. 34).

(4) With regard to UBS group governance there was: '[F]ailure to demand a holistic assessment. Whilst group senior management was alert to the general issues concerning the deteriorating US housing market, they did not demand a holistic presentation of UBS's exposure to securities referencing US real estate assets before July 2007, even though such an assessment may have been warranted earlier in view of the size of UBS's real estate assets' (2008, p. 35).

(5) The report concluded with reference to risk control that there was over-reliance on VaR and stress: 'MRC relied on VaR and stress numbers, even though delinquency rates were increasing and origination standards were falling in the US mortgage market. It continued to do so throughout the build-up of significant positions in subprime assets that were only partially hedged. Presentations of MRC to UBS's senior governance bodies did not provide adequate granularity of subprime positions UBS held in its various businesses. No warnings were given to group senior management about the limitations of the presented numbers or the need to look at the broader contextual framework and the findings were not challenged with perseverance' (2008, p. 39).

(6) Finally the report condemned the lack of independence and healthy scepticism in UBS governance: 'Fundamental analysis of the subprime market seems to have been generally based on the business view and less on MRC's independent assessment. In particular there is no indication that MRC was seeking views from other sources than business . . . Further, risk systems and infrastructure were not improved because of a willingness by the risk function to support growth' (2008, pp. 39–40).

Incentivization

The final and most critical part of the explanation of why investment banks and other financial institutions took such extreme risks with highly leveraged positions in complex securities, neglecting risk management, governance principles, and often basic business ethics, was that *they were highly incentivized to do so*. Massively incentivized irresponsibility became the operating compensation norm in the financial community, as banks and fringe financial institutions chased the super profits available as global financial markets expanded exponentially.

The management teams at the investment banks did exactly what they were incentivized to do: maximize employee compensation. Investment banks pay out 50% of revenues as compensation. So, more leverage means more revenues, which means more compensation. In good times, once they pay out the compensation, overhead and taxes, only a fraction of the incremental revenues fall to the bottom line for shareholders. The banks have done a wonderful job at public relations. Everyone knows about the 20% incentive fees in the hedge fund and private equity industry. Nobody talks about the investment banks' 50% compensation structures, which have no high-water mark and actually are exceeded in difficult times in order to retain talent. (Einhorn, 2008a, p. 11)

The report on the vast write-downs at UBS examines how the compensation structure directly generated the behaviour which caused the losses, as staff were motivated to utilize the low cost of funding to invest in subprime positions.

Employee incentivization arrangements did not differentiate between return generated by skill in creating additional returns versus returns made from exploiting UBS's comparatively low cost of funding in what were essentially carry trades . . . The relatively high yield attributable to subprime made this asset class an attractive long position for carry trades. Further, the UBS funding framework amplified the incentives to pursue compensation through profitable carry trades. The compensation structure generally made little recognition of risk issues or adjustment for risk/other qualitative indicators (e.g., for group internal audit ratings, operational risk indicators, compliance issues etc.). (Einhorn, 2008a)

As a result there were insufficient incentives to protect the UBS franchise for the longer term; 'it remains the case that bonus payments for successful and senior international business fixed income traders, including those in the businesses holding subprime positions were significant. Essentially, bonuses were measured against gross revenue after personnel costs, with no formal account taken of the quality and sustainability of those earnings' (2008a, p. 42).

Regulation and governance of financial institutions

While the accumulated cost of the global financial crisis was being realized, the commitment to establish a new international financial regulatory framework increased. As the costs of all forms of intervention to alleviate the crisis by the US government ballooned out to $7.7 trillion (including credit discounts, credit extensions, securities lending, term auction facilities, portfolio funding, money market funding, TARP, assistance to specific institutions, economic stimulus packages and homeowner assistance), the general market assistance and specific rescue packages for individual financial institutions amounted to almost $11 trillion worldwide by October 2008 (Table 2.2). While these funds could be regarded as a temporary investment in the financial economy, with the hope of recouping much of the funds back at a later stage, this was an optimistic view when the crisis spread to other sectors of the economy. As the financial crisis impacted upon the real economy the fears of a prolonged recession grew, with US industrial production falling further than it had for over thirty years, and, for example, the US automotive industry becoming increasingly precarious, announcing further major redundancies and looking for support from the federal government (including support from the assistance intended for financial institutions, since the automotive companies had also become finance companies). The International Labour Organization in Geneva estimated that up to twenty million people in the world would lose their employment as a consequence of the financial crisis, and that for the first time in a decade the global total of unemployed would be above 200 million (*Associated Press*, 21 October 2008). The prospect of the whole world falling into recession at the same time became possible, something not witnessed since the 1930s.

There was a widespread sense that this regulatory failure of financial markets could not be allowed to occur again. The Chancellor of Germany, usually a stalwart ally of President Bush, derided the lack of regulation which, in her view, allowed the financial crisis to erupt in the United States and seep inexorably towards Europe. She reminded

Table 2.2 *Government support for global financial crisis 2008*

	$US
Europe	1.8 trillion
UK	856 billion
US	7.74 trillion
Sweden	205 billion
South Korea	130 billion
Australia	10.4 billion
Rest of the world	105.12 billion
Total	10.85 trillion

Source: Compiled from: BBC, 'Credit crisis: world in turmoil', available at http://news.bbc.co.uk/2/hi/business/7654647.stm and IMF, 'Global financial stability report', October 2008, available at www.imf.org/external/pubs/ft/gfsr/2008/02/ index.htm.

the German public that the United States and Britain rejected her proposals in 2007 for regulating international hedge funds and bond ratings agencies. 'It was said for a long time, "Let the markets take care of themselves",' Merkel commented. 'Now,' she added, 'even America and Britain are saying, "Yes, we need more transparency, we need better standards."' Germany's finance minister, Peer Steinbrueck, said that the 'Anglo-Saxon' capitalist system had run its course and that 'new rules of the road' are needed, including greater global regulation of capital markets (*The Washington Post*, 28 September 2008). Gordon Brown and Nicolas Sarkozy called for a Bretton Woods agreement for the twenty-first century, aimed at rebuilding the international financial system. Though the economic summit meeting of leaders of the G20 countries was arranged for Washington in November 2008, it was clear George Bush would not be taking the lead in this initiative. Yet something of a sea-change was occurring in US domestic politics in response to the financial crisis and with the sweeping election to the US presidency of Barack Obama. The experience of Congress and the White House equivocating about a rescue package of buying securities had made a deeply unfavourable impression on the US public. The UK government had recognized the deeper problem of a lack of confidence in the banks themselves, which was resolved by governments becoming the investor of last resort and the guarantor of loans between banks, and it was the adoption of a similar strategy by the US government that finally staunched the panic on Wall Street. As Andrew Moravcsik, professor of politics and international affairs at Princeton University, suggested, 'Americans, especially conservatives, have a particular view of Europe as over-regulated, therefore suffering from weak growth and Euro-sclerosis. This could change that view and create more respect for the European view of regulation more generally' (*Australian Financial Review*, 20 October 2008).

A problem in devising a new financial regulatory architecture was that Bretton Woods in 1944, though it established the International Monetary Fund and the World Bank, was essentially dealing with national financial markets. Digital and interconnected global financial markets presented a much bigger challenge. A series of measures was proposed by Gordon Brown:

(1) Improving risk disclosure by financial institutions was fundamental, together with stricter rules on bank liquidity and leveraging.
(2) Ensuring banks take bigger stakes in any loans they pass on to others through securitization might constrain irresponsible innovations.
(3) Establishing a central clearing house for complex derivatives could help to discipline their use.
(4) Increased supervision and regulation might include new standards for off-balance sheet accounting, and supervision of the largest international banks and insurance companies.
(5) Reforming executive compensation structures that encouraged excessive risk-taking and aligning reward with long-term value creation was another imperative.
(6) Finally a capacity to police the potential for future dangers to the international economy and the means of cooperation for future crises were important (*The Times*, 16 October 2008).

These principles for reforming international financial markets were broadly supported in Europe, and had public resonance in the United States where it was argued the rapid expansion of unregulated financial institutions and instruments from hedge funds to credit default swaps should be contained by extending financial reserve requirements, limiting leveraging and ensuring trading occurred on public exchanges (*The Wall Street Journal*, 25 July 2008; IPS 2008). With the international financial community still in a state of profound shock, and heavily dependent upon state aid, any protests about the dangers

of over-regulation were muted. Adair Turner, head of the Financial
Services Authority (FSA) in the UK (responsible for regulating financial institutions), commented:

> If a year and a half ago, the FSA had wanted higher capital adequacy, more
> information on liquidity, had said it was worried about the business models
> at Bradford & Bingley and Northern Rock, and had wanted to ask questions
> about remuneration, the fact is that we would have been strongly criticized
> for harming the competitiveness of the City of London, red tape, and over-
> regulation. We are now in a different environment. We shouldn't regulate
> for its own sake, but over-regulation and red tape has been used as a
> polemical bludgeon. We have probably been over-deferential to that rhet-
> oric. (*The Guardian*, 16 October 2008)

However the question is: will the deference of regulators return when
financial markets recover, and financial institutions and markets are
free again to pursue their self-interest? An early indication of how
entrenched the irresponsibility of the financial sector had become was
the astonishing news that the surviving US financial institutions were
preparing to pay end of year executive bonuses approximately equivalent to the billions of dollars of aid they had just received from
Congress. While the US economy was collapsing around them, and
the US public were becoming increasingly concerned how they might
survive a severe recession, the executives of major banks seemed
focused primarily on maintaining their bonuses.

Note

1 Oliver Stone's iconic movie *Wall Street*, set in this period, was supposed to
be about crime and punishment on Wall Street, but Michael Douglas,
playing the ruthless takeover magnate Gordon Gekko, who won an Oscar
for his 'Greed is Good' speech, now cannot have breakfast in New York
without being approached by young men saying it was seeing the movie
that made them want to become Wall Street traders.

References and further reading

Aglietta, M. and Berrebi, L. 2007. *Désordres dans le capitalisme mondiale*.
    Paris: Odile Jacob.
Aglietta, M. and Reberioux, A. 2005. *Corporate Governance Adrift:
    A Critique of Shareholder Value*. Cheltenham: Edward Elgar.
Amble, B. 2003. *The Diversity of Modern Capitalism*. Oxford University
    Press.

Auletta, K. 1986. *Greed and Glory on Wall Street*. New York: Random House.

Chesnais, F. 2008. 'Fin d'un cycle. Sur la portée et le cheminement de la crise financière', *Carré Rouge – La Brèche* 1: 17–31 January.

Clarke, T. 2009. 'A critique of the Anglo-American model of corporate governance', available at http://papers.ssrn.com/sol3/papers.cfm?abstract_id=1440853, last accessed 21 December 2010.

Coffee, J. 2006. *Gatekeepers: The Professions and Corporate Governance*. Oxford University Press.

CTR/CEPS 2005. *Deep Integration: How Transatlantic Markets are Leading Globalization*. Centre for Transatlantic Relations/Centre for European Policy Studies, Washington, DC, Johns Hopkins University.

Ee, K. and Xiong, K. 2008. 'Asia: a perspective on the subprime crisis', *International Monetary Fund* 45 (2), available at www.imf.org/external/pubs/ft/fandd/2008/06/khor.htm, last accessed 22 December 2010.

Einhorn, D. 2008a. 'Private profits and socialized risk', *Global Association of Risk Professionals Review* June/July 42: 10–18.

Einhorn, D. 2008b. *Fooling Some of the People All of the Time: A Long Short Story*. Hoboken, NJ: Wiley.

EPI 2008. *The State of Working America*. Washington: Economic Policy Institute.

Epstein, G. A. 2005. *Financialization and the World Economy*. Northampton, MA: Edward Elgar.

Erturk, I., Froud, J., Johal, S., Leaver, A. and Williams, K. 2008. *Financialization at Work: Key Texts and Commentary*. London: Routledge.

Fleckenstein, F. 2008. *Greenspan's Bubbles: The Age of Ignorance at the Federal Reserve*. New York: McGraw Hill.

Froud, J. and Johal, S. 2008. 'Questioning finance: a special issue of competition and change', *Competition and Change* 12 (2): 107–9.

Froud, J., Johal, S., Leaver, A. and Williams, K. 2006. *Financialization and Strategy: Narrative and Numbers*. London: Routledge.

Galbraith, J. K. 1993. *A Short History of Financial Euphoria*. London: Penguin.

Goodman, P. 2008. 'Taking a hard new look at the Greenspan legacy', *The New York Times*, 8 October.

Greenspan, A. 2004. 'Risk and uncertainty in monetary policy', *American Economic Association*, San Diego, CA, 3 January 2004. Federal Reserve Board, available at www.federalreserve.gov/BoardDocs/Speeches/2004/20040103/default.htm, last accessed 22 December 2010.

Hilferding, R. 1985 (original edition 1910). *Finance Capital: Study of the Latest Phase of Capitalist Development*. London and New York: Routledge.

IFSL 2008. *International Financial Markets in the UK*. London: International Financial Services.

IMF 2002. *The Globalization of Finance, Finance and Development*. Washington, DC: International Monetary Fund 39 (1).

IMF 2008. *Global Financial Stability Report: Financial Stress and Deleveraging*. Washington, DC: International Monetary Fund.

IOSCO 2003. 'Regulatory and investor protection issues arising from the participation by retail investors in (funds-of-) hedge funds', Report of the Technical Committee of the International Organization of Securities Commissions, February 2003. Available at www.iosco.org/ library/ pubdocs/pdf/IOSCOPD142.pdf, last accessed 22 December 2010.

IPS 2008. *A Sensible Plan for Recovery*, Washington, DC: Institute for Policy Studies, 15 October 2008.

Janszen, E. 2008. 'The next bubble: priming the markets for tomorrow's big crash', *Harper's Magazine*, February: 39–45.

Krippner, G. R. 2005. 'The financialization of the American economy', *Socio-Economic Review* 3: 173–208.

Krugman, P. 2008. 'Cash for trash', *The New York Times*, 21 September.

Laeven, L. and Valencia, F. 2008. 'Systemic banking crises: a new database', *IMF Working Paper, WP/08/224*, International Monetary Fund: Washington, DC.

Langley, P. 2008. *The Everyday Life of Global Finance: Saving and Borrowing in Anglo-America*. Oxford University Press.

Leroy, P. 2008. *The Subprime Mortgage Crisis: Highlighting the Need for Better Corporate Governance*. Sydney: University of Technology.

Lewis, H. 2007. '"Moral hazard" helps shape mortgage mess', 18 April, available at www.bankrate.com/brm/news/mortgages/20070418_subprime_mortgage_morality_a1.asp?caret=3c, last accessed 10 November 2008.

Lim, M. 2008. 'Old wine in a new bottle: subprime mortgage crisis – causes and consequences', Working Paper No. 532. The Levy Economics Institute.

Lockhart, D. 2008. 'The subprime crisis: is it contagious?' Federal Reserve Bank of Atlanta, 29 February, available at www.frbatlanta.org/invoke.cfm?objectid=65C8B587–5056–9F12–125B76D448344BEF&method=display, last accessed 22 December 2010.

Martin, R. 2002. *The Financialization of Daily Life*. Philadelphia, PA: Temple University Press.

Maximus, F. 2008. *Consequences of A Long, Deep Recession – Parts I, II, III*, available at http://fabiusmaximus.wordpress.com/2008/06/18/consequences-1/ -2, -3. June 18–20, last accessed 22 December 2010.

Mcavoy, P. W. and Millstein, I. M. 2004. *The Recurrent Crisis in Corporate Governance*. Stanford: Business Books.

McKinsey & Company. 2008. *Mapping Global Capital Markets: Fourth Annual Report.* San Francisco: McKinsey Global Institute.

Muolo, P. and Padilla, M. 2008. *Chain of Blame: How Wall Street Caused the Mortgage and Credit Crisis.* Hoboken, NJ: Wiley.

Narayanan, M. P. 1985. 'Managerial incentives for short-term results', *Journal of Finance* 40 (5): 1469–84.

Patel, B. 2008. 'Credit crisis and corporate governance implications: guidance for proxy season and insight into best practices', RiskMetrics Group, April, available at www.riskmetrics.com//system/files/private/CreditCrisisCorporateGovernance20080408.pdf, last accessed 22 December 2008.

Phillips, K. 2008. *Bad Money: Reckless Finance, Failed Politics, and the Global Crisis of American Capitalism.* New York: Viking Books.

Rosen, R. 2007. 'The role of securitization in mortgage lending', *Chicago Fed*, 11 October, available at www.chicagofed.org/publications/fedletter/cflnovember2007_244.pdf, last accessed 22 December 2010.

Schwarcz, S. 2008. 'Disclosure's failure in the subprime mortgage crisis', Research Paper Series, Research Paper No. 203. Duke Law School, March 2008.

Scott, W. A. 2008. 'The credit crunch and the law – a commentary on economic and policy issues', in Austin, R. P. (ed.), *The Credit Crunch and the Law.* Monograph 5, Ross Parsons Centre of Commercial, Corporate and Taxation Law: University of Sydney.

Shiller, R. 2008. *The Subprime Solution: How Today's Global Financial Crisis Happened and What to Do About It.* Princeton University Press.

Soros, G. 2008. *The New Paradigm for Financial Markets: The Credit Crisis of 2008 and What it Means.* New York: Public Affairs.

Stiglitz, J. 2008. 'Realign Wall Street's interests', *Harpers Magazine*, November: 36–7.

2008b. 'Henry Paulson's shell game', *The Nation*, 26 September.

UBS 2008 *Shareholder Report on UBS's Write Downs*, Zurich: UBS AG, available at www.ubs.com/1/ShowMedia/investors/shareholderreport?contentId=140333&name=080418ShareholderReport.pdf, last accessed 22 December 2010.

Whalen, C. 2008. *The Subprime Crisis – Cause, Effect and Consequences*, Networks Financial Institute, Indiana State University, March 2008.

3 | The failure of corporate governance and the limits of law: British banks and the global financial crisis

ROMAN TOMASIC

The global financial crisis demonstrated the fragility of the widely accepted faith in prevailing corporate governance ideas and the adequacy of legal mechanisms that were available to buttress these ideas. This was very evident from the fate of British banks after the failure of Northern Rock plc in late 2007 and the subsequent government action to rescue other leading British banks (Treasury Committee, 2008b). After more than two decades of debate in regard to the improvement of corporate governance mechanisms in Britain, it became evident that many of the ideas that had been advanced during this debate have been found to be wanting and were in need of revision or even replacement; these earlier debates had largely sought to legitimize a self-regulatory approach to corporate governance and a minimal involvement of governments in markets.

This corporate governance rhetoric can be traced back at least to the Cadbury Committee and subsequent inquiries which have helped to fashion the architecture of British corporate governance (Cadbury, 1992). These debates raised expectations in regard to the effectiveness of corporate governance codes, the monitoring roles of boards and especially of non-executive directors, the roles of institutional investors, and the effectiveness of shareholders in being able to deal with major governance matters requiring attention (Greenbury, 1995; Myners, 2001; Higgs, 2003). The recent Walker Review of corporate governance in UK banks has sought to salvage many of these prevailing ideas by looking for best practice solutions to strengthen the largely self-regulatory corporate governance structures (Walker, 2009).

This approach followed a broadly Anglo-American tradition of seeking to minimize the involvement of government in markets and led to the development of international movements to replicate this rhetoric in the fabric of international corporate governance structures; this is best illustrated in the development of the OECD's Principles of Corporate Governance and the replication of such codes widely around the world (OECD, 1999; OECD 2004). The OECD has more recently also looked for best practice mechanisms to strengthen corporate governance in banking institutions (OECD, 2010). In many countries, and particularly in the UK with its Combined Code on Corporate Governance (2006), the faith in these 'soft law' corporate governance strategies was matched by a minimal development of legal rules, such as those regarding the issue of derivatives, and by a regulatory approach to markets which accepted the prevailing orthodoxy that markets could best be left to regulate themselves.

The effect of the minimal regulatory influence of the state over financial markets was amplified by the role of government in promoting London as a leading financial centre and in encouraging foreign banks and financial institutions to base themselves in this city because of the low level of legal intervention that could be expected. As a consequence, London attracted many of the riskier financial operations of foreign firms such as Lehman Brothers and AIG, as well as securities fraudsters such as Bernard Madoff.[1] The discussion of these other catastrophic failures is, however, beyond our scope here.

This chapter will look at evidence that has emerged from the recent financial crisis regarding the weaknesses in prevailing corporate governance prescriptions; it will also examine failures in regard to legal mechanisms that had been seen as buttressing these largely private corporate governance ideas. It will focus mainly upon the UK, although similar findings could be made in regard to other markets, such as the United States and Germany (see further, Acharya *et al.*, 2009; Hopt, Kumpan and Steffek, 2009; Posner, 2009; Mulbert, 2010). Unfortunately, there is insufficient space to deal with wider issues, such as the development of effective regulatory structures to deal with financial markets and the wider, largely politically driven, imperative to support London as a major financial centre. This is because an adequate treatment of these issues does, to a significant degree, require an international approach that is beyond the capacity of any one jurisdiction (see further, Treasury Committee, 2009d).

The wider context of UK corporate governance

To understand why it was possible for such catastrophic failures of major British banks to occur so suddenly it is useful to draw attention to the interweaving of three prevailing forces. First, the ideological belief in the inherent superiority of self-regulation of financial markets was deeply entrenched in both the public and private sectors and undermined effective public oversight of markets. Secondly, the consequential belief that there was little, if any, need for government monitoring of these markets had the consequence that public legal institutions were either underdeveloped or under-mined. Thirdly, the political imperative to develop and maintain the position of London as a major financial centre meant that political pressure could also be brought to bear against intrusive regulations or regulators.

There is no doubt that there are good arguments for all of these beliefs. It is also true that any effective corporate regulatory regime must depend heavily upon corporations being committed to maintaining appropriate governance standards and values as part of their corporate culture. It is clearly unrealistic to rely exclusively upon state intervention and monitoring in the regulation of complex financial markets; but this should not mean that government should retire from the field and merely act as a cheerleader on the sidelines of the marketplace.

Alternatives to governmental regulation, such as the reliance upon private sector bodies, such as rating agencies, to evaluate the quality of financial products such as derivatives, face other problems, such as possible conflict of interest; indeed, it has been argued that rating agencies have played a significant role in generating the financial crisis (see further, Coffee, 2009). Similarly, professional gatekeepers have also failed effectively to restrain abuses in accounting practices (as we saw with the collapse of Enron) or to ensure that directors acted properly (see generally, Armour and McCahery, 2006).

Professional gatekeepers (such as auditors and lawyers) have been seen as playing an important role in ensuring corporate integrity and their failure to prevent misconduct (often due to conflicts of interest) have undermined their effectiveness (see generally, Coffee, 2006; Fuchita and Litan, 2006; Dravis, 2007, pp. 125–46). Even internal corporate risk monitors within banks who were charged with the responsibility of risk assessment proved ineffective when faced with euphoric market situations and pressures from the sell side of banks. This was most graphically illustrated by the failure of Paul Moore in HBOS to effectively communicate the gravity of the risks that were being taken by the bank.[2]

Finally, the political appeal of hosting a major financial centre needs to be balanced by the risks that excesses in such centres may lead to the need to impose heavy financial burdens on taxpayers who may be called upon to rescue failed financial institutions on the grounds that their survival was essential to the maintenance of stability in markets.

Maintaining market stability and avoiding the spread of contagion from any failed financial institution are primary considerations in times of market crisis, so that emergency action taken to rescue failing institutions may often not be well thought through and may in due course be seen as being too irksome. For this reason, effective corporate governance mechanisms cannot readily be constructed during crises, but crises do provide an opportunity to articulate more long-term solutions. This is because the evidence produced by such crises can be illuminating for corporate governance reformers.

Recent failures in British banking

The decade or so leading up to the failure of Northern Rock plc in late 2007 had seen a massive transformation in the size and nature of British banking. Long-established building societies, like Northern Rock, had demutualized and set their sights upon rapid expansion; this was facilitated by the ready availability of substantial funds from foreign investors from as far afield as East Asia and the Middle East. Little consideration was given to the possibility that the availability of funds might suddenly dry up, as occurred in September 2007.

In May 2009, the House of Commons Treasury Committee reviewed the failure of British banking since September 2007 and noted that as a result of the financial crisis:

Five of the nine FTSE 100 banks in March 2007, Bradford & Bingley, HBOS, Lloyds TSB, Northern Rock and RBS, are now partly or wholly in public ownership. None of the four demutualised building societies, Alliance and Leicester, Bradford & Bingley, HBOS and Northern Rock, now exists as a stand-alone bank in its own right. Thousands of jobs in the financial services sector have been lost . . . It is hard to estimate what will be the eventual cost to public funds of the banking crisis but the damage will be substantial and long-term. (Treasury Committee, 2009b, p. 7)

But prior to September 2007, the ready availability of borrowed funds during these boom years meant that some banks, such as the Royal

Bank of Scotland (RBS), Northern Rock and HBOS, rapidly expanded to become significant national and international players. In the case of RBS, it was to become a major international player as a result of the ease with which funds could be borrowed; this expansion was largely achieved by resort to corporate takeovers (such as the ill-fated acquisition of Dutch bank ABN Amro in 2007 by RBS, Fortis and Santander[3]) as well as to the development of new and more risky lines of business.

This led to a change in the dominant business model that was used by these banks and financial institutions; in the case of a bank's mortgage business, instead of relying on the traditional 'originate to hold' model, whereby banks would write mortgages and then hold these until lenders had paid their mortgages out, banks moved to an 'originate to distribute' model in which they would repackage or securitize mortgages and often transfer these to off-shore special purpose vehicles that would then sell these securitized assets to investors. It was believed that the use of securitization was a way of limiting the risk faced by banks by taking these securitized products off their balance sheets by dispersing risk among other investors. But, as the FSA Chairman, Lord Turner, had observed, '[t]his analysis has proved wrong. Rather than improving system resilience, the development of securitised credit has ended up producing the worst financial crisis for a century' (Turner, 2009).

The dangers presented by these new business models were not properly understood in view of the short-term horizons upon which prevailing risk models had been built (Taleb, 2007). The misplaced reliance upon faulty mathematical models also encouraged even greater risk-taking by issuers of new financial products (Tett, 2009). Accentuating this risk-taking was the system of distorted incentives, such as large bonuses, which encouraged investment divisions of banks to develop and distribute new derivative products. The system of rewarding bankers by the payment of bonuses based on short-term performance often failed to have regard to long-term risks that were inherent in the products that had been sold by these banks (see further, Treasury Committee, 2009c).

This conduct was built upon a conception of markets as ultimately being rational and efficient, assumptions that were found to be faulty; the concept of 'irrational exuberance' has been used to characterize behaviour during market bubbles (Shiller, 2000; Fox, 2009). However, despite the prevailing view of the inherent rationality of markets, some economists such as Minsky (1986) and Kindleberger and Aliber (2005) had long known that financial markets were susceptible to crises during periods of speculative booms. But, as Richard Posner (2009, pp. 259–60) has argued, contrary voices such as these were often lost or submerged during the boom years due to the 'overinvestment by economists, policymakers, and business leaders in a free-market ideology that opposes aggressive government interventions in the operations of the economy'.

These ideologies were very influential in the UK where deregulatory and *laissez-faire* rhetoric was embraced with enthusiasm by both government and business. As Chancellor of the Exchequer, Gordon Brown championed risk-taking and the 'light touch' regulatory environment that London provided. On the eve of the collapse of financial markets in 2007, in addressing civic leaders and members of the financial community in London, Chancellor Brown confidently observed:

Over the ten years that I have had the privilege of addressing you as Chancellor, I have been able year by year to record how the City of London has risen by your efforts, ingenuity and creativity to become a new world leader. Now today over 40 per cent of the world's foreign equities are traded here, more than New York:

- over 30 per cent of the world's currency exchanges take place here, more than New York and Tokyo combined,
- while New York and Tokyo are reliant mainly on their large American and Asian domestic markets, 80 per cent of our business is international, and
- in a study last week of the top 50 financial cities, the City of London came first.

So I congratulate you Lord Mayor and the City of London on these remarkable achievements, an era that history will record as the beginning of a new golden age for the City of London.[4]

This exuberant attitude had led the UK in 2002 to confer an honorary knighthood upon the former chairman of the US Federal Reserve, Alan Greenspan, the architect of the low level of regulatory intervention in financial markets, for his 'contribution to global economic stability'.[5] Two years later, the Chief Executive of the

Royal Bank of Scotland, Fred Goodwin, was also awarded a knighthood, although there were later calls for the removal of this knighthood following the collapse of RBS.[6]

More significantly, the UK had deliberately chosen an approach to market regulation that was 'principles-based' and used 'light-touch' regulatory methods. This model had been championed as a more effective response to the kinds of market abuses that had led to the passage in 2002 of the Sarbanes-Oxley Act in the United States following the Enron and Worldcom failures. Critics have claimed that the superiority of the UK principles-based system of market regulation was not well founded (Kershaw, 2005). In contrast, the success of this strategy had been asserted by Chancellor Brown in his 2007 Mansion House speech, but the weakness of this strategy was soon evident after the Financial Services Authority sought to explain its failure to prevent the failure of Northern Rock. The FSA's internal audit presented a damning account of its failures as a regulator.[7]

The Treasury Committee of the House of Commons, when reviewing the failure of Northern Rock, was also critical of the failure of the tripartite regulatory authorities (consisting of the FSA, the Bank of England and the Treasury) to act quickly enough in the face of Northern Rock's difficulties in September 2007; these bodies also seemed to lack a clear leadership structure, although the Chancellor was said to be ultimately in control (Treasury Committee, 2008a, pp. 104–13).

The FSA was subsequently to largely abandon exclusive reliance upon its 'light-touch' and 'principles-based' approach to regulation as being unsuitable in regard to financial markets as they had come to evolve in London. Instead, the FSA moved to what it was to call 'the Intensive Supervisory Model'. Hector Sants, the FSA Chief Executive, explained the rationale for this model:

Historically, the FSA characterised its approach as evidence-based, risk-based and principles-based. We remain, and must remain, evidence- and risk-based but the phrase 'principles-based' has, I think, been misunderstood. To suggest that we can operate on principles alone is illusory particularly because the policy-making framework does not allow it. Europe, in particular, has a particular penchant for rules and in any case in a number of key areas such as prudential regulation they are indeed necessary . . . Furthermore, the limitations of a pure principles-based regime have to be recognised. I continue to believe the majority of market participants are decent people; however, a principles-based approach does not work with individuals who have no principles.[8]

From the above it is clear that external corporate regulatory structures were poorly attuned to effectively monitoring 'high impact' firms such as Northern Rock. UK laws were also poorly structured to deal effectively with failing banks, leading to a scramble to draft new special resolution regimes in an effort to rescue failing banks and to maintain market stability (see further, Tomasic, 2009b). In addition, it was recognized that other legal remedies, such as the company law obligations of directors' provisions and shareholder rights' mechanisms were not adequate when dealing with financial crises such as that involving Northern Rock and other British banks (see further, Tomasic, 2009a; Tomasic, 2009c).

This then leads us to look more closely at the internal corporate governance structures within British banks. This was a matter that was touched upon in the January 2008 report of the Treasury Committee that looked into the run on Northern Rock, when criticisms were made of the lack of adequate banking qualifications of the Northern Rock Chairman and CEO. The Treasury Committee noted that the failure of Northern Rock was both a failure of the FSA as regulator as well as a failure of the Northern Rock board of directors (Treasury Committee, 2008a, pp. 33–4).

It pursued these themes further in a number of reports in the following year (Treasury Committee, 2009a; Treasury Committee, 2009d). The theme of corporate governance failure was to be further pursued in the Committee's later reports and was taken up especially in the November 2009 Walker Review into corporate governance in UK banks (Walker, 2009). It is appropriate that we now turn to look more closely at some of these corporate governance issues.

A case study: corporate governance failures in Northern Rock plc

In many ways, the rise and fall of Northern Rock plc may be seen as reflecting many of the forces at work in the UK financial system in the lead up to, and in response to, the global financial crisis.[9] It was certainly not the biggest casualty of the crisis, as Royal Bank of Scotland and HBOS had greater financial difficulties. It was, however, the only bank to be fully nationalized by the UK Treasury, although

larger amounts of public money were allocated to the rescue of some
of the other failing UK banks.

Some UK banks, such as Barclays and HSBC, managed to avoid
having to call upon the Treasury for funds to sustain them,[10] but other
banking names have now disappeared, such as Bradford & Bingley
and Alliance and Leicester, which were acquired by the Spanish bank
Santander and added to Santander's other British banking assets.
Some major building societies, such as Scotland's largest building
society, the 140-year-old Dunfermline Building Society, were absorbed
by a larger domestic financial institution.[11] A recapitalized Northern
Rock is also likely to be sold off as market conditions improve.

Like many of the institutions that had struggled in the face of the
global financial crisis, Northern Rock was a former mutual, having
been set up as a building society in 1965 following the merger of two
older building societies that had originally been established in 1850
and 1865 respectively.[12] In 1965 the Northern Rock Building Society
became the largest building society in Newcastle. It then grew rapidly,
largely as a result of the acquisition of other building societies, and
this saw its assets double to over £1 billion in 1983.

After this time the building society set up a commercial finance
division and moved into commercial lending. In 1994 it acquired the
North of England Building Society, based in Sunderland; this was
significant as it added 43,000 new borrowers and over £1.5 billion
in assets, giving Northern Rock assets of over £10 billion and making
it one of the top ten players in the industry. As one observer has noted:
'[o]ver four years it had increased its size threefold, its profits fourfold
and had halved its management expense ratios' (Walters, 2008, p. 6).

In 1997 Northern Rock demutualized and became a listed public
company; this allowed it to raise more capital from markets.[13] All
qualifying members of the mutual received 500 shares each and
became shareholders in the new company. The business grew on the
back of competitive pricing of its products and a narrow margin
between what it paid for funds and the amount that mortgage borrowers paid it in interest. Although it was called a bank, Northern
Rock did not offer a full range of banking services and tended to focus
mainly upon residential and commercial mortgages and unsecured
personal loans. In the first half of 2007 it wrote £10.7 billion in
residential mortgages and this represented 18.9 per cent of UK net
mortgage lending.

The bank's growth had not been funded by an expansion in its retail deposits but through reliance upon wholesale markets for interbank lending and by use of securitization (National Audit Office, 2009, p. 13). It had also not been greatly funded by equity capital-raising on the stock market. Nevertheless, by 2007 Northern Rock had become the fifth largest mortgage lender in the UK. However, it was under pressure due to its low levels of capitalization. It had almost the lowest level of market capitalization with only £4.8 billion in capital raised on stock markets on 2 April 2009.[14] In contrast, the market capitalization at that time of other leading UK banks was much higher: £31.6 billion for Lloyds-TSB, £39.30 billion for HBOS, £47.1 billion for Barclays, £62.8 billion for RBS and £103.1 billion for HSBC (Treasury Committee, 2009b, p. 7).

In March 2007, Northern Rock was forced to sell its profitable commercial finance division as the new Basel II Accord, introduced earlier that year, had imposed higher capital adequacy requirements for commercial lending than for mortgage-based lending. In June this commercial finance business was eventually sold for £1.6 billion to Lehman Commercial Mortgage Conduit Limited – an affiliate of the American investment bank Lehman Brothers. In the meantime, interest rates continued to rise; this was a problem for Northern Rock as it relied heavily upon borrowing funds from the money market at the interbank rate (LIBOR). This created a problem as most of Northern Rock's mortgage lending to its customers was tied to the Bank of England base rate, which was lower than the rate at which it sourced funds.

This pressure caused Northern Rock to issue a profit warning to the London Stock Exchange at the end of June 2007. This led to a 12 per cent drop in the bank's share price or a 30 per cent drop in prices since February. At the same time Northern Rock received a Basle II waiver, which meant that only 15 per cent of its funds had to be available to support its residential mortgages. However, in a company that sourced 75 per cent of its funds externally, this left Northern Rock 'particularly exposed' due to the severe shortages of capital that it faced (Walters, 2008, p. 45). But the bank did not seem to be too concerned about this problem.

This was characteristic of similar attitudes in other banks at this time, which continued to trade optimistically (see Treasury Committee, 2009b, pp. 7–8). This extraordinary lack of restraint in the face of signs that the market was beginning to collapse was found in other banks such as HBOS and RBS, which continued to do very risky deals, despite the warnings (Treasury Committee, 2009b, pp. 20–4).

On 9 August 2007 interbank lending stopped suddenly due to fears that arose from an announcement by the French bank BNP Paribas that it would suspend three of its asset-based securities funds because of concerns that these could no longer be properly valued due to difficulties that were emerging in the US subprime mortgage market (Brummer, 2008, pp. 55–74). This followed hard on the heels of revelations of severe problems with three German banks on 2 August.[15] In one insider account from within Northern Rock:

This announcement sent shock waves through an already sensitive market and it became evident to the board at Northern Rock that it would face severe problems if the markets were to stay frozen for long. The problems were especially severe for Northern Rock because its funding model required mortgage-backed securities and plain mortgages to be securitised, and its next securitisation was scheduled for September 2007. (Walters, 2008, p. 53)

The market freeze of 9 August 2007 was similarly described by one financial journalist:

The events of Thursday, 9 August, had devastating consequences for Northern Rock as it felt the full blast of the credit crunch. The bank's risk committee, headed by Sir Derek Wanless, had failed to act as a restraining force on the strategy of the executive members . . . Now that the credit markets around the world, on which it depended for 75 per cent of its funding, were freezing up it found itself caught in a perfect squeeze, unable to fund the loans on its mortgage book, many of which had been sold too cheaply. (Brummer, 2008, p. 67)

The senior officers of Northern Rock were also severely shocked by the multiple failures that occurred at this time. As the Commons Treasury Committee observed:

Mr Applegarth [the CEO] told us that Northern Rock had wrongly 'believed that high-quality assets and transparency [were] the way to maintain liquidity.' Sir Derek Wanless [a non-executive director] told us that Northern Rock's 'first line of defence [was] good credit quality . . . Northern Rock had not foreseen all its funding markets closing simultaneously, as happened after 9 August . . . The idea of all markets closing to Northern Rock was repeatedly characterised to us by Northern Rock officials as 'unforeseeable'. (Treasury Committee, 2008, p. 16)

September did indeed prove a decisive moment for Northern Rock; on the 13th the Bank of England's emergency loan to Northern Rock was made public as a result of a leak to the BBC; this precipitated a bank run by Northern Rock depositors. As one financial journalist observed:

Within minutes of the BBC bulletin, consumers began logging on to Northern Rock's website and withdrawing their cash. The website then crashed, fuelling panic. The next morning, Northern Rock savers flocked to the bank's branch offices, and pictures of terrified savers in a long line in front of the bank beamed on to computers, television screens . . . across the world. By mid-morning, a full-scale bank run was under way. (Tett, 2009, p. 229)

The board of Northern Rock finally announced on 17 September that the Bank of England had given it a guarantee of 100 per cent of its deposits. A number of concerns had led the Bank of England to keep its support for Northern Rock secret as it examined legal issues connected with the provision of state support. Previously, the Bank of England had been reluctant to provide support to private banks because of arguments around the problems of moral hazard that had often been used to prevent government support for failing companies; these economic arguments were to be almost universally discarded as the financial crisis gathered momentum.

The corporate governance problems facing Northern Rock were closely examined by the Treasury Committee of the UK House of Commons which concluded that:

The directors of Northern Rock were the principal authors of the difficulties that the company faced since August 2007. It is right that members of the Board of Northern Rock have been replaced, though haphazardly, since the company became dependent on liquidity support from the Bank of England. The high-risk, reckless business strategy of Northern Rock, with its reliance on short- and medium-term wholesale funding and the absence of sufficient insurance and a failure to arrange standby facility or cover that risk, meant that it was unable to cope with the liquidity pressures placed upon it by the freezing of international capital markets in August 2007.

The Treasury Committee went on to explain the nature of this governance failure when it added that:

Given that the formulation of that strategy was a fundamental role of the Board of Northern Rock, overseen by some directors who had been there since its demutualisation, the failure of that strategy must also be attributed to the Board. The non-executive members of the Board, and in particular the Chairman of the Board, the Chairman of the Risk Committee and the senior non-executive director, failed in the case of Northern Rock to ensure that it remained liquid as well as solvent, to provide against the risks that it was taking and to act as an effective restraining force on the strategy of the executive members. (Treasury Committee, 2008a, p. 19)

In its response to these findings, the UK government agreed that the primary responsibility for minimizing risks and preventing other problems lay with the bank's directors. Criticisms were levelled at a number of key features of its board; first, the chairman of the board (Dr Matt Ridley, a well-known scientist) was seen to lack appropriate experience and expertise to chair a major banking institution; secondly, the chief executive of the bank (Adam Applegarth) was criticized on a number of counts; thirdly, the board itself did not have significant levels of banking expertise; finally, its independent or non-executive directors seem to have failed to provide the kinds of checks and balances that it was said that such directors might provide to restrain an overly adventurous chief executive. Let us look at some of these concerns more closely (see further, Tomasic, 2008b, pp. 330–5).

As we have seen, the House of Commons Treasury Committee laid responsibility for this failure to respond to the bank's changing risk situation squarely on the shoulders of its board.[16] The senior independent director of Northern Rock, Sir Ian Gibson, had argued before the Committee, in the board's defence, that it had sought advice from the FSA and the UK Listing Authority on the state of its business model; it also sought advice from its own legal advisors, and as a result the Northern Rock board was 'fully satisfied that we did follow the best advice and follow[ed] it to the letter' (Treasury Committee, 2008a, p. 19). This confidence is in stark contrast to the subsequent findings of the Treasury Committee and many of those experts that it relied upon.[17] Whether this effort to seek external advice is enough to satisfy the business judgment rule and principles of reliance is open to question.

It is interesting to refer to wider reactions in the financial media to the patterns of behaviour at Northern Rock, which were apparently sanctioned by the Northern Rock board. This might help to better assess what would be seen as reasonable action on the part of the board. Some corporate governance authorities have accused the

Northern Rock board of lacking in due diligence.[18] Other comments have focused on the differing roles of executive and non-executive directors, as well as on the role and skills base of the bank chairman and its CEO. Writing generally about the difficulties facing board members, Paul Myners, at the time the City Minister and a former member of the UK Financial Reporting Council, stressed the increasing importance of corporate governance in regard to banks:

Proposals to overhaul the banking system have largely ignored the governance of our banks. But if other reforms are to have any traction, it is essential to shake up the boardrooms that oversee the rest of the operation. First, board members should never forget that the most vital part of their job is to challenge executives . . . Are board members asking the right questions and with enough persistence? . . . The business of banking is exponentially more complicated than a generation ago, and the panel [the board] guiding it must be able to follow its dealings. At the very least the chairman and senior independent director or chairman of the risk committee should have recent and relevant banking experience. (Myners, 2008, p. 15)

In regard to non-executive directors, Ruth Sunderland, writing in *The Observer*, noted that:

Northern Rock's downfall highlights persistent weaknesses in corporate governance, not just there but at other blue-chip companies. The independent directors, who are supposed to act as a check on executive folly, did not restrain Adam Applegarth, the chief executive, from his turbo-charged business model, which was a bit like putting a Ferrari engine into a Micra.

Sunderland went on to ask why none of the non-executive directors 'seems to have made the simple inquiry as to why a modest mortgage bank in Newcastle upon Tyne was playing at the casino end of the capital market'.[19] But Anthony Hilton, writing in September 2007, thought that the non-executive directors of Northern Rock were 'not lightweight people' as they had considerable experience in the financial services industry and yet they either did not see the risks that the bank was running or, if they did, they were unable 'to persuade the management to be more prudent'. He added that some non-executive directors may find it difficult to seek to restrain an overly zealous CEO who was at the same time being cheered on by the wider business community.[20] This was a point emphasized by Hilton when he wrote: 'Adam Applegarth, the [Northern Rock] chief executive, was a much-admired man in the fund management community until last month. What chance do non-executive directors have to rein him in when the entire fund management community is on the other side urging him on?' He added pointedly that '[w]e might conclude that the problem lies not in the quoted companies, but among the analysts and institutional shareholders who in their thirst for rewards too often drive executives to those very excesses of risk which end in tears.'[21] It could also be argued that the board may have been encouraged to have less to fear of the risks inherent in its business strategy because these risks were being securitized and then passed on to Granite, Northern Rock's special purpose vehicle.

As it turned out, this was not as effective a way of avoiding these risks as they might have expected. In any event, it seems from the comments of independent director Sir Ian Gibson that the board would seek shelter in legal arguments to the effect that they acted reasonably and that they took advice from appropriate experts. However, some courts have become increasingly uncomfortable with arguments upon reliance where directors might be expected to know better or to be more diligent.[22]

The old view of a director's standard of care and diligence, as expressed by Romer J in *Re City Equitable Fire Insurance Co Ltd*,[23] has come to be criticized with the rise of community expectations concerning the qualities that directors should bring to the boardroom. In developing a standard of 'reasonable care' to be followed by directors, Romer J had drawn upon the discussion of the notion of reasonable care in the nineteenth-century decision in *Overend & Gurney Co v. Gibb*. This was, of course, a case involving a company that was at the heart of the last major run on a British bank (see further, Collins and Baker, 2003, pp. 86–91). In that case it was said:

. . . whether or not the directors exceeded the powers entrusted to them, or whether if they did not so exceed their powers they were cognisant of circumstances of such a character, so plain, so manifest, and so simple of appreciation, that no men with any ordinary degree of prudence, acting on their own behalf, would have entered into such a transaction as they entered into?[24]

This view of the notion of reasonable care has been echoed to some degree by the New South Wales Court of Appeal in *Daniels t/as Deloitte Haskins & Sells* v. *AWA Ltd*.[25] However, this Court went on to call for a higher standard of care than that propounded by Romer J and called for a more active engagement by directors in the scrutiny of company decisions.

Influenced by more objective standards for directors of companies facing insolvency, there has been a movement in some courts to adopt a more objective standard of care than was evident in earlier cases such as *Re City Equitable*. This may be illustrated by the view taken in the UK of the duty of care owed by a director.[26] For example, Professor Davies has noted:

. . . the change over time in the type of person appointed to the board has also led to a shift of view within company law about the appropriate standard of care for directors . . . The primary focus of the law's scrutiny is on whether the board took reasonable steps to inform itself before it took the decision in question and not on whether the substantive decision taken was reasonable. (Davies, 2002, pp. 155–7)

In the Australian case of *Daniels* v. *Anderson*, the NSW Court of Appeal sought to go beyond early twentieth-century British case law and drew upon US authority to update legal principles derived from Britain on the extent to which directors could rely upon others when making decisions.[27] However, Northern Rock shareholders were not able to obtain much comfort from these developments as there remained some doubt in the UK that legal actions against its directors would be successful.

Following its nationalization, on advice from their lawyers, the new controllers of Northern Rock therefore decided that there were insufficient legal grounds to pursue such an action against the former bank directors.[28] When Northern Rock shareholders subsequently sought compensation for the loss of their shares, as a consequence of the forced nationalization of the bank, their causes of action did not focus upon the duties of the directors of Northern Rock, but unsuccessfully relied largely on human rights grounds concerned with the unfair misappropriation of their property by government (see further, Tomasic, 2009c).

In light of this discussion of evolving legal principles regarding the appropriate duties of directors, it is interesting to note the level of qualifications held by members of the board of Northern Rock; this had been discussed by the Commons Treasury Committee and has been the subject of pointed comments in the press. Although the chairman of Northern Rock's Risk Committee was seen as being 'an extremely experienced banker', the report of the Treasury Committee found:

We are concerned that the Chief Executive of Northern Rock [Mr Adam Applegarth] was not a qualified banker, although of course he has significant experience. The Financial Services Authority should not have allowed nor even again allows two appointments of a Chairman and a Chief Executive to a 'high-impact' financial institution where both candidates lack relevant financial qualifications; one indication that an individual has been exposed to the relevant training is an appropriate professional qualification. Absence of such a qualification should be a cause of concern. We therefore recommend that the FSA undertake an urgent review of the current qualifications of senior directors in financial firms . . . (Treasury Committee, 2008, pp. 33–4)

The qualifications of the former chairman of Northern Rock, Dr Matt Ridley, also did not escape comment; it was noted in the *Financial Times* that he was a zoologist and a successful science writer (Myners, 2008, p. 15). He had joined the board of Northern Rock in 1994 and then served as non-executive chairman from 2004 until 2007; he resigned after being criticized in Parliament for harming the reputation of British banking and for lacking financial experience.[29] His aristocrat father (Viscount Ridley) had previously been chairman of the bank from 1987 to 1992 and had sat on the board for three decades. It is not a strong defence for the board to say that the FSA had sanctioned actions taken by Northern Rock, especially when one reads the heavy criticism of the role of the FSA in this collapse that was made in the House of Commons (Treasury Committee, 2008, p. 34).

However, industry leaders since the time of Walter Bagehot (1873) have for some time called for the adoption of a higher standard of care than that which UK courts have been prepared to articulate; the judicial view was that it was the responsibility of Parliament to state any higher duty of care and not the courts. For example, in more recent times, Sir Adrian Cadbury, writing about the role of the chairman of a public listed company, highlighted the rise in expectations of directors that has occurred and went on to point to the need for the training of directors; he pointed to paragraph A.2.1 of the then UK Combined Code on Corporate Governance which stated that 'every director should receive appropriate training on the first occasion that he or she is appointed to the board of a listed company, and subsequently as necessary' (Cadbury, 2002, p. 24). Cadbury went on to discuss risk management and the role of the board in this regard and noted that:

A key point is that companies are continually having to adjust their plans and strategies in the light of a changing competitive environment and thus the risks they face, and the priorities to be assigned to them, are continually changing as well . . . It is for boards to set internal control policies and to assure themselves that they are working as they should. It is the job of management to put those policies into effect. (Cadbury, 2002, p. 220)

Interestingly, the government-appointed Walker Review was also to criticize the standards of directors and called for amendments of the Combined Code to require them to be more actively involved in monitoring company matters. Walker, however, refrained from seeking to express this higher standard in legislative form, preferring the voluntary 'comply or explain' model that had prevailed for some time. In the context in which domineering CEOs were able to influence boards to adopt excessively risky strategies, Walker called into question patterns of behaviour on British bank boards and noted that: 'The most critical need is for an environment in which effective challenge of the executive is expected and achieved in the boardroom before decisions are taken on major risk and strategic issues' (Walker, 2009, p. 12).

Walker's preferred solution was to strengthen corporate governance mechanisms that were already in place because of the fact that many corporate governance problems were 'organic, dynamic and behavioural' and better dealt with by non-legal mechanisms (Walker, 2009, p. 28). This view is only partly correct, as there is much scholarly research to show that sole reliance on private regulatory enforcement alone will fail to secure improved regulatory objectives (see generally, McBarnet *et al.*, 2007; Braithwaite, 2008).

In any event, Walker focused on making improvements, such as in the composition of the board, obtaining greater time commitment by non-executive directors to their board duties, seeking a more active involvement of the chairman, increased board-level engagement in risk oversight and greater involvement of shareholders (and especially institutional shareholders) in discharging their responsibilities as owners. This has led the UK Financial Reporting Council to draft a Stewardship Code and to review provisions of the former Combined Code of Corporate Governance (see further FRC 2009; FRC 2010). The key question here will be whether these 'soft law' solutions will be sufficient.

It is too early to say whether such corporate governance changes are likely to prevent the collapse of another leading banking institution. The collapse of Northern Rock clearly highlighted major deficiencies in the internal and external regulation of British banks and identified corporate governance issues as being important reasons for this failure. The academic literature would suggest that there is more room for improvement than that identified in the Walker Review. But the fact that the FSA has become more active in regulating British banks and financial institutions is a major departure from earlier patterns of governmental regulation of this sector.

Some conclusions

The failure of so many British banks during the global financial crisis has highlighted the centrality of corporate governance issues. These have widely been perceived to have been important in explaining why banks failed to respond to the risks that were to cause them to fail. In part, this failure has been attributable to an uncritical adherence to market self-regulation; in this context it was widely considered that soft-law codes of corporate governance were more effective than legislation or government regulatory action. To some degree this view has been echoed in the academic literature, which has pointed to the limits of law and the centrality of corporate culture in explaining corporate conduct (see further, Stone, 1975).

Although formal legal rules and government regulation alone have limitations in being able to ensure corporate accountability, the simple pursuit of self-regulatory or soft-law mechanisms is not adequate either. This has been demonstrated by recent events, where the virtual withdrawal of government action in fostering improved corporate governance has undermined the operation of self-regulatory strategies in British banks. It is clear that there is room for a range of mechanisms in achieving better corporate governance.

The failure of British banking regulation during the recent financial crisis calls for a more thoroughgoing review of existing corporate governance mechanisms. This applies both within banks and to bank boards in particular. It also calls for more effective external monitoring and control of corporate governance failures. Simply tinkering with the self-regulatory 'comply or explain' approach and renaming the Combined Code, are unlikely to be effective, especially in periods of market euphoria or booms. A history of successive bank and other corporate failures has demonstrated this lesson. As evident in the above discussion, the well-documented events surrounding the failure of British banks such as Northern Rock, RBS and HBOS, to mention but a few, call for a more radical review of prevailing corporate governance and self-regulatory strategies than has occurred to date.

Notes

1 In regard to Lehman Brothers and AIG see further McDonald, 2009; Sorokin, 2009 and in regard to the Ponzi scheme orchestrated by Bernard Madoff, see further Arvedlund, 2009; Markopolos, 2010.

2 See further, BBC News, 'HBOS whistleblower probe demanded', 11 February 2009, available at www.news.bbc.co.uk/1/hi/uk_politics/7882119.stm.

3 See further, Robbins, Mathieu, 'Was ABN the worst takeover deal ever?', *The Independent*, 20 January 2009, available at www.independent.co.uk/news/business/analysis-and-features/was-abn-the-worst-takeover-deal-ever-1451520.html.

4 Speech by the Chancellor of the Exchequer, the Rt Hon. Gordon Brown MP, to Mansion House, City of London, 20 June 2007, available at http://www.hm-treasury.gov.uk/press_68_07.htm.

5 BBC News, 'Alan Greenspan to be knighted', 7 August 2002, available at www.news.bbc.co.uk/1/hi/business/2177814.stm.

6 Churcher, J., 'Harman admits blunder over Goodwin's knighthood', *The Independent*, 4 March 2009; available at www.independent.co.uk/news/uk/politics/harman-admits-blunder-over-goodwins-knighthood-1637347.html.

7 See further, Financial Services Authority, *The Supervision of Northern Rock: A Lessons Learned Review; Report*, March 2008, available at www.fsa.gov.uk/pubs/other/nr_report.pdf. See further, Tomasic, 2010.

8 Sants, H., 'Delivering intensive supervision and credible deterrence – Speech by Hector Sants, Chief Executive, FSA', 12 March 2009, Financial Services Authority, available at www.fsa.gov.uk/pages/Library/Communication/Speeches/2009/0312_hs.shtml. Also see Wilson, H., 'Hector Sants calls time on FSA's "light touch" regulation', Telegraph.co.uk, 12 March 2010, available at www.telegraph.co.uk/ finance/newsbysector/banksandfinance/7431645/Hector-Sants.

9 In addition to extensive material from public inquiries, much has been written about the failure of Northern Rock; see further Keasey and Veronesi, 2008; Lastra, 2008; Tomasic, 2008a and Tomasic, 2008b.

10 Banks like Barclays may, however, have obtained indirect benefit from the fact that the UK government has put in place an asset protection scheme to guarantee bank debts, although it had not, as such, signed up

to joining this scheme; see further, Farrell, S. and Aldrick, P., 'Barclays, the Houdini bank', *The Telegraph*, 13 February 2010, available at www. telegraph.co.uk/finance/newsbysector/banksandfinance/7229425/Barclays-the-Houdini-bank.html. Also see generally, Power, H. and Coates, S., 'Barclays Bank comes out fighting against Treasury', *The Times*, 19 January 2009, available at http://business.timesonline.co.uk/tol/business/industry_sectors/banking_ and_finance/article5543107.ece.

11 See further: Wood, Z. and Hinsliff, G., 'Dunfermline Building Society to be broken up', *The Guardian*, 28 March 2009, available at http://www.guardian.co.uk/business/2009/mar/28/dunfermline-building-society/print.

12 These were the Northern Counties Permanent Benefit and Investment Building Society (formed in 1850) and the Rock Building Society (formed in 1865).

13 Other building societies to have demutualized included Abbey National (1989), Alliance & Leicester (1997), Birmingham Midshires (1999), Bradford & Bingley (2000), Bristol & West (1997), Cheltenham & Gloucester (1995), Halifax (1997), National & Provincial (1996) and Woolwich (1997); see further Treasury Committee, 2009b, p. 29.

14 Only Bradford & Bingley was weaker, with a market capitalization of £2.9 billion; see further, Treasury Committee, 2009b, p. 7.

15 These three German banks were IKB Deutsche Industriebank, Sachsen LB and West LB.

16 The following discussion draws in part upon Tomasic, 2008b, pp. 332–5.

17 These included the Governor of the Bank of England, who described the Bank's business strategy as being 'fundamentally flawed'. Also, Professor William Buiter from the London School of Economics pointed out that Northern Rock was 'clearly engaged in high-risk behaviour' and that 'its funding policies were reckless' – quoted in: Treasury Committee, 2008a, pp. 16–18.

18 This was the view of Professor Bob Garratt, a founding member of the Commonwealth Association for Corporate Governance; see further, Battersby, L., 'Don't turn your back on your board', *The Age*, 14 March 2008, available at http://thebigchair.com.au/news/focus/don't-turn-your-back-on-the-board.

19 Sunderland, R., 'Comment: King not only culprit in a right royal mess', *The Observer*, 23 September 2007.

20 It is too early to know what really motivated the Northern Rock non-executive directors as some, like Nichola Pease, insist that they do not want to talk about their experience at Northern Rock; see further, Burgess, K., 'Little time to talk about the Rock', *Financial Times*, 12 May 2008, p. 25.

21 Hilton, A., 'Why non-execs failed to rein in risk-taking at Northern Rock', *Evening Standard*, 20 September 2007.
22 There is a useful discussion of the development of this body of law in Austin, Ford and Ramsay, 2005 at pp. 250–7.
23 [1925] Ch 407.
24 (1872) LR 5 HL 480 at 486–7.
25 (1995) 13 ACLC 614.
26 This more objective standard may be seen in view of the duty of care owed by a director taken in two decisions of Hoffman LJ in the UK, see *Norman & Anor* v. *Theodore Goddard & Or* [1992] BCC 14 and *Re D'Jan of London Ltd* [1993] BCC 646. Also see further, Deane, 2001, pp. 65–70.
27 *Daniels (formerly practising as Deloitte Haskins & Sells)* v. *Anderson* (1995) 37 NSWLR 438.
28 'No legal action against Northern Rock bosses', *The Independent*, 14 October 2008. See the further discussion of the background considerations that would have explained this approach in Tomasic, 2009a, pp. 7–9.
29 Werdigier, J., 'Northern Rock chairman quits after criticism from lawmakers', *International Herald Tribune*, 19 October 2007.

References

Acharya, V. V., Carpenter, J. N., Gabaix, X., John, K., Richardson, M., Subrahmanyam, M. G., Sundaram, R. K. and Zemel, E. 2009. 'Corporate governance in the modern financial sector', in Acharya, V. and Richardson, M. (eds.), *Restoring Financial Stability: How to Repair a Failed System*. New York: John Wiley & Sons, pp. 185–96.
Armour, J. and McCahery, J. A. 2006. *After Enron: Improving Corporate Law and Modernising Securities Regulation in Europe and the United States*. Oxford: Hart Publishing.
Arvedlund, E. 2009. *Madoff: The Man Who Stole $65 Billion*. London: Penguin Books.
Austin, R. P., Ford, H. and Ramsay, I. M. 2005. *Company Directors: Principles of Law and Corporate Governance*. Sydney: LexisNexis Butterworths.
Bagehot, W. 1873. *Lombard Street: A Description of the Money Market* (1999 edn). New York: John Wiley & Sons.
Braithwaite, J. B. 2008. *Regulatory Capitalism: How It Works, Ideas for Making It Work Better*. Cheltenham: Edward Elgar Publishing.
Brummer, A. 2008. *The Crunch: The Scandal of Northern Rock and the Escalating Credit Crisis*. London: Random House Business Books.
Cadbury, Sir A. 1992. *Report of the Committee on the Financial Aspects of Corporate Governance*. London: Gee & Co.

2002. *Corporate Governance and Chairmanship*. Oxford University Press.

Coffee, J. C. 2006. *Gatekeepers: The Professors and Corporate Governance*. New York: Oxford University Press.

2009. 'What went wrong? An initial inquiry into the causes of the 2008 financial crisis', *Journal of Corporate Law Studies* 9 (1): 1–22.

Collins, M. and Baker, M. 2003. *Commercial Banks and Industrial Finance in England and Wales, 1860–1913*. Oxford University Press.

Davies, P. 2002. *Introduction to Company Law*. Oxford University Press.

Deane, J. 2001. *Directing Public Companies*. London: Cavendish Publishing.

Dravis, B. F. 2007. *The Role of Independent Directors after Sarbanes-Oxley*. Chicago: American Bar Association.

Fox, J. 2009. *The Myth of the Rational Market: A History of Risk, Reward, and Delusion on Wall Street*. New York: HarperCollins.

FRC 2009. *2009 Review of the Combined Code: Final Report*. London: Financial Reporting Council.

2010. *Consultation on a Stewardship Code for Institutional Investors*. London: Financial Reporting Council.

Fuchita, Y. and Litan, R. E. (eds.) 2006. *Financial Gatekeepers: Can They Protect Investors?* Washington, DC: Brookings Institution Press.

Greenbury, Sir R. 1995. *Directors' Remuneration: A Report of a Study Group Chaired by Sir Richard Greenbury*. London: Gee & Co.

Higgs, D. 2003. *Review of the Role and Effectiveness of Non-Executive Directors*. London: UK Department of Trade and Industry.

Hopt, K. J., Kumpan, C. and Steffek, F. 2009. 'A new framework for bank rescue in Germany – regulatory challenges for modern company, corporate insolvency and constitutional law', available at http://ssrn.com/abstract=1501187.

Keasey, K. and Veronesi, G. 2008. 'Lessons from the Northern Rock affair', *Journal of Financial Regulation and Compliance* 16: 8–18.

Kershaw, D. 2005. 'Evading Enron: taking principles too seriously in accounting regulation', *Modern Law Review* 68 (4): 594–625.

Kindleberger, C. P. and Aliber, R. Z. 2005. *Manias, Panics and Crashes: A History of Financial Crises* (5th edn). Houndmills: Palgrave Macmillan.

Lastra, R. M. 2008. 'Northern Rock, UK bank insolvency and cross-border bank insolvency', *Journal of Banking Regulation* 9: 165–86.

Markopolos, H. 2010. *No One Would Listen: A True Financial Thriller*. Hoboken, NJ: John Wiley & Sons.

McBarnet, D., Voiculescu, A. and Campbell, T. (eds.) 2007. *The New Accountability: Corporate Social Responsibility*. Cambridge University Press.

McDonald, L. 2009. *A Colossal Failure of Common Sense: The Incredible Inside Story of the Collapse of Lehman Brothers*. New York: Crown Business, Random House.

Minsky, H. P. 1986. *Stabilizing an Unstable Economy*. New York: McGraw Hill.

Mulbert, P. 2010. 'Corporate governance of banks after the financial crisis: theory, evidence, reforms', available at http://ssrn.com/abstract=1448118.

Myners, P. 2001. *Myners Report on Institutional Investment*. London: HM Treasury.

   2008. 'Reform of banking must begin in the boardroom', *Financial Times*, 25 April, p. 15.

National Audit Office 2009. *HM Treasury: The Nationalisation of Northern Rock: Report by the Comptroller and Auditor General, HC 298 Session 2008–2009, 20 March 2009*. London: The Stationery Office.

OECD 1999. *Principles of Corporate Governance*. Paris: Organisation for Economic Co-operation and Development.

   2004. *Principles of Corporate Governance* (Revised). Paris: Organisation for Economic Co-operation and Development.

   2009. *Corporate Governance and the Financial Crisis: Key Findings and Main Messages*. Paris: Organisation for Economic Co-operation and Development.

   2010. *Corporate Governance and the Financial Crisis: Conclusions and Emerging Good Practices to Enhance Implementation of the Principles*. Paris: Organisation for Economic Co-operation and Development.

Posner, R. A. 2009. *A Failure of Capitalism: The Crisis of '08 and the Descent into Depression*. Cambridge, MA: Harvard University Press.

Shiller, R. J. 2000. *Irrational Exuberance* (2nd edn). New York: Random House.

Sorokin, A. R. 2009. *Too Big to Fail: Inside the Battle to Save Wall Street*. New York: Viking.

Stone, C. 1975. *Where the Law Ends: The Social Control of Corporate Behaviour*. New York: Harper & Row.

Taleb, N. 2007. *The Black Swan: The Impact of the Highly Improbable*. London: Penguin Books.

Tett, G. 2009. *Fool's Gold: How Unrestrained Greed Corrupted a Dream, Shattered Global Markets and Unleashed a Catastrophe*. London: Little, Brown.

Tomasic, R. 2008a. 'Corporate rescue, governance and risk taking in Northern Rock: part 1', *The Company Lawyer* 29: 297–303.

   2008b. 'Corporate rescue, governance and risk taking in Northern Rock: part 2', *The Company Lawyer* 29: 330–7.

   2009a. 'Raising corporate governance standards in response to corporate rescue and insolvency', *Corporate Rescue and Insolvency* 2: 5–9.

   2009b. 'Creating a template for banking insolvency law reform after the collapse of Northern Rock: part 2', *Insolvency Intelligence* 22: 81–8.

2009c. 'Shareholder litigation and the financial crisis: the Northern Rock shareholder appeal considered', *Company Law Newsletter* (262): 1–5, 29 October.

Treasury Committee 2008a. *The Run on the Rock: Fifth Report of Session 2007–08, Volume 1. House of Commons Treasury Committee HC 56–1.* London: The Stationery Office.

2008b. *The Run on the Rock: Government Response to the Committee's Fifth Report of Session 2007–08. House of Commons Treasury Committee HC 56–11.* London: The Stationery Office.

2009a. *Banking Crisis: Regulation and Supervision: Fourteenth Report of Session 2008–09. House of Commons Treasury Committee HC 767.* London: The Stationery Office.

2009b. *Banking Crisis: Dealing with the Failure of the UK Banks: Seventh Report of Session 2008–09. House of Commons Treasury Committee HC 416.* London: The Stationery Office.

2009c. *Banking Crisis: Reforming Corporate Governance and Pay in the City: Ninth Report of Session 2008–09. House of Commons Treasury Committee HC 519.* London: The Stationery Office.

2009d. *Banking Crisis: International Dimensions: Eleventh Report of Session 2008–09. House of Commons Treasury Committee HC 615.* London: The Stationery Office.

2010. 'Beyond "light touch" regulation of British banks after the financial crisis', in MacNeil, I. and O'Brien, J. (eds.), *The Future of Financial Regulation.* Oxford: Hart Publishing.

Turner, Lord A. 2009. *The Turner Review: A Regulatory Response to the Global Banking Crisis.* London: Financial Services Authority.

Walker, Sir D. 2009. *A Review of Corporate Governance in UK Banks and Other Financial Industry Entities: Final Recommendation, 26 November 2009.* HM Treasury. Available at www.hm-treasury.gov.uk/Walker_review_information.htm.

Walters, B. 2008. *The Fall of Northern Rock: An Insider's Story of Britain's Biggest Banking Disaster.* Petersfield, Hampshire: Harriman House.

4 | *Where was the 'market for corporate control' when we needed it?*

BLANAID CLARKE

A totally unfettered market for corporate control is literally all that is needed for near ideal corporate governance.

(Manne, 2008, p. 14)

The 2008 banking crisis was the result of 'a perfect storm of economic conditions' (Lipton *et al.*, 2008, p. 1) which included the subprime mortgage crisis, the property collapse, the liquidity crisis, market volatility and an accommodating accounting and regulatory environment. Most commentators also agree that corporate governance failings played a contributory role. In particular, there has been widespread criticism of the chronic and reckless risk-taking by management, which was fuelled by the banks' remuneration policies. A myriad of reports and recommendations have identified these failings and proposed solutions to ensure that these same mistakes are not repeated.

Against this background it is interesting to consider the implications of the theory of the market for corporate control. This theory, first proposed by Henry Manne in 1965, suggests that mismanagement is reflected in share price because shareholders sell their shares rather than replace management. An opportunity thus arises for a bidder to acquire the company cheaply, replace the inefficient managers and turn the company around. The theory suggests that takeovers have a disciplinary effect on managers. As recently as 2008, Manne has argued that if there is a competitive market for corporate control, there will be no need for any of the other mechanisms for corporate governance other than those voluntarily adopted by contracts and norms. He dismisses the view that there need to be detailed controls over the tenure, constituency and power of boards of directors on the

This chapter is based on a paper presented as part of the ESRC Corporate Governance, Regulation and Development Seminar Series at the University of Central Lancashire (5 June 2009).

basis that the displacement of ineffective boards is at the centre of
the workings of the market for corporate control. In light of recent
calls for changes to our remuneration practices and the EU Recommendation on remuneration, it is particularly striking to note Manne's
comment that 'One of the happiest results of a totally unregulated
market for corporate control will be that the regulators can get out of
the business of limiting or fixing executive compensation' (Manne,
2008, p. 15).

The market for corporate control has received widespread acceptance outside the academic community. In the course of drafting Directive 2004/25/EC ('the Takeover Directive') the European Commission
appointed a High Level Group of Company Law Experts under the
chairmanship of Professor Jaap Winter to examine certain matters
relating to takeover bids. The resulting report ('the Winter Report')
noted that 'in the light of available economic evidence . . . the availability of a mechanism which facilitates takeover bids is basically beneficial'. It cited three reasons for this: the exploitation of synergies, the
opportunity to sell at a premium on market price and, finally, the
market for corporate control. In respect of the latter, it stated categor-
ically that 'such discipline of management and reallocation of resources
is in the long term in the best interests of all stakeholders and society at
large'. The Winter Report also stated quite clearly that these views
'form the basis for the Directive' (Winter *et al.*, 2002, p. 19).

The purpose of this chapter is to consider the following questions:
Why did the market for corporate control not lead to share price
reductions in firms where there was poor risk management and
inadequate oversight by the board? Why were these firms not subsequently acquired by buyers who replaced the board and management
and introduced appropriate risk management structures? Alterna-
tively, why did the fear that this would happen not constitute a
sufficient deterrent to prevent poor risk management in the first
place?

Efficient markets

The challenge to efficient market theory has consequences for the extent to
which we can rely on market discipline rather than regulatory action to
constrain risks. (Turner, 2009, p. 45)

There are a number of assumptions upon which the market for corporate control depends for its validity. The first is that the market for securities is efficient or, as Manne has explained recently, 'relatively efficient and liquid' (Manne, 2008, p. 10). The notion of capital markets efficiency means that all available information about a company is fully reflected in share price (Fama, 1970). The view generally put forward is that the markets are 'semi-strong' in the sense that prices adjust rapidly in response to public information (Gilson and Kraakman, 1984). This hypothesis is crucial to securities regulation as it underlies mandatory disclosure of information and many investor protection rules (Moloney, 2009, p. 95). However, it is fair to say that the assumptions underlying the efficient market theory have been subject to increasingly effective criticism 'drawing on both theoretical and empirical arguments' (Turner, 2009, p. 40). One problem is that the hypothesis does not factor in socio-psychological factors. Bubbles and crashes are an endemic feature of financial markets (Shiller, 2005). There is also evidence of pervasive and systemic biases in the marketplace (Kahneman *et al.*, 1982; Black, 1986). The efficient market hypothesis suggests that arbitrage should correct any irrationality in the marketplace (Gilson and Kraakman, 1984). However, even Gilson and Kraakmann have accepted that investor irrationality is likely to matter to price episodically:

[C]ircumstances of abnormal trading – when a spike in the number of individual investors suggests that noise traders will share a common mistaken belief – will give rise to a shift in arbitrageur strategy that drives prices further from efficiency. On these occasions, arbitrage constraints on price are relaxed, and the effects of cognitive biases on prices are likely to be of significantly greater magnitude than cost-based deviations. (Gilson and Kraakman, 2003, p. 31)

The efficient market hypothesis depends on an even flow of information through to the market. As will be discussed below, there was clear evidence in the recent crisis of relevant information, for example in relation to risk management, not being made available either to boards or to the public. Furthermore, the UK Financial Services Authority (FSA) has acknowledged that information asymmetries between informed contracts for difference (CfD) holders and uninformed 'ordinary' investors can result in price inefficiency in the market. It noted:

Uninformed investors may be unable to acquire valuable information because it is held with informed traders. Valuable information in the context of CfDs which could affect pricing of the referenced shares could include information on those holders of large CfD positions who are able either currently or prospectively to exercise ownership rights over the reference shares. (FSA, 2007, para. 3.14)

It is also important to note, in the context of derivatives, that there is clear evidence that the share prices of banks were artificially altered by short selling. The International Organization of Securities Commissions (IOSCO) noted that there are circumstances in which short selling can be used as a tool to mislead the market (IOSCO, 2008). It can be used in a downward manipulation whereby a manipulator sells the shares of a company short and then spreads inaccurate rumours about a company's negative prospects. This harms issuers and investors as well as the integrity of the market. IOSCO noted that short selling may be particularly problematic in the midst of a loss in market confidence, such as occurred in the credit crisis, where certain otherwise-solvent banks faced liquidity challenges. In such circumstances, the decrease in share prices induced by short selling led to further credit tightening for the banks in question. This was one of the reasons that led most regulators, including those in the UK and Ireland, to introduce a temporary ban on short selling of securities of listed financial services firms. Indeed in certain jurisdictions, such as Australia, the ban extended to all listed securities. However, such measures do not represent an ideal solution and many bans have been lifted since. Short selling does play an important role in market efficiency. It provides more efficient price discovery, mitigates market bubbles, increases market liquidity, facilitates hedging and other risk management activities, and limits upward market manipulations (Powers *et al.*, 2003). The need for greater disclosure in this area has been acknowledged. In October 2009, the FSA announced its intention to pursue enhanced transparency of short selling through disclosure of significant short positions in all equities. However, it stated that it would work towards agreement on future requirements at an international level rather than introducing a separate domestic regime. In order to achieve a harmonized approach, in September 2010, the European Commission published a proposal for a regulation on short selling and certain aspects of credit default swaps (European Commission, 2010) which, if adopted, would apply from July 2012. This will require all share orders on trading venues to be flagged as 'short' if they involve a short sale and will require investors to disclose significant net short positions in shares to regulators at one threshold (0.2 per cent of issued share capital), and to the market at a higher threshold (0.5 per cent). The proposal responds to naked short selling by requiring investors who wish to enter a short sale to have borrowed the instruments concerned, entered into an agreement to borrow them, or have an arrangement with a third party to locate and reserve them for lending in order to allow delivery by the settlement date. The proposal also gives national regulators clear powers in exceptional situations to temporarily restrict or ban short selling in any financial instrument, subject to coordination by the European Securities and Markets Authority (ESMA). In addition, if the price of a financial instrument falls by a significant amount in a day, national regulators will have the power to restrict short selling in that instrument until the end of the next trading day. ESMA will also have the possibility, in certain circumstances, to adopt temporary measures itself, with direct effect, restricting or prohibiting short selling.

Gilson and Kraakmann admit to underestimating 'the institutional complexities that attend the production, processing, and verification of market information, as well as its reflection in share prices' (Gilson and Kraakman, 2003, p. 35). They acknowledge that they failed to appreciate the magnitude of the incentive problems in the core market institutions that produce, verify and process information about corporate issuers. Empirical evidence would appear to prove that financial market prices can diverge substantially and for long periods of time from estimated economic values, with the calculated divergences at times so large that policymakers can reasonably conclude that market prices have become irrational (Shiller, 2005). In the aftermath of the banking crisis in the UK, the Chancellor of the Exchequer asked Lord Turner, the FSA Chairman, to review and make recommendations for reforming UK and international approaches to the way banks are regulated. The resulting report published in March 2009 ('the Turner Review') concluded that policymakers have to recognize that 'all liquid traded markets are capable of acting irrationally, and can be susceptible to self-reinforcing herd and momentum effects' (p. 41).

A further factor to detract from the efficiency argument is that financial markets have proven themselves incapable of regulating themselves (De Grauwe, 2008). This deregulation made it possible for banks to be fully involved in financial markets thus exposing shareholders to the vagaries of the stock markets.

Inefficient behaviour

It is also true to say that the market for corporate control depends on a particular type of efficiency. It depends on the existence of a high positive correlation between 'corporate managerial efficiency' and the market price of shares (Manne, 1965, p. 112). Manne noted that: 'Apart from the stock market, we have no objective standard of managerial efficiency' (p. 113). In the context of the current crisis, the question to be asked is: was inefficient behaviour reflected in share price?

To answer this question, one needs to consider exactly what is meant by 'inefficient behaviour' or as Manne calls it 'bad behaviour'. We can then determine whether the performance of the bank boards in the run-up to the banking crisis could have been considered 'inefficient'. One then needs to consider whether the markets react to this inefficiency by a reduction in share price. Manne has explained 'corporate managerial efficiency' as any action, or inaction, of the managers 'that kept the price of the shares lower than a potential raider thought he could raise it to (minus the costs of the takeover)'. He explained this as follows:

A mere failure to engage in actions (e.g. a merger unattractive to the incumbents, or a liquidation that would cost the incumbents their jobs) that the raider thought would benefit the price of the shares could be enough to call the scheme into action. It thus reached deficiencies like simple inattention to work matters that litigation, with its necessary business-judgment safe harbor, could never touch. It corrected misguided efforts (certainly from the shareholders' point of view) to benefit stakeholders at the expense of shareholders. (Manne, 2008, p. 11)

It appears self-evident now that the management of the banks did not perform effectively. The OECD Steering Group on Corporate Finance (Kirkpatrick, 2009) and the European High Level Group on Financial Supervision in the European Union (De Larosière *et al.*, 2009) both identify failures in risk management systems, incentive structures and board oversight. The question then is: was this reflected in share price?

The share prices of financial institutions did not begin to decline until mid 2007 and the decline then became most dramatic in the third quarter of 2008. However in the run-up to mid 2007, bank share prices failed to indicate that risks were increasing. The share sales predicted by Manne simply did not occur. Quite the contrary in fact – the Turner Review commented that the banks 'delivered strong market price reinforcement to management's convictions that their aggressive growth strategies were value creative' (Turner, 2009, p. 46). In a paradigm shift, during the 1990s the business model for banks had moved towards an equity culture with a focus on faster share price growth and earnings expansion (Blundell-Wignall *et al.*, 2008, p. 5). The Turner Review suggested that, in part, falling spreads and volatility prices drove up the current value of a range of instruments, marked to market value on the books of the banks and the hedge funds. This led to higher book profits and 'reinforced management and traders' certainty that they were pursuing sensible strategies' (Turner, 2009, p. 25). The Senior Supervisors Group noted that 'some firms found it challenging before the recent turmoil to persuade senior management and business line management to develop and to pay sufficient attention to the results of forward looking stress scenarios that assumed large price movements' (Senior Supervisors Group, 2008, p. 5). The OECD referred to evidence which indicated that risk management information was not always available to boards or available in a form corresponding with their monitoring of risks (Kirkpatrick, 2009). It may even be the case, thus, that the boards may not themselves have been fully aware of their 'inefficiencies'.

The market for corporate control suggests that the share price should have decreased as either shareholders identified inefficiencies but sought to exercise the 'exit' rather than the 'voice' option, or shareholders were aware of underperformance but did not attribute this to their boards' inefficiencies. In reality, corporate values did not decrease and there is no evidence of boards being replaced at this stage. Quite the contrary, boards were rewarded by increasing remuneration packages. Clearly shareholders did not perceive the actions of the boards as inefficient. In fact, share prices in the entire industry increased at this time.

Although it is clear that there was poor risk management, part of the problem was that this was not a feature of one bank but apparently of almost all. Nearly all of the banks reviewed by the Senior

Supervisors Group failed to anticipate fully the scale of market stress. Although competition is often cited as a primary form of external control, competition did not restrict the high risk behaviour of banks' management as the majority of banks maintained similar risk profiles. Strong investor demand, facilitated by an accommodating regulatory framework, encouraged many banks to hold assets off their balance sheets and to adopt an 'originate to distribute' model (Purnanandam, 2009). For example, in Ireland, despite warnings from the Central Bank of the inherent dangers in the bank's property-lending practices (Central Bank of Ireland, 2007), all banks grew their property portfolios. The Turner Review refers to the existence of a self-reinforcing cycle of falling risk aversion and rising irrational exuberance (Turner, 2009, p. 25). It thus appears that the challenging competitive conditions encouraged rather than restricted management, and the herd mentality referred to above prevented most institutions from stepping out of line. In July 2008, Chuck Prince, CEO of Citibank, explained that '[W]hen the music stops, in terms of liquidity, things will be complicated. But as long as the music is playing, you've got to get up and dance. We're still dancing' (*Financial Times*, 2007).

For Manne, sales by dissatisfied shareholders are necessary to trigger the mechanism and this simply did not happen. Indeed as share prices increased, shareholders were very satisfied indeed. It is clear now that the risks facing the banks were misunderstood by the market. Plath, on behalf of Moody's Investors Service, explained the difficulty for investors in appreciating the relevant risks. He noted: 'Assessing the quality of risk management practices . . . presents inherent challenges for investors, who are not privy to certain confidential information and who may lack a standard means of company risk management practices among peer groups and across peer industries' (Plath, 2008, p. 2). One might have thought, however, that while this was likely to reflect a correct assessment of individual shareholders, institutional shareholders and credit rating agencies would have been in a different position. While institutional shareholders may no longer have access to confidential information, one would expect that they would have sufficient financial expertise and experience to assess risk management practices more accurately. Of course they may not have possessed sufficient information to appreciate the risks. As noted above, the various corporate governance reviews have indicated that insufficient information was available to investors to allow them to assess the quality of risk management in the firms. Levine has noted that banks are generally more opaque than non-financial firms (Levine, 2004). Although information asymmetries plague all sectors, evidence suggests that these informational asymmetries are larger with banks (Furfine, 2001). Thus the primary rule of securities regulation – ensure investors have sufficient information to make a timely and informed investment decision – failed. It is also possible that investors relied on regulators to determine the level of risk which was acceptable or rather unacceptable. They might have assumed that the absence of regulation inferred that risk levels were deemed safe.

A second possibility is that even if the practices were regarded as risky, they may not have been considered as detrimental to the company and thus may not have impacted share price. Shareholders may have decided not to sell. The Turner Review accepted that all liquid traded markets are capable of acting irrationally, and can be susceptible to self-reinforcing herd and momentum effects. Investors may have considered that in order to compete, banks had to become less risk averse.

Bidders can envisage an adequate return from an acquisition

A further premise of the market for corporate control is that a bidder would be able to reap a sufficient reward from replacing the inefficient directors to be able to afford the acquisition. Recouping a sufficient reward depends, first, on the cost of the company reflecting its under-performance and not being inflated in other ways. The bidder's reward also depends on the directors' inefficiency being significant enough to be reflected in the share price. As noted above, this did not happen and share prices remained robust until at least mid 2007. Then the market value of the global banking industry more than halved in 2008. Particularly in the second half of 2008, the banking industry's market value fell by $2.5 trillion in the space of six months (Boston Consulting Group, 2009). The industry's total shareholder returns (which included capital gains and free cash flows) fell to −53.6 per cent in 2008. The total market value of the thirty largest banks dropped from $3.2 trillion in 2007 to $1.7 trillion in 2008 (47 per cent decline). Every bank in the top thirty saw a decrease in share price ranging from 75 per cent (Citigroup) to 3 per cent (Wells Fargo). The question could perhaps be asked why the market for corporate control did not lead to ownership transfers after that, i.e., when the share prices began to fall.

The answer to this may be that by the time the share price began to reflect the risks appropriately, it was too late to attempt to turn the target around. Although it is clear that the banks continued to take excessive risks for a further period, the banks were already committed to high-risk policies. The substantial losses caused by inefficient management can seldom be restored. Consequently, the level of risk required to accept a financially distressed company is high. See for example the RBS takeover of ABN AMRO for €71 billion (approximately three times the market value) in 2007. The offer was made in May 2007 and by the time the deal was closed in October, many banks were trading at around book value and dropping. This takeover has since been accepted as a risky mistake. This supports the contention that extremely badly managed companies may become indigestible. They are immune from attack precisely because of their pervasive inefficiency. As Coffee explained, companies where the level of inefficiency is 'so extreme as to surpass the bidder's level of risk aversion' fall outside the range and will not be considered as targets (Coffee, 1984, p. 1204). Furthermore, as time progressed, other external events occurred, such as the lack of liquidity in the market, which would have made it extremely difficult to finance any acquisition. It would also have affected the ability of shareholders to exit a company without incurring a loss.

Bidders can effect a takeover, i.e., there are no barriers to control

Barriers to takeovers can arise as a result of agency problems, which impede the market for corporate control. Two separate agency problems have been identified in this respect. First, the market for corporate control can be avoided if directors are allowed to engage in actions which serve to pre-empt or frustrate hostile bids. Secondly, where blockholders exist, capital and control structures in the company may grant disproportionate control rights to these shareholders and this may operate to frustrate an otherwise successful bid for the company.

The Winter Report supported the commonly stated view (see Dodd, 1980; Easterbrook and Jarrell, 1984; Dann and DeAngelo, 1988; Cotter and Zenner, 1994; Bebchuk *et al.*, 2002) that, left to their own devices, managers would be inclined to frustrate a bid. It noted that:

managers are faced with a significant conflict of interests if a takeover bid is made. Often their own performance and plans are brought into question and their own jobs are in jeopardy. Their interest is in saving their jobs and reputation instead of maximising the value of the company for shareholders. (Winter *et al.*, 2002, p. 21)

It concluded that even if board resistance might in some circumstances be justified, 'any regime which confers discretion on a board to impede or facilitate a bid inevitably involves unacceptable cost and risk' (p. 21). It thus suggested that a guiding principle of any European company law regulation aimed at creating a level playing field should be the right of shareholders to make the ultimate decision in respect of whether to tender their shares and at what price. As a result, Article 3(1)(c) of the Takeover Directive includes a General Principle providing inter alia that 'the board of an offeree company . . . must not deny the holders of securities the opportunity to decide on the merits of the bid'. Article 9(2), giving effect to this principle, requires the specific prior authorization of shareholders for 'any action . . . which may result in the frustration of the bid other than seeking alternative bids' and specifically 'before issuing any shares'. Under Article 9(2) approval is required at least from the time the offeree is approached but it may be earlier if Member States so choose. Article 9(3) introduces a requirement for shareholder approval of 'decisions taken . . . and not yet partly or fully implemented' before the beginning of the period during which Rule 9(2) applies where the decisions do not form part of the normal course of the company's business and where their implementation 'may result in the frustration of the bid'. These restrictions are reflected in Rule 21 of the City Code on Takeovers and Mergers.

An alternative category of structural barrier may exist in the form of special control rights for the board, voting caps and depository receipt structures. These structures may originally have been designed to create a strong minority shareholder who controls the company from the inside and thus protects a company with dispersed ownership against a small minority such as a board dominating the general meeting in the usual absence of the vast majority of shareholders. As such, the Winter Report noted that these structures 'may have helped to overcome the problems related to disciplining management of companies with dispersed ownership' (p. 24). However, the effect may be to endow a blockholder with disproportionate control over the outcome of a takeover bid. This also may thwart the market for corporate control. The Winter Report noted: 'the disproportionate control rights can be used, and are likely to be used, to authorize the board to frustrate the bid if the board or the minority share-holder controlling the board wishes to oppose it' (p. 3). As a result, Article 11(2) and 11(3) of the Directive disapplies certain restrictions when a bid has been made public. During the acceptance period, Article 11(2) disapplies vis-à-vis the offeror restrictions on the transfer of securities provided for in the articles of association of the offeree and restrictions on the transfer of securities in contracts between the offeree and its shareholders or between shareholders entered after the adoption of the Directive. Article 11(3) provides that restrictions on voting rights provided for in the articles of association of the offeree and restrictions on voting rights in contracts between the offeree and its shareholders or between shareholders entered after the adoption of the Directive shall not have effect at the general meeting of sharehold-ers 'deciding on any defensive measures' in accordance with Article 9. In addition, Article 11(3) provides that multiple-vote securities will carry one vote each at the general meeting of shareholders which 'decides on any defensive measures' in accordance with Article 9. Article 11(4) provides that where, following a bid, the offeror holds 75 per cent or more of the capital carrying voting rights, none of the above restrictions and none of the 'extraordinary rights' of share-holders in the articles of association concerning the appointment/removal of board members shall apply. Furthermore, multiple-vote securities will carry one vote each at the first general meeting of shareholders following closure of the bid, called by the offeror to amend the articles or appoint/remove directors. The offeror is entitled to call such a meeting on short notice once at least two weeks' notice is given. Article 11(6) and 11(7) provides an exception to the application of Article 11(3) and 11(4) if the restriction on voting rights 'is compensated for by specific pecuniary advantages' or if the rights are held by Member States. If bank shares do not trade actively in efficient equity markets, this will further hinder the market for corporate control. Indeed, a pre-crisis study shows that banks around the world were typically not widely held; rather, 75 per cent of banks have a single owner that holds more than 10 per cent of the voting rights (Barth *et al.*, 2002). This will be discussed further below.

However, it is important to note that the market for corporate control in the EU is weakened by two further provisions in the Directive. First, Article 12(1) of the final version of the Directive makes the prohibition on frustrating action in Article 9 and the breakthrough rule in Article 11 optional. It provides that Member States may decide not to require companies registered in their jurisdiction to apply the prohibition on frustrating action in Article 9 and the breakthrough rule in Article 11. Article 12(2) provides that if Member States 'make use of this option' they must still grant companies the reversible option of applying the Articles. By February 2007, an EU Commission report indicated that eighteen of the twenty-seven Member States had introduced, or were expected to introduce, Article 9 on board neutrality (European Commission Staff Working Document, 2007). However, before this can be claimed as an achievement of the Directive, it should be noted that the board neutrality obligation was only new in one of these Member States, Malta. All the other Member States that had no strict board neutrality obligation before the implementation of the Directive, decided not to introduce one. What is more worrying, however, is that in five (France, Greece, Hungary, Portugal and Slovenia) of the eighteen Member States where the obligation pre-dated the Directive, the reciprocity exception has also been introduced. Thus, in these five Member States managements' power to take frustrating measures without the approval of shareholders has actually increased as a consequence of the Directive. A further two of the Member States, which currently have board neutrality in place but had not transposed the Directive by the time of the publication of the report, Cyprus and Spain, informed the Commission about their intention to implement the Directive by introducing reciprocity. The vast majority of Member States have not imposed the breakthrough rule, choosing to make its application merely optional for companies. It is expected to be imposed only by the Baltic states and thus a mere 1 per cent of listed companies in the EU will apply this rule on a mandatory basis. Secondly, a further weakening of Articles 9 and 11 is introduced by the reciprocity provision in Article 12(3). This allows Member States 'to exempt companies which apply' the Articles 'if they become the subject of an offer launched by a company which does not apply the same Articles as they do' or a company controlled by such a company. To do so, however, Article 12(5) provides that they need the authorization of their shareholders at a meeting granted no more than eighteen months before the bid. Unfortunately, the majority of Member States have chosen to adopt the reciprocity provision in Article 12(3).

Three further elements of the Takeover Directive are worth mentioning in this context: the squeeze-out and sell-out rules in Articles 15 and 16 respectively and the mandatory bid rule in Article 5. Köhler argues that although the squeeze-out rule has increased the efficiency of the market for corporate control, the sell-out rule has reduced it (Köhler, 2009). He claims further that the mandatory bid rule fails to have an effect on takeover activity in countries with dispersed ownership structures but has increased managerial entrenchment in countries with concentrated ownership structures. As a result he maintains that it has reduced the efficiency of the market for corporate control, particularly in those countries in the EU where it aims at increasing it.

It is also argued that CfDs may be used to covertly build stakes in quoted companies without making the normal disclosures (FSA, 2007, para. 3.19). These interests are then converted into direct equity by acquiring the physical shares from the CfD writer who holds these shares as a hedge. The problem is that these 'toeholds' could discourage other potential bidders from contesting the takeover, as they are at a competitive disadvantage relative to a bidder who already has a toehold. This may discourage competitive bidding and reduce corporate contestability to the detriment of the market for corporate control. The Winter Group stated that the lack of transparency of the ownership structure could result in malfunctioning of the market for corporate control. This led to the inclusion of a provision in the Takeover Directive requiring significant direct and indirect shareholdings to be published in annual reports. (Of course this cannot deal with situations where the company is unaware of the indirect shareholdings.) Overall, the FSA has concluded that uncertainties relating to share ownership can reduce the efficiency of the market for corporate control, and dissuade some parties from participation in the market. It thus introduced a new disclosure regime effective in June 2009 requiring long CfD positions and similar derivative products to be disclosed under the Disclosure and Transparency Rules at an initial threshold of 3 per cent of total voting rights and every 1 per cent thereafter. The Rules now include long CfDs or similar derivative products which are not qualifying financial instruments but are referenced to shares and have a similar economic effect to qualifying financial instruments. This will be the case if the holder has, in effect, a long position on the economic performance of the shares. This requirement will be additional to that imposed by the City Code. The importance of disclosure as a means of facilitating the market for corporate control cannot be underestimated. However, this is a complicated area and as Schouten correctly indicates, 'setting the trigger for disclosure at the appropriate level is key' (Schouten, 2009, p. 44). Acknowledging the differences in disclosure throughout the EU, the European Securities Markets Expert Group in November 2009 recommended harmonizing the reporting obligation regarding cash settled derivatives (European Securities Markets Experts Group, 2009). It suggested a requirement to disclose significant cash settled derivative positions, both long and short positions, at a 5 per cent or 10 per cent threshold. Expressly in order to achieve true transparency on the *potential* of hidden ownership, it recommended that netting not be allowed. Finally, it suggested that global regulators should attempt to harmonize reporting obligations in other global markets to avoid forum shopping. In 2010, the European Commission consulted on the disclosure of holdings of cash settled derivatives in the context of the Transparency Directive 2004/109/EC (European Commission, 2009).

Other barriers may take the form of government regulation (Levine, 2004). Because of the importance of banks in the economy, governments impose additional regulations on banks. As Levine notes, most governments restrict the concentration of bank ownership and the ability of outsiders to purchase a substantial percentage of bank stock without regulatory approval. Of the 107 countries in the Barth, Caprio and Levine (2002) database of bank regulation and supervision, forty-one have a limit on the percentage of bank capital owned by a single entity that is less than 50 per cent and thirty-eight have limits less than 25 per cent. Furthermore, in some countries there may also be constraints on who can own banks (for instance, limits on ownership by non-bank firms). Obtaining regulatory approval can be a long-drawn-out process and this tends to make hostile takeovers in banking rare (Prowse, 1997). Levine also comments on the very large percentage (75 per cent) of not widely held banks and the fact that half of the controlling owners are families. He thus suggests that there exists a situation where regulatory restrictions are not able to limit the family dominance of banks but yet restrictions

on purchasing equity actually defend the existing owners from competition for control, obstructing this source of corporate governance.

Prior to the current financial crisis, evidence suggests that government ownership of banks had been consistently declining since 1970.
This pattern accelerated over the past ten years (consistent with bank
deregulation). Studies indicate that government ownership of banks,
while prevalent around the world in 1995, has declined significantly
since then (La Porta *et al.*, 2002). A study by Taboada indicates that
the average government ownership of banks experienced a 42.7 per
cent decline over the past ten years, dropping from 35.5 per cent in
1995 to 20.3 per cent in 2005. As it decreased, foreign and domestic
blockholder ownership of banks has increased (Taboada, 2008). It is
not consistent throughout Europe, however. A study by Köhler found
significant differences between the UK (where the median largest
blockholding is 11.09 per cent) and continental Europe (where it is
47.23 per cent). Clearly, in the UK's dispersed ownership context,
agency problems of the first type are more prevalent (Köhler, 2009).
It should be relatively easier to acquire control if no defensive tactics
exist. In the UK, Article 9 has been implemented and the reciprocity
provision has not. In continental Europe, as a result of concentrated
ownership, acquisitions are less likely. Even Manne emphasized that
the market for corporate control depended on there being 'a number
of voting shares sufficient to guarantee control . . . floating in the open
market' (Manne, 2008, p. 11).

Conclusions

This chapter has set out some of the reasons why the market for
corporate control did not operate to control inefficient management
in the run-up to the banking crisis. It argued that the fundamental prerequisites for the operation of this disciplinary force were not in place.
The share prices of the banks did not reflect the inefficiencies which
subsequently proved so costly to the global market. There were no
opportunities to acquire the banks cheaply and even if there had been,
it is not clear that there would have been support for a change in risk
management structures either at board or at investor level. The Turner
Review concluded that: 'A reasonable conclusion is that market discipline expressed via market prices cannot be expected to play a major
role in constraining bank risk taking, and that the primary constraint

needs to come from regulation and supervision' (p. 47). The current response in most jurisdictions appears to acknowledge that in the case of banking firms this is the correct approach. Although the focus of this chapter has been on the banking sector, it does have wider implications for the corporate market as a whole. Can we rely on the market for corporate control and its emphasis on deregulation in other sectors? Are the securities markets likely to be equally inefficient in other sectors? The dot-com bubble suggests that they are. Although the barriers to takeover activity may be reduced in less strategically important and systemic sectors, there are impediments that have not been completely removed. Thus one might conclude that from a corporate governance perspective, the weaknesses in the market for corporate control theory have been exposed and the banking crisis may act as a clarion call towards greater regulation (self or otherwise) in all sectors. Finally, it should be noted that the issues raised in this chapter give rise to a further and more challenging problem. This has also been identified in the Turner Review, which states:

A strong case can be made that the events of the last five years have illustrated the inadequacy of market discipline: indeed, they suggest that in some ways market prices and market pressures may have played positively harmful roles. (p. 45)

It seems, thus, that not only will regulation be required to resolve corporate governance problems that the market for corporate control cannot, but it may also be required to deal with the very mechanics of the market processes which underlie the operation of the market for corporate control.

References

Barth, J., Caprio, G. and Levine, R. 2002. 'Bank regulation and supervision: what works best?' NBER Working Paper No. W9323, available at http://ssrn.com/abstract=351423, last accessed 25 March 2010.

Bebchuk, L., Coates, IV. J. and Subramanian, G. 2002. 'The powerful antitakeover force of staggered boards: theory, evidence, and policy', *Stanford Law Review* 54: 887–951.

Black, F. 1986. 'Noise', *Journal of Finance* 41: 529–43.

Blundell-Wignall, A., Atkinson, P. and Se Hoon Lee 2008. 'The current financial crisis: causes and policy issues', *OECD*, available at www.oecd.org/dataoecd/47/26/41942872.pdf, last accessed 25 March 2010.

Boston Consulting Group 2009. 'Living with new realities: creating value in banking 2009', available at www.bcg.com/documents/file15429.pdf, last accessed 25 March 2010.

Central Bank of Ireland, 2007. 'Financial stability report', available at www.centralbank.ie/frame_main.asp?pg=fns_srep1.asp&nv=pub_nav. asp, last accessed 25 March 2010.

Coffee, J. 1984. 'Regulating the market for corporate control: a critical assessment of the tender offer's role in corporate governance', *Columbia Law Review* 84: 1145–296.

Cotter, J. and Zenner, M. 1994. 'How managerial wealth affects the tender offer process', *Journal of Financial Economics* 35: 63–97.

Dann, L. and DeAngelo, H. 1988. 'Corporate financial policy and corporate control', *Journal of Financial Economics* 20: 87–127.

De Grauwe, P. 2008. 'The banking crisis: causes, consequences and remedies', CEPS Policy Brief No. 178, available at http://econ.xmu.edu. cn/UploadFile/2009–04–13–16–01–15.pdf, last accessed 25 March 2010.

De Larosière et al., 2009. 'The High Level Group of financial supervision in the EU report', available at http://ec.europa.eu/internal_market/finances/docs/de_larosiere_report_en.pdf, last accessed 25 March 2010.

Dodd, P. 1980. 'Merger proposals, management discretion and stockholder wealth', *Journal of Financial Economics* 8: 105–37.

Easterbrook, F. and Jarrell, G. 1984. 'Do targets gain from defeating tender offers?', *New York University Law Review* 59: 277–97.

European Commission, 2009. 'Consultation document on the modernisation of the Directive 2004/109/EC on the harmonisation of transparency requirements in relation to information about issuers whose securities are admitted to trading on a regulated market', available at http://ec.europa.eu/internal_market/securities/docs/transparency/directive/consultation_questions_en.pdf, last accessed 29 November 2010.

European Commission, 2010. *Proposal for a Regulation of the European Parliament and of the Council on Short Selling and Certain Aspects of Credit Default Swaps* COM (2010) 482 final.

European Commission Staff Working Document, 2007. 'Report on the implementation of the directive on takeover bids', *SEC* (2007) 268, 21 February.

European Securities Markets Expert Group, 2009. 'Views on the issue of transparency of holdings of cash settled derivatives', available at http://ec.europa.eu/internal_market/securities/docs/esme/tdcash_en.pdf, last accessed 25 March 2010.

Fama, E. F. 1970. 'Efficient capital markets: a review of theory and empirical work', *Journal of Finance* 25: 383–417.

FSA 2007. 'Disclosure of contracts for difference', Consultation Paper CP07/20, November, available at www.fsa.gov.uk/pubs/cp/cp07, last accessed 29 November 2010.

Furfine, C. 2001. 'Banks as monitors of other banks: evidence from the overnight federal funds market', *Journal of Business* 74: 33–57.

Gilson, R. and Kraakman, R. 1984. 'The mechanisms of market efficiency', *Virginia Law Review* 70: 549–644.

Gilson, R. and Kraakman, R. 2003. 'The mechanisms of market efficiency twenty years later: the hindsight bias', Columbia Law and Economics Working Paper No. 240, available at http://ssrn.com/abstract=462786, last accessed 25 March 2010.

IOSCO, 2008. 'Technical committee members' initiatives relating to restrictions on short sales', Media Release (2 October), available at www.iosco.org/news/pdf/IOSCONEWS129.pdf, last accessed 29 November 2010.

Kirkpatrick, G. 2009. 'The corporate governance lessons from the financial crisis', *Financial Market Trends* 96 (61) OECD, available at www.oecd.org/dataoecd/32/1/42229620.pdf, last accessed 25 March 2010.

Köhler, M. 2009. 'Blockholdings and corporate governance in the EU banking sector', ZEW – Centre for European Economic Research Discussion Paper No. 08–110, available at http://papers.ssrn.com/sol3/papers.cfm?abstract_id=1338695, last accessed 25 March 2010.

La Porta, R., Lopez-de-Silanes, F. and Shleifer, A. 2002. 'Government ownership of banks', *Journal of Finance* 57: 265–301.

Levine, R. 2004. 'The corporate governance of banks: a concise discussion of concepts and evidence', World Bank Policy Research Working Paper No. 3404, available at http://ssrn.com/abstract=625281, last accessed 25 March 2010.

Lipton, M., Rosenblum, S. and Cain, K. 2008. 'Some thoughts for boards of directors in 2009', available at www.wlrk.com/docs/ThoughtsforDirectors2009.pdf, last accessed 25 March 2010.

Manne, H. 1965. 'Mergers and the market for corporate control', *Journal of Political Economy* 73: 110–20.

Manne, H. 2008. 'Corporate governance: getting back to market basics', Paper to Seminario Consob, available at www.consob.it/documenti/Pubblicazioni/Convegni_seminari/seminario_20081110_manne.pdf, last accessed 25 March 2010.

Moloney, N. 2009. *EC Securities Regulation* (2nd edn.). Oxford University Press.

Plath, C. 2008. 'Corporate governance in the credit crisis: key considerations for investors', Moody's Investors Service, available at http://ssrn.com/abstract=1309707, last accessed 25 March 2010.

Powers, M., Schizer, D. and Shubik, M. 2003. 'Market bubbles and waste-
    ful avoidance: tax and regulatory constraints on short sales',
    Yale SOM Working Paper No. ES-22, available at http://ssrn.com/
    abstract=391020, last accessed 25 March 2010.
Prowse, S. 1997. 'The corporate governance system in banking: what do we
    know?', *Banca del Lavoro Quarterly Review* March: 11–40.
Purnanandam, A. 2009. 'Originate-to-distribute model and the sub-prime
    mortgage crisis', AFA 2010 Atlanta Meetings Paper, available at http://
    ssrn.com/abstract=1167786, last accessed 25 March 2010.
Schouten, M. 2009. 'The case for mandatory ownership disclosure',
    Stanford Journal of Law, Business & Finance, forthcoming, available
    at http://papers.ssrn.com/sol3/papers.cfm?abstract_id=1327114, last
    accessed 25 March 2010.
Senior Supervisors Group, 2008. 'Observations on risk management practices
    during the recent market turbulence', available at www.newyorkfed.org/
    newsevents/news/banking/2008/SSG_Risk_Mgt_doc_final.pdf, last acc-
    essed 25 March 2010.
Shiller, R. 2000. *Irrational Exuberance* (2nd edn.). Princeton University
    Press.
Taboada, A. 2008. 'Impact of changes in government ownership of banks on
    the allocation of capital: international evidence', available at http://
    ssrn.com/abstract=1273243, last accessed 25 March 2010.
Turner, A. 2009. 'The Turner Review, a regulatory response to the global
    banking crisis', FSA, available at www.fsa.gov.uk/pubs/other/turner_
    review.pdf, last accessed 25 March 2010.
Winter, J., Garrido Garcia, J. M., Hopt, K., Rickford, J., Rossi, G., Schans
    Christensen, J. and Simon, J. 2002. 'Report of the High Level Group of
    company law experts on issues related to takeover bids', European
    Commission, available at http://ec.europa.eu/internal_market/company/
    docs/takeoverbids/2002–01-hlg-report_en.pdf, last accessed 25 March
    2010.

5 | Information asymmetry and information failure: disclosure problems in complex financial markets

STEVEN L. SCHWARCZ

Disclosure of information has been a key to regulation of the financial markets in the United States. Indeed, some have argued that the 'exclusive focus [of federal securities regulation] is on full disclosure' (Hazen, 2005). Yet there is relatively little dispute that although most if not all of the risks giving rise to the collapse of the market for structured securities backed by subprime mortgages were disclosed,[1] the disclosure was ineffective. Disclosure failed because of the complexity of those securities and transactions.

This chapter examines disclosure's insufficiency in addressing information asymmetry, arguing that complexity can cause information failure. There are multiple layers to complexity, the most obvious being complexity caused by increasingly complicated financial securities. But price volatility and liquidity of securities can be nonlinear functions of the interactive behaviour of independent and constantly adapting market participants,[2] producing not only cognizant complexity (i.e., too complex to understand) but also a temporal complexity within securities markets in which events tend to move rapidly into a crisis mode with little time or opportunity to intervene. Complexity also can cause information failure by exacerbating the misalignment of interests both between firms and their managers, especially technically proficient secondary managers, and also between individual firms and third parties. The chapter concludes that complexity makes reliance on disclosure insufficient, and that solutions will be only second best.

The financial crisis and 'securitization'

The financial crisis, starting in 2007, was a chain reaction of defaults and losses in the financial markets, triggered by the bursting of the US housing bubble. With house prices unexpectedly plummeting and adjustable-rate

This chapter is based in part on text drawn from the author's following articles: Schwarcz, 2008a, 2008b, 2009a, 2009b, 2009/10.

mortgage (ARM) interest rates skyrocketing,[3] many more borrowers defaulted than anticipated,[4] causing collections on subprime mortgages to plummet below the original estimates. Thus, equity and mezzanine classes of structured securities backed by those mortgages were impaired, if not wiped out, and in many cases even senior classes were impaired. Investors in these securities lost billions,[5] creating a loss of confidence in the financial markets and credit ratings. Furthermore, large financial institutions which invested heavily in these securities appeared to be (and, in many cases, were) undercapitalized, creating counterparty risk.

The issuance of securities backed by subprime mortgages and other assets constitutes a form of 'securitization' (also referred to as 'securitisation', especially in Europe) (Schwarcz, 1999). In a securitization transaction, rights to payment from income-producing financial assets (e.g., subprime mortgage loans) are transferred to a special-purpose vehicle (SPV – also called a special-purpose entity or SPE). The SPV, directly or indirectly, issues securities to capital market investors and uses the proceeds to pay for the mortgage loans or other income-generating assets. The investors, who are repaid from collections of the income-generating assets, buy the securities based on their assessments of the value of those assets.[6]

These securities are customarily categorized as mortgage-backed securities (MBS), asset-backed securities (ABS), collateralized debt obligation (CDO), or ABS CDO.[7] MBS are securities whose payment derives principally or entirely from mortgage loans owned by the SPV. ABS are securities whose payment derives principally or entirely from receivables or other financial assets (other than mortgage loans) owned by the SPV.

The term 'securitization' clearly includes transactions in which SPVs issue MBS or ABS securities. More broadly, the term is sometimes used to include CDO and ABS CDO transactions, although these transactions are perhaps better classified as subsets, like securitization, of 'structured finance' (sometimes called 'structured transactions'). CDO securities are backed by, and thus their payment derives principally or entirely from, a mixed pool of mortgage loans and/or other receivables owned by an SPV. ABS CDO securities, in contrast, are backed by a mixed pool of ABS and/or MBS securities owned by the SPV, and thus their payment derives principally or entirely from the underlying mortgage loans and/or other receivables ultimately backing those ABS and MBS securities.[8] For this reason, ABS CDO transactions are sometimes referred to as 're-securitization'.

The classes, or 'tranches', of MBS, ABS, CDO and ABS CDO securities issued in these transactions are typically ranked by seniority of payment priority. The highest priority class is called senior securities. In MBS and ABS transactions, lower priority classes are called subordinated, or junior, securities. In CDO and ABS CDO transactions, lower priority classes are usually called mezzanine securities – with the lowest priority class, which has a residual claim against the SPV, called the equity.[9]

The senior and many of the subordinated classes of these securities are more highly rated than the quality of the underlying receivables.[10] For example, senior securities issued in a CDO transaction are usually rated AAA even if the underlying receivables consist of subprime mortgages, and senior securities issued in an ABS CDO transaction are usually rated AAA even if none of the MBS and ABS securities supporting the transaction are rated that highly. This is accomplished by allocating cash collections from the receivables, first to pay the senior classes and thereafter to pay more junior classes (the so-called 'waterfall' of payment).[11] In this way, the senior classes are highly over-collateralized to take into account the likelihood of delays and losses on collection.

Securitization and other forms of structured finance are generally used to diversify and transfer risk to parties – for example, investors in the securities – better able to bear the risk. Where these transactions transfer substantive risk away from the company originating, or sponsoring, the transaction (called the 'originator'), it may justify the originator's booking the transaction as a sale ('off-balance sheet financing'). Additionally, these transactions are often used to obtain financing with lower costs because (among other reasons) intermediaries, such as bank lenders, between the originator and the ultimate source of funds are removed. Thus, securitization and structured transactions are normally viewed as socially desirable.

Despite their social desirability, actual securitization transactions are extremely complex and often rely on multiple SPVs (see, e.g., Hill, 1996). Furthermore, in order to integrate disparate disciplines such as bankruptcy, tax, securities law, commercial law, accounting and finance, securitization transactions often appear to be highly convoluted.[12]

Disclosure requirements and the rationale

In the United States, securities regulation relies heavily on disclosure,[13] it being believed that sophisticated investors and analysts with sufficient opportunity to evaluate the merits of an investment will bring market prices into line with the disclosure. This reflects rational choice theory: if full information is provided, rational investors can make rational choices to maximize their wealth and minimize their costs.

However, rational choice theory assumes an economic reality where disclosed information is transparent and understandable. In structured transactions, disclosure of a complex and convoluted structure may well be either too detailed for many investors, even institutional investors, to understand and assimilate, or too superficial to allow investors to fully assess the transaction and its ramifications. The problem is compounded where an originator engages in numerous such transactions.

Because of the complexity of structured transactions, even sophisticated institutional investors can lack the ability to understand the securities.

Complexities of financial markets and inherent information failure

Complexity in financial markets arises in response to 'demand by investors for securities that meet their investment criteria and their appetite for ever higher yields'[14] and in order to facilitate the transfer and trading of risk to those who prefer to hold it, promoting efficiency.[15] For example, more complex securities can offer investors the opportunity to gain exposure to new asset types and markets – such as foreign currency, commodities or residential mortgages – in turn enabling them to earn higher returns and more precisely hedge risk (Bethel and Ferrel, 2007, p. 7). Complex securities issued by SPVs and backed by pools of financial assets[16] also enable firms to raise low-cost financing by accessing the ultimate source of funds, the capital markets, without going through banks or other financial intermediaries.[17] Complexity thus can add efficiency and depth to financial markets and investments.

Nonetheless, complexity can impair markets and investments. Complexities of the assets underlying modern investment securities and the means of originating those assets can lead to a failure of lending standards and unanticipated defaults. Complexities of the investment securities themselves can lead to a failure of investing standards and financial-market practices. Those complexities add information asymmetry and information failure problems in financial markets. Furthermore, the complexities of modern financial markets can aggravate the market failures, in part because of the information uncertainty and the high sensitivity of markets to information.

Complexities can derive from the intricate combining of parts of the underlying assets, creating complications that increase the likelihood that information failures would occur and diminish the ability of investors and other market participants to anticipate and avoid these failures.[18] For example, each type of underlying asset can require a separate approach to modelling, including estimation of default risk, interest rate risk and prepayment risk.[19] To further complicate matters, prepayment risk is correlated with interest rate risk.[20] These risks are also dynamic in that they fluctuate over time.[21]

Complexities also can arise from the terms and conditions of the underlying assets. In the subprime crisis, for example, loan originators made mortgage-loan products more varied and sophisticated, and offered these products to a wider range of borrowers, purportedly in order to meet market demand (Murphy, 2006). Because of this complexity, some borrowers did not fully understand the risks they were incurring (McCoy and Renuart, 2008) and, as a result, defaulted at a much higher rate than would be predicted by the historical mortgage-loan default rates relied on by loan originators in extending credit (Eggert, 2007; Golding *et al.*, 2008).

Complexity can deprive investors and other market participants of the understanding needed for markets to operate effectively (see generally, Schwarcz, 2004b). Even if all information about a complex structure is disclosed,[22] complexity increases the amount of information that must be analysed in order to value the investment with a degree of certainty. This additional analysis entails higher cost.[23] According to rational ignorance theory, there is a point at which the benefit obtained from additional analysis can be outweighed, or at least appear to be outweighed, by the costs of performing that analysis.[24]

Furthermore, when securities are highly complex, parties reviewing, or even structuring, the securities may not always appreciate all the consequences.[25] In the subprime crisis, for example, although ABS CDO transactions were backed by what appeared to be significantly diverse securities, there was an underlying correlation in the subprime mortgage loans backing many of those securities (Schwarcz, 2008a). Not even rating agencies saw this correlation.[26]

The complexities of modern financial markets can aggravate the market failures and investment losses discussed above, in part because of the information uncertainty and the high sensitivity of markets to information. Financial markets rely critically on the supply of liquidity in the form of credit (Kohn, 1994; Stiglitz and Greenwald, 2003). The ability to contract for credit, in turn, depends on information not only about the economic health of the party seeking credit and its ability to repay but also about how the structure of the credit transaction more generally exposes the parties to risk (Kohn, 1994; Stiglitz and Greenwald, 2003). Markets consisting of securities that pool together multiple classes of assets can create a 'complex system' in which price volatility and liquidity are nonlinear functions of patterns arising from the interactive behaviour of many independent and constantly adapting market participants.[27] This not only can produce cognizant complexity[28] but also a 'tight coupling' within credit markets in which events tend to move rapidly into a crisis mode with little time or opportunity to intervene.[29] This additional nature of complexity is temporal;[30] in a complex system, signals are sometimes inadvertently transmitted too quickly to control.[31]

Information failure and non-aligned incentives

The previous section shows that increasing complexity can create information uncertainty and failure. That uncertainty and failure, in turn, can be magnified, such as when market participants engage in 'herd' behaviour, simply following the direction of other participants. In this way, information failure can lead to market failure, in which price signals do not reflect the underlying values of products.

Furthermore, the incentives of managers do not appear to be fully aligned with those of their institutions. Corporate governance scholarship has long grappled with conflicts of interest between a firm (meaning its owners, typically shareholders) and the firm's top managers, such as chief executive officers. Costs associated with this conflict are referred to as agency costs because managers are agents of the firm. It is widely acknowledged that top managers sometimes act to benefit themselves, to the detriment of the firm. To mitigate these agency costs, corporate governance scholars traditionally focus on two topics: reducing top-management conflicts of interest, and improving board governance.

Scholars have largely ignored, however, conflicts of interest between a firm and its middle- to lower-level management ('secondary managers'). There appear to be several reasons for this oversight. Most obviously, secondary managers report to, and thus are already theoretically subject to control by, top managers. Moreover, to the extent decisions of secondary managers are not deemed to be pivotal to the direction of a firm or its strategic goals, the consequences of secondary management conflicts would not be deemed to be – and in the past probably were not – significant. However, as financial markets and the securities traded therein become more complex and as firms become more highly leveraged, these conflicts are increasingly likely to trigger the collapse of firms that invest in those securities and possibly also of the markets themselves.

The conflict centres on compensation. Secondary managers are typically compensated for performing their assigned tasks, without regard to the long-term consequences of the tasks to their firms. For example, secondary managers who structure, sell, or invest in market securities on behalf of a firm are customarily compensated for those tasks even if, ultimately, the structure proves inadequate or the securities turn out to be poor investments. This conflict can create perverse incentives. For example, as the VaR, or value-at-risk, model for measuring investment-portfolio risk became more accepted, financial firms began compensating secondary managers not only for generating profits but also for generating profits with low risks, as measured by VaR. Secondary managers therefore turned to investment products with low VaR risk profile, like credit-defaults swaps, which generate small gains but only rarely have losses. The managers knew, but did not always explain to their seniors, that any losses that might eventually occur would be huge (Nocera, 2009).

There are several reasons, all relating to complexity, why monitoring and supervision by top management can fail to prevent secondary managers from acting in conflict with their firms. One reason is that complexity causes over-reliance on signals. In the face of complexity, human beings often resort to simplifying heuristics such as the 'signals' provided by rating-agency ratings and by mathematical models.[32] Being compensated for performing specific tasks without regard to long-term consequences to the firm, secondary managers are tempted to take a relatively short-term view when performing tasks. This temptation makes secondary managers especially susceptible to

over-rely on signals, particularly when the signals align their performance with their economic benefit. Over-reliance then makes those
managers more likely to act in conflict with their firms.

In the recent financial crisis, for example, secondary managers
over-relied on signals, in the form of rating-agency ratings and mathematical models, which aligned secondary-manager performance
and economic benefit. In the face of complexity, top managers will
similarly be tempted to over-rely on these simplifying heuristics.
Although top managers will not be as susceptible as secondary managers to over-rely due to conflicts, top managers will be susceptible
to over-rely for another reason: where the task being performed is
highly technical, they will know less, and thus find the task more
complex, than secondary managers. The secondary manager typically
will have considerably more, or at least more recent, technical
training and experience regarding the securities than the supervising
top manager.

The most direct way to limit conflicts is by aligning incentives.
Because compensation is at the root of the conflict between firms and
their secondary managers, the most effective way to align incentives
is to tie secondary-manager compensation to long-term interests of
the firm. This could be done in various ways, such a firm retro-
actively recovering compensation paid to secondary managers who
have structured, sold or invested in market securities on behalf of the
firm if, within some time period, the structure proves inadequate or
the securities turn out to be poor investments. Similarly, a firm might
pay a portion of a secondary manager's compensation contingently
over time or in the form of equity securities with long-term lock-
down constraints on selling the securities. The amount of compensation subject to clawback or paid contingently or in equity must be
material enough in context to affect secondary management
incentives.

In determining that amount, a firm will have to take into account,
of course, how the deferred, contingent or equity compensation will
affect the firm's ability to compete for the best secondary managers.
This creates a collective-action problem: any firm that employs a
deferred or contingent (or equity) compensation scheme will be dis-
advantaged in its ability to compete for the best secondary managers.
Government action may well be needed to help resolve this collective-
action problem.

Conflicts also can be limited by better monitoring. This might include better monitoring by top management. It also might include, for example, hiring technically trained 'control' officers who do not have conflicts to supervise relevant aspects of the quality of tasks performed by secondary managers. This could be very expensive, though, because any control officer so hired would face the prospect of losing expertise over time.

The discussion above focuses on misaligned incentives between firms and their secondary managers. In the context of systemic risk,[33] there is an even more fundamental misalignment: between institutional and financial-market interests. Especially in complex markets, where the consequences of risk-taking are blurred, discipline is inherently limited because no firm has sufficient incentive to limit its risk-taking in order to reduce the danger of systemic contagion for other firms. Even if market participants were able to collectively act to prevent systemic risk, they might not choose to do so because the externalities of systemic failure include social costs that can extend far beyond market participants, such as widespread poverty, unemployment and crime.[34] Therefore, like a tragedy of the commons, the benefits of exploiting finite capital resources accrue to individual market participants, each of whom is motivated to maximize use of the resource, whereas the costs of exploitation, which affect the real economy, are distributed among an even wider class of persons. The author has argued, however, that these costs can be at least partly internalized by establishing a market liquidity provider of last resort, funded by fees assessed against market participants (Schwarcz, 2009/10).

Concluding remarks

Complexity is undermining the traditional financial-market regulatory approach of full disclosure to address information asymmetry. Disclosure also fails to address the problems of market misalignment exacerbated by complexity, such as conflicts between firms and their secondary managers and between individual market-participants and third parties.

Although, as discussed in the previous section, conflicts may well be able to be managed, there do not appear to be any perfect solutions to disclosure's insufficiency. Even with full disclosure, the most sophisticated and largest financial institutions were the very investors that lost the most money in the subprime financial crisis.[35] And attempting to restrict complex transactions, even if otherwise feasible, would be highly risky because of the potential for inadvertently banning beneficial transactions.[36]

Economic theory on asymmetric information, especially that dealing with the so-called Lemons problem, suggests that one solution might be to require sellers of complex structured securities to retain risk, such as by requiring them to retain at least a portion of the lowest-ranked tranche of securities being sold. This generally makes sense, and indeed is typically mandated by investors in securitizations of non-mortgage assets. With highly complex securities, however, it should be cautioned that this approach can operate perversely. For example, investment bankers in some ABS CDO transactions have purchased portions of the equity tranches at least in part in order to demonstrate their (subsequently unjustified) confidence in the securities being sold. This induced many investors who otherwise might not have done so to purchase these securities, thereby working against investor caution. Thus, sometimes things are so complex that the problem is not merely information asymmetry but also information failure *on both sides* – a 'mutual misinformation' problem.[37]

Yet another theoretical solution is certification of quality. This, in fact, already exists in the form of rating agencies (which are private companies notwithstanding the 'agency' moniker) (Gorton, 2008, p. 2), which rate debt securities based on their likelihood of timely payment.[38] Rating agencies, however, have not always proved effective in the face of complexity,[39] and they are being accused of contributing to the subprime mortgage meltdown.[40] Although rating agencies are now attempting to improve their credit rating capabilities (Standard & Poor's, 2008), it is too soon to predict the outcome.[41] It is, however, important to strive to improve rating capabilities because rating agencies constitute a public good, creating an economy of scale to help individual investors assess the creditworthiness of complex securities.

Notes

1 In certain pending lawsuits, disclosure regarding the 'quality of the [underlying mortgage] loans' was insufficient. See Crimmins *et al.*, 2007.
2 Nonlinear feedback effects can result from interactivities among market participants. See Johnson *et al.*, 2003 (also describing this as the difficulty of distinguishing exogenous from endogenous factors).

3 Brooks and Ford, 2007, at A1 (analysing high-rate mortgages). Although rate increases on ARM loans (through rate resets) were not per se unexpected, the end of the liquidity glut made it harder for subprime borrowers to refinance into loans with lower, affordable interest rates.

4 Sanders, A. B. and Herberger, B., 2007. 'Incentives and failures in the structured finance market: the case of the subprime mortgage market', paper presented to the Federal Reserve Bank of Cleveland Workshop (20 November, notes on file with author). But cf. Simon, 2007, at A1 (reporting that many mortgages defaulted even before interest rates increased).

5 See Mollenkamp and Ng, 2007, at A1 (reporting on the downgrade of one CDO's AAA-rated tranches to junk status).

6 For a more complete analysis of securitization, see Schwarcz, 1994, 2004a and 2006.

7 There are arcane variations on the CDO categories, such as CDOs 'squared' or 'cubed'.

8 'Synthetic' CDOs own derivative instruments, such as credit-default swaps, rather than receivables, ABS or MBS.

9 In MBS and ABS transactions, the term 'equity' is not generally used because the company originating the securities (the originator) usually holds, directly or indirectly, the residual claim against the SPV.

10 CDO was defined as an investment-grade bond backed by a diversified pool of bonds, including junk bonds. The equity class is generally not rated.

11 See Investopedia, www.investopedia.com/terms/w/waterfallpayment. asp (defining waterfall payment as '[a] type of payment scheme in which higher-tiered creditors receive interest and principal payments, while the lower-tiered creditors receive only interest payments. When the higher-tiered creditors have received all interest and principal payments in full, the next tier of creditors begins to receive interest and principal payments').

12 See Schwarcz, 2004b, p. 5 (illustrating a 'simplified' schematic of a healthcare securitization conduit established by a leading investment firm, with the author's counsel, in order to provide low-cost financing to hospitals).

13 Hazen, 2002, § 8.1[1][B], p. 740; see also *ibid.* § 1.2[3], p. 27 (explaining that '[t]he focus on disclosure was based on the conclusion that sunlight is the best disinfectant') (paraphrasing Brandeis, 1932, p. 92).

14 Green and Jennings-Mares, 2008, p. 14. The supply-side of this investor demand is that financial innovators likewise see customized financial products as a means of staying competitive by 'constantly introduc[ing]

new financial products when [profit] margins on products decline quickly' (Hu, 1993, p. 1495).

15 Bethel and Ferrell, 2007 (explaining that structured products can promote efficiency in this way). See also Schwarcz, 1994 (explaining that by separating a corporation's liquid assets from its risks, it may obtain lower cost financing than if it were to directly issue debt or equity).

16 The term 'financial assets' includes any type of asset, such as accounts receivable, rental payments, franchise payments, loans or other rights to payment, which, over a finite period of time, converts into cash. Iacobucci and Winter, 2005. Cf. SEC Rule 3a-7 (17 CFR § 270.3a-7) (related definition of 'Eligible Asset').

17 Schwarcz, 2002a. Capital markets are now the nation's and the world's most important sources of investment financing. See, e.g., McKinsey Global Institute, *Mapping the Global Capital Markets: Third Annual Report* (2007), reporting that as of the end of 2005, the value of total global financial assets, including equities, government and corporate debt securities, and bank deposits, was $140 trillion, available at www.mckinsey.com/mgi/publications/third_annual_report/index.asp.

18 Cf. Merriam-Webster Online, 'complex', www.merriam-webster.com/ dictionary/complex; Merriam-Webster Online, 'complicated', www. merriam-webster.com/dictionary/complicated (defining 'complicated' as 'consisting of parts intricately combined' or 'difficult to analyze, understand, or explain').

19 Ho and Lee, 2004. Some assets, such as credit card loans, are further complicated because, unlike mortgage loans, they have no fixed payment amount or amortization schedule. Borrowers may pay in full, pay a minimum payment (usually 2 per cent of the outstanding balance), or even increase their balance up to a specified credit limit. Furletti, M., 2002, 'An overview of credit card backed securities', unpublished manuscript (on file with author); Baig, 2008. To address these challenges, credit card securities are typically issued separately through a revolving master trust, within which several credit accounts are pooled together to allow for multiple bond issues as well as a revolving flow of receivables. *Id.*

20 Adelson, 2006 (describing the property of negative convexity in mortgage-backed securities).

21 Ho and Lee, 2004 (discussing Monte Carlo simulations, which condition prepayment risk upon hypothetical interest rate fluctuations); *Advanced Analytics v. Citigroup*, 2008 WL 2557421, 1 (describing as 'complex' the computerized process used to estimate prepayment risk).

22 Cf. Gladwell, 2007 (distinguishing between transactions that are merely 'puzzles' and those that are truly 'mysteries'). To the extent complexity is merely a puzzle, investment bankers theoretically could understand it. In practice, though, '[m]any investors do not possess the resources to fully analyze complicated structured products' (Kravitt, 2008, p. 18).

23 Shah and Oppenheimer, 2006, p. 207 (describing costs of information analysis as identification of relevant data, storing of that data, assessing the weight of each piece of data, integrating alternative sources of data, and parsing or analysing the data to produce actionable information).

24 Community Leader's Letter, The Theory of Rational Ignorance, Community Leader's Letter: Econ. Brief N. 29, available at www.strom. clemson.edu/teams/ced/econ/8-3No29.pdf; Schwarcz, 2004b, pp. 13–15 (explaining why institutional investors face declining incentives to hire experts to parse information relating to structured products as those products increase in complexity). Schwarcz, 2008b.

25 Hu, 1993, p. 1480 (observing in a derivatives context that '[t]he complexity can overwhelm even experts'). A related concern arises to the extent securities become so highly complex that, as Professor Kenneth Klee has suggested, parties sometimes have difficulty understanding their documentation. Kenneth Klee, Remarks at the International Insolvency Institute's Eighth Annual International Insolvency Conference (10 June 2008; notes on file with author).

26 Schwarcz, 2008a. Rating agencies make their business in carefully assessing the creditworthiness of investment securities. See generally Schwarcz, 2002b.

27 Cf. Drazin, 1992 (observing that nonlinear systems represent 'a feedback loop in which the output of an element is not proportional to its input').

28 Cf. Kravitt, 2008 (observing that 'the more complicated a system becomes, and the more interconnected . . . the odds of a breakdown in a portion of the system increases (because of complexity)').

29 I thank Rick Bookstaber for introducing the term 'tight coupling', originally borrowed from engineering nomenclature, to financial markets. See Bookstaber, 2007, p. 144. Tight coupling is most pronounced when markets are illiquid and market participants are highly leveraged.

30 The effects of these types of complexity (i.e., cognizant and temporal) can combine, however, such as the cognizant complexity caused by the unexpected consequences of marking to market, which (like a complex engineering system subject to nonlinear feedback effects) resulted in a downward spiral of prices when marking to market occurred in unstable markets.

31 Cf. Arthur, 1999, p. 107 (defining economic complexity as the tendency for patterns to emerge from systems, organizations, or products with many interdependent parts or actors that would not be predicted from classical linear economic models).

32 For a discussion of rating agencies and their ratings, see Schwarcz, 2002b.

33 See Schwarcz, 2008a (observing that systemic risk is the risk that an economic shock such as market or institutional failure triggers (through a panic or otherwise) either by (i) the failure of a chain of markets or institutions or (ii) a chain of significant losses to financial institutions, resulting in increases in the cost of capital or decreases in its availability, often evidenced by substantial financial-market price volatility).

34 The widespread poverty and unemployment caused by the Great Depression, for example, apparently fostered a significant increase in crime. See Kirchmeier, 2002 (discussing an explosion of executions as probably resulting from increased crime due to the Great Depression).

35 See, e.g., Anderson, 2008, at C1 ('[M]ajor banks ... have already written off more than $120 billion of losses stemming from bad mortgage-related investments'); Smith, 2007, at A4 (reporting a total of $20 billion in write-downs by large investment banks).

36 See, e.g., Whetten and Adelson, 2005; Tavakoli, 2007. In this context, the tort law doctrine of 'unavoidably unsafe products' may help to inform a regulatory analysis. In tort law, an 'unavoidably unsafe product' is subject to strict liability unless its utility outweighs its risk. Galbreath, 1989. For example, the vaccine for rabies is inherently dangerous, but rabies can result in death, so the vaccine is not subject to strict liability. *Restatement (second) of Torts*, § 402A cmt. k (1965).

37 Cf. Schwartz and Creswell, 2008, at BU 1, 8 ('[e]ven the people running Wall Street firms didn't really [always] understand what they were buying and selling' (quoting Byron Wien, Chief Investment Strategist, Pequot Capital)).

38 See Partnoy, 1999; recall that securities issued in securitization transactions are virtually always debt securities.

39 See, e.g., *Rating the Raters: Enron and the Credit Rating Agencies Hearing Before the S. Comm. on Governmental Affairs* 107th Cong. (2002) (hearing on rating agency failure to predict Enron's collapse).

40 *The Role of Credit Rating Agencies in the Structured Finance Market Before the Subcomm. on Capital Markets, Insurance, and Government Sponsored Enterprises of the H. Comm. on Financial Services*, 110th Cong. 47 (2007) (investigating the extent to which credit rating agencies may have contributed to the subprime mortgage meltdown).

41 One scholar has proposed that the Big Four auditing firms should consider providing 'ratings based on an audit-like inquiry' which would, he claims, 'make much more sense than our current system under which the rating agency's letter grade is wholly based on information provided by the issuer that it assumes to be true' (Coffee, 2008, p. 14).

References

Adelson, M. 2006. 'MBS basics', *Nomura Fixed Income Research*, Nomura Securities International, Inc.

Anderson, J. 2008. 'Wall St. banks confront a string of write-downs', *The New York Times*, 19 February.

Arthur, W. B. 1999. 'Complexity and the economy', *Science*, 2 April.

Baig, S. 2008. 'CDO of ABS: a primer on performance metrics and test measures', available at www.yieldcurve.com, last accessed 5 March 2008.

Bethel, J. and Ferrell, A. 2007. 'Policy issues raised by structured products', *Brookings-Nomura Papers on Financial Services*, 7.

Bookstaber, R. 2007. *A Demon of Our Own Design: Markets, Hedge Funds, and the Perils of Financial Innovation*. Hoboken, NJ: John Wiley & Sons.

Brandeis, L. D. 1932. *Other People's Money and How the Bankers Use It*. New York: Stokes.

Brooks, R. and Ford, C. M. 2007. 'The United States of subprime', *The Wall Street Journal*, 11 October.

Coffee, Jr, John C. 2008. 'The securitization bubble', *National Law Journal*, 17 March, p. 14.

Crimmins, S. J., Morris, A. J. and Brown, D. T. 2007. 'Subprime mortgage lending: possible securities litigation exposure', 39 *Securities Regulation & Law Report*, 24 September.

Drazin, P. G. 1992. *Nonlinear Systems*. Cambridge University Press.

Eggert, K. 2007. 'Subprime mortgage market turmoil: examining the role of securitization, testimony before Senate Subcommittee on Securities', *Investments and Insurance*, 17 April, p. 4, available at http://banking.senate.gov/public/_files/eggert.pdf, last accessed 2 March 2008.

Galbreath, J. R. 1989. 'Annotation, products liability: what is an "unavoidably unsafe" product?', 70 A.L.R. 4th: 34.

Gladwell, M. 2007. 'Open secrets: Enron, intelligence, and the perils of too much information', *New Yorker*, 8 January.

Golding, E., Green, R. K. and McManus, D. A. 2008. 'Imperfect information and the housing finance crisis', Joint Center for Housing Studies, Harvard University, February, available at www.jchs.harvard.

edu/publications/finance/understanding_consumer_credit/papers/ucc08–6_golding_green_mcmanus.pdf, last accessed 25 November 2008.

Gorton, G. B. 2008. 'The panic of 2007', *NBER Working Paper* 14358, p. 2.

Green, P. and Jennings-Mares, J. 2008. 'Letter to the Editor', *Financial Times*, 4 July, p. 14.

Hazen, T. L. 2005. *The Law of Securities Regulation*. West Publishing Company, § 8.1[1][B].

Hill, C. A. 1996. 'Securitization: a low-cost sweetener for lemons', *Washington University Law Quarterly* 74: 1061–3.

Ho, T. S. Y. and Lee, S. B. 2004. *The Oxford Guide to Financial Modeling: Applications for Capital Markets, Corporate Finance, Risk Management, and Financial Institutions*. Oxford University Press.

Hu, H. T. C. 1993. 'Misunderstood derivatives: the causes of informational failure and the promise of regulatory incrementalism', *Yale Law Journal* 102: 1495.

Iacobucci, E. M. and Winter, R. A. 2005. 'Asset securitization and asymmetric information', *Journal of Legal Studies* 34 (1): 161–2.

Johnson, N. F., Jefferies, P. and Hui, P. M. 2003. *Financial Market Complexity: What Physics Can Tell Us about Market Behaviour*. Oxford University Press.

Kirchmeier, J. L. 2002. 'Another place beyond here: the death penalty moratorium movement in the United States', *Colorado Law Review* 73: 1–116.

Kohn, M. 1994. *Financial Institutions and Markets*. New York: McGraw Hill.

Kravitt, J. 2008. 'Foreword: some thoughts on what has happened to the capital markets and securitization and where securitization is going', p. 18, available at www.pli.edu/public/17984/foreword.pdf, last accessed 28 November 2008.

McCoy, P. A. and Renuart, E. 2008. 'The legal infrastructure of subprime and nontraditional home mortgages', Joint Center for Housing Studies, Harvard University, February, available at www.jchs.harvard.edu/publications/finance/understanding_consumer_credit/papers/ucc08–5_mccoy_renuart.pdf, last accessed 2 December 2008.

McKinsey Global Institute 2007. 'Mapping the global capital markets third annual report', January, available at www.mckinsey.com/mgi/publications/third_annual_report/index.asp, last accessed 16 March 2008.

Mollenkamp, C. and Ng, S. 2007. 'Wall Street wizardry amplified credit crisis: a CDO called Norma left "hairball of risk"; tailored by Merrill Lynch', *The Wall Street Journal*, 27 December.

Murphy, E. V. 2006. 'Alternative mortgages: risks to consumers and lenders in the current housing cycle', CRS Report RL33775, 27 December, pp. 5–6, available at http://assets.opencrs.com/rpts/RL33775_20061227.pdf, last accessed 8 March 2008.

Nocera, J. 2009. 'Risk mismanagement', *The New York Times*, 4 January, (Sunday magazine), p. 46.

Partnoy, F. 1999. 'The Siskel and Ebert of financial markets? Two thumbs down for the credit rating agencies', *Washington University Law Quarterly* 77: 619.

Schwarcz, S. L. 1994. 'The alchemy of asset securitization', *Stanford Journal of Law, Business & Finance* 1: 133, 135–44.

1999. 'The inherent irrationality of judgment proofing', *Stanford Law Review* 52 (1): 6.

2002a. 'Enron and the use and abuse of special purpose entities in corporate structures', *The University of Cincinnati Law Review* 70: 1309–15.

2002b. 'Private ordering of public markets: the rating agency paradox', *University of Illinois Law Review* 1: 1–28.

2004a. 'Securitization post-Enron', *Cardozo Law Review* 25: 1539, 1540–3.

2004b. 'Rethinking the disclosure paradigm in a world of complexity', *University of Illinois Law Review* 1: 1–38.

2006. *Structured Finance: A Guide to Principles of Asset Securitization.* (3rd edn.). New York: Practicing Law Institute.

2008a. 'Systemic risk', *Georgetown Law Journal* 97 (1): 193–249.

2008b. 'Disclosure's failure in the subprime mortgage crisis', *Utah Law Review*: 1109–14.

2009/10. 'Regulating complexity in financial markets', *Washington University Law Review* 87: 211.

2009a. 'Understanding the "subprime" financial crisis', *South Carolina Law Review* 60: 549 (2009 Keynote Address).

2009b. 'Conflicts and financial collapse: the problem of secondary-management agency costs', *Yale Journal on Regulation* 26 (2): 457.

Schwartz, N. D. and Creswell, J. 2008. 'What created this monster?', *The New York Times*, 23 March.

Shah, A. K. and Oppenheimer, D. M. 2006. 'Heuristics made easy: an effort-reduction framework', *Psychological Bulletin*, March.

Simon, R. 2007. 'Rising rates to worsen subprime mess', *The Wall Street Journal*, 24 November.

Smith, R. 2007. 'Merrill's $5 billion bath bares deeper divide', *The Wall Street Journal*, 6 October.

Standard & Poor's 2008. 'Descriptions of new actions to strengthen ratings process and better serve markets', 7 February, available at http:www2.

standardandpoors.com/spf/pdf/media/Leadership_ Action_Details.pdf, last accessed 15 June 2008.

Stiglitz, J. E. and Greenwald, B. 2003. *Towards a New Paradigm in Monetary Economics*. Cambridge University Press.

Tavakoli, J. 2007. 'Leverage and junk science: a credit crunch cocktail', *Total Securitization*, 20 September, available at www.totalsecuritization.com.

Whetten, M. and Adelson, M. 2005. 'CDOs-squared demystified', Nomura Fixed Income Research, 12–13, available at www.math.ust.hk/~maykwok/courses/MAFS521_07/CDO-Squared_Nomura.pdf, last accessed 21 May 2008.

6 | Finance, governance and management: lessons to be learned from the current crisis

ROLAND PÉREZ

Queen Elizabeth II's request for explanations of the contemporary financial crisis affecting the whole world was widely reported in the press (*Le Monde*, 28 July 2009). 'Why didn't anybody notice?' the Queen was reported to have asked during a visit to the London School of Economics. The convoluted answer from the celebrated institution's professors deserves to be quoted: 'The failure to foresee the timing, extent and severity of the crisis and to head it off, while it had many causes, was principally a failure of the collective imagination of many bright people, both in this country and internationally, to understand the risks to the system as a whole' (British Academy Forum, 2009).

Yet there were people who had seen how the system was veering out of control and predicted its inevitable implosion. A certain number of researchers had been highly critical of the way finance was developing and the risk that those developments would lead the system off course. The criticisms came from a range of scientific and social areas: economics (e.g., Orléan, 1999; Shiller, 2000; Aglietta and Rebérioux, 2004; Morin, 2006; Akerlof and Shiller, 2009), sociology (e.g., MacKenzie, 2006), philosophy of economics (e.g., Jorion, 2008), mathematics (e.g., Mandelbrot, 1997; Mandelbrot and Hudson, 2004) and finance practitioners (e.g., Soros, 1998; Taleb, 2007). Most of them pointed out that finance activities do not belong to simple models such as those that are widely used in practice.

The crisis was initially restricted to the US banking sectors (the subprime crisis), but it subsequently spread throughout the international financial system to set off a major economic crisis with social consequences that are still unfolding. The following question arises:

Acknowledgements are due to readers of early drafts of this chapter, especially to the anonymous reviewers for this book. For another version in French, see Pérez (2009).

Does the current financial and economic crisis call into question our approach to management and governance issues? Supplying a simple, straightforward answer to this legitimate question would appear to be impossible. Nonetheless, the researcher, especially in the field of economics, cannot avoid reference to a phenomenon of such a scale that it is changing not only the way the economic system operates but also the relevant analysis grids and even the underlying epistemo-logical, theoretical and normative positions.

In this chapter discussions will be restricted to some reflections on the finance–governance–management spiral which span out of control and ultimately led to the current crisis, followed by some proposals to offer better regulation. The considerations essentially concern aca-demic research, even though its responsibility for this major crisis is not exclusive.

The finance–governance–management spiral

In order to function, firms – and organizations in general – need to be able to procure the resources necessary to undertake their activities; these resources may be diverse (tangible or intangible, human, finan-cial, etc.) and contribute to defining their 'economic model'. In addition, every organization is subject to a governance regime of a socio-political nature, defining the 'game rules' for its managers and monitoring of their actions. Management is defined as the combin-ation of the two ensembles consisting of the economic model and the governance regime (Pérez, 2006).

The key argument to be developed, which the author believes is central to interpretation of the current crisis starting from 2007, is schematically as follows: finance, instead of keeping to its 'serving' position (to use the eloquent expression of Dembinski, 2009), has become dominant, even 'arrogant' (Bourguinat and Briys, 2009) and rule management through its governance regime.

Hubris-seized finance

Research in modern finance, in the wake of the pioneering work by Markowitz (1952), Tobin (1956) and Modigliani and Miller (1958), has been conceived as though finance could be treated as a scientific discipline comparable to the physical and chemical sciences. Concep-tualization and modelling of financial phenomena have thus been broadly inspired by the concepts and models of these benchmark disciplines (Tirole, 2006).

These concepts and models have too often contained assumptions (both explicit and implicit) of normal distribution. This tendency is clearly illustrated by the treatment of risk – which is nothing if not a major theme in micro-economics and management research.[1] Its importance is justified if we acknowledge that a market economy involves risk-taking, which for the entrepreneur justifies this 'residual, differential and random' factor that is profit (Perroux, 1926; 1960).

In finance particularly, an important stage in modelling was defined by Markowitz (1952), measuring the risk on an asset (stock) or revenue (cash flow) by the variance in its hypothetical movement, following a normal distribution. 'Portfolio theory', on which the whole edifice of 'scientific' or 'modern' finance is founded, brought its author and many of his successors the highest academic recognition, including several Nobel prizes in economics (Markowitz, Modigliani, Miller, Sharpe, Merton, etc). For many decades now, an imposing structure has been built up, with each level adding a further degree of sophistication: more in-depth examination of portfolio theory (Fama, 1970; Myers, 1977), option theory (Black and Scholes, 1973; Merton, 1973), agency theory (Jensen and Meckling, 1976) and signalling theory (Ross, 1977).

This is the structure which, like buildings shaken or brought down by an earthquake, is now feeling the tremors of the financial crisis that originated in a US real estate credit compartment and that has sent out a shockwave across the entire planet. As is often the case before large earthquakes, there were warning signs, such as the collapse of the LTCM (Long Term Capital Management) fund in 1997, despite the scientific guarantee provided by the involvement of two Nobel prize winners (Merton and Scholes).[2]

If the worldwide financial crisis has several roots, then modern finance theory is one of them. The main reason for this part of responsibility is that portfolio theory since Markowitz (1952) had offered an attractive but too narrow conceptual framework, based on the mean-variance approach.

Over-financialized governance

'The return of the shareholder', in the words of L'Hélias (1997), has been visible in recent decades in the United States. Various researchers have analysed this historic change of direction (Thiveaud, 1994; Tunc, 1994; Aglietta, 1997), emphasizing how important 'financialization' of the economy and the growing influence of institutional investors have come to be there.

This financialization is apparent from the markets' key role in funding the US economy, the international dimension of the country which is both the world's largest investor and largest debtor, the increasing importance of operations on those markets with different groups of players (households and businesses), their balance sheet structures and assets, and more.

Institutional investors reflect the growing intermediation of household savings, which are less often managed by the savers themselves and increasingly entrusted to professionally managed organizations with extensive resources. This concerns various types of investment, particularly those associated with pension funds, which, as we know, are the standard system for pensions in the United States. These pension funds can cover employees of a particular state, city, profession or large company, and they manage large volumes of assets: the twelve largest funds have more than a thousand billion dollars under their management.[3]

These two trends combine to make institutional investors major players on the financial markets, in an increasingly financialized economy (Hawley and Williams, 2000). The new players have gradually come to manage enormous volumes of financial assets, leading them to diversify their portfolios in order to reduce risks. As a result, they have invested often significant amounts in the capital of a certain number of large companies, especially companies included in the benchmark indices.

This involvement led them to take an interest in the way those companies were managed, ask the management for information they considered necessary, and finally to contact the management for explanations on past activities and performance, then on the business strategies under consideration and their impact. Corporate governance came into being in its current form, reflecting shareholder vigilance, and it is significant that the first principles of corporate governance formally expressing this trend were issued by the Californian CalPERS fund, which was a pioneer in the field.[4] The movement then spread rapidly; investment funds and associations for the protection of individual shareholders vied to outdo each other in what is generally called 'shareholder activism', intended to oblige managers of listed companies to release more information on their management, and to influence policies to make them more favourable to shareholders.

The effects of this shareholder-oriented governance are well known (Pérez, 2003; 2009). Most of them are related with creating shareholder value (Rappaport, 1987; Jensen, 2001) by several means: increasing the average rate of return by concentration on the most profitable activities, decreasing the cost of capital by leverage (the cost of debt being lower than the cost of equity), priority to the market price, short vision, etc. The over-financialized governance to which such practices lead is manifested by an 'instrumented' management.

Instrumented management

The major trends of the modern economy have been clearly identified: they are carried along by a combination of two underlying movements: market globalization and scientific and technical innovations. 'Market globalization', the ultimate phase in the globalization of economies, concerns the markets for goods and services, the associated production and consumption patterns, and the capital and financial instruments markets that mobilize them. 'Technological progress', generated by ongoing advances in scientific knowledge, is reflected in an increasing flow of innovations in the form of new products and sometimes drastic changes in production processes.

Faced with this dual undercurrent, firms were obliged to respond ('adaptive strategies') and if possible to plan ahead ('proactive strategies'). The progressive globalization of the main markets for goods and services requires market actors to specialize, as even a large firm cannot hope in the long run to hold strong profitable positions on a large number of product-market couples at a worldwide level. Technological advances are a harsh source of selection between the players who use and promote them (or are able to purchase them) and the players who are subjected to them.

Of the scenarios observed, a typical situation is increased shareholder pressure with calls in the name of corporate governance for more supervision of management and better income for shareholders, either in terms of dividends or in terms of stock market appreciation for a listed firm. To meet these demands, in addition to the demands of competition dynamics, managers are obliged to redirect their 'strategic vision' and possibly adopt a new one. The approach to competitiveness, which had previously focused on the relative market position and market growth, must now pay more and more attention explicitly to profitability.

This concern for the demands of profitability lies at the origins of refocusing policies to concentrate business on activities that offer strong market positions (current and potential) and satisfactory profitability (current and future). But this refocusing does not only affect the portfolios of businesses through withdrawal from activities with apparently jeopardized prospects. For a given business, it may also affect the organization of its production system. What should the 'structural configuration' be? Should a firm 'do it itself' or 'have it done'? The solution often put forward for a profitability problem lies in outsourcing of an increasing share of the value chain, enabling the firm to concentrate on the most effective segments of that chain, assessed on the basis of the criteria referred to above (market position and profitability).

Outsourcing certain components of the production system generally has two consequences for the value creation process. The first consequence concerns management of the components of the production system, those that remain in the organization and those that were already outsourced or that it has been decided to outsource. Internally, priority will be given to raising the productivity of both equipment and labour, quality improvement, reduction of delivery times, stocks, breakdowns, etc. (see the 'seven zeros' in the consulting literature). Externally, the emphasis will be on the terms of trade and cooperation with other actors in the supply chain: the terms of prices, delivery times, traceability, etc.; calling for 'relationship management', covering everything from normal trading relations to what is practically integration, via all the forms of partnerships and network organization. The second consequence concerns the structure of assets and funding. Clearly, outsourcing part of the production system frees up the relevant production assets. This 'slimming down' on assets (lean capital) has a similar effect on financing, making it possible to reduce the funds invested. Reducing investments naturally improves financial performance expressed in terms of rates and coefficients, through the automatic 'accretive' effect.

Decisions on successive reconfigurations of the scopes of firms and groups are thus central to decisions on strategic management of these value creation-oriented entities in a financialized governance context. These successive decisions are generally based on performance criteria from internal reporting, which measure out the lives of the employees, executives and management of the firms concerned to an increasing extent and with greater frequency. This 'instrumentation' of decision-making transforms the nature of management, reducing the scope for discretionary latitude. There is a movement towards a kind of 'steering by instruments' comparable to air navigation, which is known to be satisfactory but only as long as flight conditions, especially the weather, are favourable. This kind of management is available with a 'normal' environment; it is not adapted when this environment becomes difficult, indeed chaotic, as is the period studied here.

It is possible to illustrate a time sequence of the finance–governance–management spiral. The case of Danone group is a significant example (Pérez, 2006). During thirty years (1966–95) this firm, called BSN, was a typical case of 'managerialism'. The main goal was rate of growth (both by internal and external means) and not the price of shares; the governance was not financialized and the management was strong under the charismatic chair and CEO Antoine Riboud. In the mid 1990s the enterprise changed its name to Danone group and the new chair and CEO Frank Riboud – son of the founder – decided to list his firm's shares on the New York Stock Exchange (NYSE). Institutional investors required that the protective measures related to the control of the company be abandoned and a new model of governance, shareholder-oriented, became prevalent. The strategic decisions made by the top management were in accordance with this new governance: sell-off of the less profitable activities, leverage, shares buybacks, etc.

Avenues for improvement

As mentioned earlier, the aim of this chapter is not to present a structured set of solutions to a major crisis that has not yet shown all its effects, but to put forward proposals, particularly in the academic field, that could improve the current situation and prevent the same type of crisis happening again. These proposals can be deduced 'between the lines' of the previous analysis regarding the finance–governance–management progression.

Sensible finance

The importance of this crisis calls for renewal of research and education practices, particularly for risk analysis and modelling in finance. The proposals will focus on the following two points, which are viewed as being connected: we need to encourage the emergence of a new paradigm in finance, and on that basis, review the way financiers are educated.

For a new paradigm in finance

The philosopher of science, Kuhn (1962), studying the times of crisis a science passes through during its development, considers that there is a 'scientific revolution' when an established scientific theory – forming a paradigm – is rejected and replaced by a new theory – a new paradigm.

Based on the critical assessments presented above, the author is convinced that finance is currently in such a position. The dominant paradigm born in the 1950s from the founding work by Markowitz, Tobin, Modigliani and Miller, is currently – despite the immense developments it has engendered and despite the half-dozen Nobel prizes in economics that have punctuated its history – in its dying phase, because it is unable to deal with the problems posed by the current financial crisis. Moreover, it has a share of responsibility for those problems.

It is no longer useful to add a further floor to the impressive edifice built up over the last half-century, which has now become a 'giant with feet of clay'. What is required is a review of the entire structure, starting with the foundations. In short, contemporary finance needs a new paradigm.

Defining this new paradigm obviously falls outside the scope of this chapter, and should furthermore be considered in the framework of a collective programme. However, some avenues can usefully be debated and examined here:

(1) Resituating finance in the field of human and social sciences, giving up the illusion of finance as an autonomous discipline comparable to the physical sciences. This means accepting the contingency of financial events and behaviours, requiring differentiation according to the economic, legal, political and cultural environments of the companies that produce them, and in which those events and

behaviours participate. For example, financing corporate invest-ment, self-financing, banking credit, financial market are all avail-able, but the 'mix' of financing is dependent on many factors, notably institutional and human factors. In other words, financial decisions are contingent and not to be reducible to 'one best way'.

(2) Broadening the analysis framework for financial risks to factors other than price, rates and random variations in these prices and rates. Risk concerns also the upholding of the firm as an autonomous entity and, at large, the upholding of the different positions of concerned actors, especially top management. Different conceptions of risk – based, for example, on variations in rates of return, in debt default, in independence – bring about different results for financial decisions related with each conception. As MacKenzie (2006) says about the actual finance framework: it is 'an engine, not a camera'.

(3) Use of formalization as one possible type of analysis among others. Over the last few decades, analysis, modelling and fore-casting tools have seen considerable development in finance, used with apparently limitless creativity. In terms of risk modelling, conception of a universe structured in terms of random variables has engendered excessive use of the axioms and laws for calculat-ing probabilities (El Karoui, 2009); these practices look highly questionable today. Mandelbrot (1997), Taleb (2007) and Walter and de Practontal (2009) all pointed to the consequences of this excessive use of basic probabilistic rules. The current range of tools used (actuarial techniques, probabilities) should be extended to include other mathematical tools (game theory, fractal theory, etc.). But the best of mathematical tools remain tools, and a finance decision is, first of all, a human decision.

For reform of financiers' education

Many teachers/researchers in finance have a background in math-ematics, and inadequate knowledge of economics, law, sociology, etc., not to mention accounting. Too many students can gain their qualifications (such as a masters in finance) while presenting the same inadequacies, which may be worsened or masked by rash trust in the 'scientific' nature of their modelling tools.

The author does not believe it is possible to ignore the education of financiers, particularly traders working in the front office of the international financial markets. As we know, most of these professionals have trained for their careers in the financial industry through an education consisting almost entirely of mathematical techniques. This has two unfortunate consequences:

- It firmly establishes the idea that finance, like physics or chemistry, is an autonomous science that can be expressed through appropriate modelling.
- It brings financial decision-makers onto the market in the form of (often young) agents who have no experience of economic or corporate life, nor any training in law, economics, management or more broadly social and human sciences, which could have given them basic preparation for their future jobs. Not to mention classes in ethics . . .

In liaison with the desired emergence of a new paradigm in finance, a review of financiers' education appears vital. Here again, some directions will simply be sketched out. Any 'finance masters'-type course should include:

- a grounding in the 'anthropology of finance': classes based on research by economic anthropologists/sociologists (Levi-Strauss, Polanyi, etc.) and historians (Braudel (1985), Wallerstein, etc.);
- extensive training in economics (particularly international economics), law (particularly commercial) and management (firms and organizations);
- knowledge of tools and languages (mathematics, statistics, information systems, including accounting and internal control) involving 'deciphering' of their conceptual bases and their modes of use;
- specific modules concerning, respectively, epistemology and methodology, the psycho-sociology of decision-making,[5] professional ethics and business ethics.

Open governance: a new youth for the 'German model'?

The situation in Germany has long been highly specific; bank–industry relations are strong in terms of both investment financing, and shareholdings and control. In correlative terms, the financial markets played a more modest role in Germany than in Anglo-American countries. The Federal Republic had set up a co-management system in which employee unions took part in meetings of the firm's supervisory boards.[6] The state, as a result of its federalist structure, takes a less interventionist approach than in countries such as France, even though it has influence at the level of its *Länder*. All the circumstances explain that corporate governance in Germany is a case apart, called the 'Rhine model' by M. Albert (1991).

This model of governance was, some years ago, considered as obsolete – as was that of Japan. This 'Germano-Nippon model' was less shareholder-oriented than the 'Anglo-American model', which gave a prominent role of financial markets to corporate governance. This assessment is now relevant because of the resilience of this 'Rhine model' during the recent crisis. The reasons for these better performances – or less negative effects – are multiple: confident context related with links between management and employee unions, as well as with the banking system, and sometimes with local institutions like *Länder* (as reflected for example in the Lower Saxony *Land*'s acquisition of shares in Volkswagen). But the main reason for this resilience is easily understandable: the German model, giving a lesser place to financial markets, was less affected by the effects of the current crisis that concern, first of all, these markets and the financial-based corporate governance model.

So, it would perhaps be beneficial to roll out this governance system across Europe. The best angle for attack appears to be through discussions – which began a long time ago, but regularly come to a standstill – on the 'European company' status. The debate should be resumed with the aim, as sketched out above, of giving a specific status to large companies in the EU, at least in Germany, France and other countries willing to join them.

This proposal boils down to 'giving the enterprise an explicit status'. Embryonic plans exist – for instance, in labour law, and for the slightly heterogeneous set of laws and regulations called 'economic law'. We need to go further, situating these factors in an architecture that is coherent, functional and innovative, centred on 'the enterprise as a collective actor'. This would necessarily require a break from current company law: abandoning 'French-style' governance structures with board of directors and chair-CEO in favour of two-tier 'German-style' governance with a 'management board' and a 'supervisory board' (an option that is currently possible in France but rarely used).

Clearly, a new status for the enterprise in its capacity as a social actor recognized as a legal entity would significantly change the role of the financial markets. This is not an unrealistic prospect, as the central reform would concern the governance regime rather than the ownership regime:

- The financial markets are able, when necessary, to do business with listed companies whose control structure makes them 'takeover-proof', either because they are family-controlled (LVMH, Michelin, Peugeot) or because of their special status (for example mutual banks like Credit Agricole).
- Some operators, such as hedge funds, may have objections, but controlling them more effectively would be precisely one of the objectives sought.
- The other institutional investors will be encouraged to be patient (Porter's 'still capitalism') and reap the harvest of a corporate development policy. Given the index-linked structure of most portfolios held by these institutional investors, they could no longer ignore large European groups prepared to adopt this governance structure.

Responsible management

It is tempting to say 'this will never happen again', but history illustrates how much people and the elites are capable of forgetting. All the same, it is to be hoped that we will no longer hear peremptory statements like 'The economy doesn't lie' (Sorman, 2008)[7] or recommendations for greater deregulation, with the markets themselves responsible for self-regulation.

On the level of management instruments, certain indicators that were praised to the skies a few years ago are becoming dramatically obsolescent: for example EVA (Economic Value Added), and other indicators of shareholder value creation. Similarly, analysis of the risk must be reconsidered on both the conceptual and operational levels. For example the indicator called VaR (Value at Risk) is now criticized because it does not examine the consequence – which may be dramatic – of events with weak probability ('The black swan': Taleb, 2007). In the world of accounting, the debate concerns the recent reforms based on IFRS (International Financial Reporting Standards) which have created a pro-cyclic effect in the recent financial crisis (Capron, 2005; Bignon *et al.*, 2009; Colasse, 2009; Marteau and Morand, 2009).

Above all, it is to be hoped that the managers themselves will be able to guard against the abuses that resulted from the combined influence of globalization, financialization and excessively short-term behaviour that is indifferent to the negative externalities generated. Let us hope that management can 'evolve in an appropriate system, stimulating the creative capacity of individuals while also providing links of solidarity within society' (Urban, 2008; Sun, 2009).

Conclusion

The progression from finance seized with hubris, to excessively financialized governance, and finally to instrumented management led to the breakdown we have witnessed in successive waves since September 2007. This breakdown also reflected 'failing regulations' or, more precisely, the end of the myth of self-regulation, either by the markets themselves – the old neo-liberal premise – or via professional bodies supposed to be sufficiently clear sighted to decide on regulation and sufficiently well structured to ensure compliance with their decisions.

A new framework seems necessary; it concerns first a new paradigm of finance considered as a social science and not as a physical one, then a corporate governance system less shareholder- and more stakeholder-oriented, and, last but not least, a broader and more responsible management vision. This management of tomorrow awaits invention.

Notes

1 Since Knight (1921), micro-economic analysis has tended to single out uncertain situations considered 'random', meaning that the laws of probability can be used to represent them. The best known of these are the Laplace-Gauss or 'normal' laws of distribution, defined by their first two moments (mean and variance).

2 An anecdote from 'scientific' finance: when he received the Nobel prize, R. C. Merton ended his presentation speech with a quotation vaunting the LTCM investment fund he had set up with Scholes and other renowned researchers as 'The best finance faculty in the world' (see http:// nobelprize.org, last accessed 10 December 2010). This was in 1996, less than one year before the fund's spectacular collapse.

3 See www.pioline.com, last accessed 10 December 2010.
4 See www.calpers-governance.org, last accessed 10 December 2010.
5 To refer back to a note quoted earlier, financier education could learn as much from Merton senior (1948) ('The self-fulfilling prophecy') as Merton junior (1973) ('Theory of rational option pricing').
6 On the origins of German co-management, see the interesting essay by P.-Y. Gomez and P. Wirtz (2008) highlighting the role of the Church as a 'founding institution' during the period of history concerned (1945–50).
7 The author, a leading figure of free market economics, asserts rather naively that 'economics is no longer an opinion but a science', even adding – in a bold assertion for spring 2008 – 'the age of the great crises seems to be over'.

References

Aglietta, M. 1997. *Régulation et crises du capitalisme* (2nd edn.). Paris: O. Jacob.
Aglietta, M. and Rebérioux, A. 2004. *Dérives du capitalisme financier.* Paris: Albin Michel.
Akerlof, G. A. and Shiller, R. J. 2009. *Animal Spirits: How Human Psychology Drives the Economy and Why it Matters for Global Capitalism.* Princeton University Press.
Albert, M. 1991. *Capitalisme contre capitalisme.* Paris: Seuil.
Bignon, V., Biondi, Y. and Ragot, X. 2009. 'Une analyse économique de la "juste valeur": la comptabilité comme vecteur de crise' (*Prisme* no. 15), Paris: Centre Cournot pour la Recherche en Economie.
Black, F. and Scholes, M. 1973. 'The pricing of options and corporate liabilities', *Journal of Political Economy* 81 (3): 637–54.
Bourguinat, H. and Briys, E. 2009. *L'arrogance de la finance.* Paris: La Découverte.
Braudel, F. 1985. *La dynamique du capitalisme.* Paris: Flammarion.
British Academy Forum 2009. 'The global financial crisis: why didn't anybody notice?', *British Academy Forum*, London, 17 June.
Capron, M. 2005. *Les normes comptables internationales: instruments du capitalisme financier.* Paris: La Découverte.
Colasse, B. 2009. 'La normalisation comptable internationale face à la crise', *Revue Eco. Fin.* 95: 387–99.
Dembinski, P. H. 2009. *Finance: Servant or Deceiver? Financialization at the Crossroad.* London: Palgrave.
El Karoui, N. 2009. 'Un moment de l'expérience probabiliste: théorie des processus stochastiques et pratiques dans les marchés financiers', *Prisme*

n° 17, November, Paris: Centre Cournot pour la Recherche en Economie.

Fama, E. F. 1970. 'Efficient capital markets: a review of theory and empirical work', *Journal of Finance* 25 (2).

Gomez, P.-Y. and Wirtz, P. 2008. 'Institutionnalisation des régimes de gouvernance et rôle des institutions socles: le cas de la co-gestion allemande', *Économies et Sociétés*, 42 (10): October, p. 1869.

Hawley, J. P. and Williams, A. T. 2000. *The Rise of Fiduciary Capitalism*. Philadelphia: University of Pennsylvania Press.

Jensen, M. C. 2001. 'Value maximization, stakeholder theory and the corporate objective function', *Journal of Applied Corporate Finance* 14 (3): 8–21.

Jensen, M. C. and Meckling, W. H. 1976. 'Theory of the firm: managerial behavior, agency costs and ownership structure', *Journal of Financial Economics*, October.

Jorion, P. 2008. *La crise: des subprimes au séisme planétaire*. Paris: Fayard.

Knight, F. 1921. *Risk, Uncertainty and Profit*. New York: M. Kelley.

Kuhn, T. S. 1962. *The Structure of Scientific Revolution*. University of Chicago Press.

L'Hélias, S. 1997. *Le retour de l'actionnaire*. Paris: Galino.

MacKenzie, D. A. 2006. *An Engine, Not a Camera: How Financial Models Shape Markets*. Cambridge, MA: MIT Press.

Mandelbrot, B. 1997. *Fractals and Scaling in Finance: Discontinuity, Concentration and Risk*. New York: Springer.

Mandelbrot, B. and Hudson, R. 2004. *The (Mis)Behavior of Markets: A Fractal View of Risk, Ruin and Reward*. New York: Basic Books.

Markowitz, H. 1952. 'Portfolio selection', *The Journal of Finance* 7 (1): 77–91.

Marteau, D. and Morand, P. 2009. *Normes comptables et crise financière: propositions pour une réforme du système de régulation comptable*. Paris: La Documentation Française (report to the Minister for the Economy).

Merton, K. C. 1948. 'The self-fulfilling prophecy', *Antiech Review*, Summer: 193–210; reprinted in *Social Theory and Social Structure*. New York: Free Press, 1949.

Merton, R. C. 1973. 'Theory of rational option pricing', *Bell Journal of Economics*, Spring.

Modigliani, F. and Miller, M. 1958. 'The cost of capital, corporation finance and the theory of investment', *American Economic Review* 48 (3): 261–97.

Morin, F. 2006. *Le nouveau mur de l'argent: essai sur la finance globalisée*. Paris: Seuil.

Myers, S. C. 1977. 'Determinants of corporate borrowing', *Journal of Financial Economics* 6 (5): 147–75.

Orléan, A. 1999. *Le pouvoir de la finance*. Paris: edn. O. Jacob.

Pérez, R. 2003. *La gouvernance de l'entreprise*. Paris: La Découverte.

  2006. 'Les relations capital humain–capital financier: l'exemple de l'évolution du groupe BSN-Danone 1984–2004', *Gestion 2000*, No. 3, May, pp. 213–42.

  2009. 'Finance, gouvernance et management: quelles leçons tirer de la crise actuelle', in Kalika, M. (ed.), *Les hommes et le management: des réponses à la crise*. Paris: Economica, pp. 211–24.

Perroux, F. 1926. *Le problème du profit*. Paris: Giard.

  1960. *Le capitalisme*. Paris: PUF.

Plihon, D. 2003. *Le nouveau capitalisme* (3rd edn, 2009). Paris: La Découverte.

Polanyi, K. 1944. *The Great Transformation: The Political and Economic Origin of Our Time*. Boston: Beacon Press.

Rappaport, A. 1987. *Creating Shareholder Value: The New Standard for Business Performance*. New York: The Free Press.

Ross, S. A. 1977. 'The determination of financial structure: the incentive-signalling approach', *Bell Journal of Economics* 8: 23–40.

Shiller, R. 2000. *Irrational Exuberance*. Princeton University Press.

Sorman, G. 2008. *L'économie ne ment pas*. Paris: Fayard.

Soros, G. 1998. *The Crisis of Global Capitalism*. New York: Perseus Books.

Sun, W. 2009. *How to Govern Corporations So They Serve the Public Good: A Theory of Corporate Governance Emergence*. Lewiston, NY: Edwin Mellen Press.

Taleb, N. N. 2007. *The Black Swan: The Impact of the Highly Improbable*. New York: Penguin.

Thiveaud, J.-M. 1994. 'De la gouvernance des grandes sociétés', *Revue économique et financière* 31: 243–76.

Tirole, J. 2006. *The Theory of Corporate Governance*. Princeton University Press.

Tobin, J. 1956. 'Liquidity preference as behavior towards risk', *Review of Economic Studies* 26 (1): 65–86.

Tunc, A. 1994. 'Le gouvernement des sociétés anonymes: le mouvement de réforme aux États-Unis et au Royaume-Uni', *Revue internationale de droit comparé* 1.

Urban, S. 2008. 'Financial markets' expectations and human development', *S.B.R.* 3 (2): 162–71.

Wallerstein, I. 1983. *Historical Capitalism*. London: Verso.

Walter, C. and de Pracontal, M. 2009. *Le virus B. Crise financière et mathématiques*. Paris: Seuil.

Ownership, internal control and risk management: the roles of institutional shareholders and boards

Introduction to Part II

The contributions in this section concentrate on examining the failure of the internal governance system in the financial crisis and exploring how we may address the problems with the role of institutional shareholders, board effectiveness, internal control and risk management. Robert A. G. Monks starts the section with a focus on the complex and conflicting role of institutional shareholders, which has caused the systemic dysfunction of shareholders' rights and responsibilities to monitor the corporation. While there is no genuine commitment to an ownership-based governance system at present, he suggests two main policy initiatives to tackle this issue: the first is enabling effective shareholder engagement in corporate governance through explicit legislation and commitment to enforcement by all branches of government, and the second is encouraging shareholder activism by arrangement for financing 'activism' either as an appropriate corporate expense or as a designated portion of the investment management fees.

Roger Barker further investigates the impotence of institutional shareholders in monitoring the decision-making of bank boards and other financial companies in the UK prior to the financial crisis, and examines the reasons for the impotence. He argues that the underlying cause of poor engagement between shareholders and boards is the diversified portfolio strategy of most institutional fund managers. This basic problem is not overcome by the Stewardship Code for institutional shareholders in the UK. He concludes that the regulatory approach to corporate governance may make sense for the financial sector, but would be undesirable for the rest of the economy due to the frequent occurrence of regulatory failure. The alternative solution to shareholder engagement problems might need to be a return to the ownership structure itself: less ultra liquidity and more captive company ownership.

Jay W. Lorsch's chapter moves the focus from institutional shareholders to the functioning of the board. He starts with a reflective conclusion that the board failures in the 2008 financial crisis, as compared to that of 2002, were attributable primarily to the growing complexity of large companies in which an adequate and accurate flow of information from the lower level to the upper is problematic. His empirical investigations of forty-five board directors of financial institutions and other complex companies demonstrate that board effectiveness rests not on legislative prescriptions but on what transpires within individual boards. He presents a triangular model for board effectiveness in which boards' roles, their understanding of the company and board–management relationship are three key determinants that shape boards' behaviour. He concludes that the most challenging task for boards is to maintain a delicate balance in their relationship with management. Boards must be challenging and critical on the one hand and supportive on the other. They have to sustain an open and candid flow of communication in both directions. And they must seek sources of understanding outside management without offending management.

In recent years, corporate governance reforms worldwide have emphasized the role of independent directors in making the board more effective. But many people are concerned about whether the functioning of independent directors in corporate governance really could work. Chunyan Liu, Jianlei Liu and Konari Uchida's empirical research demonstrates that independent directors have played a positive role in disciplining management against its performances (through management turnover) and protecting shareholder wealth (via maintaining dividend policy) during the financial crisis. Their research supports the view that well-designed corporate governance structures serve an important role during crisis times when agency conflict becomes severe.

While a basic regulatory framework is essential for internal control and risk management, Christoph Van der Elst's chapter reviews the regulatory practices across Western Europe over the last decade and during the financial crisis, with a focus on five countries and their different or similar approaches on risk management. His review is complemented by a case study of the real estate investment industry. He notes that significant progress towards integrated regulations on risk management in Europe has been made in recent years, with a shift from risk management being considered as a financial and operational issue to it being a pivotal element of good corporate governance.

Regulatory provisions have been particularly strengthened after the financial crisis, yet the regulatory integration of risk management and internal control in the corporate legal framework is still fragmented and incomplete. He recognizes several regulatory gaps that need to be addressed further.

7 | A review of corporate governance in UK banks and other financial industry entities: the role of institutional shareholders

ROBERT A. G. MONKS

What is wrong with the British and American system is that far too many shareholders, both institutional and individual, do not behave like owners. *The Economist*, 5 May 1990.

How far have we moved, if at all, from this state described by Rupert Pennant-Rea twenty years ago? The Treasury Committee suggests there has been inadequate progress, if indeed there has been any.[1] The Walker Review of Corporate Governance of UK Banking Industry addresses the policy considerations underlying institutional responsibility which he styles 'stewardship'.

(5.7) . . . The potentially highly influential position of significant holders of stock in listed companies is a major ingredient in the market-based capitalist system. It needs to be accorded an *at least implicit social legitimacy*. As counterpart to the obligation of the board to the shareholders, this implicit legitimacy can be acquired by at least the larger fund manager through assumption of a reciprocal obligation. This obligation should in particular involve attentiveness to the performance of the investee companies over a long as well as a short term horizon. On this view, those who have significant rights of ownership which enjoy the very material advantage of limited liability should see these as completed by a duty of stewardship. (Walker Review, 2009, emphasis added)

To shareholders in a typical public company in America or Britain – call it Anglo-Saxon Inc – a share is now little more than a betting slip. It is bought at what a shareholder thinks are good odds, to provide winnings that he hopes will be large. The notion that he owns part of Anglo-Saxon Inc makes as much sense to him as it would the average gambler to imagine that he owns part of Lucky Lady, running in the 2:30 tomorrow afternoon.[2]

This chapter was originally a paper written on 30 September 2009 commenting on the UK Walker Review, in response to its chapter 5: 'The role of institutional shareholders: communication and engagement'.

134

Today's consolidated US/UK shareholder roster typically shows that 30 per cent of the outstanding shares are invested in index mode and a further 20 per cent are invested pursuant to a variety of computer-driven algorithms, generally in the search for value anomalies among various industries, companies and currency denominations. In both these cases, choices are made by mechanistic formulae and do not reflect a human being's decision to buy or sell. Another 30 per cent of investors know the stock market solely through their friendly broker. Although brokers are of all kinds, they are paid if their customers buy or sell, the more frequently the better. None of these groups has the long-term, informed engagement with their holdings necessary for them to be activist owners.

So, quite quickly, we are left with 20 per cent of the total who might be thought of as real proprietors and even potential activist investors. These are the owners who consider the long-term disposition of their funds; who follow the conduct of their portfolio companies; and who are prepared, if necessary, to take steps to ensure that defects in the governance or strategy or execution by managements are addressed. In the simplest terms, these are the only shareholders who actually know the companies in which they hold shares. McKinsey, the premier consulting firm for corporate management, describes these 'intrinsic investors' as basing their decisions on a deep understanding of a company's strategy, its current performance, and its potential to create long-term value. We can begin, at this point, to appreciate Lord Myners' recent suggestions about the possible desirability of two classes of stock – which, ironically enough, echo Proprietors and Punters (*The Economist*, 5 May 1990).

However, even this one investor in five who may be considered a real owner is further diluted by the dirty little secret of benign neglect of conflict of interest. Let's briefly re-screen the major categories of institutional investors from the perspective of activity *encouraging conflict of interest* and thus *inhibiting responsible activist ownership*.

(1) A 'golden rule' among company executives at corporate pension funds goes as follows: My pension fund will leave you alone so long as your pension fund leaves me alone. In the United States, there has never been an activist intervention by a pension fund governed by the Employee Retirement Income Security Act.

Never. For its part, the US Department of Labor has an unblemished record over the last twenty-five years of *not* bringing suit against a fiduciary having a conflict of interest for failure to monitor portfolio companies.[3] I am unaware of any government action otherwise in the UK.

(2) Most trustees of public pension funds are appointed or elected and are thus both politically vulnerable and politically conflicted. Why would any company locate new jobs in a region that uses its pension resources to oppose management?

(3) Conflicts abound equally for financial service firms. Why would any company go out of its way to talk with analysts from an investment group company that does not support it? Why would a 'focus company' hire such an investment group to run its retirement programme?

(4) Banks and insurance companies have a myriad of sometimes conflicting connections with companies, the securities of which they hold in trust accounts. Often the financial importance of the trust arrangement is substantially smaller than that of the other business concerns.

(5) Many of the trustees of our august universities and foundations depend on the favour – collegial, psychological and financial – of the enterprises whose securities comprise their endowment.

Passing from institutions to the leading individual investors, the 'collective action problem' is daunting. Warren Buffett recently said, 'when we own stock, we are not there to try and change people'.[4] Buffett 'rescued' Salomon Brothers as a minority owner. While he made an adequate return, the overall impact of his effort was to make money for people whose conduct caused the problem in the first place. The Gates Foundation professes no interest in activism. Volunteering to be a leader of shareholder activism created unwelcome problems of publicity and conflict of interests for Fidelity's Ned Johnson; Lloyd Blankfein, CEO of Goldman Sachs, says simply: 'It doesn't make business sense for us or for our customers.' Frank Cahouet,[5] then CEO of the UK-owned Crocker Bank, wrote to me on 17 August 1995:

We are very reticent to position ourselves as an activist shareholder in domestic or international securities. The problem for us is how we are perceived by our customer base. The risks are such that it probably does not make sense for us to take an aggressive position. I can imagine many of your partners do have a lot more freedom since they apparently have no other business interests with portfolio companies.

Can Cahouet's concern for his customers' reactions be fully met by *implicit social legitimacy* for activism, or will more be required – such as legal obligation – in order to ensure a level playing field among competitors? Alan Greenspan speaks for the conventional wisdom: 'After considerable soul-searching and many congressional hearings, the current CEO-dominant paradigm, with all its faults, will likely continue to be viewed as the most viable form of corporate govern-ance for today's world. The only credible alternative is for large – primarily institutional – shareholders to exert far more control over corporate affairs *than they appear to be willing to exercise*.'[6] The emphasis is mine, added to demonstrate Greenspan's apparent ignor-ance of fiduciary law. He writes as if obedience to the law is a discretionary matter for fiduciaries. Therefore, activist fiduciaries would be perceived as 'volunteers', almost 'officious intermeddlers' if they depart from the conventional. Yet Greenspan does, however inferentially, confirm the right place to begin.

The core problem has been the disappearance of any practical or legal respect for the fiduciary standards (even for Frank Cahouet, a profoundly ethical man) that assure a beneficiary of the loyal compe-tence of the person responsible for managing his property. We have tolerated conflicts of interest throughout the commercial system with the result of enriching service providers and impoverishing beneficiar-ies. Worse, this regulatory neglect has placed the conscientious fidu-ciary at a competitive disadvantage.

We arrive at the current place where 'activism' is not generally attractive, either from the perspective of value-adding incentive or of avoiding discipline or fine for fiduciary failure.[7] Put simply, the 'carrot' is not sufficient inducement and the 'stick' is insufficiently daunting. The result is that – with a few honourable exceptions: TIAA/CREF in America, BTPS and Hermes in the UK – activism has been limited to union and public employee pension funds, which – notwithstanding their virtues – do not appear to have the experience or orientation necessary to act as credible maximizers of shareholder value. In sum, only the least credible tranche of shareholders is prepared to act for the class as a whole; the preponderance – for their own reasons – prefer non-action.

This systemic dysfunction necessitates the involvement of an external catalyst – government. Only government can definitively locate the
responsibilities of shareholders – shares loaned, shares sold short,
shares whose vote is contracted away from the economic beneficiary,
and, not least, government as shareholder – UK Financial Investments
Ltd (UKFI). There is a need clearly to place responsibility for stewardship on one of the parties in the fiduciary chain. The pattern of trustees
delegating functions is well established; often the voting responsibility
is de facto delegated to a voting service. If active ownership is to serve
its intended purpose, there needs be a single responsible body. Nor
can a UK regime bind institutions with domiciles elsewhere. As the
Walker Report duly notes, a voting regime can only be imposed
on UK-domiciled funds. 'The aim is to embed commitment to the
Stewardship Code (on a "comply or explain" basis) on the part of
UK-authorised entities and thereafter to encourage voluntary participation by SWFs and other non-resident investors on the basis that this
is likely be in their own interest and in that of their clients as ultimate
beneficiaries' (para. 5.41).

Short-term activists – arbitrageurs, 'locusts', hedge funds – need no
encouragement. Their business model rewards thrusts into the marketplace. We are left with two components of potential long-term
activists – the unthinking index and computer shareholders and the
activist portion of McKinsey's 'intrinsic' holders. They have very
different characteristics. The index funds are in competition with
active managers for the portion of investors' funds allocated to equity.
One of the principal competitive advantages they have is lower costs.
If the index funds are to be an element of the activist shareholder of
the future, some economic arrangement will be necessary in order not
to prejudice their competitive posture. Their perspective will inevitably be systemic. Following the guidance of Alastair Ross Goobey,
they will relate to the market place as a whole, they will not usually
focus on individual companies. Alas, there is no clone of Ross Goobey.
We will need to overcome present reluctance of indexers with carrot or
stick. The intrinsic holders, by contrast, will focus on individual companies. Probably, their incentive structure always needs to be reconsidered. Do we want two kinds of activism? And if not, which one?

The Institutional Shareholders' Committee ('ISC') is comprised of
industry-based associations of institutional investors. Whether or not
a particular fiduciary is an insurance company or a pension fund or a

mutual fund is not germane to its appropriateness as an activist investor. Each institution will inevitably have holdings that are indexed, that are managed by computer program. Most will have some intrinsic investors. The ISC has no particular credibility or competency in being responsible for passive or intrinsic shareholder activists. While there have been instances in the past of ISC activity focused on particular companies and there have been leaders – Mike Sandland of Norwich Union and Donald Bryden in his Barclays days come to mind – with ambitious agendas, overall it has been rare that the ISC has committed substantial time or resources to governance challenges. In light of the incongruence between the institutional classification of its component members and the nature of the two kinds of potential activists, it must be questioned whether the ISC is the appropriate agency to carry this work forward.

The threshold question must be whether we feel stewardship objectives can be achieved within the current framework of 'comply or explain' or whether significant alterations will need to be made to the incentives and penalties governing the ongoing system. There are such a myriad of conflicting considerations that new transcending and binding resolution has appeal. We have to deal with real problems – how is our hypothetical honourable chief executive going to reconcile stewardship with his customers' reasonable expectations if there is not an unequivocal requirement that his competitors comply with the same requirements? How are we going to induce those institutional categories, being strangled by conflict of interest, without legal insistence that they act as stewards solely in the interest of their beneficiaries? Is it fair to impose a burden of additional expense on 'stewards' without making possible a reallocation of rewards?

Does the critical voice have the ring of truth? 'Unfortunately, Walker's proposals lack teeth and risk becoming nebulous when economic health returns and investors must look to prevent the next crisis, not cast an eye over their shoulder at the last. What will they really achieve in seriously promoting long-term investment? Where is the "incentive" for the ultimate shareholders – the institutional investors – to become owners with their eyes fixed firmly on durable returns and their service providers clearly aligned in this direction also?' (Note that fund manager votes against corporate management remain pitifully low: Wheelan, 2009.)

With Allen Sykes, I have elsewhere (Monks and Sykes, 2002) articulated four comprehensive proposals in aid of a system of effective stewardship:

- Governments should affirm, in support of the fundamental principle that there should be no power without accountability, that creating an effective shareholder presence in all companies is in the national interest and that it is the nation's policy to aid effective shareholder involvement in the governance of publicly owned corporations. A national level council should be created so as to ensure effective involvement of authorities, stock exchanges and other similarly involved entities.
- All pension fund trustees and other fiduciaries (insurance companies, mutual funds) holding shares must act solely in the long-term interests of their beneficiaries and for the exclusive purpose of providing them with benefits. The scope of required shareholder activism is to ensure, on a continuous basis, the functioning of an appropriate board of directors.
- To give full effect to the first two proposals institutional shareholders should be made accountable for exercising their votes in an informed and sensible manner above some sensibly determined minimum holding ($15 m/£10 m). Votes are an asset (voting shares always have a market premium over non-voting ones). Accordingly they should be used to further beneficiaries' interests on all occasions. In effect, the voting of all institutionally held shares would be virtually compulsory.
- To complete and powerfully reinforce the other three proposals shareholders should have the exclusive right and obligation *to nominate* at least three non-executive directors per major quoted company.

Our conclusion is that involvement by the full spectrum of institutional investors – without which the legitimacy of ownership activism is seriously diluted – is only possible through explicit legislation and commitment to enforcement by all branches of government. Allen Sykes and I speak to the 'stick' aspect of incentivizing institutional stewardship.

Our approach can be expanded (and improved) by focusing a little on the carrot side. I have cited often the 'Punters or

Proprietors' article in *The Economist* of twenty years ago. It may be that the passage of two decades has managed to change a conjunction and today the answer is Punters AND Proprietors. It must be clear that amidst the panoply of stock ownership, there is a difference of kind between those who invest through impersonal mechanism and those whose investments are a matter of sentient choice. Lord Myners' suggestion of two classes of stock might well reflect this difference. A further dichotomy might be drawn between those shareholders – passive and active – who choose to function as stewards and those who do not. Again, dual classes of stock might be appropriate. It is well to remember that when Warren Buffett invests in marketable securities, he is usually able to secure a special classification that reflects the value added by his involvement. Nor has the dual class prevalent in Scandinavia lowered long-term equity returns. Even American scholars comment favourably on such a notion: 'Providing long-term shareholders a greater number of votes per share should become a permissible option' (Lipton *et al.*, 2009).

Further improvement would result from the determination that stewardship, being in the interest both of the corporation and of society, is appropriately an expense of the corporation. If a sum is to be made available for those willing to undertake the costs and exposure of stewardship, there would be reduced difficulty in enlisting the index funds to perform the key long-term role. It might well be that this is the best answer, as what is wanted is both long-term stewardship and a perspective for the investment world as a whole, in contrast to individual companies.

This chapter asks the question:

- Is there genuine commitment to an ownership-based governance system? (It must be said that no such commitment exists at present.) If so,

The chapter suggests two main policy initiatives:

- there must be effective enforcement of existing law so as to *require* fiduciaries to take appropriate action to protect and enhance the value of portfolio securities, and
- there must be arrangements for financing 'activism' either as an appropriate corporate expense or as a designated portion of the investment management fees.

Notes

1 The Treasury Committee Report provides an answer in the affirmative. 'Institutional Investors have failed in one of their core tasks, namely the effective scrutiny and monitoring the decisions of boards and executive management in the banking sector, and hold them accountable for their performance.' House of Commons, Treasury Committee, 'Banking Crisis: Reforming corporate governance and pay in the City', 12 May 2009, para. 29. 'We also believe that one of the most important lessons from the crisis is that institutional investors responsible ownership needs to be strengthened in order to be fit for purpose.' UNEP Finance Initiative, Fiduciary Responsibility, July 2009, p. 11.

2 *The Economist*, 5 May 1990.

3 United States Government Accountability Office, 'Pension plans: additional transparency and other actions needed in connection with proxy voting' (GAO-04-749, August 2004).

4 Global Edition of *The New York Times*, 9–10 May 2009.

5 In the interest of full disclosure I gratefully acknowledge that Frank Cahouet, later CEO of Mellon Bank, has been a friend and classmate for the last sixty-five years. I know of no one with greater personal integrity. I have used his name in this chapter in order to personalize the difficulties that fine people, responsible for fiduciary institutions, encounter under the present regimes of failure of enforcement of fiduciary duties.

6 Alan Greenspan, 'Remarks at the Stern School of Business', 26 March 2002.

7 An honourable exception is the late Alastair Ross Goobey, who, while CEO of Hermes Investment Management, devised a business scheme pursuant to which those to whom he was responsible were enriched at the same time as his subsidiary activist funds, initially Hermes Lens Asset Management, and introduced activism into the UK marketplace. His view was that index investors have no choice but to allocate assets to ensuring the continuing integrity of the marketplace in which they invested.

References

Lipton, M., Lorsch, J. W. and Mirvis, T. N. 2009. 'Schumer's shareholder bill misses the mark', *The Wall Street Journal*, 12 May.

Monks, R. and Sykes, A. 2002. *Capitalism without Owners Will Fail: A Policymaker's Guide to Reform*. London: Centre for the Study of Financial Innovation.

Walker Review 2009. 'A review of corporate governance in UK banks and other financial industry entities: final recommendations', available at www.hm-treasury.gov.uk/d/walker_review_261109.pdf, last accessed 6 December 2010.

Wheelan, H. 2009. 'We must incentivize long-term investment to help prevent systemic risk', *Responsible Investor* 4 August, available at http://www.responsibleinvestor.com/home/article/systemic/P1.

8 Ownership structure and shareholder engagement: reflections on the role of institutional shareholders in the financial crisis

ROGER BARKER

The central role of shareholders in corporate governance is embodied in company law and corporate governance codes around the world. Company law in the UK, for example, states that a primary duty of directors is to run the firm in a way that promotes the success of the company for the benefit of its shareholders.[1]

The quid pro quo for the shareholder primacy in corporate governance is an expectation that shareholders will carefully monitor the activities of the company, and potentially intervene if they have concerns about the performance or motivations of the board of directors. In most countries, the law provides them with voting and other shareholder rights to enable them to fulfil this role.

However, in the years leading up to the financial crisis, there appears to have been a widespread acquiescence by institutional investors – the dominant form of shareholder in many developed economies – in respect of rapidly rising levels of leverage at banks and other financial institutions.

Despite being major holders of the equity of major financial institutions, institutional shareholders failed to inhibit bank boards from adopting aggressive business models, inadequate risk management systems and remuneration policies that did not take sufficient account of performance or risk.

A study by Manifest (2009) showed little evidence of shareholder dissent in relation to the activities of banks prior to 2008. For example, the level of shareholder dissent against the remuneration report of banks between 2002 and 2007 was around 9 per cent, the same as for companies in other sectors. By 2008, dissent was slightly higher, amounting to 10 per cent at a number of banks, but still very low.

Institutional investors were particularly impotent with respect to the disastrous takeover of ABN Amro, in 2007, by a consortium of European banks led by Royal Bank of Scotland and Fortis. Despite the scepticism expressed by financial journalists and other commentators concerning the cost of the deal and its threat to the capital position of the acquiring banks,[2] 95 per cent of shareholders of both banks voted in favour of the transaction.

Furthermore, at the two shareholder meetings required by Fortis to gain approval, the voter participation was only 36 per cent, a tiny participation in view of the crucial nature of the transaction. The takeover subsequently proved fatal to the balance sheets of both banks, and resulted in their subsequent nationalization, in 2008, by the governments of the UK and Belgium.

There is hence significant evidence to suggest that institutional investors did not provide an effective governance counterweight to the poor decision-making of bank boards and other financial companies prior to the financial crisis, either by being too passive or insufficiently engaged, or by even encouraging the adoption of high-risk business strategies.

These shortcomings have been recognized by policymakers. The former UK Treasury Minister, Lord Myners, has described institutional investors as 'absentee landlords' during the financial crisis (Myners, 2009). Hector Sants, chief executive of the FSA, has argued that investors were 'too reliant and unchallenging' with regard to their companies under ownership despite having extensive rights to directly or indirectly influence their governance (Sants, 2009).

The same sentiments were succinctly expressed by the Dutch Minister of Finance in a speech to shareholders in March 2009: 'We cannot avoid asking ourselves what you, shareholders, have done to prevent and manage the crisis. Unfortunately, and I know you don't like to hear this, the answer is almost nothing'.[3]

Consequently, although investors may justifiably argue that other corporate governance actors – such as financial regulators, government policymakers, and the directors and senior managers of the banks themselves – must accept a share of the blame for the financial crisis, institutional investors themselves cannot escape some degree of culpability.

The remainder of this chapter considers the current state of company–shareholder engagement in the main developed economies, and evaluates the reasons for its relative impotence. It then considers recent proposals designed to forge a closer relationship between institutional investors and companies. The chapter concludes by arguing that, despite the obstacles that must be overcome, shareholder engagement is an essential means of improving the effectiveness and legitimacy of national systems of corporate governance in the post-crisis era.

The case for shareholder engagement

Shareholder engagement is a generic term used to describe the ongoing relationship between shareholders and company boards, and designed to deal with concerns about underperformance.

From the perspective of corporate governance theory, shareholders are exposed to the agency problem which arises from the gap between owners and managers, and the potential for misalignment of interest between them. Any such misalignment creates the potential for loss of performance or the pursuit of inappropriate corporate objectives. The justification for shareholder engagement is to narrow this gap.

Engagement procedures typically include shareholder policy on voting and voting disclosure. However, voting is just one (and a perhaps over-emphasized) aspect of engagement. Engagement also covers the entire range of processes employed by investors for monitoring investee companies. It will involve meeting and establishing a dialogue with a company's chairman, senior independent director, other directors and senior management. It may also define a strategy for more detailed shareholder intervention in a company's affairs in certain circumstances.[4]

A key objective of engagement is to foster greater investor confidence in the medium- and longer-term strategy of the company, and in the board's capacity to oversee its implementation. A potential benefit of this kind of relationship is to reduce the focus of investors on earnings announcements and other short-term performance metrics. This should allow the company to adopt a longer-term strategic orientation.

Such mutual understanding is also likely to be of benefit to the company in difficult times. By improving the quality of communication with institutional shareholders in 'normal' situations, a good basis of understanding and trust can be embedded. As a result, situations involving tension and potentially strong differences of view between boards and shareholders can be more easily diffused at an early stage.

A distinction should be made between encouraging engagement between investors and boards and increasing shareholder pressure on boards to perform in the short term.

Prior to the financial crisis, there were significant short-term performance pressures on many financial institutions. Stock market analysts and activist investors argued for increased leverage, spin-offs, acquisitions or share buybacks, aimed at boosting the share price and corporate earnings in the short term. But such initiatives were often achieved at the expense of increased leverage and credit risk.

In contrast, shareholder engagement is about dialogue and interaction between investors and companies where the investors are likely to be relatively long-term shareholders.

Engagement is not the only investment strategy that can be followed by shareholders. A commonly utilized alternative involves active trading in stocks. Fund managers following such an active trading strategy tend to have little interest in forming relationships with the boards of their investee companies. If they dislike a stock, they simply sell it on the secondary equity market.

However, such a disengaged approach to ownership has negative implications for corporate governance. Although selling the stock may send a signal to the management of the company, its impact on their behaviour or policies, beyond a slight increase in the company's weighted average cost of capital, and possibly an increased vulnerability to takeover, will be limited. Furthermore, it may stimulate a short-termist approach from company management.

For passive investors that take ownership stakes in companies according to externally defined index benchmarks, thereby limiting their ability to exit underperforming investments, stock trading is not an available investment strategy. For these investors, the adage that 'if you can't sell, you must care' is highly relevant.

Furthermore, the benefits of active stock trading for the majority of institutional investors are questionable. While rare (or lucky) fund managers with superior insight and timing may beat a benchmark index through trading activities for a while, this will not be possible, by definition, for the average market participant. Market trading is, in effect, a zero sum game; for every trader who wins another must lose.

In contrast, some form of involved governance or engagement activity offers a means of increasing absolute returns for all investors by addressing performance issues in the company. It is a positive sum game from which all market participants can potentially gain.

There is also a moral case for shareholder engagement rather than share trading. In his recent review of UK corporate governance, Sir David Walker argues that 'those who have significant rights of ownership and enjoy the very material advantage of limited liability should see these as complemented by a duty of stewardship'. According to Sir David, the influential position of shareholders in listed companies can only be regarded as socially legitimate if it involves a reciprocal obligation of the investor to engage with the investee company (Walker, 2009, p. 70).

While recognizing its potential benefits, it is important that the limits to the scope of shareholder engagement are properly understood. For example, both companies and investors would agree that it is not practicable or desirable for institutional shareholders to attempt to micromanage or 'second guess' the boards or managements of their investee companies from a distance. External investors are also not likely to be in a position to identify and assess specific business risks.

In most cases, engagement will focus on areas of company activity that shareholders are in a position to monitor effectively from outside the firm, and which they are able to influence in the long-term interests of the enterprise. This may lead to a concentration on issues that institutional shareholders are well placed to evaluate due to their ability to compare governance structures across business entities.

This may include assessing the quality and capability of the leadership of the company, most notably the chairman and chief executive; gaining reassurance that the board and its committees are appropriately composed and are functioning effectively; evaluating the company's principal strategies and objectives, including in particular the approach to remuneration and its risk appetite; and appraising the company's performance in delivering the agreed strategy.

The current state of shareholder engagement

The quality and extent of engagement between institutional investors and boards has in recent years been mixed. Some institutions, such as CalPERS in the United States and Hermes in the UK, have well-established track records in playing an active ownership role. In addition, some hedge funds and private equity groups have, from time to time, effectively performed the role of active shareholders.

However, there is also a growing body of research, based on the disclosure of voting records, which suggests only limited engagement with investee companies by mainstream institutional investors.

For example, a recent study by Goergen *et al.* (2008) suggests that the largest shareholders in most listed UK firms do little company monitoring. Choi and Fisch (2008) found that many public pension funds in the United States kept a low, non-confrontational profile. In addition, an increasing number of institutions rely on proxy advisors to either advise them how to vote or to directly exercise their voting rights.

A more wide-ranging survey undertaken by the International Corporate Governance Network (ICGN) in 2009 found low levels of trust between companies and their investors in many countries, and this acted as a serious barrier to constructive engagement (Wong, 2009, p. 60).

There was also a concern among companies that not all share-holders were well equipped – in terms of level of human resources and expertise – to make informed decisions on board composition, remuneration and other corporate governance matters. Furthermore, companies were frustrated with the lack of coordination between governance specialists and fund managers, resulting in inconsistent messages being conveyed to companies.

The legal framework appears to have a substantial impact on engagement practices. In the Netherlands and the UK, for example, securities law has been more conducive to dialogue between companies and shareholders compared to other countries.

In contrast, in the United States, low levels of engagement with share-holders on corporate governance matters have partly been attributed to concerns over infringing securities regulations, in particular Regulation Fair Disclosure (Regulation FD). To comply with Regulation FD, US companies may insist on highly restrictive interactions with sharehold-ers. This may include having legal counsel in attendance, stipulating the agenda in advance to ensure that discussion does not venture beyond pre-defined boundaries, and limiting discussion to receiving the views of shareholders rather than a two-way exchange of views.

In many countries, national corporate governance codes are one of the main mechanisms used to encourage shareholder engagement. In most European jurisdictions, for example, corporate governance codes are applied according to the 'comply or explain' principle, which seeks to promote a dialogue between companies and shareholders on appropriate corporate governance practices. Such an approach is often referred to as a 'soft law' approach to corporate governance, as companies can deviate from the requirements of the code as long as they explain their reasoning to shareholders.

The Dutch code, for instance, explicitly calls for shareholders to be willing to 'engage in a dialogue with the company and their fellow shareholders'. In 1992, the seminal Cadbury Report in the UK stated that 'we look to the institutions in particular to use their influence as owners to ensure that the companies in which they have invested comply with the Code'. The current version of the UK Corporate Governance Code (which was until 2010 known as the Combined Code) stipulates that 'institutional shareholders should enter into a dialogue with companies based on the mutual understanding of objectives'.

The success of European corporate governance codes in encouraging shareholder engagement was evaluated in a recent study conducted by RiskMetrics and several other business organizations on behalf of the European Commission (Riskmetrics *et al.*, 2009).

Although the study found that both companies and institutional investors across Europe broadly supported the 'comply or explain' approach, particularly relative to a more regulatory-oriented approach to corporate governance, there was also a wide consensus that investors were not sufficiently exercising their monitoring and engagement responsibilities. Companies also provided an inadequate level of disclosure and explanation to shareholders on their implementation of the codes.[5]

One of the study's main observations was that the institutional investor community consisted of two distinct parts: a small active minority and a majority of more passive investors. The former tended to exercise their shareholder rights actively. They usually had a corporate governance policy, actively communicated and engaged with companies, used their voting rights and disclosed their voting record. However, the overwhelming majority of investors belonged to the latter group, and were much more reluctant to actively participate in the governance of their investee companies (Riskmetrics *et al.*, 2009, p. 174).

From the perspective of shareholder voting, the passivity of many investors was further confirmed by recent data on shareholder voting in Europe. The data relating to the first half of 2009 indicated that voter turnout rates, i.e., the total number of votes cast at a given shareholder meeting as a percentage of total voting rights, was only 61 per cent (similar to the preceding year).

Many influential governance organizations – including those reflecting the views of institutional investors themselves – have concluded that investors are often inactive and that more engagement is required. In a statement in March 2009, the International Corporate Governance Network explicitly recognized that 'many investors did not invest the time or resources to provide effective oversight' (ICGN, 2009).The European Fund and Asset Management Association, as well as a number of national asset management associations, have also come to similar conclusions.[6]

The obstacles to effective engagement

Most commentators agree that improved engagement between boards and shareholders would be beneficial, and could have obviated the excesses of the financial crisis. Given such a consensus, what stands in the way of effective shareholder engagement?

The shift in savings patterns over time towards collective savings vehicles (e.g., pension funds, mutual funds, insurance companies) has encouraged the aggregation of listed company ownership in the hands of institutional investors.

This ownership trend has been particularly prevalent in the Anglo-Saxon economies, although it is a growing feature of company ownership in most developed economies around the world. For example, by 2006 institutional investors accounted for 60 per cent of equity ownership in the United States. In contrast, there has been a substantial decline in the equity holdings of private individuals and other non-institutional investors (OECD, 2009, p. 50).

Modern portfolio theory encourages institutional fund managers to adopt highly diversified portfolios. A large number of small percentage stakes in numerous companies is seen as preferable, from the perspective of risk-return optimization, to a small number of large blockholdings.

With such diffuse shareholdings, many institutional investors find it difficult, if not impossible, to act as owners in the way that would be normal where there is concentrated ownership.

Investors are commonly of the view that their small percentage ownership stakes do not allow them to exert much influence over company boards. Furthermore, their investments are spread over too many companies to justify paying much attention to individual companies. It is hence easy for such investors to neglect their engagement activities, and to concentrate on a trading approach to investment strategy.

Investors are also conscious of the free-rider benefit that would be provided to other institutional investors which did not contribute to the engagement process. Given that many of these investors are their business competitors, there is little incentive for institutions to engage on a unilateral basis or to attempt some form of collective engagement. As a result, many investors are deterred from investing too much resource in engagement efforts.

This contrasts with the situation in an unlisted enterprise or a private equity-owned company in which ownership is normally dominated by a controlling shareholder or blockholder. In such companies, the owners have a material proportion of their wealth tied up in an individual enterprise and have limited opportunities to exit their ownership stakes. In such companies, the agency gap between owner and manager is minimized by the fact that the owner has a strong incentive to become directly involved in the company and exercise a more intensive level of monitoring.

Although diffuse ownership is the most important factor that deters institutional investors from active engagement, a range of other factors create practical difficulties for investors. A first is that stock market regulatory arrangements may restrict the form of communication between boards and shareholders. This may increase the reticence of both companies and boards to engage in meaningful dialogue.

A second issue relates to the continued prevalence of barriers to the exercise of voting rights in many markets. Investors may find it difficult to vote at general meetings due to cross-border voting restrictions, short notice periods, share blocking and the shareholder-unfriendly practices of custodians.

Thirdly, investors may also fear that criticism of a company – or a vote against a company's proposals at an Annual General

Meeting – could reduce their subsequent access to company management. They may also be concerned that disagreements with a company could leak into the public arena, causing the stock price to fall.

A further issue that deters shareholder engagement is the practice of securities lending. Long-term institutional shareholders may be tempted to generate extra returns for their portfolio by lending their shares to other market participants for a period of time. This may interfere with their ability to exercise their voting rights, and may not be conducive to the long-term engagement of investor and investee company.

The disinclination of many institutional investors to devote significant resources to engagement – for all of these reasons – has a knock-on effect on the attitudes of boards. Chairmen often express misgivings and dissatisfaction at the level and quality of shareholder dialogue. This deters them from further engagement efforts.

Furthermore, companies find that close engagement with shareholders only materializes in problem situations. However, in such circumstances, specific differences of view may be already entrenched and difficult to resolve.

In addition, a commonly expressed frustration on behalf of boards is that shareholder engagement, when it does occur, tends to focus on issues such as remuneration rather than wider strategic issues.

Improving engagement: the search for a solution

The corporate governance debate in many countries over the last two decades has focused on strengthening shareholder rights in order to permit a meaningful activist role for shareholders.

However, if institutional shareholders are not prepared to fully utilize these rights – through voting and other forms of engagement – a logical response is to attempt to shift the focus of the debate on to the responsibilities rather than the rights of shareholders.

In the UK at least, there have been a number of historical attempts to promote shareholder engagement among institutional investors. As early as 1991, the Institutional Shareholders' Committee (ISC) – a forum of UK institutional shareholding trade associations – published a statement on 'The responsibilities of institutional shareholders in the UK'. This was updated and re-issued on various occasions over the subsequent fifteen years.

In November 2009, the ISC converted its Statement of Principles into a code (ISC, 2009a). The objective of the Code was to 'set out best practice for institutional investors that choose to engage with the companies in which they invest'. Furthermore, it aimed to 'enhance the quality of the dialogue of institutional investors with companies to help improve long-term returns to shareholders, reduce the risk of catastrophic outcomes due to bad strategic decisions, and help with the efficient exercise of governance responsibilities'. The new code was intended to be voluntary but called on institutions to state publicly – on a 'comply or explain' basis – how they applied its principles (ISC, 2009b).

However, in December 2009, the Walker Review into the governance failings of financial institutions during the financial crisis recommended that the ISC code should be renamed the Stewardship Code and adopted as an official UK code of practice for institutional investors (under the aegis of the Financial Reporting Council, the UK's independent corporate governance regulator). This proposal is currently under evaluation by the government and the FRC. The UK's financial regulator – the FSA – also plans to consider introducing a mandatory rule that would require regulated investment management firms to 'comply or explain' with the Code (FSA, 2010).

The concept behind the Stewardship Code is to increase the accountability of fund managers to their ultimate beneficiaries with respect to engagement activities. It will require fund managers to publicly disclose their commitment to a stewardship obligation or to explain their alternative investment approach if they are unwilling to assume such a commitment.

It is assumed that many ultimate beneficiaries – such as pension fund trustees and other end investors – will be supportive of a stewardship obligation, and the specific engagement with investee companies that it may encourage. A public declaration that a fund manager is ready to commit to principles of stewardship could hence be important in the winning of new business mandates by fund managers.

Will this new code succeed in significantly improving engagement between companies and shareholders? In its favour, the proposed code represents a clear statement of societal expectations with respect to the stewardship role of institutional investors. Over time, this could serve to influence the norms and business practices of the fund management industry (including non-domestic investors in UK companies, such as sovereign wealth funds). It may also assist the beneficial owners of investment products in demanding a more engaged and long-term ownership strategy from their asset managers.

However, as previously argued, the underlying cause of poor engagement between shareholders and boards in the UK is the diversified portfolio strategy of most institutional fund managers. This basic problem is not overcome by the Stewardship Code. As a result, many institutional fund managers will continue to be deterred from devoting significant resources to engagement due to the costs involved and the 'free-rider' benefits that would accrue to competitor fund managers.

Furthermore, it should not necessarily be assumed that actual or potential beneficial owners of shares (e.g., trustees, policyholders, retail investors) will demand a stewardship orientation from their investment suppliers. Beneficiaries may simply not understand or accept the accountability role that the Code is inviting them to play.

Indeed, stewardship activities could be seen as exerting a negative impact on investment returns (e.g., through higher administration costs or by inhibiting the flexibility of the investment process). If such a perception emerges among beneficial owners, the declaration of a stewardship orientation could, ironically, be a source of competitive disadvantage for institutional investors.

Last but not least, only UK institutional investors will be required to 'comply or explain' in respect of the Stewardship Code. However, the importance of foreign investors in UK company ownership has increased dramatically in recent years. As recently as 1990, foreign investors held less than 12 per cent of UK shares. However, by 2008, this had risen to more than 41 per cent. Traditional UK institutional investors – such as insurance companies and pension funds – now hold only around 26 per cent of the total (down from 52 per cent in 1990) (ONS, 2010, p. 4). Consequently, the Stewardship Code will only apply to a relatively narrow section of UK company ownership.

In short, although it represents a worthwhile step for UK corporate governance, the Stewardship Code faces an uphill battle in order to exert a meaningful effect on board–shareholder engagement.

A second way of encouraging greater shareholder engagement has involved considering how institutional investors can work together. In other words, although each investor may hold insignificant percentage stakes in individual companies, by collaborating, shareholders could increase their collective control over companies and thereby engage in a more meaningful way.

In the past, institutional investors have argued that listing and takeover rules in many leading equity markets have prevented them from working collectively on the corporate governance of individual companies. Such rules are designed to prevent investors from seeking to manipulate markets by obtaining control of a company without being subject to any takeover regulations: a so-called concert party situation.

In the United States, for instance, some large institutional investors have justified their unwillingness to work with other investors on the grounds that they would be required to make a Schedule 13D filing with the Securities and Exchange Commission. In Australia, institutional investors have expressed concern that collaborative activities on corporate governance matters outside shareholder meetings would contravene the Corporations Act (McKay, 2007). In the UK, investors have claimed that the regulations outlined in Rule 9 of the Takeover Code, and in the FSA's controllers' regime (which was implemented to comply with the EU's Acquisitions Directive) have deterred collective engagement (OECD, 2009).

In response to these potential impediments to collective action, the UK's FSA has recently issued guidance to market participants, which states that existing market regulations do not 'prevent collective engagement by institutional shareholders designed to raise legitimate concerns on particular corporate issues, events or matters of governance with the management of investee companies'.[7] The UK Takeover Panel has also issued similar guidance (Takeover Panel, 2009).

In Germany, the Risk Limitation Act of 2008 has reaffirmed that 'singular arrangements' among investors – such as with respect to several agenda items at one shareholder meeting or the same matter at different companies – fall outside the scope of a 'concert party' (Shearman and Sterling, 2008). The same applies to actions among shareholders outside shareholder meetings, in particular the pursuit of a common strategy to 'substantially' or 'permanently' alter the strategic direction of an investee company.

It will be important for authorities in other countries to clarify the scope of 'concert party' rules in order to facilitate investor cooperation on corporate governance matters at investee companies. However, in many markets, it appears that there is no substantive regulatory barrier that prevents investors from collective engagement if they are minded to do so.

A third way of facilitating the collective engagement of investors – particularly in terms of exercising their voting rights – is through proxy voting agencies. Large institutional investors in many countries outsource a significant amount of their corporate governance activities to proxy advisors. This is likely to be particularly true in relation to portfolio companies in which they have smaller stakes and foreign holdings.

A recently published American Bar Association report noted that 'with some exceptions, mutual funds tend not to invest significant monies in their analysis of corporate governance issues . . . the result is that some mutual funds defer to proxy advisors to determine how to vote their shares and focus their resources on determining when to buy, hold and exit' (American Bar Association, 2009).

There are, however, a number of problems with outsourcing corporate governance to proxy advisors. The quality of their voting recommendations can vary significantly by company and by market (OECD, 2009). Furthermore, the market for global proxy voting advisory services in North America and Western Europe has become highly concentrated, with the growing dominance of one firm. In addition, there is the issue of conflicts of interest arising from proxy advisors that serve both corporate and institutional investor clients. This conflict proved to be a toxic combination for the rating agencies prior to the financial crisis, particularly in relation to their credit ratings of mortgage-backed securities.

Nonetheless, a more competitive and appropriately regulated market for proxy advice has the potential to assist investors in fulfilling their engagement responsibilities.

A fourth area of recent policy initiative has involved improving the engagement awareness of foreign investors. As mentioned above, equity holdings by foreign investors have risen dramatically in recent years in most major stockmarkets. For example, as well as the increases already quoted for the UK, the holdings of foreign investors in German companies jumped from 20 per cent of the DAX 30 in 2005 to 52.6 per cent in 2007. In the Netherlands, non-Dutch investors now own 85 per cent of the shares in the AEX 25 index (Manifest, 2007).

Empirical findings show that in many markets foreign shareholders vote a smaller portion of their holdings than domestic investors. In Finland, for example, only 18.5 per cent of the shares owned by foreign investors participated in shareholder meetings, compared to 54 per cent for domestic shareholders (European Commission, 2006).

While the failure of foreign investors to exercise their voting rights is partly attributed to shareholder passivity, voting obstacles such as share blocking and cumbersome powers of attorney requirements also play a part. In some cases, elimination of legal voting obstacles has not cascaded down the voting chain. For example, in the Netherlands, legislators have eliminated share blocking as a legal requirement but some custodians continue to demand the deposit of shares prior to voting (OECD, 2010, p. 30).

A lack of familiarity with local practices may also have hampered foreign investor participation. For instance, although Americans are significant portfolio investors in the UK, many US institutional investors – due in part to differences in regulatory frameworks and commercial practices – are reluctant to follow an active engagement approach with investee companies. Similarly, foreign investors are less likely to sit on the nomination committees of Swedish companies, even where they are among the largest shareholders.

Policymakers are attempting to address some of these issues. An EU directive is seeking to prohibit share blocking for listed companies. In the Netherlands, the institutional shareholder association Eumedion has opened its membership to non-Dutch institutional investors. In the UK, the Walker Review has urged the Financial Reporting Council and major UK institutional investors to 'invite potentially interested major foreign institutional investors, such as sovereign wealth funds and public sector pension funds' to participate more actively in engagement activities (Walker, 2009).

A number of more radical proposals have been mooted since the financial crisis in order to deter short-termist investment strategies and promote a longer-term approach from investors. These all involve a more active policy approach to fostering shareholder engagement than has so far been countenanced in the mainstream corporate governance debate.

The thinking behind some of these proposals is to provide a clear financial incentive for investors to retain ownership of stocks for longer periods, to avoid lending them to market counterparties, and to focus on generating returns through greater engagement with companies. In the words of Paul Myners, a UK Treasury minister, 'we need to look at ways in which we can offer a carrot to some financial institutions to take the issue of ownership more seriously'.[8]

For example, a first idea involves the granting of a loyalty dividend to shareholders conditional on shares not being sold or lent during, say, a period of two to five years. An alternative option could be to give enhanced voting rights to longer-term or committed investors. A further reform could include favouring longer-term shareholdings through capital gains tax policy (with higher tax rates for shares sold within one or two years). Stamp duty could also be introduced on stock lending (Burgess, 2009; Butler, 2009).

Needless to say, such proposals have not been enthusiastically welcomed by the institutional shareholder community. Many of these ideas threaten the hard-won principle of 'one share, one vote', which has been central to protecting the interests of minority shareholders with small percentage ownership stakes.

In particular, institutional investors fear that shares with enhanced rights and privileges could become concentrated in the hands of non-institutional shareholders, such as families or other blockholder interests enjoying long-term relationships with incumbent management. Such an ownership structure is common in the blockholder-dominated corporate sectors of continental Europe (Barker, 2010a). This could prevent institutional investors from being able to exercise much influence over the management of the companies in which they invest (Burgess, 2009).

However, this is a rather self-interested criticism. Institutional investors appear to be jealously guarding a wide range of rights and privileges for minority shareholders but without accepting any obligation on their behalf to fulfil stewardship responsibilities. It appears that they are unwilling to accept changes that could encourage the emergence of a more engaged class of owners due to the threat it would pose to their own position as an interest group.

However, their criticisms are on stronger ground in the sense that there is no guarantee that long-term shareholders are necessarily engaged shareholders. Significant numbers of institutional investors – such as index investors – are forced to hold the shares of large listed companies on a long-term basis in order to comply with the requirements of their investment mandates. However, this does not mean that they will necessarily devote significant resources to engagement. In such instances, dividend and tax benefits for 'loyalty' would accrue to them for simply doing nothing.

The future of shareholder engagement

After considering the problems with these alternative policy proposals, it might be tempting to conclude that there is no obvious way of inducing institutional investors to engage with investee companies on a significant scale.

What does this conclusion imply for corporate governance? A core requirement for any corporate governance system is the existence of a mechanism by which the management of companies can be held accountable for their behaviour and performance. If institutional investors are not able to provide that accountability, it needs to come from elsewhere. Otherwise, there is a danger of a 'non-system' of corporate governance, in which company management is neither accountable nor legitimate in the eyes of society as a whole.

The main alternative to a governance model of shareholder monitoring is one of monitoring by regulators. Such a regulatory model is the path being followed in respect of the governance of the UK financial sector in the wake of the financial crisis (Barker, 2010b). For example, the FSA has recently announced that it will seek to monitor the entire governance and risk oversight framework of regulated financial institutions. It will directly involve itself with the appointment of senior banking executives and non-executive directors, particularly the senior independent director and the chairs of key board committees (FSA, 2010).

This is a far more intrusive supervisory approach to financial sector governance than was the case prior to the financial crisis. In earlier years, the FSA's main governance involvement was simply to vet the probity (but not the competence) of potential bank board directors, and leave the bulk of governance monitoring to shareholders.

A greater role for the regulator in company monitoring may make sense for the financial sector. As became clear during the financial crisis, systemically important financial institutions have the potential to transmit significant negative externalities to the rest of the economy (particularly the taxpayer). Financial regulators may therefore be justified in directly monitoring the risk appetite and risk governance of the financial sector.

However, such a restrictive approach to corporate governance would be an undesirable model for the rest of the economy. State-employed supervisors lack the financial resources and human capital to effectively monitor corporate behaviour on a significant scale. Furthermore, in contrast to shareholders, they are incentivized to focus overwhelmingly on downside risks. This would foster a corporate governance culture that was detrimental to the wealth-creation process in the broader economy.

Corporate governance based on regulatory edict rather than dialogue with shareholders would also be highly inflexible, encouraging a 'box-ticking' approach focusing on minimum compliance rather than adhering to the spirit of good governance.

Furthermore, compliance with corporate governance regulations inevitably has significant cost implications. In the United States, the onerous regulatory requirements of the Sarbanes-Oxley Act 2002 gave rise to massive implementation costs for US business (and generated substantial revenues for consultants). The American Enterprise Institute has quantified the cumulative compliance cost to the US economy at $1.4 trillion.

In short, the regulatory model does not appear to be an attractive model for corporate governance (except in the financial sector, due to the open-ended liabilities of the taxpayer and associated problems of moral hazard that afflict the management of banks and other financial institutions).

There seems little alternative to making shareholder engagement work. Despite the challenges, institutions and companies are, quite literally, stuck with each other. In the interests of good governance and effective wealth creation, a way must be found to encourage institutional shareholders to fulfil their governance role.

Going forward, this may require some re-evaluation of the previously sacrosanct policy objective of ultra-liquid public equity markets. From a governance perspective, it may be preferable to have less liquidity and more captive company ownership if the result is improved shareholder engagement.

The solution may even involve reconsidering the value of certain shareholder rights and privileges – such as 'one share, one vote' – if

such rights are not justified by the exercise of stewardship responsibilities by the main institutional shareholder groups.

Unlike in the political sphere, shareholder rights are not an end in
themselves, but a means to an end. Unless they are used to catalyse a
spirit of meaningful engagement between companies and shareholders, they lose much of their justification. The current shareholder
ideology of 'one share, one vote' will only survive if it becomes more
supportive of an engaged relationship between companies and
shareholders.

Notes

1 This duty is codified in Section 172 of the Companies Act 2006.
2 *The Guardian*, 10 February 2009.
3 Speech to the ICGN as reported in *Global Proxy Watch* 18 (10), 6 March
   2009.
4 In engaging with shareholders, companies should take care to abide with
   the general requirements of company and securities law in respect of
   granting shareholders equal access to information. Engagement would
   not normally involve the sharing of inside information with investors.
5 According to the survey, companies from Ireland, the Netherlands,
   Sweden and the UK scored highest in the quality of the information that
   they provided to shareholders (RiskMetrics *et al.*, 2009, p. 170).
6 These bodies have included the UK Institutional Shareholders' Committee, the German Bundesverband Investment und Asset Management, the
   French Association Française de Gestion Financière, the Polish Chamber
   of Fund and Asset Management and the Swedish Pension Fund Association (RiskMetrics *et al.*, 2009, p. 176).
7 Dewar, S. 2009. 'Shareholder engagement and the current regulatory
   regime', Letter from Financial Services Authority to Institutional Shareholders' Committee, UK.
8 BBC interview, 1 August 2009.

References

American Bar Association 2009. *Report of the Task Force of the ABA
   Section of Business Law Corporate Governance Committee on Delin-
   eation of Governance Roles and Responsibilities*. August.
Barker, R. M. 2010a. *Corporate Governance, Competition, and Political
   Parties: Explaining Corporate Governance Change in Europe*. Oxford
   University Press.

2010b. 'The new governance of UK finance: implementing the Walker Review', *Butterworths Journal of International Banking and Financial Law*, May.

Burgess, K. 2009. 'Investors wary of Myners' idea on voting rights', *Financial Times*, 4 August.

Butler, P. 2009. 'Is comply or explain still fit for purpose?', Presentation to Corporate Governance Circle, Institute of Directors, London, 6 May.

Choi, S. and Fisch, J. 2008. 'On beyond CalPERS: survey evidence on the developing role of public pension funds in corporate governance', *Vanderbilt Law Review* 61 (2): 315–54.

European Commission 2006. *Commission Staff Working Document – Impact Assessment* (COM(2005) 685 final), 17 February.

FSA 2010. *Effective Corporate Governance: Significant Influence Controlled Functions and the Walker Review.* January. London: Financial Services Authority.

Goergen, M. *et al.*, 2008. 'Do UK institutional shareholders monitor their investee firms?', TILEC Discussion Paper, DP 2008–016.

ICGN 2009. *Second Statement on the Global Financial Crisis. 23 March.* London: International Corporate Governance Network.

ISC 2009a. *Improving Institutional Investors' Role in Governance.* Institutional Shareholders' Committee, London.

ISC 2009b. *Code on the Responsibilities of Institutional Investors.* 16 November. London: Institutional Shareholders' Committee.

Manifest 2007. *Cross-Border Voting in Europe: A Manifest Investigation into the Practical Problems of Informed Voting across EU Borders.*

2009. *Treasury Select Committee Inquiry into the Banking Crisis*: Memorandum by Manifest Information Services Ltd.

McKay, R. 2007. 'Collective action by institutional investors is more than a passing fad', *Report by the Australian Council of Superannuation Investors.*

Myners, P. 2009. 'Speech to the conference at the Association of Investment Companies', 21 April. London: HM Treasury.

OECD 2009. *Corporate Governance and the Financial Crisis: Key Findings and Main Messages.* June. Paris: Organisation for Economic Co-operation and Development.

2010. *Corporate Governance and the Financial Crisis: Conclusions and Emerging Good Practices to Enhance Implementation of the Principles.* February. Paris: Organisation for Economic Co-operation and Development.

ONS 2010. *Statistical Bulletin: Share Ownership Survey 2008.* January. Office for National Statistics.

RiskMetrics 2009. *Voting Results in Europe: Understanding Shareholder Behaviour at General Meetings.* 8 September.

RiskMetrics *et al.* 2009. *Study on Monitoring and Enforcement Practices in Corporate Governance in the Member States.* 23 September.

Sants, H. 2009. 'The crisis: the role of investors', Speech to the NAPF Investments conference. 11 March. London: FSA.

Shearman & Sterling LLP 2008. *German Risk Limitation Act Enacted.* August 2008. Germany.

Takeover Panel 2009. *Practice Statement No. 26.* 9 September.

Walker, D. 2009. *A Review of Corporate Governance in UK Banks and Other Financial Institutions.* 24 November. United Kingdom: HM Treasury.

Wong, S. 2009. *Shareholder–Company Engagement: A Comparative Overview.* ICGN 2009 Yearbook.

9 | *Board challenges 2009*

JAY W. LORSCH

Numerous corporate scandals and failures have characterized the early twenty-first century: from the bursting dot-com bubble in 2000 to malfeasance at Enron, Tyco, Worldcom and elsewhere in 2002 to the demise of once-great automotive companies and the failures of banks and financial institutions in 2008 and 2009. Each wave of business problems has been greeted by accusations of failure on the part of corporate boards and calls for government action. Indeed, passage of the Sarbanes-Oxley Act in 2002 was a result of the failures of Worldcom, Enron and other mismanaged companies. Pressure from shareholders, the media and politicians has prompted the SEC to stiffen requirements for reporting executive compensation in company 10-Ks and recent proposals for 'say-on-pay' legislation seek to provide a non-binding shareholder vote on executive compensation. Moreover the SEC has floated a proposal granting shareholders the right to nominate candidates for corporate boards.

This flurry of attention to boards and to corporate governance has not gone unnoticed at Harvard Business School. Early in 2009, members of the faculty's Corporate Governance Initiative discussed the impact of the economic crisis on corporate governance and boards in particular.[1] We recognized the legitimacy of many issues raised by the media, the public and politicians about boards' ineffective oversight of complex companies whose actions contributed to the recession.

As we reflected on how and why boards had fallen short, we came to a conclusion. The problems that surfaced in 2008 and 2009 largely differed, we believed, from those of 2002, when boards failed to identify and stop management malfeasance and fraud. By contrast,

This chapter was based on interviews conducted by my colleagues, Joe Bower, Srikant Datar, Ray Gilmartin, Steve Kaufman, Rakesh Khurana, Clayton Rose, Bill George, and Jay Lorsch.

the more recent boardroom failures were primarily attributable to the growing complexity of the companies that boards are charged with governing.

By *complex companies*, we meant those that operate multiple businesses (in terms of both products and geographies). We concluded these companies create unprecedented challenges for the executives who lead them and the boards that oversee them. Such companies typically have at least two levels of general managers – those responsible for individual product or geographic units, making strategic, resource-allocation and human-resource decisions within their purview. These general managers in turn report to the upper echelon of general managers, including the CEO. Assuring an adequate and accurate flow of information from the lower level to the upper is a significant challenge. Atop this management structure sits the board of directors. Board members are largely dependent on management for an accurate and transparent flow of information. We questioned whether the boards of complex companies receive adequate information to understand the performance issues and risks their companies face. Another challenge for these boards, we postulated, is how to oversee such complexity within the limited time that directors can devote to their task. Time constraints clearly impose strict limitations on the thoroughness of board oversight.

We agreed that the best way to test these conclusions was to go directly to the source: directors on the boards of financial institutions and other complex companies. We decided to seek answers to two broad questions: how well did such boards function before the recession, and, more importantly, what aspects of board functioning troubled board members as they looked to the future?

The approach we chose may seem unorthodox to other academics, but we concluded that it would provide the most accurate answers to our two questions: eight senior members of our faculty, all directors themselves, agreed to interview at least five directors each. Each faculty member selected as interviewees (1) members of boards of complex public companies whom the faculty member both (2) knew personally and (3) believed to be both dedicated and respected by fellow board members. Clearly, this was not a random sample. It was intentionally biased towards experienced directors with whom we had prior relationships and therefore believed would be candid with us. We think that this approach has paid off handsomely.

Table 9.1 *Interviewees' companies by industry and size in 2008*

Industry	Number of companies	Average market capitalization, 2008 (in $ million)	Average sales, 2008 (in $ million)
Consulting	2	12,745	18,722
Consumer discretionary	18	28,485	47,618
Energy	2	34,064	34,164
Financials	14	16,601	24,535
Healthcare	11	30,797	19,475
Industrials	8	32,639	42,661
Information technology	16	23,812	18,713
Materials	4	6,776	18,816
Telecommunications	2	106,051	07,323
Utilities	1	15,739	13,094
Total	78	26,210	31,346

We interviewed forty-five directors. Table 9.1 characterizes the companies they represented (while preserving the anonymity of both director and company, a condition we established to encourage candour). We believe that the interviewees were frank about their boards' strengths and about specific needs for improvement.

Interviewees' opinions varied about the difficulties that complexity poses for boards, but there was strong consensus that the key to improving boards' performance is not government action but action on the part of each board. Several directors, however, worried that the government would take action if boards themselves did not. One director articulated the challenge: 'How should the board help the company avoid embarrassment and reputational damage, and not allow the government to run the companies because we don't step up and do what we're supposed to do?' More state or federal regulations and rules were seen as unneeded and apt to produce unintended consequences that could damage boardroom effectiveness. In the view of these directors, each board must develop structures, processes and practices that fit the needs of the company; the notion that 'one size fits all' is viewed with extreme scepticism. In essence, there was a strong consensus that the key to successful governance rests in the hands of each board. Specifically, it resides in how directors work together and with management to oversee the company and make decisions. In the directors' view, these are matters that cannot be regulated by government.

The directors also expressed the view that organizations representing shareholders are too formulaic and prescriptive. This has led to a check-the-box mentality whose efficacy several directors questioned. 'I think there's a lot of focus put on meeting metrics set by outside parties today. I'm not entirely certain that's a good thing, but certainly . . . so-called proxy governance firms, like RiskMetrics and so forth, have become the de facto regulators as it relates to corporate governance,' one director said. 'And increasingly these guidelines shift annually, requiring boards to monitor changes that are going on, and to adjust. So it's kind of become a bit of a shifting-sand environment in that regard.' Another director concurred: 'I saw . . . a certain attitude which was form over substance. In many board meetings, I realized, just "Let's address the formal issues – tick, tick, tick the box – and now let's get to business."' The directors also agreed that they should be long-term stewards of their companies. Therefore, it is not surprising that they also worried about the focus on short-term shareholder value that dominates the US economy. Specifically, they were critical of the agency theory promulgated by Michael Jensen. According to this theory, directors are agents for their companies' shareholders. While recognizing their fiduciary duty to the shareholders who technically elect them, our respondents are typically acutely aware that they also have a legal responsibility for the long-term health of the company. Furthermore, they recognize that shareholders are often short-term investors with no long-term commitment to the company. In sum, these directors tend to be uncomfortable with the notion that they can or should act as shareholders' agents. As one senior executive put it: 'We are transitory managers of a permanent institution.'

I will next briefly explain how the interviewees characterized the strengths of their boards and then examine in more depth areas in which they identified needs for improvement.

Pre-recession boards

The interviewees generally reported that their boards had grown more effective in recent years, and that the quality of their fellow directors had improved. For one thing, the number of independent directors had increased. These new directors also seemed better qualified than their predecessors. 'I think the boards that I am on have all recruited new members,' one director told us, 'and I would say have significantly upgraded the board – fewer of the cronies and the old-timers, and more of the real professionals, experienced people who have some "value added" to the board.' Another commented: 'I'm impressed by the quality of the people that are willing to provide time. They're frequently a mix of people who have expertise in a particular area that is important to the company, people who have operations or CEO experience, or people who have financial or Street experience. They typically are very impressive. I think it is important to make sure that there is some breadth of experience, because it does provide you with insights that are hard to get otherwise.'

Some directors who remained uneasy about the insufficiency of relevant experience on boards questioned the emphasis on independence. 'I don't think independence is anywhere near as important as people thought it was,' one such director commented. 'I think it was a red herring.' Independence – a focus of recent regulatory changes – is a subject to which I shall return, related as it is to the question of how well directors understand their company.

Another positive sign is the growing comfort of directors about meeting the requirements of the Sarbanes-Oxley Act. 'I think by 2007 we kind of felt that the pendulum was swinging back,' one director commented. 'We felt comfortable about the company we were involved in, that there wasn't any monkey business, there weren't any backdated options, there were none of the various types of scandals that we tested for in all of these companies. And so I think we felt good about that, and so therefore could begin by 2007 to think again about strategy, big picture. Where are we really going, and where are the opportunities?'

Issues highlighted by the recession

Though most directors believed that their boards had been on a positive trajectory, the credit crisis and recession raised deeper and more basic issues for many. Most frequently mentioned were two linked questions: What role is appropriate for the board? And how can the directors understand enough about the company to meet their responsibilities effectively?

The board's role

One reason so many directors were focused on the board's role rests in the fact that regulations and laws offer little guidance about what boards are supposed to do. In most US states the basic statute that describes the purpose of boards is very broad. For instance in Delaware, which sets the standard for other states, directors find little help in the statute that defines their job: 'The business and affairs of every corporation shall be managed by or under the direction of a board of directors.'[2] This statute also permits directors to delegate the running of the company to its officers. The pertinent court decisions, related to director conduct, are largely focused on matters of process – that is, on *how* boards are to carry out their duties. For example, directors must exercise good business judgment and be loyal to the corporation.

Given this broad mandate, most boards have developed an implicit understanding of what their job should be. As long as the business was thriving, and management was comfortable with what the board was and was not doing, there was no need for greater explicitness. But the economic shock of 2008 caused many directors to reconsider what their boards had been doing and to question whether they could or should be acting differently.

Directors' reflections on the board's role had multiple dimensions. For some, the question was how much the board should focus on compliance with laws and regulations. In their view, the board's primary role is to be rules-oriented. Others viewed compliance as the job of lawyers and conceived of the board's job much more broadly. 'I'm more comfortable on some boards than I am on others,' one director told us. 'Some people have really taken the value of governance, the importance of governance, to heart and it pervades the company. Others have been slower to that realization and tend to view governance as something that the lawyers are driving. And therefore it is something that, at the attitude level, slows things down; it's a cost to the enterprise. It gets in the way of being efficient about decision-making and moving forward.'

This director and a handful of others seemed to be struggling with a hangover from the effects of Sarbanes-Oxley and other regulations, which absorbed so much board time a few years ago. To others, the financial crisis itself meant that boards should intensify their efforts at compliance: 'In adversity, boards become more active by definition,' one director said. 'But what one has to ask is: Should they be more active when things are good, to make sure that the risk-management processes are in place, that the financial-control processes are in place, so that they're assured that the organization has the controls and procedures that will red-light or highlight risks when they need to be highlighted?'

Other directors disagreed, believing that the board should devote less time to compliance and more to substantive business matters. Doing both is not easy, as one director pointed out: 'Just the challenge of fitting all of the compliance activities that boards and their committees have to execute on, while still doing these broader and perhaps more interesting things that boards are supposed to do – in terms of providing oversight of the business, oversight of management, particularly oversight of the CEO, as well as engaging in the strategy and the direction of the company – is difficult.'

One director pointed out a significant problem that arises when boards contemplate becoming more engaged: 'I think the board is more involved. I think it's busier. I think boards have to be more focused. And I think they have to be careful that they don't start trying to manage the company. They have to give the guidance, or set the trends, but they can't be managing the company.' Where to draw the line between the board and management troubled our interviewees. Two directors' comments effectively capture the two sides of the debate. One said: 'In today's environment, where there is so much pressure on directors, I think there can be a tendency for directors to want to cross the line a little too much sometimes, on the operating side, probing committees on every little subject that comes up.' In sharp contrast, another director said: 'At the moment, boards are reluctant to be intrusive into the day-to-day operations. And I think they are reluctant to be intrusive on the personnel management, beyond the top guy and maybe the heir apparent, if there's a change coming. And so they isolate themselves from understanding where the risks are coming from and what those risks are. I don't think they can do the job without becoming more involved.'

While these directors puzzle over where to draw the line between management and the board, others believe that the crucial issue is how the board interacts with management around major decisions. 'I've always thought the board should be a catalyst,' one director said. 'They need to make sure that there's really good open dialogue and all the dimensions and possibilities are at least given some air time. I think the board's role is to make sure that management, if they are not having these discussions with the board, does have these discussions with the board.' Another director asserted that boards should be even more proactive: 'I think the board has to lead more. And the shareholders may not even like that too much, and the management may not like it. But I think the board has to say, "Wait a minute, what steps are we taking while we're still making that profit on one product? What are we going to do so that we're ready in five years with another new product?"'

As we shall see, directors' preoccupation with better defining the board's role is also linked to their views on board involvement in shaping company strategy. And both questions turn on how well the board understands the company.

The board's understanding of the company

The thoroughness of the board's understanding of its company was second only to the issue of the board's role in frequency of references during our interviews. I use the term *understanding* because it expresses what the directors seemed to be seeking. They often used the words *knowledge* and *information* as well, but their underlying concerns were clearly insufficient understanding on the part of some boards, the causes of this and what directors could do about it. This issue must be examined in the context of growing corporate complexity, since the companies in question are the complex corporations alluded to earlier. Such companies are particularly difficult for their directors to understand.

One director spoke about what can transpire when a company is complex, and about the possible corrective effect of an expectation that the board should understand the company's transactions: 'I think a head of a company looking at the sustainability and the long-term future of the company should never allow somebody in the company to get in any deal which is not fully understood by the board and by the shareholders. And the best check is that the CEO should be able to speak about all deals which are made.' The same director emphasized the need for directors to fully comprehend the company's business model: 'My experience is that it's of utmost importance that the board has a full understanding of the business model . . . entry barriers, competitors, technological changes and so on.'

As important as they believed it to be to understand the company, some directors admitted that complete understanding is an impossibility: 'You really can't understand everything that's going on in the company and the notion that you can is misguided,' one director said. 'Unfortunately, I think people do expect directors to know a lot more than they sometimes do.'

A disproportionate number of those who attested to the elusiveness of adequate understanding were directors of financial services firms. 'We had the Enron era; now we have the financial era, where we're taking down the whole world with us and it can't be because all these people are stupid,' one director said. 'It has more to do with the depth of understanding of what's really going on.' Another was even more pointed: '[Two banks] – I think they crashed and burned. Neither one of them had anybody that I could detect on the board that's had any serious financial skills. And it doesn't look to me like those boards demanded to know what was happening off balance sheet.' A third director concurred but questioned top management's financial skills as well: 'The bank boards and the bank CEOs and leadership, obviously, with the exception of maybe one or two, did not understand the risks that they were managing. Clearly, the bank boards were in over their heads, just like the CEOs were. They didn't understand the paper they were issuing and how the risk was being syndicated, all that.'

Finally, one director pointed out that even when a board meets as often as ten times a year (the typical US board meets six times) it is impossible for directors to understand complex financial companies: 'One has to understand that, at the beginning of this, board members show up, at a maximum, let's say fifteen to twenty days a year. Maximum. And the idea that board members would be close enough, informed enough, experienced enough, engaged enough to have seen some of this coming, and even more, to have been wise enough to figure out how to duck, is just naïve in the extreme.'

Such comments raise the obvious question: why do directors have such difficulty understanding their companies? Several directors commented on the scarcity of specific industry knowledge on most boards. 'I think our thinking is going to be forced to be changed by virtue of the financial crisis, in that I think we're going to place higher value on industry-specific knowledge and less on general knowledge of governance and the general experiential things that come with an all-purpose board', one director said. Another echoed this view: 'The board needs to be asking the right questions. One thing that I've seen just over the last couple of years, and been a champion of, is having at least one board member who is very knowledgeable about the business you're in . . . It really is helpful, particularly in executive sessions, when you don't have the management there, and you're debating something, or wondering whether you should be worrying about something, to have someone who understands the business a little bit better than you do.'

A third director went further, linking the shortage of specific company knowledge to corporate-governance reforms calling for more independent directors: 'Strategy is harder, because it requires a familiarity with the business and an understanding of it, in order to make any sort of informed suggestion. And clearly, I think if you were to look at boards, there are still huge deficits in certain technical expertise and understanding of the business that persists at boards . . . One of the things that's been lost, in this notion of full independence and limited insiders and split chairmen and CEOs, is that boards have lost insight into the business as a result of not having, if you will, as free and consistent access to people who are steeped in the business as they might otherwise have.'

This final point deserves emphasis. I believe that a major reason directors find it difficult to understand their companies is that the typical board of a large public US company consists entirely of directors who must meet the test of independence. As a practical matter, it is difficult, if not impossible, to find directors who possess deep knowledge of a company's process, products and industries but who can also be considered independent.

A second reason that directors have difficulty understanding their companies' business is that they are heavily dependent on management, especially the CEO, to know what is going on. One director explained the frustrations of such dependence: 'Whether [an automobile manufacturer] should close their European operation, [management has] much more insight and information than the board has and they have gone through a thorough evaluation. They make a recommendation and you're more likely to agree with it than not, even after you have questioned them very closely, because you do not have nearly the amount of information they have. It's not that they're withholding the facts from you, but you're just not as close to it. I find that very frustrating.'

A second director itemized specific aspects of the challenge that directors face in judging the validity and veracity of what management tells them; he also described the changes his board had implemented in response to a recent crisis: 'It was significant in terms of information that we requested and management began to bring forward: the kind of information, the way it was brought forth, the form in which it was presented and the amount of time spent on some kinds of reports rather than others. We didn't change the board structure or the committee structure. But we changed the info flow and the feedback and the transparency, one might say, between the board and management on certain issues.'

Directors do not merely have difficulty assessing the answers they get from management; they also have trouble knowing which question to ask. 'A board only knows what it's told. You can ask a question and be given an answer – but maybe it's not the right question, or maybe the answer is true but doesn't exactly get you where you need to go,' one director explained. 'But more fundamentally, management basically provides the material at a board meeting and if you don't live day to day in the company, you're not going to know whether in fact you are hearing all the relevant aspects of it, the good, the bad and the ugly. You're not going to know. And I've got to tell you, I've lived through too many of those.'

So what can directors do to achieve greater understanding and deeper insights? Our directors discussed two approaches. The first was, as they put it, to 'dig deeper' in discussions with management. 'We always run with this concern that we don't want to manage the company. But we want to direct the company . . . Asking detailed questions to understand more fully what's going on in a company is, I think, a requirement to be an effective director, not managing,' one director told us. He added: 'I have no insight about what we should do until I have significant insight as to what's really going on and you can't get that by somebody doing a PowerPoint presentation.'

Such comments imply that, to be effective, directors must be willing to keep pushing and questioning until they are confident that they thoroughly understand the issues involved in any decision or assessment they make. As we shall see, a complication of this approach is that it is off-putting to management to be pressed for answers. And, as we shall also see, directors want to maintain a cordial relationship with management.

A second approach – the two are not mutually exclusive – is to seek sources of information and knowledge beyond the management team. One director suggested that directors need to seek out company stakeholders other than management to talk to: 'Whether it's once in a while meeting with shareholders, once in a while meeting with the representatives of the employees, whatever, I think it's really important, particularly in difficult times like we are in and are going to be in for some time, for the board to see actual underpinnings of the company.'

A second director advocated seeking broader sources of information but acknowledged that such approaches take time: 'There is no substitute for time spent meeting with management of the different divisions or sectors that are the next level down the corporate ladder, having them present directly to the board, visiting operations . . . getting in the field, getting a sense of operations – not interfering, but understanding on a more hands-on level.'

As this comment indicates, digging more deeply takes time and directors already have limited time, both for preparation and for meetings. The directors we interviewed seemed willing to invest the time needed, but at some point even they will encounter limits to devoting time to gain greater understanding. Furthermore, as our informants noted, it is important to be sensitive to management's feelings and to find ways to seek more profound understanding of the company without putting more strain on their relationship with management.

The relationship between the board and management

When directors spoke of management, they were often implicitly referring to the CEO. However, they were aware that the board's relationship with the CEO is impacted by its relationships with other senior executives.

According to our informants, the board's relationship with management has several dimensions. The most obvious is the division of decision-making responsibility between the board and management – what both parties call 'the line between the board and management'.

This line is not drawn in concrete; it is like a line drawn on a sandy beach, according to these directors, because it can be erased and moved in response to circumstances.

One factor affecting the position of the line is the nature of the challenges the company faces. As one director told us: '[At one company] that has gone through some recent challenges, I would say the board started at a high level, and, with the challenges the company has had, it descended into deeper and deeper, longer meetings and deeper involvement in the business. And in that case management is trying to figure out quite how this works. So the board and management are sort of working with each other, with respect and a high level of collegiality, but are also a little wary of each other as we try to redefine what the role is and how deep we get and how deep we don't get.' Another director was more succinct: 'Even when a company is in trouble, the board gets more involved but still is limited in what it can accomplish other than replacing the CEO.'

A second factor that influences where directors draw the line is their degree of confidence in the CEO. 'Where the CEO hasn't changed recently, my sense is – and my own experience is – that committee activity, board activity and board leadership, as opposed to CEO leadership, are still on the immature side,' one experienced director observed. 'Where something cathartic has happened – there have been life-threatening experiences, CEOs change, maybe new people have come onto the board – my sense and my experience is that [board activity is] more advanced and people take it more to heart and tend to see the value of it.'

'And when the board is seriously challenged, the need for information also becomes more acute,' as another director explained. 'And the board members try to ask more insightful questions, to be supportive and helpful to management in making their decisions. I think we've been doing this well at [company name] because [the CEO] encourages it, but still we may have to put more pressure on him.' As this comment indicates, reciprocal attentiveness to the emotions stirred up on both sides is another important aspect of the relationship between the board and management.

When directors press management for more information, they report taking pains to do so tactfully and to communicate their continuing confidence in management. As one director recounted:

'When [management] walked in and sat down around the edge of the room, I said, "Folks, we've very aware of all the work you've done. We've had a great review of all that. But there is an enormous amount of information here. You all, we know, have made very significant decisions to get to the conclusions you've come to. We suspect they are the right decisions. But the only way we will know and be able to put our judgment on that, is if you'll permit us the opportunity to test you in many ways during the next couple of days of discussions, so that we can get through the same small knotholes and decisions you did, in the same way that you did. And you're going to need to be patient with us, if you'll do that with us." They did, we did and we got to a very common ground. But it took a lot more intense discussion and an environmental change between the management and the board that says asking questions, probing deeply, is not bad, it's good.'

The same director described his delicate dealings with individual managers: 'I go very close to the line, I know that. But seldom have I crossed the line where I said, "Hey, Mike, I think you ought to do this," or "John, you ought to do that." But I do constantly inquire of them what is going on. I cross off the input that I get from all the different places and where it's not matching up right for me, I go back and say, "Hey, this isn't fitting yet. I think you ought to go look at this, because I'm concerned that you think this will happen and I'm concerned that this is what's really happening." And I think that involvement is necessary. Look, I'm not smarter than the people that are managing this day-to-day. But I've got the benefit of not being burdened by having 100 meetings on my calendar day-to-day and I can take advantage of what it is I learned over forty years and then help them see things that are getting by them that they don't see just because they're on the playing field.'

Yet another board member described what happens when a board lets the CEO dominate the discussion: 'I think that what happens is you get this kind of groupthink on the board, where the CEO sets the agenda and after a while people stop objecting.'

According to these directors, what actually transpires in a boardroom depends not only on the role the board adopts, implicitly or explicitly, or the understanding of the company the board gains. It also depends on how successfully the board builds a constructive relationship with management, especially the CEO.

Many directors emphasized that the board's relationship with management depends heavily on the leadership of the board itself. Although there have been many calls in recent years for American companies to separate the job of board chair from that of CEO, most of the companies whose directors we interviewed had gone a different route, creating the position of lead director, occupied by an independent director, whose main job was to lead discussion when management was not present.

As a number of our interviewees pointed out, selection of an effective lead director was important in improving management–board relationships. For one thing, a skilled lead director can assure open communication with management. 'I'm really happy that on all my boards we have a lead director who can be very blunt with the CEO,' one director said. 'And if people don't have a person like that on the board, or as part of the board structure, it must be set up.' Another director expressed a similar perspective: 'Lead director is an idea whose time really has come and should come. It gives a focal point for the board and is a good information conduit. And board members who don't want to say to the CEO, "Look, I think you're all wet on this idea" can tell the lead director.'

The lead director, we were told, can also enable the CEO to raise sensitive issues with the board without damaging their relationship with him. 'If you want the CEO to be transparent . . . then you can't take every little thing that he tells you is wrong in the company and then drill down on it and beat him up on it. That's what gets management sometimes gun-shy about letting boards really know what's going on,' one director said. 'There's a role there for a lead director, to help the management and the communications between management and the board be totally transparent, but on the other hand not be abused.'

Having a lead director also helps boards deal with crises. When a board faces suddenly enhanced complexity and uncertainty, such a leader can help guide them. 'Most people have lead directors now or presiding directors, or some such person. And I think that is one area that, in this crisis, had needed to be made a real job,' one director told us. 'And boards who do well in this crisis are ones that are well led. It's not just the naming of such a person, or presiding over [executive sessions] – it's much, much more than that.'

The lead director typically works closely with the CEO to assure that the board's agendas include issues of importance and that the board gets the information it wants. 'Several directors say to the chairman of the governance committee, who might also be the lead director: "Look, we're concerned about this. Would you bring it up with management when you have your regular chat and ask management to set aside some time at the next board meeting to discuss whatever the issue is?"' one director explained. 'I don't think individual directors doing things is likely to work. But I think working through the governance committee or the lead director . . . I think management would be responsive if it's done that way.'[3]

The board's activities

The directors pinpointed three activities that they believed their boards should address differently in the future: company strategy, management development and succession, and risk management. (Obviously missing from this list is compliance with laws and regulations; since passage of the Sarbanes-Oxley Act, and partly because of it, the directors believed that their boards were already handling these matters well.) When discussing these activities, the directors often related them to redefinition of the board's role.

Board involvement in strategy

The directors clearly agreed that defining company strategy belongs to management; the board's job is testing, assessment and approval. As a director said: 'Certainly, boards should be there to keep management honest and to ask the right questions and to really figure out how we want to do it – appropriate milestones, appropriate questions, appropriate dashboard, to continue to monitor how things are going.'

Another interviewee expressed a similar perspective: 'In my experience, the strategy comes from management, not from the board. The board hears about the strategy, approves the strategy, insists that there *is* a strategy – but it is the management's strategy, not the board's strategy.'

Directors did have ideas about how the board might oversee strategy better. Several wanted to see the board press for a longer-term perspective in strategic planning. As one director said, 'In terms of things that I think could be better, I still think – especially in this financial crisis – that the long-range planning tends to get put aside too much. And it's very hard to see really where we're going for more than about 90 to 120 days. We have plans and so forth, but I just think the long-term – where are we going to be in the three-to-five-year range? – I think that is still not paid enough attention to.'

Others disagreed on the grounds that, in a financial downturn of this magnitude and scope, boards ought to focus on the short term, particularly in the financial services industry. 'At this time, there's a focus on understanding the nearer-term implications before returning to long-range planning,' one said. 'In fact, we actually decided that. We do a long-range strategic plan offsite every spring and we decided that it really doesn't make sense for management to spend a lot of time between now and then trying to gin up another five-year plan or three-year plan and they would be better off focusing on nearer-term and making sure that we see the opportunities in the near term. Because in market dislocations like these, or economic dislocations, there are opportunities as well as risks and so we really want them thinking about that.'

Other directors argued that their boards ought to be more pro-active in shaping discussions with management about strategy. 'And so what I am starting to see at some boards is the board is being more proactive and perhaps a bit more directive, about framing the strategy discussion,' one director reported. 'So what do I mean by that? Management may want to talk about a series of interesting new investments and initiatives as the centerpiece of their strategy discussion, but the board may want to talk about competition, relative performance, other issues like that. So I'm starting to see boards say, "Let's look at an outline of how you, management, want to discuss the strategy." And the non-executive chair, the lead director, would share that with the other directors and kind of solicit input. It would sometimes be face-to-face, sometimes by phone and [they would] say, "OK, does the strategy discussion that management is proposing, does that fulfill your needs and answer your questions, or are there other topics that you want to talk about?" And that way, the board perhaps asserts more control over the direction and the composition of the strategy discussion, as opposed to what management solely wants to talk about.'

A number of directors asserted that how a board involves itself in strategy should depend on company circumstances. One observed: 'Board role in strategy is going to vary a lot by industry and by director ability to contribute on the strategy side. So in a leading-edge, high-tech company, most directors are not going to understand the market, or the products or the technologies, well enough to play a substantive role in terms of contributing to strategy. The best they can do is making sure that management in its discussion and application of the strategy is internally consistent and is true to the things that they believe about market and strategy.'

In sum, in spite of differences of opinion, these directors considered it critically important to assure that management develops a strategy that the board can assess and approve and which can serve as a template to judge company performance against. And they were searching for better ways to do so.

Involvement in management succession and development
These directors considered a successful transition from one CEO to the next to be the board's critical responsibility. 'I think succession planning – thoughtful, careful succession planning – is critically important,' one director said. 'And not just at the juncture whereby succession needs to pass, but years in advance to make sure there is depth of understanding.' Another director used McDonald's as an example to argue that boards should always have a ready supply of CEO candidates: 'I think a board should never be in a position where they have no candidates in-house for the CEO. The poster boy for really good board planning on management succession is McDonald's. Two guys die and within eighteen months! Remember that? Heart attack, cancer. Each time, they had a guy ready to go, and they're doing fine now. Here you are, three CEOs in eighteen months, tragically, and the third guy, I think, is still in charge. That's the management succession that you need to be doing.'

A number of directors acknowledged that their boards need to improve in this arena. 'I have some experience with that, as I've been brought into three CEO positions now from the outside,' one said. 'And what I found behind me upon arrival is a real dearth of detailed succession planning from the board.' Another described efforts to avoid other companies' mistakes: '[Boards are] spending a lot of time on succession planning because we know a lot of companies haven't done a good job with that.'

One director noted that one impediment to good succession planning is limited opportunity to expose up-and-coming managers to the board: 'There are relatively few companies that have had the luxury, in this period of enormous growth and highly specialized activity, to broadly expose somebody through cycles to enough of what's going on that you'd be confident he or she could take the seat.' A second director noted the difficulty of assessing how well the CEO, who actually made the management-career decisions, was doing so: 'How do we really evaluate the CEO, and, more importantly, what's the CEO's succession plan beyond just putting a book together and letting it gather dust on the shelf between meetings?'

Another director explained why boards often defer this issue: 'I'd say to some extent with all three companies, now that we have relatively new CEOs, we're probably less into a succession-planning dialogue because, at least right now, there's nothing imminent on the horizon other than the proverbial get-hit-by-a-truck kind of problem. And the real issue is much more of really beginning to identify some potential leaders deeper in the organization.'

Often, thinking about succession and management development was deferrable. When boards typically have more tasks than time, the board is understandably relieved when a set of issues can be deferred. But deferring the topic can be problematic, too often leading to time-pressured recruitment from the outside. And as has been pointed out, selecting successors from outside the company can be problematic and costly.[4]

Risk management

Another activity uppermost in the thoughts of the directors was, unsurprisingly, risk management. They had witnessed other companies, and in some cases their own, fail to anticipate and control risk during the financial decline. One director spoke for many: 'I think now there is more and more concern that risk has to be a board-level activity.' Though there was consensus on this point, opinions varied about who should manage which risks. One point of view was that all risks, even broad business risks, are the responsibility of the audit committee. 'I would say, yes, risk assessment is an area that has taken on a lot of importance over the last couple of years,' one director told us. 'I've seen it handled quite effectively within the context of the audit committee.'

An alternative point of view is that boards facing substantial financial risk need a risk management committee. 'Just judging by what I'm
reading and hearing, the knee jerk seems to be "Let's create a risk
committee and we got it done." And I think that's appropriate for [a
large bank]. I don't think it's appropriate for [manufacturing com-
panies],' one director asserted. 'I think it is a board-level, not
committee-level, responsibility to go through the major risks – after
all, they're supposed to be in the 10-K every year.'

Others insisted that the responsibility for risk management rests
with the entire board because of the broad experience required.
'I think a big part of that is to help the management assess risk,'
one director said. 'It's one of the things that a good board can do,
because of all the experiences around that table from various industries. They can also help a lot with identifying those so-called
strategic risks . . . They may not know the business as well as the
management, but they can certainly help identify risk outside the
company.'

Still other directors observed that boards are highly dependent on
their CEOs for judging risk. 'I think my lesson is that ERM only goes
so far and that in the end I almost think what we depend on as
shareholders – I'm going to step back from being a director, and then
we can go back into the director's chair – but as shareholders, with
these big, complex companies that we have, what we almost depend
on is that the CEO has an intuitive feel for risk,' one director said. 'It,
sadly, can't all depend on oversight. But the directors are in a position
to have a feel for the CEO's risk intuition. And in the end, that's a very
valuable protective tool.'

Many directors acknowledged that the preoccupation with risk is a
reaction to recent events. 'In this economy, I think, first, it has changed
what the board is focusing on right now,' one director said. 'And
I think the second thing that it's done has just so heightened the sense
of risk, unknowability and, frankly, vulnerability of any institution
and the kinds of consequences that can come from decisions.' Others
considered it vitally important to take a longer-term and broader view
of financial crises. 'Now there's no excuse. Everybody – financial
business or industrial business – has to have risk management as a
much more important function.'

Still other directors agreed that risk management is something that
boards should always have concentrated on: 'I think risk management

in general has to be much more on the radar screen. And financial risk – even in how you manage your cash, how you manage your investments, pension funds and other things, if there is such a thing, and all those are going to have to be re-looked at,' one director said. 'My sense is that a lot of management teams and boards gave lip service to risk, maybe looking at the more obvious risks. But I think the lesson of the last two years is: there are a lot of risks that we haven't really thought about and we need to consider.'

These directors clearly believed that it ought to be a priority for their boards to focus on business risks, especially financial risks. But they disagreed about how to do so, or about how doing so would mesh with their other activities. This uncertainty is unsurprising, since the magnitude of financial risks is a recent discovery for many boards. As often happens when an institution confronts a new set of issues, some of the directors' worries may turn out to be excessive, or to have to be addressed in a way that will not compromise their other activities.

The key to improving boards

What is most noteworthy in our interviews is the overall thrust of the directors' thoughts on what makes for effective boards. In their view, effectiveness has little to do with regulators and laws and everything to do with what transpires within individual boards. The determinants that shape boards' behaviour, in the eyes of our interviewees, are illustrated in Figure 9.1. What really matters, they told us in a variety of ways, is for each board to achieve clarity about its role – that is, about the extent and nature of its involvement in strategy, management succession, risk oversight and compliance.

This conception of the board's activities has several important implications. If, as our interviewees insisted, each board's effectiveness is directly attributable to its activities, it follows that boards have a responsibility to define their own roles with precision and to decide how to perform those roles in light of the nature of the firm, its industry and its particular challenges. Furthermore, if boards are reluctant to look to others – whether regulators or other boards – for much guidance in deciding on their goals and activities, they must expect to invest extended time in hard-headed discussions of both, leading to concrete and actionable conclusions.[5]

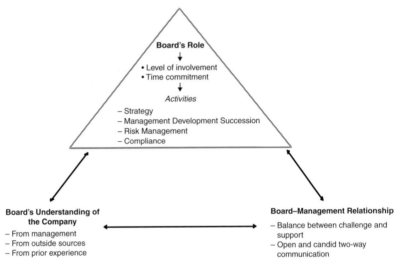

Figure 9.1 Three interrelated issues

    Whatever choices a board makes about its role, they must be consistent with the members' shared understanding of their company. Furthermore, though legally the board wields the ultimate power in the corporate hierarchy, as a practical matter it can execute its role successfully only if it develops and maintains a sound relationship with management. Such a relationship calls for explicit agreement, on the part of the board and management, about the role of each in leadership of the company. It also requires open two-way communication and mutual respect between the two parties.

    To be effective, in sum, boards have to maintain a delicate balance in their relationship with management. They must be challenging and critical on the one hand and supportive on the other. They have to sustain an open and candid flow of communication in both directions. And they must seek sources of understanding outside management without offending management.

    None of this is easy. It is all essential, however, for effective governance. Failure to achieve any component of this prescription can undermine the effectiveness of the board. And ineffective boards have contributed to the corporate failings that have recently been far too conspicuous on the landscape of the US and other economies.

Notes

1 The Corporate Governance Initiative has served since 1999 as a forum to discuss and encourage faculty research.
2 Section 141(a), Delaware General Corporation Code Annotated, Title 8, available at http://delcode.delaware.gov/index.shtml (last accessed 29 November 2010).
3 For more about the board's relationship to its CEO, see Kaufman, 2008.
4 For more about the board's role in management succession, see Khurana, 2002 and Bower, 2007.
5 For a complementary perspective see Carter and Lorsch (2004).

References

Bower, J. L. 2007. *The CEO Within: Why Inside Outsiders Are the Key to Succession Planning*. Boston: Harvard Business School Press.
Carter, C. B. and Lorsch, J. W. 2004. *Back to the Drawing Board: Designing Corporate Boards for a Complex World*. Boston: Harvard Business School Press.
Kaufman, S. 2008. 'Evaluating the CEO', *Harvard Business Review*, October.
Khurana, R. 2002. *Searching for a Corporate Savior: The Irrational Quest for Charismatic CEOs*. Princeton University Press.

10 | Do independent boards effectively monitor management? Evidence from Japan during the financial crisis

CHUNYAN LIU, JIANLEI LIU AND
KONARI UCHIDA

The financial crisis that originated in the collapse of the US subprime loan market had a serious impact on the global economy; various companies in all industries experienced serious performance declines. For example, Toyota Motor Corp., a Japanese representative automobile manufacturer, fell into a negative operating income situation for the accounting year ended March 2009, reporting red ink for the first time since the end of World War II. Such serious performance decline engenders severe conflicts among corporate stakeholders.

This chapter investigates whether outside directors effectively monitor management in the interest of shareholders. Specifically, the chapter examines the relationship between board independence, management turnover and dividend policy in Japan during the financial crisis. Corporate board structures recently have received much research attention. This increased attention is largely attributable to the Sarbanes-Oxley Act (SOX), which mandates that the audit committees of listed companies comprise a majority of independent members. Similarly in Japan, the Tokyo Stock Exchange (TSE) announced a new rule in December 2009 that has required listed companies to adopt at least one independent director to their boards. It is important to evaluate the regulatory movement from a viewpoint of shareholder wealth maximization, because Japanese corporate governance reforms since the late 1990s have been principally intended to align interests of managers with those of shareholders.

As shown in previous studies, companies that perform poorly tend to suffer management turnover (Warner *et al.*, 1988; Kaplan,

This research is financially supported by JSPS Grants-in-Aid for Scientific Research and Kyushu University Interdisciplinary Programs in Education and Projects in Research Development.

1994). Typically, firms replace management to accelerate substantial corporate restructuring in response to poor performance. If outside directors are effective in monitoring management in the interest of shareholders, firms that have more independent boards will tend to experience more management turnovers. In addition, there are likely conflicts that exist regarding the distribution of decreased cash flow; managers have an incentive to decrease dividends in order to retain cash holdings. Particularly in Japan, managers tend to care more about employee wealth than shareholder interests (Yoshimori, 1995; Allen and Zhao, 2007). While it is beneficial for managers and employees to retain firm solvency by decreasing dividends, shareholders would desire managers not to do so. However, if outside directors monitor management to the benefit of shareholder interests, over-reduction in dividends should be prohibited.

To test those views, the authors investigate the relationship between board independence and the likelihood of management turnover and dividend cuts. The authors principally adopt the fraction of outside directors over the total board members as a measure of board independence because, in Japan, board reforms have typically referred to an increase in outside directors. In the Japanese Commercial Code, outside directors are defined as board members who have no experience working for, or serving as, an executive officer at the firm or its controlling company. However, it is well documented that outside directors do not critically monitor management if the sender company has a business relationship with the receiver firm (Coles *et al.*, 2008). In addition, outside directors appointed from banks have an incentive to monitor management in the bank's interests; potentially forcing managers to cut dividends (Pinkowitz and Williamson, 2001). Indeed, the TSE announced a rule that requires Japanese firms to include at least one 'independent' director on their boards. To address this issue, the authors also investigate the relation between the proportion of independent directors and the likelihood of management turnover and dividend cuts.

The authors argue that financial crisis data has two advantages in addressing the role of outside (or independent) directors. First, the authors could collect data from numerous companies that experienced serious performance declines over a very short period, allowing the authors to investigate management turnover and corporate dividend policy in a homogeneous setting. Second, financial crisis data allowed the authors to avoid an endogeneity problem, which commonly plagues corporate governance researchers (Mitton, 2002). Deteriorating performance during a crisis is a sudden and unpredictable event; it is extremely difficult for firms to adjust corporate governance structure in advance of the crisis. Therefore, the authors could effectively analyse pure effects of board independence on management turnover and dividend policy after such shocks.

Mitton (2002) noted that minority shareholder expropriation can become more severe during a crisis when the expected return on investments falls; therefore, crisis may force investors to recognize and understand corporate governance weaknesses. For this reason, several papers investigated the relationship between corporate governance structure and stock price performance during a financial crisis. For example, studies of emerging markets during the East Asian financial crisis provided evidence that corporate higher stock price performance was related to governance structures that mitigate expropriation of minority shareholders (Mitton, 2002; Lemmon and Lins, 2003; Baek *et al.*, 2004). By contrast, Nogata, Uchida and Moriyasu (forthcoming) have suggested that firms that adopted stock option plans suffered more from deteriorating stock price performance during the present financial crisis than firms that did not adopt such option plans. However, to the best of our knowledge, there are few studies that effectively investigate how corporate governance structures in industrial countries affect management turnover and corporate financial policies during a financial crisis. Accordingly, this chapter contributes to existing literature by analysing whether corporate governance has a real effect when firms face macroeconomic, negative shocks.

The rest of this chapter is organized as follows. The first section reviews previous studies and describes our hypotheses. The second section presents sample selection procedures and data. The final section shows empirical results, followed by a brief summary of the chapter.

Previous studies and hypotheses

The corporate board is expected to monitor and advise management (Coles *et al.*, 2008). In general, it is difficult for inside directors to critically monitor management, although they provide valuable information about the firm's activities. In contrast, outside directors are likely to contribute both expertise and objectivity in evaluating the managers' decisions (Byrd and Hickman, 1992). This idea gives rise to the prediction that independent boards contribute to higher firm value. However, previous studies show mixed results as to the effect of board independence on firm value. Using an event study methodology, Rosenstein and Wyatt (1990) found significantly positive stock price reactions to the announcements of firms regarding the addition of outsiders to their boards. Examining 128 tender offer bids during the period from 1980 to 1987, Byrd and Hickman (1992) showed that bidding firms in which independent outside directors hold at least 50 per cent of the seats have significantly higher announcement returns than other bidders. Nogata *et al.* (2011) found that Japanese firms experience more favourable stock price reactions to their acquisition announcements when there are more outsiders on the companies' boards. Musteen *et al.* (2010) showed evidence that firms with a greater proportion of outside directors exhibit a better reputation than those with a higher proportion of insiders. However, Yermack (1996) and Miwa and Ramseyer (2005) did not find clear evidence that board independence has a positive impact on firm value. Further, it is extremely difficult to evaluate the performance effect of board independence accurately because firms endogenously choose their board structures (Denis and Sarin, 1999; Mak and Li, 2001; Lehn *et al.*, 2004; Boone *et al.*, 2007; Coles *et al.*, 2008; Guest, 2008; Linck *et al.*, 2008).

Several researchers offered evidence that board independence affects managerial incentives. In general, agency theory suggests that management turnover and compensation should be linked to observable performance measures (Warner *et al.*, 1988; Kaplan, 1994) to give managers an incentive to maximize shareholder value. However, managers desire to occupy seats even after serious performance declines. Indeed, Goyal and Park (2002) showed evidence that management turnover becomes less sensitive to firm performance when the CEO and board chairman roles are vested in the same individual. Well-designed corporate boards are likely to play a role in mitigating the problem. Weisbach (1988) found that the sensitivity of CEO turnover is greater for firms with a higher proportion of outside directors. Investigating firms that experience serious performance declines, Perry and Shivdasani (2005) found that 13 per cent of firms

with boards in which independent directors account for the majority
of the total experience disciplinary CEO removal as opposed to only
5 per cent of firms that do not; though the difference is not statistically
significant. In a similar vein, Ryan and Wiggins (2004) provided
evidence that firms with more outsiders on their boards tend to use
more stock-based compensations than their insider-controlled counterparts. The authors follow these studies to investigate the relationship between management turnover and board independence during
financial crisis.

H1: *Management turnover is more likely to occur in firms with more
independent board members during a financial crisis.*

Dividend payments serve as an important mechanism to mitigate
expropriation of minority shareholders. La Porta *et al.* (2000)
offered evidence that firms in common law countries in which
investor protection is typically better, make higher dividend
payouts than firms in civil law countries. However, serious performance reductions potentially engender conflicts between shareholders and other stakeholders for dividend payments. Managers
have an incentive to cut dividends in order to retain the firm's
financial health. In particular, Japanese firms typically form cross-
shareholdings to block potential hostile takeover bids (Sheard,
1989; Morck and Nakamura, 1999). Cross-shareholdings release
managers from the threat of hostile takeovers while engendering
entrenchment effects. As a result, Japanese firms traditionally care
more about employee wealth than shareholder wealth (Aoki, 1990;
Allen and Zhao, 2007). In addition, main banks that play an
important role in Japanese corporate governance are likely to
monitor management in the interest of creditors (Morck and
Nakamura, 1999; Pinkowitz and Williamson, 2001). Such agency
problems inevitably affect Japanese corporate dividend policies.
Yoshimori (1995) showed survey evidence that almost all (97 per
cent) of Japanese managers thought that employee job security is
more important than dividend payments to shareholders. Indeed,
Dewenter and Warther (1998) showed evidence that Japanese firms
were less reluctant to cut or omit dividends than their American
counterparts. Accordingly, a financial crisis provides Japanese
managers with an incentive to substantially decrease dividends. By
contrast, if outside directors effectively monitor management in the
interest of shareholders, firms that have more independent board

members will not decrease dividends. Such discussions give rise to the following hypothesis.

H2. *Firms with more independent board members are less likely to decrease dividends during a financial crisis than those with insider-controlled boards.*

Sample selection and data

Ivashina and Scharfstein (2010) defined the present financial crisis period as between August 2007 and December 2008. This definition is based on the view that the current financial crisis originated in the US subprime loan market collapse during the summer of 2007. However, Japanese firms' operating performance was not as seriously damaged for the accounting year 2007; it was less likely that Japanese companies recognized management turnover and substantial restructurings as essential for shareholder value creation during the accounting year 2007. However, the economic condition became much worse after Lehman Brothers fell into bankruptcy in September of 2008. Indeed, Nogata *et al.* (forthcoming) have reported that the average Japanese firm experienced more serious stock price reductions during the August 2008 to December 2008 period than during the August 2007 to July 2008 period. Accordingly, the authors focus on management turnover and dividend policy in Japan for the accounting year 2008.[1]

The authors selected sample firms from those listed on the first or second section of the TSE. The authors deleted banks and insurance companies from the analysis because they have different styles of financial statements. Corporate financial data were obtained from Nikkei NEEDS FinancialQuest. The authors merged Nikkei NEEDS Cges, which includes various corporate governance data, with the financial data. Following Perry and Shivdasani (2005), who investigated corporate voluntary restructuring and adopted 33 per cent decline in pre-tax income as a cut-off point for identifying firm performance declines, the authors picked up firms for the accounting year 2008 that experienced 33 per cent or greater declines in operating income before depreciation. Of the 2,190 companies for which necessary data are available, 885 firms (about 40.4 per cent) met this criterion.

Table 10.1 *Definition of variables*

Variable	Definition
TURNOVER	Dummy variable that takes a value of one for firms that replace the president or CEO and zero for all others.
Dec_DIVIDEND	Dummy variable that takes a value of one for firms that decrease dividends per share from the previous year, and zero otherwise. It takes a missing value if the firm does not pay dividends in the previous year.
OUTDIR	The fraction of board outsiders to total board members.
INDDIR	The fraction of independent directors to total board members. The authors define independent directors as outside board members who have no experience working at banks and affiliated companies.
BANKDIR	The fraction of outside directors appointed by banks to total board members.
BOARDSIZE	The number of board members.
SOD	Dummy variable that takes a value of one for firms that adopt stock options and zero otherwise.
MANAGEROWN	The percentage of manager ownership.
MBOWN	The percentage of main bank ownership.
FOREOWN	The percentage of foreigner ownership.
ROA	Operating income before depreciation divided by assets.
MtBr	Market value of common stocks and liabilities divided by book value of assets.
LEVERAGE	Liabilities divided by assets.
Ln(Asset)	Natural logarithm of assets.
TENURE	The length of years for which the incumbent manager holds his/her position.

To test H1 and H2, the authors adopted two dummy variables as dependent: TURNOVER; Dec_DIVIDEND (See Table 10.1 for variables definitions). The authors identify management turnover as when the firm's president or CEO is replaced, because the highest-ranking or most powerful person in the typical Japanese company is the president or CEO. TURNOVER takes a value of one for firms that replace the president or CEO, and zero for others. Turnover data were obtained from the annual reports and press releases of the included firms. Dec_DIVIDEND takes a value of one for companies that decrease dividends per share from the previous year, and zero otherwise.[2]

The most important independent variable is OUTDIR, which is a measure of outside directors to total board members. Our hypotheses predict that OUTDIR has a positive impact on TURNOVER and a negative effect on Dec_DIVIDEND. The authors also used INDDIR, which is the proportion of independent directors over the total board members. Independent directors are defined as outside board members who have no experience working at banks or companies that have business relationships with the receiver company.

It is likely that managers who have strong negotiation power will try to remain in their positions even after a serious performance decline (Goyal and Park, 2002).[3] To test this idea, the authors also included percentage ownership by the president (MANAGEROWN). The authors also included the number of board members (BOARD-SIZE) because several researchers argue that large boards suffer from free-rider problems (Lipton and Lorsch, 1992; Jensen, 1993). Yermack (1996), Eisenberg *et al.* (1998) and Bennedsen *et al.* (2008) showed evidence that small boards are accompanied by high firm values. Japanese firms have conducted substantial board downsizing since the late 1990s. Miyajima and Nitta (2006) reported that the mean board size of Japanese companies listed on TSE decreased from 16.6 in 1993 to 9.8 in 2004; in Japan, it is becoming a prevailing idea that large boards do not work well. Inclusion of BOARDSIZE allows the authors to investigate whether board restructuring enhances managerial decisions for shareholder wealth maximization during financial crisis. Stock option dummy takes a value of one for firms that adopt stock option plans, and zero for others (SOD). The Japanese Commercial Code was amended in 1997 to allow stock option usage. Since then, many Japanese companies have adopted stock option plans as managerial and senior employee compensations (Kato *et al.*, 2005; Uchida, 2006). Previous studies suggested that managers who receive stock options have an incentive to cut dividends (Lambert *et al.*, 1989; Fenn and Liang, 2001).

The authors also adopted proxy variables for traditional Japanese corporate governance. Previous studies suggested that main banks play an important role in Japanese corporate governance, especially when the firm performs poorly. Kaplan and Minton

(1994) found that the appointments of directors from banks increase with earnings losses. Kang and Shivdasani (1995) found that the sensitivity of non-routine management turnover to poor earnings performance is higher for firms that retain a closer relationship with the main bank than those that do not. Kang and Shivdasani (1997) reported that firms owned more by a main bank conduct more restructuring plans when they experience serious performance declines. The authors included main bank ownership (MBOWN) to test the view that main banks play an important role in poorly performing companies. Main banks are also likely to affect corporate dividend policy. Pinkowitz and Williamson (2001) showed evidence that Japanese banks exert monopoly power and require firms to retain large cash holdings. This fact gives rise to prediction that main banks are likely to require management to cut dividends during performance declining periods in order to retain their creditor value. Non-Japanese investors tend to require management to pursue maximum shareholder wealth. Consistent with this notion, previous studies of Japanese firms suggested that the percentage of foreign ownership is positively associated with firm value (Hiraki *et al.*, 2003). It is likely that firms with high non-Japanese investor ownership are more likely to replace incumbent management. In addition, Baba (2009), who investigated Japanese corporate dividend policy during the period 1998–2005, showed evidence that percentage ownership by foreigners is positively related to the likelihood that the firm will pay or increase dividends. To test this view, the authors included the percentage ownership by foreigners (FOREOWN).

Several control variables are also addressed. Management turnover and dividend policy are substantially affected by current year operating performance. To control for this relationship, the authors included return on assets (ROA). Agency theory suggests that firms with rich growth opportunities pay lower dividends; market-to-book ratio is included in our analyses (market value of common stocks and liabilities divided by their book value of assets; hereafter denoted by MtBr). The authors used LEVERAGE (liabilities divided by assets) because high-leveraged firms have a strong incentive to restructure to address financial distress. In addition, high-leveraged firms have lesser ability to pay dividends. The authors adopted the natural logarithm of assets (Ln(Asset)) as a proxy for firm size.

Finally, the authors included the number of years for which the manager has occupied his or her seat (TENURE). The authors predicted that managers with long tenures will be more likely to be replaced when the firm experiences serious performance drops.

The authors used year 2006 data (data before the subprime loan market collapse) for most independent variables in order to mitigate endogeneity problems. Year 2008 data were used for ROA while year 2007 data were used for TENURE. Firms for which necessary data were not available were deleted from the analysis. As a result, 804 companies were adopted for our sample. In the turnover analysis, the authors deleted two observations in which the president left the position due to illness. Thus, 802 firms were adopted. In the analysis of Dec_DIVIDEND, the number of observations was decreased to 731 because the authors deleted seventy-three firms that did not pay dividends in 2007.

Table 10.2 presents descriptive statistics. Panel A shows that 116 (14.5 per cent) of the performance-declining companies experience management turnover. This figure is similar to the turnover rates reported by Kaplan (1994) (14.9 per cent), Abe (1997) (11.6 per cent), and Kang and Shivdasani (1995) (12.9 per cent) who investigated the relationship between Japanese management turnover and firm performance.[4] For the 116 turnovers in our sample, the authors collected press releases that suggest that many companies conducted turnover to reorganize the management structure and business lines in response to severe business environments. Table 10.2 suggests that over 60 per cent of the sample firms decreased dividends after performance declines. This figure, which is much higher than the fraction of companies that decreased dividends in Baba (2009) (31.4 per cent), is attributable to our sample characteristics. Panel B shows that the median OUTDIR is zero; the mean is 8.0 per cent. As of year 2006, adding outsiders to the board is less common for Japanese companies. Independent directors account for a major part of outside directors; the mean INDDIR is about 5.1 per cent. The authors also reported the fraction of outside directors who came from banks (BANKDIR). In the Japanese corporate governance, banks play an important role in sending personnel to firm boards. However, our data show that the mean BANKDIR is only 0.6 per cent; Panel B also shows that the average board size is about 9.3. As a result of recent board downsizing, Japanese corporate board sizes

Table 10.2 *Descriptive statistics*

Panel A of this table describes frequencies of management turnover and dividend cuts as well as the percentage of companies that adopt stock options in the sample firms. Panel B of this table shows descriptive statistics for non-dummy variables. Management turnover is defined as replacement of the president. Sample firms include 804 companies that experience 33% or more declines for the year 2008 in operating income before depreciation. For TURNOVER data, the authors delete two firms in which the president is replaced due to death or illness. For DEC_DIVIDEND data, the authors have deleted seventy-three companies that do not pay dividends in the prior year. See Table 10.1 for definitions of variables.

Panel A: Dummy variables

	The number (%) of observations that take a value of one		The number (%) of observations that take a value of zero		N
TURNOVER	116	14.46%	686	85.54%	802
DEC_DIVIDEND	494	67.58%	237	32.42%	731
SOD	269	33.46%	535	66.54%	804

Panel B: Non-dummy variables

	Mean	Standard deviation	Minimum	Median	Maximum	N
OUTDIR	0.080	0.127	0.000	0.000	0.786	804
INDDIR	0.051	0.097	0.000	0.000	0.667	804
BANKDIR	0.006	0.028	0.000	0.000	0.250	804
BOARDSIZE	9.300	3.838	3.000	9.000	30.000	804
MANAGEROWN	0.031	0.077	0.000	0.001	0.535	804
MBOWN	0.023	0.019	0.000	0.023	0.207	804
FOREOWN	0.146	0.125	0.000	0.114	0.702	804
ROA	0.009	0.071	−1.017	0.015	0.180	804
MtBr	1.266	0.538	0.506	1.144	8.821	804
LEVERAGE	0.521	0.189	0.013	0.538	1.305	804
Assets (millon yen)	427766	1596647	2562	77154	32600000	804
TENURE	5.430	7.487	0.000	3.000	50.000	804

become almost identical to those of the United States (Uchida, 2010). It is noteworthy that the mean ROA is not negative (0.9 per cent). Although our sample firms experienced serious performance decline, the sample companies on average did not fall into a red ink situation or suffer financial distress.

Empirical results

Univariate test results

Testing H1 and H2, the authors divided the sample firms into three groups based on OUTDIR to compare the frequencies of management turnover and dividend cuts. Specifically, the authors devised a group that comprises firms that have no outside directors (Group 0). Then, the authors divided the remaining firms that have at least one outside director into two groups based on their median OUTDIR (approximately 18.2 per cent). Thus, Group 1 consists of firms with lower OUTDIR and Group 2 consists of the highest OUTDIR companies.

Panel A of Table 10.3 shows results for TURNOVER. The frequency of management turnover does not monotonically increase with OUTDIR. However, it is much higher for Group 2 (19.1 per cent) than Group 0 (13.4 per cent) and Group 1 (12.4 per cent); the frequency difference is significant at the 10 per cent level between Group 0 and Group 2. This result is at least partly consistent with H1. Panel B presents results for Dec_DIVIDEND. Again, the frequency of dividend cuts does not monotonically decrease with OUTDIR. However, the fraction is much lower for Group 2 (55.6 per cent) than for Groups 0 and 1 (69.1 per cent and 75.0 per cent, respectively); the difference between Group 0 and Group 2 is significant at the 1 per cent level. Consistent with H2, this result suggests that firms with more outside board members are less likely to decrease dividends than those with no or fewer outsiders.

Regression results

In order to avoid potential multicolinearity problems, the authors examined the correlations matrix among independent variables. Table 10.4 finds no high correlation between the board independence variable (OUTDIR and INDDIR) and other variables. Table 10.5 presents results of regression analyses. In all the regression analyses, the authors add industry dummy variables and TSE second dummy that takes a value of one for firms listed on the TSE Second Section. The TSE Second Section is an exchange for medium-sized companies that receive less attention from the public. The authors include the

Table 10.3 *Univariate test results*

This table presents univariate test results on the relationship between the fraction of outside directors and frequencies of management turnover and dividend cuts. Management turnover is defined as replacement of the president. Sample firms are those that experience 33% or more declines for the year 2008 in operating income before depreciation. The firms are divided into three groups. Specifically, the authors make a group that consists of 455 firms with no outside directors (Group 0). Then, the authors divide the 349 firms that have at least one outside director into two groups based on their median OUTDIR (approximately 18.2%); Group 1 consists of firms with lower OUTDIR and Group 2 comprises highest OUTDIR companies. Analysis of management turnover deletes two companies from the sample in which the manager leaves the seat due to death or illness. Analysis of dividend reduction deletes seventy-three firms that do not pay dividends in the prior year.

Panel A: Management turnover (N = 802)

	The number (%) of firms that replace management		The number (%) of firms that do not replace management	
Group 0 (OUTDIR = 0)	61	13.41%	394	86.59%
Group 1	21	12.43%	148	87.57%
Group 2	34	19.10%	144	85.90%
Z-statistics	1.680*			

Panel B: Dividend reduction (N = 731)

	The number (%) of firms that decrease dividends		The number (%) of firms that do not decrease dividends	
Group 0 (OUTDIR = 0)	286	69.08%	128	30.92%
Group 1	123	75.00%	41	25.00%
Group 2	85	55.56%	68	44.44%
Z-statistics	2.905**			

**Significant at the 1% level
*Significant at the 10% level

TSE second dummy because those characteristics potentially affect the likelihood of management turnover and dividend policy.

Our basic results are shown in Models (1) and (2). The logit regression of TURNOVER (Model (1)) engenders a negative and significant

Table 10.4 Correlation matrix

	OUTDIR	INDDIR	BANKDIR	BOARDSIZE	SOD	MANAGEROWN	MBOWN	FOREOWN	ROA	LEVERAGE	MtBr	Ln (Asset)
OUTDIR	1.000											
INDDIR	0.855	1.000										
BANKDIR	0.317	0.082	1.000									
BOARDSIZE	−0.023	−0.049	0.015	1.000								
SOD	0.241	0.232	0.104	−0.020	1.000							
MANAGEROWN	−0.060	−0.018	−0.045	−0.189	0.149	1.000						
MBOWN	−0.222	−0.195	−0.035	0.011	−0.162	−0.169	1.000					
FOREOWN	0.199	0.205	0.094	0.246	0.252	−0.083	−0.211	1.000				
ROA	−0.049	−0.015	−0.061	0.110	−0.079	−0.160	0.046	0.047	1.000			
LEVERAGE	0.050	0.017	0.068	0.077	−0.076	−0.051	0.075	−0.114	−0.123	1.000		
MtBr	0.175	0.171	0.051	0.008	0.161	0.071	−0.259	0.221	0.030	−0.135	1.000	
Ln(Asset)	0.177	0.111	0.148	0.472	0.154	−0.211	−0.113	0.642	0.051	0.204	0.021	1.000

This table presents the correlation matrix among independent variables. See Table 10.1 for definition of the variables.

Table 10.5 *Logit regression results (1)*

This table presents logit regression results. The dependent variables are TURNOVER and Dec_DIVIDEND. Sample firms are those that experience 33% or more declines for the year 2008 in operating income before depreciation. Management turnover is defined as replacement of the president. Models (1) and (3) delete two firms from the analysis in which the president leaves the position due to death or illness. Models (2) and (4) delete 73 companies from the analysis that paid no dividends in the prior year. See Table 10.1 for definition of the variables.

	(1)	(2)	(3)	(4)
	TURNOVER	Dec_DIVIDEND	TURNOVER	Dec_DIVIDEND
OUTDIR	1.841**	−2.304***		
	(2.33)	(−3.04)		
INDDIR			2.181**	−2.826***
			(2.15)	(−2.75)
BANKDIR			−3.519	4.316
			(−0.88)	(1.35)
BOARDSIZE	0.038	0.020	0.034	0.024
	(1.36)	(0.79)	(1.25)	(0.96)
SOD	−0.162	0.402**	−0.140	0.365*
	(−0.70)	(2.01)	(−0.60)	(1.83)
MANAGEROWN	−6.442**	0.355	−6.708**	0.618
	(−2.39)	(0.30)	(−2.46)	(0.53)
MBOWN	−13.263**	0.505	−13.754**	1.116
	(−2.12)	(0.10)	(−2.21)	(0.23)
FOREOWN	−0.888	−0.415	−1.064	−0.242
	(−0.79)	(−0.40)	(−0.95)	(−0.23)

	(1)	(2)	(3)	(4)
ROA	−1.247	−15.866***	−1.671	−16.010***
	(−1.00)	(−6.03)	(−1.28)	(−6.04)
LEVERAGE	0.236	1.146**	0.231	1.117**
	(0.38)	(2.11)	(0.37)	(2.05)
MtBr	−0.118	0.851***	−0.084	0.846***
	(−0.46)	(3.56)	(−0.35)	(3.60)
Ln(Asset)	0.071	−0.032	0.103	−0.073
	(0.63)	(−0.33)	(0.93)	(−0.74)
TENURE	0.029**		0.029**	
	(2.04)		(2.03)	
Constant	−2.628**	−0.016	−2.909**	0.347
	(−2.23)	(−0.02)	(−2.50)	(0.34)
Industry dummy			Yes	
TSE 2nd dummy			Yes	
Pseud R^2	0.046	0.103	0.045	
N	802	731	802	731

*** Significant at the 1% level
** Significant at the 5% level
* Significant at the 10% level

coefficient on MANAGEROWN. This result suggests that managers who have more controlling power on firms are likely to refuse to leave their positions even when their firms experience serious performance reductions (Goyal and Park, 2002). In addition, Model (1) engenders a negative and significant coefficient on MBOWN. The result, which shows a sharp contrast with the findings of Kang and Shivdasani (1995), suggests that bank shareholders protect the incumbent management position during financial crisis. In spirit, the result is consistent with previous studies, showing evidence that bank ownership decreases firm value (Morck *et al.*, 2000; Uchida, 2009). Such findings suggest that in Japanese firms, conflicts of interest exist between shareholders and other stakeholders during the financial crisis. Importantly, Model (1) carries a positive and significant coefficient on OUTDIR, suggesting that firms with more outside directors are likely to replace management when they face serious performance reductions. As with Weisbach (1988), this result suggests that outside directors make management turnover more sensitive to poor performance.

As mentioned, managers have an incentive to reduce dividends during financial crisis to prevent large declines in cash holdings; other stakeholders will also desire the manager to do so. If outside directors monitor management in the shareholder interest, they will prevent managers from readily decreasing dividends. Model (2) (logit regression results of Dec_DIVIDEND) shows that OUTDIR has a negative and significant coefficient; firms that have more outsiders on their boards are less likely to decrease dividends, even when they face serious performance declines. This result suggests that outside directors keep managers from transferring wealth from shareholders to non-shareholder stakeholders. Consistent with Weisbach (1988) and Ryan and Wiggins (2004), our results suggest that outside directors play a role in monitoring management on behalf of shareholders.[5]

Univariate test results suggest that firms that have a positive, but low fraction of outside directors (Group 1 of Table 10.3) have lower (higher) frequency of management turnover (dividend cuts) than those with no outside directors. In non-reported analyses, the authors use outside director dummy that takes a value of one for companies that have at least one outside director and zero for those that have no outside directors instead of OUTDIR. The analysis engenders an insignificant coefficient on the outside director dummy, which suggests that adopting only one outside director (especially for large boards) is not enough to effectively monitor management; a certain percentage of directors should be appointed from outside the company.

Model (3) indicates that INDDIR has a positive and significant coefficient while BANKDIR has an insignificant coefficient. Similarly, Model (4) engenders a negative and significant coefficient on INDDIR, but an insignificant coefficient on BANKDIR. This suggests that the results of prior analyses mainly come from independent directors, who serve as an effective monitor of management; they discipline managers and protect shareholder wealth.

Examining other variables, Models (1) and (3) show that TENURE has a positive and significant coefficient. Managers who have held their positions for many years are more likely to leave the position for performance declines. BOARDSIZE has an insignificant coefficient in all models. As with Uchida's (2010) finding, the result does not support the idea that small boards have fewer free-rider problems and effectively monitor management. Models (2) and (4) carry a positive coefficient on SOD. Consistent with previous studies, this result suggests that managers who receive stock options have an incentive to cut dividends to increase their option values (Lambert *et al.*, 1989; Fenn and Liang, 2001).

Previous studies suggested that in Japan, foreign ownership is positively related to firm value and dividend payments (Hiraki *et al.*, 2003; Baba, 2009). Baek *et al.* (2004) showed evidence that Korean firms with higher ownership concentrations by unaffiliated foreign investors suffered less from deteriorating stock performance during the East Asian financial crisis of 1997. These results suggest that foreign shareholders mitigate expropriation of minority shareholders. However, the authors do not find evidence that FOREOWN has a significant impact on management turnover and dividend policy during the current financial crisis. Foreign shareholders do not play an important role in the current financial crisis, which originated in the US market (Nogata *et al.*, 2010). MtBr has a positive coefficient in Models (2) and (4). Consistent with agency theory, firms with rich growth opportunities are likely to decrease dividends. ROA has a significantly negative coefficient and LEVERAGE has a significantly positive coefficient in the regression of dividend cuts. Highly-leveraged, poorly performing firms are more likely to cut dividends.

Additional tests

Thus far, the authors define management turnover simply as president or CEO changes. Although the most frequently reported reasons for turnover were responses to severe business conditions and management and business line reorganizations, twelve firms announced that the president will leave his or her seat simply because the term ends. Potentially, outside directors have no influence on such routine turnovers. As an additional test of the disciplinary role of outside directors, the authors conducted the same logit regression after deleting those firms from the sample. Models (1) and (2) of Table 10.6 carry a positive and significant coefficient on OUTDIR and INDDIR, which suggests that outside directors serve a disciplinary role for management. Consistent with the former analysis, MANAGEROWN and MBOWN have a negative and significant coefficient.

As an additional test, we investigated whether outside directors increase the likelihood that the replaced manager will leave the board. However, our sample included only fifty replaced managers leaving the board. The logit regression result (Models (3) and (4) of Table 10.6), which used a dummy as the dependent variable that takes a value of one for those fifty companies, and zero for others, engenders an insignificant coefficient on OUTDIR and INDDIR. The authors argue that in terms of management turnover, outside directors have a moderate disciplinary role.

Discussions

Our results offer evidence that independent boards have monitored management in the interests of shareholders during the financial crisis. Traditionally, Japanese companies had large, insider-dominated boards. However, since the late 1990s, there have been increased calls for board reforms. For example, CalPERS launched the Corporate Governance Principle, which required Japanese companies to adopt small, independent boards. As a result, Japanese companies have substantially downsized boards by adopting an officer system, which organizationally separates executive officers from boards of directors (Uchida, 2010). However, Japanese firms remain reluctant to increase board independence. As a result, the TSE only requires listed

Table 10.6 *Logit regression results (2)*

This table presents logit regression results. Sample firms are those that experience 33% or more declines for the year 2008 in operating income before depreciation. Models (1) and (2) delete firms from the analysis that replace management due to term ends, using TURNOVER as a dependent variable. Management turnover is defined as replacement of the president. In Models (3) and (4), the dependent variable takes a value of one for companies in which the replaced manager leaves the board, and zero for all other firms. All models delete firms from the analysis in which the manager leaves the position due to death or illness. See Table 10.1 for a definition of the variables.

	(1)	(2)	(3)	(4)
	TURNOVER	TURNOVER	TURNOVER and leave the board=1	TURNOVER and leave the board=1
OUTDIR	1.948**		−0.189	
	(2.39)		(−0.16)	
INDDIR		1.928*		−0.733
		(1.86)		(−0.38)
BANKDIR		−2.505		−4.524
		(−0.64)		(−0.70)
BOARDSIZE	0.039	0.034	−0.010	−0.012
	(1.32)	(1.16)	(−0.20)	(−0.25)
SOD	−0.175	−0.139	−0.364	−0.334
	(−0.71)	(−0.56)	(−0.98)	(−0.89)
MANAGEROWN	−6.502**	−6.775**	−11.452**	−11.536**
	(−2.09)	(−2.15)	(−2.16)	(−2.17)
MBOWN	−12.331*	−13.312**	−23.389***	−23.265***
	(−1.90)	(−2.08)	(−2.58)	(−2.60)

Table 10.6 (*cont.*)

	(1)	(2)	(3)	(4)
	TURNOVER	TURNOVER	TURNOVER and leave the board=1	TURNOVER and leave the board=1
FOREOWN	−0.553	−0.682	−0.703	−0.619
	(−0.47)	(−0.58)	(−0.43)	(−0.37)
ROA	−1.254	−1.581	−1.914	−2.159
	(−0.90)	(−1.03)	(−1.16)	(−1.25)
LEVERAGE	0.180	0.198	0.995	1.033
	(0.27)	(0.29)	(1.34)	(1.35)
MtBr	−0.278	−0.233	−0.069	−0.042
	(−0.92)	(−0.80)	(−0.20)	(−0.12)
Ln(Asset)	0.078	0.109	−0.168	−0.161
	(0.67)	(0.94)	(−1.01)	(−0.95)
TENURE	0.035**	0.035**	0.019	0.019
	(2.47)	(2.43)	(0.87)	(0.86)
Constant	−2.663**	−2.926**	−0.381	−0.484
	(−2.16)	(−2.39)	(−0.20)	(−0.26)
Industry dummy	Yes			
TSE 2nd dummy	Yes			
Pseud R^2	0.053	0.050	0.070	0.072
N	790	790	802	802

*** Significant at the 1% level
** Significant at the 5% level
* Significant at the 10% level

companies to adopt at least one independent director. Our evidence supports this regulatory movement.

A possible criticism of our research is that independent boards play a disciplinary role only in limited situations, such as the present financial crisis period. Indeed, the authors conducted a similar analysis for the year 2007 and found no evidence that board independence significantly affected management turnover and dividend policy. Those results suggest that outside (or independent) directors may effectively monitor management when severe conflicts of interest exist between shareholders and other stakeholders. However, the authors argue that this outside directors' role is important, especially in Japan, where the market for corporate control is less active. Japanese companies must have internal corporate governance mechanisms that effectively discipline management. The authors argue that independent boards play a certain disciplinary role in Japan.

Conclusions

Corporate board structure has received more attention in the recent corporate governance literature. The topic is important because some major stock exchanges, like the New York Stock Exchange and the Tokyo Stock Exchange, require listed companies to appoint independent directors. To examine whether outside (or independent) directors monitor management in the shareholder interest, the authors collected Japanese companies that experienced 33 per cent or more performance declines during the financial crisis (for the 2008 accounting year) and investigated how board independence affects management turnover and corporate dividend policy. Poor firm performance associated with the current financial crisis engenders severe agency conflicts. In severe business environments, firms must conduct management turnovers, which accelerate restructuring to create shareholder value. In addition, managers have an incentive to substantially decrease dividends in order to retain the firm's financial health at the expense of shareholder wealth; other stakeholders desire the same. Such situations offer a sufficient environment to test the effectiveness of internal corporate governance mechanisms.

The authors find that the fraction of outside (or independent) directors over total board members is positively related to the frequency of management turnover, whereas managerial and bank ownership are negatively related to the likelihood of turnover. This suggests that independent boards have critically monitored management and made turnovers more sensitive to poor firm performance. In addition, the proportion of outside (or independent) directors to total board members is negatively related to the likelihood that a firm will decrease dividend payments. Such results suggest that independent boards have disciplined management and protected shareholder wealth. From a viewpoint of shareholder wealth maximization, we argue that the recent regulatory movement is in the right direction.

Our results contribute to prior studies in several dimensions. First, the authors provided additional evidence, using data from the present financial crisis, that outside directors make management turnover more sensitive to poor performance (Weisbach, 1988). Second, the authors provide evidence that supports the view that well-designed corporate governance structures serve an important role during crisis periods when agency conflicts become severe. Unlike previous studies (Mitton, 2002; Lemmon and Lins, 2003; Baek *et al.*, 2004), the authors find that internal corporate governance mechanisms have a positive role in management turnover and dividend policy. To the best of our knowledge, this is the first report to show that independent boards reduce the frequency of dividend cuts: direct evidence that outside directors protect shareholder wealth.

Notes

1 For most Japanese companies, the 2008 accounting year ends 31 March 2009. It would be also interesting to investigate the issue for the accounting year 2009, because the global financial crisis could be still occurring and affect management turnover and dividend policy for that year. However, data availability does not allow this.

2 Many previous studies use dummy variables that indicate dividend cuts (or increases) to investigate corporate dividend policies (e.g., DeAngelo and DeAngelo, 1990; Dewenter and Warther, 1998; Baba, 2009).

3 Jensen (1993) suggested that high managerial ownership can allow the CEO to create a board that is unlikely to monitor.

4 Kaplan (1994) found that Japanese management turnover is related to earnings and stock returns as much as US management turnover is. Abe (1997) found that the long-run performance measures of individual CEOs

(the annualized average of cumulative performance as a CEO) are significantly related to Japanese CEO turnover. Kang and Shivdasani (1995) focused on the relation between corporate governance structure and the sensitivity of management turnover to firm performance.

5 The authors investigate whether the proportion of outside directors affects a firm's likelihood of omitting dividend payments, but do not find a significant relation. This result is attributable to the fact that the average sample firm reports a positive ROA, which makes it difficult for managers to omit dividends. Indeed, only eighty-eight firms (about 12 per cent) of the 731 sample companies omit dividend payments.

References

Abe, Y. 1997. 'Chief executive turnover and firm performance in Japan', *Journal of the Japanese and International Economies* 11 (1): 2–26.

Allen, F. and Zhao, M. 2007. 'The corporate governance model of Japan: shareholders are not rulers', *PKU Business Review* 36: 98–102.

Aoki, M. 1990. 'Toward an economic model of the Japanese firm', *Journal of Economic Literature* 28 (1): 1–27.

Baba, N. 2009. 'Increased presence of foreign investors and dividend policy of Japanese firms', *Pacific-Basin Finance Journal* 17 (2): 163–74.

Baek, J.-S., Kang, J.-K. and Park, K. S. 2004. 'Corporate governance and firm value: evidence from the Korean financial crisis', *Journal of Financial Economics* 71 (2): 265–313.

Bennedsen, M., Kongsted, H. C. and Nielsen, K. M. 2008. 'The causal effect of board size in the performance of small and medium-sized firms', *Journal of Banking and Finance* 32 (6): 1098–109.

Boone, A., Field, L., Karpoff, J. and Raheja, C. 2007. 'The determinants of corporate board size and composition: an empirical analysis', *Journal of Financial Economics* 85 (1): 66–101.

Byrd, J. W. and Hickman, K. A. 1992. 'Do outside directors monitor managers? Evidence from tender offer bids', *Journal of Financial Economics* 32 (2): 195–221.

Coles, J., Daniel, N. and Naveen, L. 2008. 'Boards: does one size fit all?', *Journal of Financial Economics* 87 (2): 329–56.

DeAngelo, H. and DeAngelo, L. 1990. 'Dividend policy and financial distress: an empirical investigation of troubled NYSE firms', *Journal of Finance* 45 (5): 1415–31.

Denis, D. and Sarin, A. 1999. 'Ownership and board structure in publicly traded corporations', *Journal of Financial Economics* 52 (2): 187–223.

Dewenter, K. L. and Warther, V. A. 1998. 'Dividends, asymmetric information, and agency conflicts: evidence from a comparison of the dividend policies of Japanese and U.S. firms', *Journal of Finance* 53 (3): 879–904.

Eisenberg, T., Sundgren, S. and Wells, M. 1998. 'Larger board size and decreasing firm value in small firms', *Journal of Financial Economics* 48 (1): 35–54.

Fenn, G. W. and Liang, N. 2001. 'Corporate payout policy and managerial stock incentives', *Journal of Financial Economics* 60 (1): 45–72.

Goyal, V. K. and Park, C. W. 2002. 'Board leadership structure and CEO turnover', *Journal of Corporate Finance* 8 (1): 49–66.

Guest, P. M. 2008. 'The determinants of board size and composition: evidence from the UK', *Journal of Corporate Finance* 14 (1): 51–72.

Hiraki, T., Inoue, H., Ito, A., Kuroki, F. and Masuda, H. 2003. 'Corporate governance and firm value in Japan: evidence from 1985 to 1998', *Pacific-Basin Finance Journal* 11 (3): 239–65.

Ivashina, V. and Scharfstein, D. 2010. 'Bank lending during the financial crisis of 2008', *Journal of Financial Economics* 97 (3): 319–38.

Jensen, M. 1993. 'The modern industrial revolution, exit, and the failure of internal control systems', *Journal of Finance* 48 (3): 831–80.

Kang, J.-K. and Shivdasani, A. 1995. 'Firm performance, corporate governance, and top executive turnover in Japan', *Journal of Financial Economics* 38 (1): 29–58.

1997. 'Corporate restructuring during performance declines in Japan', *Journal of Financial Economics* 46 (1): 29–65.

Kaplan, S. N. 1994. 'Top executive rewards and firm performance: a comparison of Japan and the United States', *Journal of Political Economy* 102 (3): 510–46.

Kaplan, S. N. and Minton, B. A. 1994. 'Appointments of outsiders to Japanese boards: determinants and implications for managers', *Journal of Financial Economics* 36 (2): 225–58.

Kato, H., Lemmon, M., Luo, M. and Schallheim, J. 2005. 'An empirical examination of the costs and benefits of executive stock options: evidence from Japan', *Journal of Financial Economics* 78 (2): 435–61.

Lambert, R. A., Lanen, W. N. and Larcker, D. F. 1989. 'Executive stock option plans and corporate dividend policy', *Journal of Financial and Quantitative Analysis* 24 (4): 409–25.

La Porta, R., Lopez-De-Silanes, F. and Vishny, R. W. 2000. 'Agency problems and dividend policies around the world', *Journal of Finance* 55 (1): 1–33.

Lehn, K., Patro, S. and Zhao, M. 2004. 'Determinants of the size and structure of corporate boards: 1935–2000', *Working Paper*. University of Pittsburgh.

Lemmon, M. L. and Lins, K. V. 2003. 'Ownership structure, corporate governance, and firm value: evidence from the East Asian financial crisis', *Journal of Finance* 58 (4): 1445–68.

Linck, J. S., Netter, J. F. and Yang, T. 2008. 'The determinants of board structure', *Journal of Financial Economics* 87 (2): 308–28.

Lipton, M. and Lorsch, J. 1992. 'A modest proposal for improved corporate governance', *Business Lawyer* 48 (1): 59–77.

Mak, Y. and Li, Y. 2001. 'Determinants of corporate ownership and board structure: evidence from Singapore', *Journal of Corporate Finance* 7 (3): 231–56.

Mitton, T. 2002. 'A cross-firm analysis of the impact of corporate governance on the East Asian financial crisis', *Journal of Financial Economics* 64 (2): 215–41.

Miwa, Y. and Ramseyer, J. M. 2005. 'Who appoints them, what do they do? Evidence on outside directors from Japan', *Journal of Economics and Management Strategy* 14 (2): 299–337.

Miyajima, Y. and Nitta, K. 2006. 'Nihongata torishimariyakukai no tagenteki shinka: sono ketteiyoin to performance koka' ('Multilateral evolution of Japanese corporate boards: determinants and performance effects'), *Working Paper 06–003*. Waseda University, Japan (in Japanese).

Morck, R. and Nakamura, M. 1999. 'Banks and corporate control in Japan', *Journal of Finance* 54 (1): 319–39.

Morck, R., Nakamura, M. and Shivdasani, A. 2000. 'Banks, ownership structure, and firm value in Japan', *Journal of Business* 73 (4): 539–67.

Musteen, M., Datta, D. K. and Kemmerer, B. 2010. 'Corporate reputation: do board characteristics matter?', *British Journal of Management* 21 (2): 498–510.

Nogata, D., Uchida, K. and Goto, N. 2011. 'Is corporate governance important for regulated firms' shareholders? Evidence from Japanese mergers and acquisitions', *Journal of Economics and Business* 63 (1): 46–68.

Perry, T. and Shivdasani, A. 2005. 'Do boards affect performance? Evidence from corporate restructuring', *Journal of Business* 78 (4): 1403–31.

Pinkowitz, L. and Williamson, R. 2001. 'Bank power and cash holdings: evidence from Japan', *Review of Financial Studies* 14 (4): 1059–82.

Rosenstein, S. and Wyatt, J. G. 1990. 'Outside directors, board independence, and shareholder wealth', *Journal of Financial Economics* 26 (2): 175–91.

Ryan, H. E. Jr and Wiggins, R. A. 2004. 'Who is in whose pocket? Director compensation, board independence, and barriers to effective monitoring', *Journal of Financial Economics* 73 (3): 497–524.

Sheard, P. 1989. 'The main bank system and corporate monitoring and control in Japan', *Journal of Economic Behavior & Organization* 11 (3): 399–422.

Uchida, K. 2006. 'Determinants of stock option use by Japanese companies', *Review of Financial Economics* 15 (3): 251–69.

    2009. 'Reduction in bank ownership and firm performance: evidence from Japan', *Working Paper 1460344*. SSRN.

    2010. 'Does corporate board downsizing increase shareholder value? Evidence from Japan', *International Review of Economics and Finance*, in press.

Warner, J. B., Watts, R. L. and Wruck, K. H. 1988. 'Stock prices and top management changes', *Journal of Financial Economics* 20: 461–92.

Weisbach, M. S. 1988. 'Outside directors and CEO turnover', *Journal of Financial Economics* 20: 431–59.

Yermack, D. 1996. 'Higher market valuations of companies with a small board of directors', *Journal of Financial Economics* 40 (2): 185–212.

Yoshimori, M. 1995. 'Whose company is it? The concept of the corporation in Japan and the West', *Long Range Planning* 28 (4): 33–44.

11 | Risk management in corporate law and corporate governance

CHRISTOPH VAN DER ELST

Risk management is high on the agenda of lawmakers, policymakers, supervisory bodies, academics, corporate advisors and corporate constituents. Risk management was acknowledged as early as World War II but the terrorist attack on the World Trade Center twin towers and the collapse of Enron, Worldcom and other companies, together with the recent financial crisis, the alleged Goldman Sachs' fraudulent structuring and marketing of a synthetic mortgage bond, the (continuation of) skyrocketing bonus schemes and Greece's flirting with bankruptcy, prevent any dwindling of interest in risk management.

Previously, risk management was considered as a typical management activity in which most social sciences, and in particular corporate law, hardly had any interest. The aforementioned events and incidents changed that awareness. Risk management and internal control became a major concern in corporate law and corporate governance. A number of reforms introduced regulatory requirements regarding risk management. In general risk management is similar or even identical in different countries in regard to the operations, the finance and the strategy of companies. Hence, it can be expected that the regulatory requirements are similar regarding the aforementioned topics. The compliance framework should differ more due to the other differences in regulatory frameworks.

In the following sections risk management and the development of risk management in corporate governance will be addressed. Section 1 starts with the identification of risk management frameworks. Section 2 discusses the early requirements of corporate constituents and in particular the board of directors vis-à-vis risk management. Section 3 compares the new corporate law and corporate governance requirements in five Western European countries for appropriate internal control and risk management systems.[1] Section 4 reports the

I am grateful for the assistance and cooperation of Marijn van Daelen in section 3.

development of risk management reporting of the real estate invest-ment industry over the last decade. It illustrates both the significant increase of the role and importance of risk management and the difficult process of balancing entrepreneurship and risk management. Section 5 concludes with a discussion of the state of the art on internal control and risk management. The research subject is the regulatory framework for the general industrial and commercial companies listed on a regulated stock exchange market. This review will not analyse the specific governance and risk management rulebooks of the financial, pharmaceutical, food, defence or other industries, for which many specific and detailed (operational) risk management constraints are in operation, nor will it investigate the particular requirements for mitigating fraud.

Holistic risk management frameworks and responsible behaviour

The leading framework of internal control and enterprise risk man-agement is provided in the COSO I and COSO II Reports (van Daelen and van de Ven, 2010, p. 6). This chapter therefore adopts the defin-ition of enterprise risk management that is given by the 2004 report (COSO, 2004, p. 2):

Enterprise risk management is a process, effected by an entity's board of directors, management and other personnel, applied in strategy setting and across the enterprise, designed to identify potential events that may affect the entity, and manage risk to be within its risk appetite, to provide reason-able assurance regarding the achievement of entity objectives.

A risk management framework should help companies in achieving their strategic, operations, reporting and compliance objectives (COSO, 2004, p. 3). The financial crisis stressed the importance of the strategic oversight role of the board of directors in this process. In its thought paper, *Effective Enterprise Risk Oversight: The Role of the Board of Directors*, COSO requires the board of directors to play a critical role in 'overseeing an enterprise-wide approach to risk man-agement', which includes the understanding of the risk philosophy and the concurrence with the entity's risk appetite, inquiry into the effect-iveness of the risk management system, review of the portfolio of risks and regularly being informed of the risk response to key risk exposures

(COSO, 2009a, pp. 2–3). The paper is accompanied by the paper *Strengthening Enterprise Risk Management for Strategic Advantage*, providing guidance to senior management in how to assist the board of directors' monitoring role (COSO, 2009b, p. 24).

Legislators and regulators used these risk management developments to require companies to install risk management systems and report on them. The next two sections briefly address the legislative processes, both at the European level and in five European Member States. These sections provide the impetus to analyse the risk management systems that the business community is using.

First generation of regulatory risk management and internal control

Over the last decade risk management has become more and more embedded in corporate law and corporate governance. The entrenchment followed the development of interpreting the duties of the board of directors and management of large (listed) companies. Different steps in this development can be identified.

In older editions of Companies' Acts it was generally stated that 'the business of the company shall be managed by the directors who may exercise all the powers of the company'.[2] According to the Dutch, Belgian and French Codes it was, and still is, the duty of the board of directors to govern the company.[3] In the two-tier German structure the management board is responsible for the management of the company and the supervisory board must monitor the management of the company.[4] An article or section regarding the representation of the company follows this management duty.[5]

In some countries, like the Netherlands, the requirement to govern is further explained as the duty to properly manage and protect the assets of the company.[6] However, most Acts remain silent or point at specific duties such as the duty to prepare and provide timely (financial) information[7] and to answer all questions with regard to the items on the agenda of the general meeting and the reports.[8] Any further clear legal guidelines as to what the board is required to do in order to meet this general duty of governing are lacking. Some corporate legal scholars fill the absence of legal directives. De Wulf analyses the Belgian implied obligations. The board of directors has a legal duty to assess the continuity of the company, which requires a decent internal control system. The board of directors must adjust the valuation rules as soon as discontinuity is discovered (De Wulf, 2002, p. 282). The analysis shows that the internal control system must (only) provide reasonable assurance that the (internal and external) financial reporting is adequate but there are no requirements as to which framework must be used.

Corporate governance entered into the spotlight in the last decade of the previous millennium, and has remained there ever since. According to the Cadbury Code 'corporate governance is the system by which companies are directed and controlled' and 'boards of directors are responsible for the governance of their companies' (Committee on the Financial Aspects of Corporate Governance, 2002, para. 2.5). In the different corporate governance codes the duties of the board of directors vis-à-vis internal control and risk management were further developed and fine-tuned.

The Cadbury Committee argued that the legal duty to manage the company requires the board of directors to establish a 'system of internal control over the financial management of the company'. The board must report 'on the effectiveness of their system of internal control and that the auditors should report thereon' (Committee on the Financial Aspects of Corporate Governance, 2002, paras. 4.31–4.32). The 1994 Rutteman Report added the requirement of the board to report their responsibility regarding the internal control system, to provide a description of the procedures and an assessment of the effectiveness including a confirmation of this assessment and a statement that internal control only provides reasonable assurance (Spira and Page, 2003, p. 649; Rayton and Cheng, 2004, pp. 29–30).

The Cadbury Code was a forerunner to internal control and risk management. Similar first generation corporate governance reports on the continent were less developed as regards internal control and risk management requirements. In France, the first Vienot Report of 1995 required the establishment of an audit committee which must verify the internal procedures for collecting information and checking its reliability (CNPF-AFEP, 2005, p. 20). The scope was clearly limited to the effectiveness of the system to provide reliable financial information. Two of the three Belgian corporate governance reports that were published in 1998 recommended that the board of directors 'ensures that an efficient internal control system is in place' and that 'executive management develops and implements the tools necessary to allow appropriate and effective internal control' (Belgian Commission on Corporate Governance, 1998, para. 4.4; VBO/FEB, 1998, para. 4.5).[9] The Dutch 1997 Peters Report contained more detailed guidelines for both the management board and the supervisory board. According to recommendations 4.2 and 4.3 the management board was required to report to the supervisory board as to which risks strategy and policy entail and the results of the assessment of the internal control system for financial reporting. Simultaneously the board was required to establish effective systems for internal control. The supervisory board had to discuss at least once a year the 'risks of the company' as well as the results of the assessment of the management board of the systems of internal control (Committee on Corporate Governance, 1997, para. 3.4). In Germany, corporate governance codes were only developed after the first legislative changes regarding internal control systems were issued.

Overall, the corporate governance requirements regarding internal control and risk management were of a general nature and immature. First, only the Rutteman Report defined internal control. As a consequence, internal control was often, but not exclusively, related to the internal or external financial reporting process, which is considered as one of the three – and later four – objectives of the broader risk management. Secondly, the process of achieving this objective was not identified. At best the internal control-related guidelines identified some of the different duties to assure an appropriate internal control framework was in place, which included the identification of risks, the effectiveness of *the system* and reporting to the shareholders or the supervisory board. Thirdly, the recommendations contained hardly any clear guidance as to which corporate constituent is responsible for the different types of internal control objectives. In some governance codes duties were assigned to *owners* which were identifiable from a management perspective, but not from a legal perspective. Fourthly, notwithstanding that many aspects of internal control and risk management are similar or even identical in different industries and countries, different bodies were responsible for similar duties. The Dutch management board, the British board of directors and the French audit committee are accountable for the assessment of the internal control system for financial reporting. Finally, some of the recommendations seem to conflict with each other. The Dutch management board must report on the evaluation of the internal control system for financial reporting but the supervisory board has to receive the assessments of all the different systems of internal control. While some of the members of the different committees on corporate governance were familiar with the developments of the Committee of Sponsoring Organizations (COSO), the first generation of corporate governance codes clearly opted for a formal approach of best practices.

After the publication of the first generation of corporate governance codes, but before the triggering events on the stock markets at the turn of the millennium, the German Parliament started with specific corporate legislative requirements regarding operational internal control in the German Control and Transparency in Business Act (KonTraG). According to the German Companies Act the management board has to establish an early risk recognition system. The system must provide assurance that material risks that can endanger the going concern of the company or, according to the German literature, can impair the net worth, financial position and results of the company in a sustainable matter (Schmidt and Lutter, 2008, p. 1035), will be identified. The German law requires a system to be set up but only to the extent that risks that can cause material damage can be identified at an early stage. The management report must also report on the risks of the future development of the company. Moreover, auditors must control the risk early recognition system. The German Accounting Standards Board issued the German Accounting Standard number 5, assisting the German auditors in their control assessment of the management report. The Standard goes beyond the legal requirements, and as a consequence, the risk report provides information that exceeds the information that is acquired by the early recognition system (Dobler, 2003, p. 3).

It is generally argued that KonTraG does not require the management board to establish a risk management system that covers all different areas. However the first German corporate governance code emphasizes that the management board must regularly inform the supervisory board 'about all relevant matters regarding business development, risk exposure and risk management of the company and major group subsidiaries' and immediately if the risk exposures 'change significantly against plan' (German Panel on Corporate Governance, 2000, pp. 3–4). The audit committee that should be established at the supervisory board level must address risk management

(German Panel on Corporate Governance, 2000, p. 11). German best practices broadened the legislative scope of KonTraG.

State of the art of internal control and risk management in corporate law

The corporate scandals on both sides of the Atlantic drove politicians to new legal initiatives. The aim of most plans was to restore trust and ensure that companies have adequate controls to mitigate the identified risks. Some Parliaments issued new mandatory requirements regarding risk management and internal control, like the French NRE Act and LSF Act.[10] In Germany, the UK and the Netherlands a more balanced approach that combines features of mandatory requirements with best practices was adopted. In 2010 Belgium followed this approach.

These legislative and regulatory developments coincided and as a consequence convergence is not guaranteed, the exception being the European Corporate Governance Forum, as will be illustrated next.

European developments

At the European level, the 2004 Transparency Directive requires that issuers' annual and interim reports include 'a description of the principal risks and uncertainties that [it] face[s]'.[11] The requirement to disclose the principal risks and uncertainties obliges companies to install at least a risk and uncertainty identification system. Similar requirements can be found in the Prospectus Directive 2003/71/EC and Commission Regulation 809/2004, which oblige companies to include risk factors in the prospectus (van Daelen, 2008). The list of risk factors must comprise company-specific risks and/or risks related to the securities issued that are material for taking investment decisions.[12]

The 2006 amendment to the Fourth and Seventh Company Law Directives requires an annual corporate governance statement from listed entities. This statement must contain 'a description of the main features of the company's internal control and risk management systems in relation to the financial reporting process'.[13] On the consolidated level, 'a description of the main features of the group's internal control and risk management systems in relation to the process for preparing consolidated accounts' must be provided.[14] The statement can be integrated in the management report or be published as a separate report. There are some legal differences between the two publication methods but in both cases the auditor's opinion is required to cover the consistency of the main features of the company's internal control and risk management systems in relation to the financial reporting process. As a minimum, the auditor will have to control the availability in the corporate governance statement of the description of the main features of the system in relation to the financial reporting process and issue a consistency opinion. The Directive did not provide any guidance as to the level of work required nor did it oblige the auditor to start a forensic audit (FEE, 2009, p. 36).

The 2006 Directive on statutory audits stipulates that public-interest entities must establish an audit committee (or alternative body) to monitor the financial reporting process and to monitor the effectiveness of the company's internal control, internal audit where applicable and risk management systems.[15] The statutory auditor must also 'report to the audit committee on key matters arising from the statutory audit, and in particular on material weaknesses in internal control in relation to the financial reporting process'.[16] In its Statement on Risk Management and Internal Control, the European Corporate Governance Forum confirmed that company boards are responsible for monitoring the effectiveness of internal control systems but pleaded against a legal obligation for boards to certify the effectiveness of internal controls (European Corporate Governance Forum, 2006, p. 5). The European Commission's recommendation on independent directors and committees of the board recommends the audit committee to assist the board in its task to review the internal control and risk management systems and the effectiveness of the external audit process and to ensure the effectiveness of the internal audit function (European Commission, 2005, p. 61).

The UK approach

The UK immediately opted for a 'comply or explain' corporate governance regime. The London Stock Exchange introduced a requirement into the Listing Rules for companies to include a statement of (non-)compliance with the provisions of the report in their annual report and accounts. This approach is more or less maintained but is thwarted by the mandatory European requirements. After an update of the remuneration guidelines in the 1995 Greenbury Report, the Hampel Committee issued its report in January 1998.[17] This report emphasized that the board should maintain a sound system of internal control to safeguard shareholders' investment and the company's assets. The Hampel Report furthered internal control by arguing that this system not only covers financial controls but also operational and compliance controls, as well as risk management (Hampel Committee, 1998, p. 21). Following the recommendations of the Hampel Committee, the London Stock Exchange issued the Combined Code on Corporate Governance in June 1998. In the UK the Institute of Chartered Accountants of England and Wales provided further guidance regarding internal control and risk management via the Turnbull Report in 1999. The report sets out best practices on internal control and assists listed companies in applying this internal control principle. The board of directors is responsible for maintaining a sound system of internal control and must ensure that the system is effective in managing risks in a manner approved by the board (Turnbull Committee, 1999, section 16).

According to the Turnbull Report, management is responsible for implementing the board's policies on risk and control. Management should also provide the board with a balanced assessment of the significant risks and the effectiveness of the system of internal control in managing those risks (Turnbull Committee, 1999, sections 18 and 30). The board itself should make a public statement on internal control and it should therefore undertake an annual assessment that should consider the changes in the nature and extent of significant risks, as well as the company's ability to respond to changes.

In the UK corporate governance rules, and as an integrated part of the Turnbull Report, the risk management system is regularly under review. After the Smith Report and the Higgs Review of 2003 the main principle regarding internal control reads: 'The board should maintain a sound system of internal control to safeguard shareholders' investment and the company's assets' (Financial Reporting Council, 2003, para. C.2). It is the board's responsibility to annually review 'the effectiveness of the group's system of internal controls and [it] should report to shareholders that they have done so. The review should cover all material controls, including financial, operational and compliance controls and risk management systems' (Financial Reporting Council, 2003, para. C.2.1). This approach is confirmed in the Guidance on Audit Committees (Financial Reporting Council, 2008, para. 4.6). The previous interpretation of the City and the accounting profession that the requirement was limited to the internal financial controls was completely set aside.

In 2004 the independent Financial Reporting Council ordered a committee chaired by Douglas Flint to review the Turnbull guidance and to update it in light of the new national (Combined Code) and international (Sarbanes-Oxley Act) developments. The revised Turnbull guidance of October 2005 is still applicable. The guidance refined the Combined Code principle and stressed that a sound internal control system facilitates the company's 'effective and efficient operation by enabling it to respond appropriately to significant business, operational, financial, compliance and other risks to achieving the company's objectives. This includes the safeguarding of assets from inappropriate use or from loss and fraud and ensuring that liabilities are identified and managed' (Financial Reporting Council, 2005, p. 7). Testing the effectiveness of the internal control system is the board of directors' responsibility.

The publication of the Walker Review of Corporate Governance in the UK Banking Industry in November 2009 raised questions as to whether the risk management systems and frameworks of the other industries also needed a more modernized approach. The Financial Reporting Council acknowledged that further improvement of the internal control guidelines and reporting requirements was necessary, in particular regarding risk appetite assessment, tolerance and maintaining of the system. The modernization is scheduled for 2010 and a first step was taken with the publication of the UK Corporate Governance Code in June 2010. The new main principle regarding internal control and risk management reads: 'The board is responsible for determining the nature and extent of the significant risks it is willing to take in achieving its strategic objectives. The board should maintain sound risk management and internal control systems' (Financial Reporting Council, 2010, para. C.2). The latest developments confirm and emphasize the policies which were already installed in the pre-financial crisis era.

The alternative French approach

The French Companies Act – integrated in the Commercial Code – requires the board of directors to perform all controls and verifications that it considers expedient.[18] Since 2003 it has been a requirement that the chairman of the board present a report to the general meeting of shareholders with the internal control procedures and the risk management established by and in the company. The report must highlight those procedures related to the gathering and treatment of the accounting and financial information, both for the annual and the consolidated accounts. This French legal requirement caused companies many compliance difficulties, in particular due to the lack of guidelines. To overcome these problems, the French supervisory authority recommended the use of the referential framework 'Le dispositif de contrôle interne: cadre de référence' of the *Groupe De Place* which the AMF sponsored. In 2008 a *light* edition 'Cadre de référence du contrôle interne: guide de mise en œuvre pour les valeurs moyennes et petites' for small and medium-sized listed companies was published.[19] Both reports clearly distinguished (reporting) requirements related to the general internal control framework and the more elaborated specific requirements with respect to the internal control over reporting of financial information. Next, the requirements are aligned but not identical to the COSO I report on internal control that includes an appropriate organizational structure, internal communication of information, a system to identify and manage the risks, control activities and continuous monitoring. However, the French Commercial Code requires the chairman not only to report on the internal control procedures but also on risk management. Conversely, and as opposed to the three objectives in COSO I, the French framework identifies four objectives which resemble the four objectives of COSO II, namely compliance, follow-up of the instructions and the orientations of the executive board, good internal operations, in particular to protect the company's assets, and reliable financial information. The financial crisis has not (yet) changed the French approach.

The Dutch 'in control statement'

The compliance with the Dutch Peters Report was unsatisfactory and the Dutch Minister of Finance and Minister of Economic Affairs invited Euronext Amsterdam, the Employers' Association and several other interested associations to develop a new corporate governance code, commonly known as the Tabaksblat Code. It was issued in 2003 and at the end of 2004 the Code and its 'comply or explain' regime was legally acknowledged. The main internal control and risk management provisions are set out in para. II.1 of the Tabaksblat Code. The principle deals with the responsibility of the management board for complying with laws and regulations, managing the risks associated with the company's activities, and financing the company. Furthermore, it stipulates that the management board has to report related developments to, and discuss the internal risk management and control systems with, the supervisory board and its audit committee. The best practice provisions required the management board to have an internal risk management and control system that is suitable for the company and declare in the annual report that the internal risk systems are adequate and effective (Tabaksblat Committee, 2003, paras. II.1.3 and II.1.4). The latter best practice provision is commonly known as the 'in control statement'.

The Dutch monitoring commission provided guidelines to comply with the financial reporting risks and the other – operational, strategic and compliance – risks. It also offered good practices to portray the risk profile and the internal control and risk management system in the 'in control statement'. The proposals have been incorporated in the new edition of the Dutch Corporate Governance Code of 2008 (DCGC 2008). The DCGC 2008 requires companies to have an internal risk management and control system suitable for the company with, as instruments of the system, risk analyses of the company's operational and financial objectives and a monitoring and reporting system (Corporate Governance Code Monitoring Committee, 2008, para. II.1.3). Besides being responsible for complying with all relevant primary and secondary legislation and managing the risks associated with the company's activities, the management board is also responsible for the company's risk profile. In line with the Tabaksblat Code, the management board has to report related developments to, and discuss the internal risk management and control systems with, the supervisory board and the audit committee (Corporate Governance Code Monitoring Committee, 2008, para. II.1). The DCGC 2008 has amended the 'in control statement' by requiring the management board to declare in the annual report that the systems provide a reasonable assurance that the financial reporting does not contain any errors of material importance and that the systems have worked properly (Corporate Governance Code Monitoring Committee, 2008, para. II.1.5). Thus, instead of declaring that the systems are adequate and effective, the management board has to declare that the systems provide reasonable assurance, which is a major reduction of the requirement. Since 2009 the declaration only has to address the financial reporting – not other aspects of the system such as strategy, operations and compliance – and only for errors of material importance. However, The DCGC 2008 added a provision requiring the management board to give a description in the annual report of: (1) the main risks related to the strategy of the company; (2) the design and effectiveness of the internal risk management and control systems for the main risks during the financial year; and (3) any major failings in the internal risk management and control systems, including significant changes made to the systems and the major improvements planned, and a confirmation that these issues have been discussed with the audit committee and the supervisory board (Corporate Governance Code Monitoring Committee, 2008, para. II.1.4). The system set out by the COSO reports is cited as an example of an internal control and risk management system in the explanatory statement (Corporate Governance Code Monitoring Committee, 2008, 39). Also, the DCGC 2008 provides that the supervisory board's oversight of the management board has to include the company's risks inherent in the business activities and the design and effectiveness of the internal risk management and control systems (Corporate Governance Code Monitoring Committee, 2008, para. III.1.6). One of the key committees of the supervisory board, the audit committee, has to monitor the activities of the management board with respect to the operation of the internal risk management and control systems (Corporate Governance Code Monitoring Committee, 2008, para. III.5.4).

In light of the financial crisis the DCGC will not be strengthened. However, as in the UK, a new Banking Code was issued in September 2009. It is applicable to all Dutch-licensed banks. This code requires the Dutch-licensed bank to provide a risk appetite approval and risk monitoring procedure as well as a product approval process. A risk committee must assist the supervisory board in its risk monitoring role (NVB, 2009, p. 16). It is expected that the 'comply or explain' code will be legally endorsed. In the meantime a monitoring commission assesses the compliance with the Banking Code (De Jager, 2010, p. 2).

The German and Belgian follow-up

Above it was shown that Germany was the first Western European country to legally endorse a specific risk management system, the *Frühwarnsystem*. Conversely, Germany was very late in the development of a generally accepted corporate governance code. It was only in 2000 that a Government Panel on Corporate Governance was installed. It reported to the German Chancellor in July 2001 after which the German Minister of Justice installed a corporate governance commission. The Code was published in 2002 and obtained the status of a mandatory 'comply or explain' code via section 161 of the German Companies Act. It did not contain many guidelines regarding internal control or risk management. It explicitly recognizes the management board's responsibility for risk management and the requirement for the chairman of the management board to discuss risk management with the chairman of the supervisory board. The audit committee must 'handle issues of accounting and risk management' (Government Commission, 2002, paras. 4.1.4, 5.2, 5.3.2). In the 2005 edition the commission added that the chairman of this committee must have knowledge of and experience in internal control processes (Government Commission, 2005, 5.3.2). Other or more detailed governance regulations are not included in the Code. The financial crisis has not yet resulted in more specific risk management guidelines in the Code.

Finally, Belgium followed the developments in the other countries. Belgium established a Commission on Corporate Governance, which issued its code in late 2004. It contained several internal control and risk management-related provisions and guidelines. First, it explicitly acknowledged that the board is responsible for enabling the company to identify and to manage its risks and to define its risk appetite (Belgian Commission on Corporate Governance, 2004, paras. 1.1 and 1.2). The board must ascertain that an internal control system that effectively identifies and manages risks, including the compliance risks of which the effectiveness must be controlled by the audit committee, is in place. The executive management must establish internal controls for all different kinds of risks (Belgian Commission on Corporate Governance, 2004, paras. 1.3, 6.5 and 5.2.7).

According to the industry and a number of scientific studies the Belgian Corporate Governance Code was well received. However, it is our understanding that these studies do not analyse the functioning of the internal control systems. Therefore, it does not come as a surprise that the 2009 update of the Code hardly changed the recommendations on internal control and risk management systems. In the 2009 edition the board of directors must approve and assess the implementation of the internal control and risk management framework (Belgian Commission on Corporate Governance, 2009, 1.3). The most important characteristics of the framework must be disclosed in the corporate governance statement, a European disclosure requirement which has recently been endorsed by a new corporate governance law.[20] Furthermore, an induction programme with the fundamentals of risk management and internal control must be provided, not only for the members of the audit committee but for all board members (Belgian Commission on Corporate Governance, 2009, para. 4.8).

Risk management and internal control in practice

Research design

To gain proper insight into the identification, assessment, response and control of risks and risk management systems before and after the financial crisis, an analysis of risk management reporting in the annual reports of 2000, 2005 and 2009 of five real estate companies in the five different countries is performed. The year 2000 is selected as the year before the explosion of corporate scandals and accounting irregularities that burst over the financial markets in late 2001 and 2002. By 2005 both regulators and companies had had sufficient time to mitigate the problems that the crisis at the start of the millennium caused. Finally, in their 2009 report companies had the opportunity to address the consequences of the financial crisis. The companies in the sample are Wereldhave (the Netherlands), Cofinimmo (Belgium), British Land (UK), Unibail-Rodamco (France) and IVG Immobilien (Germany). These companies specialize in property management and property development. Wereldhave, Unibail and Cofinimmo focus strategically on the former. Over the years IVG Immobilien oriented towards the development of real estate investment products, but property management remained its core business. British Land specializes in the latter activity. As a consequence operational risk management of British Land has different priorities.

The focus of this analysis is more on the risk management report or provisions in the business review or corporate governance statement, and less on the risk reporting in the notes to the accounts. According to the COSO II framework, the risk management process should be divided in to the following activities: setting the internal environment, objective-setting (risk appetite), event identification, risk assessment, risk response, control activities, information and communication, and monitoring effectiveness. The annual report does not provide information on all the different activities. We limit the analysis of the annual reports to event identification, risk assessment, risk response and monitoring. The review illustrates the level of information that is publicly disclosed via the annual report. The risk management part of the annual report is provided in a narrative report. It goes without saying that the sample of the survey is too small to be representative for all companies. Further, the reported results could be flawed as there is a considerable risk that the surveyed reports only partially report on the practices in place. Notwithstanding these restrictions the results of the analysis can be summarized as follows.

Research results

First, according to the amendment to the Fourth and Seventh Company Law Directives, companies must disclose the main features of the risk management and internal control system for financial reporting in the corporate governance statement. Notwithstanding the fact that the law limits the requirement to financial reporting, an efficient system requires the integration of this internal control system into a broader and general risk management system. All companies reported in 2009 on the use of a – national – internal control system. While the French company Unibail-Rodamco applied the AMF framework and British Land referred to the use of Turnbull, IVG developed an adjusted accounting-related internal control system. Wereldhave did not identify any framework but stressed the appropriateness of its internal administrative organization. Only Cofinimmo explicitly acknowledged the use of COSO. The reference to the use of a framework is accompanied by the use of a code of conduct or ethical guidelines and/or a compliance guide.

The explicit identification of the framework is obviously related to the legal developments. In 2000 only British Land and IVG referred to the use of a control system, the former to the Turnbull Report, published in 1999, and the latter via an overview of the different steps of identifying, assessing, managing and monitoring risks. In 2005 Unibail provided the report of the chairman of the board describing the use of a – non-identified – internal control system and Wereldhave referred to a non-identified internal control system to meet the requirements of the Tabaksblat Code. In 2009 all companies applied an internal control framework.

Key is the identification of the portfolio of the events a business is confronted with. Due to the regulatory requirements and business strategy, only negative events – risks – are described in detail in the annual reports. In 2000 only the largest company and IVG, for which the early warning system was already mandatory, identified and reported some (financial) risks. The major turnaround took place during the first part of the millennium. Even in countries where the regulatory requirements regarding (the reporting of) risk management were installed after 2005, as in Belgium, companies invested in risk management systems. In the second half of the decade the systems were further improved, aligned with the regulatory requirements, and consolidated. Since 2005 the average number of reported risks has stabilized at around fifteen, with a minimum of around ten and a maximum of around twenty (Figure 11.1). A first analysis of all listed real estate investment funds in the Netherlands supported these findings; the annual reports refer to sixteen risks on average, with a minimum of thirteen and a maximum of twenty.[21]

The development of reporting on risks coincided with the interest in, and requirement to, manage these risks. For a long period of time only financial risk management was emphasized. In 2000 the majority of the companies only identified currency, interest and liquidity risk. By 2005 all companies identified these financial risks and the majority added a list of operational and strategic risks. The other identified risks were of a more idiosyncratic nature.

According to COSO, risk assessment is the fourth important step in the risk management process. Each risk must be classified according to

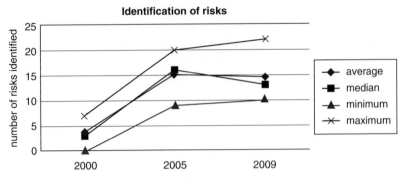

Source: own research based on annual reports

Figure 11.1 Identification of risks

its impact on the objectives of the company and likelihood of occurrence. Risk assessment employs both qualitative and quantitative
methods. Risk assessment reporting suffers from the difficulties in
standardizing qualitative methods. While no assessment reporting
could be found in the annual reports of 2000, in 2005 the impact of
the financial risks was well documented. Both in 2005 and in 2009
most companies quantitatively documented the impact of the volatility of currencies and interests. In a number of 2009 reports this information was completed with the assessment of the impact of
operational risks, such as the exposure to contract termination and
the default of tenants.

The likelihood of occurrence is barely reported. As a result, classification of risks categories in order of importance is missing in all
reports. It creates a field of tension between the appearance of compliance with a referential framework and the state of the art of the risk
management system.

According to COSO there are four types of risk response: acceptance, avoidance, sharing and reduction. In case of acceptance, the
company must monitor the risk; for the reduction of risks controls
are necessary; while insurance is the most common technique for
risk-sharing. Most companies combine all four types of response
although information on avoidance is missing: as the company elim-
inates the risk by getting out of the situation hardly any information
is provided. An exception to this rule is the currency risk. Some
companies have developed their business in the Eurozone and are

not confronted with the currency risk. Table 11.1 provides an overview of the most common risk responses of real estate investment companies. While strategic risks are monitored and financial risks are reduced, the other types of risk are more actively managed via different techniques of controls, risk-sharing and monitoring. A relatively new phenomenon is the monitoring of the reduction techniques of financial risks. Most companies have recently started to provide information on the quality of the counterparty of the derivatives.

There is no ranking of the different kinds of risk responses, and investors and other stakeholders have to assess the appropriateness of the risk response. While some companies opt for fixed interest rate loans to mitigate the interest rate developments, others explicitly select variable interest rate loans to profit from these developments. Stakeholders must examine the market developments to assess the risk response of each company. Similarly, some companies adopt a policy of spreading the (tenant) counterparty risk as much as possible, while others concentrate this risk to mitigate more cumbersome administrative procedures of tenants' compliance.

Information on the control activities and the effectiveness testing of the system is underdeveloped. In general, responsibility of the management and the audit committee is assumed and some companies have installed an internal audit function. However, companies do not frequently address questions of the feasibility of the risk management systems and the deficiencies of the systems are not disclosed. However, companies regularly report improvements to the systems, indirectly indicating the weaknesses of the previous system. One of the companies reported that in 2009 a risk inventory on the basis of individual risks was carried out for the first time, clearly illustrating the weaknesses of the previous system.

Conclusion

For a long period of time risk management was considered a financial, a reporting or, at best, an operational issue. Middle management was deemed to mitigate the impact of unexpected financial market developments, in particular fluctuations in interest rates or exchange rates, via different financial hedging arrangements. In operations many companies spend significant resources to optimize

Table 11.1 *Risks and risk responses of real estate companies*

Risk class	Risk	Risk response class	Risk responses				
Strategic and REIT status		accept	monitoring by the board	quarterly assessment finance department			
Operations (and economic)	market development	accept	monitoring	developing new properties	sell older properties	appropriate contract terms	maintenance programmes
	lease price	accept/ reduce	developing new properties	sell older properties	long-term leases	maintenance programmes	prime locations
	letting	reduce	follow-up tenants	regular contacts with tenants	active letting campaigns		
	property valuation	reduce/ sharing	internal valuation (quarterly or biannual)	external valuation (quarterly or semi-annual)	insurance		
	counterparty (tenants)	reduce/ sharing	advance payments	(bank) guarantees	pre-letting screening	diversified tenants	reputed tenants
	real estate development	reduce	close supply chain relationships	well-developed project management	first class contractors	due diligence for acquisitions	follow-up of tenants

Finance	currency	reduce	matching	hedging	use of financial derivatives	ALM committee
	interest	reduce	fixed interest loans	variable interest loans	use of financial derivatives	ALM committee
	refinancing	reduce	different bank relationships	credit facilities	reputed banks	solid solvency ratio
	financial instruments	reduce	monitoring credit exposure to derivatives	banks with credit rating		
	liquidity risk	reduce	maturities spread in time	financing facilities	monitoring covenants	cash management
Legal	regulations and administrative procedures	accept	monitoring	local companies		
Other	fraud and misstatement	accept/ reduce	transparency	segregation of duties	well-organized administrative organization	
	construction health and safety/ environment	sharing	requirements on contractors	environmental code	energy-efficient construction	

supply, to limit industrial accidents, to improve IT support, and so on. The European Union endorsed the harmonization of financial reporting, obliging companies to develop an appropriate financial administrative system.

However, over the last fifteen years, risk management and internal control have developed into a pivotal element of good corporate governance. All corporate governance codes in Western Europe refer to the implementation and maintaining of internal control and risk management systems as best practice. This development has coincided with the growth of legal requirements to establish risk management systems, in particular systems in relation to the financial reporting process. It has shifted the interest and awareness to the top levels of the company, including the board of directors, the audit committee and the external auditor.

The major efforts to raise the standards of accountability for risk management have spurred the harmonization of systems and procedures. In many countries new risk management responsibilities were followed by frameworks to help companies to implement the requirements. In the UK and France the work of the Turnbull Committee and the *Groupe de Place* Commission provided helpful insights into the translation of the recommendations into applicable tools. In other countries the interaction of the regulators with the business community reduced the gap between the regulatory expectations and the business capacities to provide risk management. In the Netherlands the 'in control statement' must now provide *reasonable assurance* instead of 'the statement of an adequate and effective system'.

The harmonization of the regulatory frameworks is visible in corporate reporting of risk management. In 2000 risk management reporting was, at best, fragmented. In 2009 all companies have included a risk management section and describe in detail the risks and risk responses. Reporting and probably implementation of risk management systems still suffer from vagueness and fragmentation of the regulatory framework. Financial risks are quantified and well addressed; the other types of risk are at best qualified and some companies start with scenario analysis to evaluate the impact of the risks incurred. The latter development must be encouraged to integrate the different risks in the risk management approach.

The regulatory integration of risk management and internal control in the corporate legal framework is still fragmented and incomplete. Despite the harmonization efforts some areas require more detailed study. At the moment many rules foresee an obligation to install and maintain both internal control *and* risk management systems. However, COSO II explicitly acknowledged the incorporation of the internal control framework in the enterprise risk framework to move forward to a mature risk management process. Many regulators refer to COSO as an appropriate framework for companies to comply with the legislative and/or regulatory requirements. It is an open question which COSO framework meets the minimum standards avoiding liability and which degree of compliance is required to meet these obligations. The lack of clarity is also visible in the systematization of the regulatory objectives. According to some regulatory bodies it is sufficient if the systems provide reasonable assurance regarding the reliability of the financial reporting process, while others require that the corporations provide processes so that all the objectives can be achieved: strategic, operational, compliance and reporting.

The mandatory requirements to establish and maintain internal control and risk management systems included the identification of corporate constituents who are accountable for setting up and maintaining the systems. Parliaments all over Europe and at the European level identified the responsibilities of the audit committee, the (supervisory and management) board, the executive management, such as the senior accounting officer pursuant to Schedule 46 to the UK Finance Act 2009, and the external auditor. In corporate governance codes other constituents, such as the internal audit department, risk officers, compliance officers and other officers and employees, were provided with responsibilities regarding (parts of) the day-to-day operations of the systems. While responsibilities of most corporate constituents have been more or less clearly identified, other aspects of (corporate) law have not been fully addressed. The chief accounting officer, the compliance officer and risk management officer are often not directors but officers subjected to the authority of the board. As employees of the company they have to work under the authority, direction and supervision of the board of directors. This employer–employee relationship impedes independent actions. Balancing the trade-off between independence and accountability and responsibility is a very difficult exercise in labour relationships.

Another, even more important, issue is the relationship between responsibility and liability regarding the new requirements to establish and maintain internal control and risk management systems. The European Directive 2006/46/EC explicitly acknowledged the collective responsibility and liability of the different boards for the accounts, the annual report and the corporate statement. However, for all other duties liability is not further specified. National and general liability rules prevail, which boils down to the liability of the board for mismanagement and officers for breach of contract. In light of the new responsibilities and corporate governance developments, boards of directors, more than ever before, set up specialized subcommittees and consist of separate classes of directors. The audit committee especially is considered as an important subcommittee in European Member States. The members of the audit committee bear important corporate responsibilities as regards the effectiveness of the risk management systems. However, in some countries (all) the directors are jointly and severally liable vis-à-vis the company as well as vis-à-vis third parties for any loss resulting from an infringement of the provisions of the relevant Companies Act.[22] Any kind of division of liability between audit committee directors and other directors is lacking. The question is also raised as to the duties of the other directors regarding the monitoring of the work of the audit committee. The mature responsibility status that these committees acquired does not (yet) correspond with the corporate liability frameworks that still date from the pre-risk management periods.

Officers must perform in accordance with the principles of good faith, due care and equity. In several jurisdictions they are liable for damages vis-à-vis the company and even third parties. In light of the new internal control and risk management responsibilities, modifications of the working conditions will not only require an appropriate board mechanism to make use of the *ius variandi* but also fleshing out the accountability of officers vis-à-vis developing risk management. Risk appetite, tone at the top and strategy are dynamic concepts which have to fit into the static labour relationships as regards the liability of the officers. Boards can unilaterally change the strategy or tone at the top which the officer must implement, apply and adhere to. It is the duty of the board of directors to develop policies. This duty is accompanied with the right (and duty) of the individual director to react and respond and ultimately (the duty) to resign in case of insurmountable disagreement. These rights and duties are – to say the least – less evident in the position of an officer who works under the authority and supervision of the board. A recent decision of the German *Bundesgerichtshof* of 17 July 2009 (Mutter and Quincke, 2009, R416), which found the compliance officer guilty and referred to a criminal *Garantenpflicht*[23] of this officer, shows a reflection is required.

Notes

1 But, of course, not in different industries or other differences between companies.
2 Regulation 70 of the UK 1985 Table A. The Companies Act 1985 is imprecise and only provides that the duty of the directors is owed to the company (section 309(2) CA 1985).
3 Book 2:129 Dutch Civil Code, Article 53 Belgian Companies Act 1935 and Article 89, French Companies Code 1966.
4 Article 76(1) and Article 111(1) German Stock Corporation Act 1965.
5 Book 2:130 Dutch Civil Code, Article 54 Belgian Companies Act 1935; in France the chairman of the board of directors represented the company (Article 113, French Companies Code 1966).
6 Book 2:9 Dutch Civil Code.
7 Articles 221, 226 and 233 Companies Act 1989, Book 2:141 Dutch Civil Code (to the supervisory board), Article 92 Belgian Companies Code, and Article 341-1 French Companies Code 1966 (amended in 1984) (to the general meeting).
8 See, for example, Article 540 Belgian Companies Code.
9 The third corporate governance report of the Belgian Banking and Finance Commission was limited to corporate governance information to be disclosed. This code contained no specific recommendations on internal control or risk management.
10 Law no. 2001-420 of 15 May 2001 relative aux nouvelles régulations économiques, *Official Gazette* no. 113 of 16 May 2001, p. 7776; Law no. 2003-706 of 1 August 2003 de sécurité financière, *Official Gazette* no. 177 of 2 August 2003, p. 13220. The Breton Law of 2005 (Law no. 2005-842 of 26 July 2005, *Official Gazette* no. 173 of 27 July 2005) has limited the scope of the internal control reporting requirements to French joint stock companies; and Law no. 2008-649 of 3 July 2008 portant diverses dispositions d'adaptation du droit des sociétés au droit communautaire, *Official Gazette* no. 155 of 4 July 2008, p. 10705, further elaborated the requirements.
11 Article 4, para. 2, subpara. (c) and Article 5, para. 4, Directive 2004/109/EG of the European Parliament and of the Council of 15 December 2004 on the harmonisation of transparency requirements with regard to

information about issuers whose securities are admitted to trading on a regulated market, OJ L 390, 31 December 2004, p. 38.

12 Article 2 under (3), Commission Regulation (EC) No. 809/2004 of 29 April 2004 implementing Directive 2003/71/EC of the European Parliament and of the Council as regards information contained in prospectuses as well as the format, incorporation by reference and publication of such prospectuses and dissemination of advertisements, OJ L 149, 30 April 2004, p. 1.

13 Article 1, para. 7, subpara. (c), Directive 2006/46/EC of 14 June 2006 of the European Parliament and of the Council amending Council Directives 78/660/EEC on the annual accounts of certain types of companies, 83/349/EEC on consolidated accounts, 86/635/EEC on the annual accounts and consolidated accounts of banks and other financial institutions, and 91/674/EEC on the annual accounts and consolidated accounts of insurance undertakings, OJ L 224, 16 August 2006, p. 1.

14 Article 2, para. 2, Directive 2006/46/EC.

15 Article 41, para. 2, subparas. (a) and (b), Directive 2006/43/EC of 17 May 2006 of the European Parliament and of the Council on statutory audits of annual accounts and consolidated accounts, amending Council Directives 78/660/EEC and 83/349/EEC and repealing Council Directive 84/253/EEC, OJ L 157, 9 June 2006, p. 87.

16 Article 41, para. 4, Directive 2006/43/EC.

17 The Hampel Committee was established in November 1995 on the initiative of the Chairman of the Financial Reporting Council (Sir Sydney Lipworth).

18 Article 225-35 section 3 of the French Commercial Code.

19 Both reports can be downloaded from www.amf-france.org, last accessed 15 June 2010.

20 Law of 6 April 2010 tot versterking van het deugdelijk bestuur bij de genoteerde vennootschappen en de autonome overheidsbedrijven en tot wijziging van de regeling inzake het beroepsverbod in de banken financiële sector, *Official Gazette* of 23 April 2010, p. 22709.

21 The detailed results are on file with the author.

22 See, for example, Article 528 Belgian Companies Code. Directors who had no part in the infringement must act in compliance with a specific procedure to be exempted from liability.

23 'Duty to guarantee'.

References

Belgian Commission on Corporate Governance 1998. *Recommendations of the Market Authority of the Brussels Stock Exchange.*
2004. *The Belgian Code on Corporate Governance.*

2009. *The Belgian Code on Corporate Governance.*

CNPF-AFEP 2005. *The Board of Directors of Listed Companies in France.*

Committee of Sponsoring Organizations of the Treadway Commission (COSO II) 2004. *Enterprise Risk Management: Integrated Framework, Executive Summary.* New York: AICPA Inc.

2009a. *Effective Enterprise Risk Oversight: The Role of the Board of Directors.* New York: AICPA Inc.

2009b. *Strengthening Enterprise Risk Management for Strategic Advantage.* New York: AICPA Inc.

Committee on Corporate Governance 1997. *Recommendations of Corporate Governance in the Netherlands.*

Committee on the Financial Aspects of Corporate Governance 2002. *The Financial Aspects of Corporate Governance.* London: GEE.

Corporate Governance Code Monitoring Committee 2008. *The Dutch Corporate Governance Code: Principles of Good Corporate Governance and Best Practice Provisions (DCGC).*

De Jager, J. 2010. 'Letter of the Minister of Finance', available at www.dnb.nl/openboek/extern/file/dnb_tcm40-197407.pdf, last accessed 15 April 2010.

De Wulf, H. 2002. *Taak en Loyauteitsplicht van het Bestuur in de Naamloze Vennootschap.* Antwerp: Intersentia.

Dobler, M. 2003. 'Auditing corporate risk management: a critical analysis of a German particularity', *LMU Paper 2001–2003*, Dresden University, Germany.

European Commission 2005. Commission Recommendation of 15 February 2005 on the role of non-executive or supervisory directors of listed companies and on the committees of the (supervisory) board, OJ L 52 of 25 February.

European Corporate Governance Forum 2006. *Statement on Risk Management and Internal Control*, available at http://ec.europa.eu/internal_market/company/ecgforum/index_en.htm, last accessed 15 April 2010.

FEE 2009. *Discussion Paper for Auditor's Role Regarding Providing Assurance on Corporate Governance Statements.*

Financial Reporting Council 2003. *The Combined Code on Corporate Governance.* London: CCH.

2005. *Internal Control: Revised Guidance for Directors on the Combined Code.* London.

2008. *Guidance on Audit Committees*, available at www.frc.org.uk/corporate/auditcommittees.cfm. last accessed 15 April 2010.

2010. *UK Corporate Governance Code.*

German Panel on Corporate Governance 2000. *Corporate Governance Rules for Quoted German Companies.*

Government Commission 2002. *German Corporate Governance Code.*

2005. *German Corporate Governance Code.*

Hampel Committee 1998. *Committee on Corporate Governance – Final Report (Hampel Report).* London: Gee.

Mutter, S. and Quincke, D. 2009. 'Vorstand und Aufsichtsrat – Garanten-stellung bei pflichtwidriger Compliance', *Die Aktiengesellschaft* 54 R: 416–R418.

NVB 2009. *Banking Code.*

Rayton, B. and Cheng, S. 2004. 'Corporate governance in the United Kingdom: Changes to the regulatory template and company practice from 1998 to 2002', University of Bath Working Paper No. 2004/13.

Schmidt, K. and Lutter, M. 2008. *Aktiengesetz Kommentar.* Cologne: O. Schmidt Verlag.

Spira, L. and Page, M. 2003. 'Risk management: the reinvention of internal control and the changing role of internal audit', *Accounting, Auditing & Accountability Journal* 16 (4): 640–61.

Tabaksblat Committee (Corporate Governance Committee) 2003. *The Dutch Corporate Governance Code: Principles of Good Corporate Governance and Best Practice Provisions.*

Turnbull Committee 1999. *Internal Control: Guidance for Directors on the Combined Code.* London: ICAEW.

van Daelen, M. 2008. 'Risk management solutions in business law: prospectus disclosure requirements', Tilburg University Business Law Working Paper, available at http://papers.ssrn.com/sol3/papers.cfm?abstract_id=1287624, last accessed 15 April 2010.

van Daelen, M. and van de Ven, A. 2010. 'Introducing risk management', in van Daelen, M. and Van der Elst, C. (eds.), *Risk Management and Corporate Governance: Interconnections in Law, Accounting and Tax.* Cheltenham: Edward Elgar Publishing, pp. 1–10.

VBO/FEB 1998. *Corporate Governance Recommendations.*

Post-crisis corporate governance: the search for new directions

Introduction to Part III

The contributions in the final part explore and point to new directions for corporate governance research and reforms as a post-crisis agenda. Peer Zumbansen begins by questioning the current functional and ahistorical approach in comparative law and corporate governance research, which is more interested in exploring and designing regulatory responses towards the quick 'fixing' of the system failures, without a fundamental understanding of the changing, evolving and increasingly complex nature of the business corporation and its regulatory environment. Examining the evolution of European capital market law and corporate governance harmonization, he recognizes the increasingly multilevel and trans-territorialized norm production in corporate governance as an ephemeral 'double movement': the attempted liberation of the national regulatory constraints as required by business globalization on the one side, and the inevitably embedded nature of corporate norms in distinct socio-economic cultures and historically grown legal and institutional frameworks on the other side. Zumbansen argues that the rapid developments of globalization of markets, information technology, knowledge economy and the 'financialization' of the corporation have opened up regulatory spaces and transformed formal rule creation in politically embedded state legal systems towards an emerging system of decentralized and specialized transnational regulatory regimes that unfolds in a web of hard and soft laws, which blur the regulatory boundaries between national and international, public and private, formal and informal. This phenomenon is what he calls 'transnational legal pluralism', the new embeddedness of the firm.

Florian Möslein is unsatisfied with the conventional explanation that the financial crisis rested upon the narrow understanding of hierarchical governance within corporations, and calls for an open and wider understanding of the governance issues in the whole contractual relationships and networks in the financial markets in which corporations are embedded, what he terms 'contract governance'. He notes that the most important developments of corporate governance reforms after the financial crisis at the European and national level have been focused mainly on the architecture of financial markets rather than on the governance of companies. He then compares contract governance with corporate governance and shows some differences, similarities and interlinks, and points to some challenges for future research between the two.

James Shinn examines the effects of the financial crisis of 2008–9 on corporate governance in a sample of developed and emerging markets, evaluating both the Investor model and the Pension Preferences model of corporate governance change (the former model refers to change through 'private ordering' mechanisms, the latter refers to change through 'public ordering' mechanisms). Using data from the Federation of European Stock Exchanges, the OECD and Risk-Metrics, he repeats a 1990s test of the effects of two independent variables – the foreign investor penetration rate that is central to the Investor model and the private pension assets to GDP ratio that is stressed by the Pension Preferences model – on the dependent variable of country-level governance rankings. As in the 1990s test, the results suggest little or no correlation between changes in corporate governance and foreign investor penetration, but a strong correlation between country-level corporate governance rankings and pension assets to GDP. Based on these results, he speculates briefly on the impact of three main features of the Great Recession – the financial sector trigger, dramatic asset repricing and ensuing fiscal deficits – on these two models of corporate governance change. He concludes that although mixed in direction and amplitude, these effects appear to have attenuated some of the mechanisms of the Investor model while amplifying some of the mechanisms of the Pension Preferences model.

Nasser Saidi's chapter leads us to corporate governance regimes in a different cultural background and examines corporate governance issues in Islamic financial institutions. Saidi finds that Islamic financial institutions have displayed more resilience amid the global financial crisis because of the stricter rules imposed on lending and investment by Islamic law. This may support the argument that sound corporate governance could be both principle-based and rule-based. However, he notes that the Islamic financial industry is not risk immune (for instance, it remains exposed in its investments to the weaknesses of the real estate market in the Gulf countries), and its risk management architecture and culture are not more robust than non-Islamic financial institutions (for example, there is a need for risk and liquidity management due to a prohibition on investing in hedging instruments in most jurisdictions and the lack of instruments with short-term maturities). Islamic finance has transcended borders and regions but many challenges lie ahead before it can make that crucial leap from being an interesting but niche market to being an integral part of the global financial market. Finally, he suggests that the way out of the global financial crisis is through *intelligent regulation*, one that does not pre-empt or hinder market-driven adjustments, but supports and strengthens financial innovation and the market, and does so through creating and maintaining a culture of transparency and accountability.

Finally, Suzanne Young and Vijaya Thyil's chapter calls for a holistic, multiple-disciplinary approach, integrating multiple lenses and perspectives in understanding corporate governance practices as a post-crisis research direction. They argue that the conventional dominance of an economic or legal approach to corporate governance is rather limited, as it excludes wider and crucial variables that collectively impact effective governance. While every variable in the governance system should be considered to ensure effectiveness, some variables are more important than others depending on the situation and environment, thus pointing to a contingency approach. In the current post-crisis time, a balance between compliance and behavioural approaches is important – regulation to ensure timely and valid disclosure and good structures, alongside a focus on ethics, culture, leadership, power and human resource practices to ensure that organizational objectives are met in an ethical manner.

12 | Corporate governance, capital market regulation and the challenge of disembedded markets

PEER ZUMBANSEN

Long before the present investigations into the role of corporate governance regulation in the coming of the financial crisis (Cheffins, 2009), corporate law had long become a highly dynamic regulatory laboratory for the study of a fast-transforming body of norms governing corporate activities worldwide. The immense attention that the field has been attracting over the past thirty years from legal scholars, economists, political scientists, sociologists and even psychologists (Aguilera *et al.*, 2004) amply testifies to the increasingly interdisciplinary nature of corporate governance. Partly, this development is owed to the dramatic transformation of corporate law over the recent past, mostly influenced by the rapid expansion of global capital markets, which have placed enormous pressure on the different existing national legal cultures pertaining to company law, labour law and industrial relations regulation. The international competition over investment and the innovation of ever-new and more flexible financial instruments have over time induced a fundamental transformation of corporate governance that is frequently referred to as a rise of 'financialism' (Mitchell, 2011; Zumbansen, 2011) and which has led to a far-reaching change in the understanding of the business corporation from an organizational entity geared towards economic growth to an investment vehicle with a very particular set of expectations attached to it (Lazonick, 1991). The nature and consequences of this transformation have been a constant cause of dispute: whereas one camp has been voicing, in sometimes triumphalist mode,[1] the inevitable convergence of corporate governance systems towards a model focused on shareholder value maximization (Kraakman *et al.*, 2009), scholars in the other camp have been questioning this alleged

This chapter builds on Zumbansen, 2009 and 2010a. It was written while I was Visiting Professor at University College Dublin 2009–2010 and my June–August 2010 Fellowship at the Hanse Institute of Advanced Study. I am grateful for conversations on the topic with Blanaid Clarke and Colin Scott.

convergence on the basis of a host of different sets of evidence, drawing on comparative political economy (Vitols, 2001; Cioffi, 2006), comparative company law (Siems and Deakin, 2009) and historical research (Deakin, 2011). Taken together, until just about the outbreak of the financial crisis, 'corporate governance' had no doubt become one among the most interesting instances for an interdisciplinary study of how market regulation rules unfold, are administered and governed. Such investigations emerged against the background of an increasingly rich body of comparative research (see the excellent overview by Hopt, 2006) and branched out into fascinating inquiries into the changing modes of corporate organization, corporate finance and corporate 'democracy' on the one hand (for example, Dhir, 2006), and into the particular nature of norms that govern corporate behaviour on the other (Baums, 2001). All along, the *political* dimensions of such research were anything but invisible: large-scale corporate scandals around firms such as Enron or Parmalat (Bratton, 2002), headline-making transnational takeovers such as the Mannesmann-Vodafone deal (Höpner and Jackson, 2001; Kolla, 2004; Maier, 2006) or the public concern over management compensation (Bebchuk and Fried, 2004; Calliess and Zumbansen, 2010) had long illustrated the political connotations of corporate governance regulation (Gourevitch, 2003; Gourevitch and Shinn, 2005; Shinn, Chapter 14 in this volume). Remarkable, however, in this debate was the discrepancy between a seemingly instant public outrage in the face of blatant corporate misdeeds and a relative amnesia with regard to the only relatively recently changed environment in which the triumph of shareholder value maximization had become the norm, not the exception. Well into the 1960s, corporations – not only in Europe, but also in the United States – had been embedded in a tightly woven regulatory infrastructure that created a politically charged environment for 'private commercial activity' (Reich, 2007).

After the 'roaring 1990s' (J. Stiglitz) and an obsession with short-term value creation over the span of the last two-and-a-half decades, the financial crisis has put all this into a new light. But the amnesia is still there, as if to show that there just is no learning from the past. While the forceful debate over convergence versus divergence of corporate governance models would be a rich reservoir of stored knowledge and insights into the different regulatory systems and company law cultures that will inevitably shape any regulatory response envisioned today, the present soul-searching is strangely disinterested in drawing on that background. Instead, the dominant concern seems to be to curb the 'excesses' and the 'failures' of the regulatory apparatus that is understood to have been at the root cause of the present calamities. There is considerable evidence that the currently explored and designed regulatory 'responses' are geared more towards the 'fixing' of the system that has prevailed over the past thirty years than towards a fundamental revisiting of the – existing – comparative and historical evidence as to the complex nature of the business corporation, its regulatory environment and the historical record of its evolution.[2]

The present chapter argues against such an ahistoric approach. It furthermore points to the comparative and legal theoretical insights into differently evolving corporate governance regimes as a basis for a better understanding of the particular nature of regulating corporate activities today.

Beyond comparisons: the emergence of transnational corporate governance

While comparative corporate or, in the English usage, *company* law researchers have come a long way in illuminating the embedded nature of historically evolved, socio-economically shaped corporate governance models (see, for example, Cioffi, 2000; Rebérioux, 2002; O'Sullivan, 2003; Deakin, 2007), it seems as if – motivated by a cross-fertilization of different disciplinary approaches (see, for example, the brilliant study by Klöhn, 2006) – scholars are now more than before engaged in both comparative and interdisciplinary studies of existing corporate governance regulations. This is surely one, but not the only, important prerequisite for any study of corporate governance today. To the degree that corporate governance has become a multilevel regulatory laboratory, in which 'hard' law overlaps and intersects with 'soft' law in numerous, fast-evolving ways, a traditional approach to the study of corporate or company law as a relatively confined doctrinal area soon reaches its limits. The present context of public and private norm creating actors engaged in the formulation, implementation and enforcement of corporate governance norms illustrates the need to expand corporate law's analytical toolkit as well as to understand corporate governance regulation in a wider context of increasingly transnational market regulation (Calliess and Zumbansen, 2010, chapter 4).

Today's transnational corporate governance regulation is a product of fundamental transformations of regulatory instruments and institutions. As corporate law is being shaped by a complex mix of public, private, state- and non-state-based norms, principles and rules, generated, disseminated and monitored by a diverse set of actors,[3] a closer look at corporate governance offers two insights: one concerns the way in which the analysis of contemporary corporate governance regulation can help us assess the emerging new framework within which corporate governance rules are evolving. The second is the way in which we begin to understand the emerging regulatory framework as an illustration of contemporary rule-making; the legal pluralist deconstruction of formal and informal legal orders can be seen in a new light. Building, on the one hand, on early legal-sociological work by Ehrlich ('living law', Ehrlich, 1962) and Gurvitch ('social law', Gurvitch, 1947), this inquiry revisits the core question of any sociology of law, namely 'to investigate the correlations between law and other spheres of culture' (Rheinstein, 1941; Gurvitch, 1947; Ehrlich, 1962).

For the purposes of this chapter, our focus will be on the tension between law and *alternative* modes of market regulation. Expanding the spectrum, on the other hand, with a view to 'legal pluralism' (Moore, 1973; Galanter, 1981; Macaulay, 1986; Santos, 1987; Teubner, 1992, 2004) contemporary assessments of 'hybrid legal spaces' (Berman, 2007, p. 1155; also Sassen, 2006) that are not sufficiently captured with references to local or national contexts can help us better understand the distinctly *transnational* character of such regulatory regimes. The transnational lens allows us to study such regimes not as entirely detached from national political and legal orders, but as emerging out of and reaching beyond them (for a discussion, see Zumbansen, 2006 and Scott, 2009). The transnational dimension of new actors and newly emerging forms of norms radicalizes their 'semi-autonomous' nature (S. F. Moore) in the following way: regulatory spaces are marked by a dynamic and often problematic instrumentalist tension between *formal* and *informal* norm-making processes, which cannot easily be subjected to a political critique because the co-existence of hard and soft laws does not necessarily or always reflect on a strategy of depoliticization. Instead, the choice of different modes of regulations has its origin most frequently in a situation in which political disagreement is only *one* among several road-blocks for effective regulation or legal reform.[4] Other problems are likely to result out of complex constellations of different overlapping and colliding norm-making authorities, something that has been shaping regulation attempts in different transnational governance regimes, from securities regulation (Black and Rouch, 2008; Möllers, 2008), corporate governance, labour law (Supiot, 1999; Atleson *et al.*, 2008), to contract law in general (Basedow, 1996) and consumer protection law in particular (Calliess, 2002a, 2006). These areas are increasingly marked by the existence of opt-out clauses and self-regulation mechanisms rather than being defined by enforceable hard-law rules. The dynamic character of such transnational regulatory regimes poses distinct challenges for a political theory of market regulation, which seems to be at least one of the several goals pursued within the present crisis-response soul-search. The framework for a distinctly political critique of crisis-response regulation is today anything but certain. As has long been recognized, even with, in the case of the EU, the goal of an internal market in view, any attempt at the harmonization of norms and the institutionalization of an administrative framework is inevitably confronted with the particular dynamics of historically grown national legal and political cultures and the still, in many ways contested, overarching economic and political project of the EU. The sobering critique of the allegedly unbearable costs of Europe's 'Social Model'[5] only aggravates the already frustrating efforts of confronting the current disembeddedness of global markets, which is one of the most important underlying themes in today's critique of 'supercapitalism' (Haunschild, 2004; Reich, 2007) and which received its most pertinent critique by Karl Polanyi in his 1944 treatise on 'The Great Transformation'.

The problem of disembeddedness

In his famous chapters on 'Societies and Economic Systems' and the 'Evolution of the Market Pattern', which we today refer to for the concept of the embeddedness of the market, Polanyi noted, that 'though the institution of the market was fairly common since the later Stone Age, its role was no more than incidental to economic life'.[6] A little later, he remarked that:

the outstanding discovery of recent historical and anthropological research is that man's economy, as a rule, is submerged in his social relationships. [. . .] Neither the process of production nor that of distribution is linked to specific economic interests attached to the possession of goods; but every single step in that process is geared to a number of social interests which eventually will be very different in a small hunting or fishing community than those in a vast despotic society, but in either case the economic system will be run on non-economic motives. (Polanyi, 1944, p. 46)

As is well known, that chapter (4) concludes with the elaboration of the three famous market-structuring and market-organizing principles: 'reciprocity' (related to family and kinship), 're-distribution' (the central collection and dissemination of production – '. . . these functions of an economic system proper are completely absorbed by the intensely vivid experiences which offer superabundant non-economic motivation for every act performed in the frame of the social system as a whole' (Polanyi, 1944, p. 48)), and 'householding' (*oeco-nomia*), which precedes the rising levels of division of labour, as well as the role of money and credit. Building on this taxonomy, Polanyi famously wrote that: 'the control of the economic system by the market is of overwhelming consequence to the whole organization of society: it means no less than the running of society as an adjunct to the market. Instead of economy being embedded in social relations, social relations are embedded in the economic system' (Polanyi, 1944, p. 57).

It is here, where, as under a magnifying glass, we not only find the kernel of the critique of capitalism unfolding in the latter half of the twentieth century (see, for example, Derrida, 1994; Rorty, 1998), but also a powerful illustration of the differentiation concept of contemporary modern sociology, most strikingly, the thesis of the hegemony of the economic system in a functionally differentiated society (Luhmann, 1988). Again, in Polanyi's words:

The vital importance of the economic factor to the existence of society precludes any other result. For once the economic system is organized in separate institutions, based on specific motives and conferring a special status, society must be shaped in such a manner as to allow that system to function according to its own laws. This is the meaning of the familiar assertion that a market economy can function only in a market society (Polanyi, 1944, p. 57).

A little further on, Polanyi added a devastatingly prophetic observation of competitive markets and short-termism by noting that 'with every step that the state took to rid the market of particularist restrictions, of tolls and prohibitions, it imperilled the organized system of production and distribution which was now threatened by unregulated competition and the intrusion of the interloper who "scooped" the market but offered no guarantee of permanency' (Polanyi, 1944, p. 66).

But in which way, if at all, can Polanyi help us think through the challenges of crisis-response market regulation? Can his observations offer analytical tools for an adequate explanation of contemporary markets? I want to suggest that we look for an answer through a detour. Using corporate governance and capital market regulation as an illustration of the evolution of transnational markets, we can canvass a number of theoretical approaches that directly or indirectly draw upon Polanyi's critique of disembeddedness. Even where contemporary regulators, policymakers and EU law, company law and securities regulation scholars do not engage with Polanyi per se, the pertinence of his assessment of the transformation of states, societies and markets is, nevertheless, both evident and crucial for our assessment of the argumentative and conceptual context in which a re-formulation of Polanyi's embeddedness theme would have to take place.

As such, the following observations can be at best cursory comments on the evolving institutional and conceptual dimensions of 'market regulation' or 'state intervention' in the areas of capital market law and corporate governance. While, geographically, the chapter draws on examples from the EU, the regulatory regimes concerned can more adequately be understood as 'global assemblages' in the sense introduced by the sociologist Saskia Sassen.[7] Building on her work, I understand these regulatory regimes as examples of *transnational legal pluralism* (Zumbansen, 2009 and 2010b). They are, on the one hand, neither exclusively national (domestic) nor international, while, on the other, they are not meant to eliminate or to overcome the nation state (Sassen, 2006, p. 325). Instead, these assemblages are constituted through persistent local activity and interpretation, and are – as such – comprised of human, institutional and technological elements, the latter resulting predominantly from the breathtaking advances in information technology ('digitalizations')[8] and the extreme acceleration in information, knowledge and capital transfer they made available. It is the precarious relation between national and global governance regimes that speaks to the continuing need for a specifically legal perspective on the reconfiguration of 'spaces and places', which Sassen depicts in her work. And it is this emphasis on the *legal* theoretical reconstruction of Polanyi's theme of embeddedness that holds considerable promise for rendering a timely concept of transnational markets.

The remainder of the chapter is structured as follows: first, I will contrast the regulatory strategies pursued in the two areas of capital market law and corporate governance in the EU. The central assumption of this complementary presentation of these two areas, which have seen a surge in regulatory activity – in both Europe and beyond – is that, in particular, the transformation of corporate finance during the last two decades has led to a far-reaching approximation of both areas. This is a remarkable development, as it raises intriguing questions regarding, for one, the methodology that informs the conceptual construction and the demarcation of legal doctrinal fields. In other words, how and why do we (continue to) distinguish between capital market law and corporate governance (law)? Secondly, the apparent overlapping and inter-twining of these two distinct regulatory areas presents formidable challenges for our understanding of the law and the specific regulatory instruments that are relied upon to govern each or both of the areas concerned.

In the next section, I will reflect on the driving forces behind the continuing regulatory reform process in both areas and discuss recurring concepts such as 'maximum', 'minimum' or 'reflexive' harmonization and regulatory competition against the analysis of Polanyi's market embeddedness and the work on the so-called 'Varieties of Capitalism' studies (Hollingsworth, 1998; Hall and Soskice, 2001). The last section seeks to provide an explanation for the particular forms of legal regulatory regimes that are emerging in the named areas by elaborating the concept of transnational legal pluralism.

Capital market regulation and corporate governance

In search of a harmonized European securities market

Only a very abbreviated overview and assessment of the developments made with regard to the regulation of capital market law in recent times can be provided here. One of the central insights one can gain from the fast evolving scholarly work in this area seems to be that long-term, economic growth in Europe is closely linked to an effectively and supportively regulated securities market. Namely, the European Commission and the European Court of Justice (ECJ) have been playing decisive roles in the context of shaping a continuously evolving, regulatory framework in this area. Central to the Commission's regulatory efforts was the 1999 release of the Financial Services Action Plan (FSAP), which spurred a tremendously dynamic series of legislative initiatives in its wake. The FSAP came into being at a time when there was very little movement and even less advancement in the area of corporate law harmonization – some even spoke of an 'almost empty' agenda (Enriques and Gatti, 2007b, p. 4). Programmatic and regulatory initiatives in the context of the FSAP have included the inauguration of the Lamfalussy Commission, which, in 2001, after the release of a preliminary report and the initiation of a consultation process, produced its comprehensive final report, in which it addressed and discussed both the challenges and the need to work towards an efficient and dynamic securities market in Europe.[9] Echoing the views shared by a wide spectrum of scholars and practitioners in the field, the Report identified, from the outset, the immediate necessity to bring swift reform to the existing regulatory framework in European financial regulation. This reform had become necessary mainly in the light of the breathtaking advances made in financial activity around the world over the previous 15–20 years, the consequences of which, for securities regulation on the one hand, and for corporate (organization and finance) law on the other, were becoming increasingly obvious (see, for example, Möllers, 2008, p. 482).

Despite the fact that the FSAP regulatory initiatives are characterized by a very recent history, the wide-ranging assessments of their structure, aspirations, their successes and their shortcomings fast filled symposia, edited collections and bibliographies, not to mention the abundance of working papers appearing, in short succession, in the Social Science Research Network (www.ssrn.com). Central to the debates surrounding the state of the European Financial Market after the introduction of a number of directives has been the concern over the inconsistency of the implementation of the directives on the part of the individual Member States. The verdict, for the time being at least, is that due to the many political differences on the one hand, and the existing variations of securities regulation institutions across Europe on the other, a harmonized securities market is still a long way off (Enriques and Gatti, 2007a). Examined closely, the Prospectus,[10] Market Abuse,[11] Takeover Bids[12] and Transparency[13] Directives and the Rating Agencies Regulation[14] allow a range of varying implementation regimes that are altogether committed to the idea of 'optionality',[15] but, as a consequence, fall short of bringing about an effectively levelled playing field for actors in the European Market. At the same time, the Lamfalussy Commission strengthened and formalized the operation of a monitoring mechanism, embodied by the European Securities Committee (ESC) on the one hand, and the Committee of European Securities Regulators (CESR) on the other. These committees play an important role in the evolving multi-polar and multilevel process of European securities regulation.[16] After the political orientation has been identified through the Council and the Parliament, the Commission and the Parliament – in collaboration with the ESC and the CESR – design the more concrete implementation and execution procedures. It is after this process that, in a third step, the CESR, through the different regulatory agencies that it brings together, produces recommendations and benchmark standards. Despite the fact that these recommendations and benchmarks are without legally binding power, they are, nevertheless, meant to provide a compellingly coherent reference mark for the implementation of the measures introduced. In a fourth and final step, the Commission is in charge to assess whether the implementation of the regulations has been successful.

The particular dynamics of this regulatory area raise significant questions concerning the way in which legislative goals are being identified, which interests are being considered, and how these feed into both the constitution and the re-constitution of distinct doctrinal and conceptual fields (see Alford, 2006). As in other areas, notably European contract law and, more specifically, European consumer protection law (Calliess, 2002b; Howells and Wilhelmsson, 2003; Mattei and Nicola, 2006), the pursuit of a European regulatory framework in capital markets law and corporate governance occurs against highly charged assessments of the underlying assumptions and goals that inform the regulatory process. In this context, market efficiency represents a highly persuasive formula which, when studied more closely, does not – in itself – contain much clarification as to the interests and goals that are actually being pursued. This dilemma, which certainly seems to plague any reform agenda in complex regulatory areas, is further exacerbated by the fact that the European securities market (or, the 'European Company Law Scene') (Schmitthoff, 1973) constitutes an even more complex arena and context than a historically evolved regulatory area in a particular state.[17] As will be argued more fully below, substantive law reforms in Europe regularly occur against the backdrop of the open-ended European integration project.

Before I briefly highlight the particular dimensions of European corporate governance regulation (ECGR), I shall pause for a moment to reflect upon the connections between capital market law and corporate governance. The different speeds at which each area has been developing in Europe could suggest that it would, indeed, be possible to distinguish neatly between them as clearly distinct, conceptually and doctrinally contained, regulatory areas. However, there are several elements at play, which point in the opposite direction, and which I briefly want to allude to under the heading of the 'financialization of the corporation'.

The financialization of the corporation

Since the 1960s, the transformation of the corporation has led to a widely held acceptance of subjecting every element of a business firm to varied processes of financialization,[18] which was spurred by a number of path-breaking innovations in financial economics that eventually prepared the ground for a new 'theory of the firm' (Alchian and Demsetz, 1972; Jensen, 2000) and was over time complemented by a fast proliferating landscape of investment actors (Partnoy and Thomas, 2007). This transformation affected corporations throughout the world and was driven by the attempt to effectively attract a highly diversified investment of global investment pools. Far-reaching deregulation with regard to capital control during the 1980s facilitated an unprecedented flow of capital across national boundaries, which permitted securitizations, often repeatedly, of a large number of assets, including pension schemes, real estate and commercial claims. With companies designing corporate strategies primarily with stock performance in mind, shareholder value became the dominating principle in assessing corporate performance, fuelled by a seemingly unstoppable growth in index values.

The focus on the short-term volatility of corporate shares in order to evaluate a company's merits and prospects quickly became the *only* perspective from which we claimed to understand a firm (Lazonick and O'Sullivan, 2002). But this narrowing of the field of vision came at a price, as both investors and managers became blind to the fact that the very environment of firms had been dramatically transformed over the course of a few decades. To the degree that the advancement of communication and information technology revolutionized the transfer of derivatives – sometimes as a company's virtual assets – across vast strategic spaces, the attention given to stock performance eventually removed the firm from its geographical environment by elevating it into a purely ethereal realm. In consequence of its financialization, the share or other security of the corporation (its 'reference asset' for the creation of another synthetic security) became radically virtualized. What architects of synthetic credit instruments call the reference asset, which can be the original subject of a loan or security, became radically virtualized in relation to the business corporation. The corporation, in turn, was reduced to an anchoring point for independently originated financial programmes, thereby positioning the corporation no longer in a real economy, but in an artificial space of financial engineering.

In the end, the firm – as we have come to understand it over the past thirty years – had outgrown even the ideal model of a nexus of contracts (Alchian and Demsetz, 1972; Jensen, 2000). In order to remain operational, the model had to be adapted to the processes of financial engineering, which – at least partially – moved the corporation out of the centre of the labyrinth of contracts in which it was, or its securities were, entangled. The financialization of the corporation and its securities entailed a radical separation of the corporation itself from the instruments that represent claims in, of or against the corporation. The corporation had become a nodal point for an ephemeral crossing, the inter-linking and overlapping of financial vectors, channelled through the glass structure of the legal person, with almost no relationship with the original 'business' of the corporation. A dream fulfilled, with money flowing in and out of the firm, the corporation had become a virtual realm for strategic investment.

The financialization of corporate governance is powerfully reflected in the fast rise in importance of financial experts on the boards of directors, the importance of financial expertise in the making of business decisions and, finally, in the transformation of the educational environment for the supporting professions – including lawyers, consultancies and accountants. The flip-side of this is the dramatic erosion of the representation of labour interests in the contemporary business corporation (Deakin, 2011). Where corporate activity had, for a long time, been marked by a lively public political discussion of the interests of the different constituencies in the firm, its financial and physical virtualization[19] increasingly erased the reference points for a general assessment of what corporations were actually doing.

As suggested above, the financialization of the corporation led to significant changes in the corporate regulatory framework. The financialization of the business corporation, which, arguably, had always been part of the corporate identity (Mitchell, 2007), does not, however, exhaust itself, either in the adaptation of corporate finance to the globally available, highly diversified investment tools and opportunities, or in the wide-ranging turn of regulatory policy towards shareholder value, which gave rise to the 'corporate governance movement' of the last decade in both corporate law theory and practice. Moreover, the financialization paradigm eventually led to a dramatic reconfiguration of the 'embedded corporation' (Jacoby, 2004) by upsetting and shifting the institutional framework of the corporation's regulatory environment (Hoffmann, 2004; Cioffi, 2006), with tremendous consequences at both the domestic *and* the transnational level. As national governments found themselves drawn into highly charged political debates regarding the goals of company law reform, which were themselves increasingly likened to existential questions of national survival (Baums, 2001), the European law-maker, too, came under growing pressure to follow up on long-standing promises and aspirations to work towards a more effective level playing field for European companies.

The turns of European corporate governance

Against this background, it is unsurprising that the history of European corporate law regulation is marked by the diversity of the interests and concerns invested in this area of regulation. While the legislative record was, until recently, not altogether comprehensive (Edwards, 1999; Wouters, 2000; Hopt, 2005), ECGR has, in recent years, become one of the most vibrant sectors of norm-creation and regulatory interaction. As such, ECGR has become a regulatory universe of its own, with a large portfolio within the Commission's Internal Market division, and a seemingly tireless expert community feeding into the policymaking and norm-making processes at every turn. With ECGR long having left the confines of the European Court of Justice, the Council and the Parliament, it has expanded into an extremely versatile, comparative and transnational legal field. ECGR constitutes a *semi-autonomous* field, comprised both of hard law and social norms, which are in a constant relationship of complementarity, fusion and irritation (Moore, 1973). As such, ECGR presents formidable challenges for legal, economic, sociological or political analysis. From the point of view of legal pluralism, the particularity and the intricacy of ECGR lies in its mixed constitution of law and 'social norms' (see, generally, Merry, 1988). Seen through the legal pluralist lens, ECGR develops as a co-evolutionary process, in which the imposition of law – which encompasses regulations, directives, recommendations and judgments – is both shaping *and* being shaped by the norms evolving outside of its imposition. Similar to the unpredictability of the consequences and the effects of rights/principles-transplants (Teubner, 2001; Pistor, 2003), ECGR faces enormous challenges in terms of both legal certainty and strategy, given its many sources of potential disturbance, irritation and complementing points, due to its complex regulatory agenda.

Adding to the difficulties arising from the multilevel and multi-stakeholder dimension in company law regulation in Europe, ECGR has amplified the tensions that underlie the conceptual and architectural distinction between 'company' and 'capital market' law, which are deeply embedded in a country's market regulation history (Wiethölter, 1961; Buxbaum and Hopt, 1988; Kübler, 2001; Merkt, 2003; Moloney, 2003; Eidenmüller, 2007; for the United States, see, only, Romano, 2005). Struggling with competing policy goals regarding the enhancement of market freedoms as they relate to capital market rules, on the one hand, and to corporate governance law, on the other, ECGR is driven to actualize 'the best of both worlds'. However, while corporate law itself appears to continue to withstand all attempts at deconstruction and demystification by other conceptual frameworks with regard to what corporations actually do (see Clark, 1986), ECGR finds itself deeply entangled in a large, increasingly amorphous market-building project. The understanding of the 'function' of the firm, as it informs ECGR, must now extend far beyond the financial-organizational dimensions that became the 'what', 'how' and 'why' of corporate law. Within the European project, in particular after the Lisbon Summit 2000 and its more recent reinvigoration in the form of a 'social makeover',[20] corporate law has become a strategic token in a complex multilevel governance game that brings a much wider range of players to the policymaking table than any single-market regulation unit would reasonably want to assume responsibility for.

ECGR, driven by pressing competitive, social, environmental and monitoring demands, continues to evolve in the particularly accentuated and contested space of the competitiveness agendas of the EU Member States. As such, ECGR has never sat comfortably within the wider market integration agenda. The real challenges of company law harmonization, however, became impressively obvious during the exhausting struggle over the adoption of a regulation concerning the creation of the European Company statute, originally initiated in the 1970s, and eventually passed, after many more compromises, in 2001. Another illustration of how ECGR has been inextricably caught up in the European 'Varieties of Capitalism' was, without doubt, the long contest over a European Takeover directive, which resulted, in 2004, in a directive full of loopholes and opt-out clauses.[21]

As the regulatory trajectory of ECGR continues to unfold, we must be even more sensitive to the degree to which this enterprise remains deeply embedded in the particular dynamics of the multilevel governance of European integration, on the one hand (Sabel and Zeitlin, 2008), and the globalization of markets and regulatory processes, on the other (see, for example, Rodrik, 2000). Under such conditions, an assessment of the concrete forms of norm-creation presents great challenges due to ECGR's complex appearance, which ranges from 'hard' to 'soft' law, to norms that are developed, promulgated and disseminated by a panoply of public and private actors (Joerges and Neyer, 1997; Trubek and Trubek, 2005). Thus, instead of trying to free ECGR from its embeddedness in this complex regulatory environment, the emphasis must be on the exact opposite. It is precisely by embracing the embeddedness of ECGR as a *transnational legal field* that we can begin to see the concrete, as well as the amorphous, forms of change more clearly. Embeddedness, here, is understood in the following four dimensions:

(1) ECGR is informed by the policy and legislative dynamics between corporate law and capital market law (securities regulation) as well as between corporate law and labour law, which are categorizations of functionally separable legal areas that can be found in all advanced industrialized societies and which are increasingly challenged through the global forces of rule-making.

(2) ECGR is entangled in the European 'Varieties of Capitalism' with regard to corporate and labour regulation, as evidenced, for example, in the struggle over the Takeover Directive and the statute of the *Societas Europaea*.

(3) ECGR is part of the larger project which aims towards the completion of the European internal market (Barnard and Deakin, 2002), in particular, in the post-Lisbon environment of knowledge society politics within the EU.[22]

(4) ECGR is a semi-autonomous field, which is both vibrant and precarious, and is always threatened by the balance between official law-making, transnational consultations, expert committee preparatory work, recommendations, communications and standardization, which we see unfolding at domestic, EU-supranational and transnational levels.

In Europe, the turn to 'law and finance' is occurring very persuasively (Fleischer, 2007; Haar, 2008), and with consequences for the continuously evolving regulatory landscape. As the European Commission continues to pursue a very effective dual agenda of revising and expanding the reach of capital market law directives on the one hand, and on indirectly reforming company law rules on the other, we find a powerful illustration of the emerging culture of interpretation. Making the 'European Company Law Scene' one of the most vibrant law-making and norm-making markets worldwide (Wymeersch, 2002; Enriques and Volpin, 2007), the European Commission has pursued one of the most sophisticated strategies of indirect, soft law-making by delegating far-reaching benchmarking and best practice formulation authorities to expert committees, on whose work the Commission has since based far-reaching recommendations which, more often than not, have been the preparation for directives (Hertig and McCahery, 2007).

These ECGR developments thus represent a series of highly diversified norm-setting processes which have resulted in a veritable explosion of corporate governance codes in Europe and elsewhere.[23] With the proliferation of corporate governance codes, influenced and driven by the international[24] and transnational activities of norm-setting, discussion and thought exchange,[25] it has become increasingly difficult to identify a single institution or author of a set of norms. Instead, the production and dissemination of corporate governance rules has, for some time now, taken on the nature of migrating standards, and a cross-fertilization of norms is now regarded as both imminent and necessary in shaping future corporate activity. A distinct feature of this de-territorialized production of norms is the radical challenge that these processes pose for our understanding of what we call law proper. With the dissemination of corporate governance codes, disclosure standards and rules, best practices and codes of conduct, not only corporate and securities law, but also other fields of law – such as labour and employment law – change. It is this strangely amorphous space which, due to its intricate relation to concrete places such as nation states, spheres of political decisionmaking, of protest and so on, creates a dramatic challenge for attempts to foster the institutional conditions for public policy debates.

Loyal to the new institutional economists' reading, this *liquidification of institutions* constituted by the decentralization of norm producers is repeated and reflected in the hybridization of the norms themselves. Everything can become an 'institution', from a fully fledged regulatory apparatus to a handshake among business partners. It is in this sense that the study of the proliferation of corporate governance codes and company law production in general, and of the rules of remuneration disclosure in particular, feeds into a broader research into the changing face of legal regulation in globally integrated marketplaces, which themselves become representations of society – which is precisely the nightmare that Polanyi so aptly depicted (Polanyi, 1944, p. 57). What shines through the particular developments in individual jurisdictions in this regard is a most poignant exhibition of particular legal and political cultures and political economies of law-making and economic regulation (Zumbansen, 2006).

The ephemeral 'double movement' in European capital market regulation and the ECGR

As has become clear, the evolution of European capital market law and corporate governance harmonization not only offers itself as a case in point for the intricate process of European integration, but also serves to illustrate the nature of legal evolution as reflected in the increasingly multilevel and trans-territorialized norm production in the law of corporate governance. On the one hand, business has, for a long time now, come to be organized in a globe-spanning manner, with historically strong attempts to liberate itself of the regulatory aspirations or constraints of nation states (Schmitthoff, 1961; Robé, 1997). This is part of the nation state's larger struggle over regulatory sovereignty with regard to the economic processes that unfold both within and beyond national borders. On the other hand, however, corporations remain, in many respects, embedded in a complex field of historically grown, institutionally and legally structured frameworks of national regulation and administration.[26] And, because national corporate laws are embedded in such distinct socio-economic cultures, and in historically grown legal and industrial regimes, scholars in comparative corporate governance have become increasingly aware of the methodological challenges in comparing different corporate governance regimes (Hopt, 2006; Donald, 2008). After early critiques of a functional approach to comparative law (Hill, 1989) had contributed to comparative legal scholarship's becoming much more nuanced, contextualized and differentiated,[27] contemporary scholars placed great emphasis upon the particular cultures of corporate governance norms, the role of institutions, policies, path dependency and innovation (see, foremost, Roe, 1997). James Fanto astutely observed that:

[c]orporate governance practices are partly cultural and historical products. In this context, culture can be defined as the conceptual framework whereby individuals, generally of the same country, understand and mediate the pressures of the world and motivate as well as explain their actions. As the corporation is a meaningful and purposeful human response to economic and social pressures, culture clearly informs corporate governance practices. (Fanto, 1998, p. 36)

Indeed, the considerably short history of European company and capital market law regulation provides numerous illustrations of this observation. There can be no doubt that there has been a strong push for streamlining in various areas of both company law and securities regulation, with changes having been initiated in particular by increased demands for transparency and more efficient management control (Enriques and Gatti, 2007a; Davies and Green, 2008). Yet despite these developments, from a comparative viewpoint, company law has been considerably less amenable to radical reform than securities regulation (Hopt, 2002; Rebérioux, 2002; Hertig and McCahery, 2004, p. 24; Enriques, 2005) and even here the road towards a fully harmonized securities market is not a straight or easy one (Enriques and Gatti, 2007b). European company law reflects the persisting challenges to European integration in that it highlights the difficulties of creating a body of law for social actors who have been relying on national rules, institutions and customs within the nation state (Kübler, 2003; Reich, 2005; Deakin, 2007). This process has consistently highlighted the immense political and socio-economic obstacles emerging from the different 'varieties' and 'models' of capitalism of the different Member States (Knudsen, 2005; see also, Rhodes and van Apeldoorn, 1998), which are often associated with the substantive costs in bringing about an effective regulatory regime for companies operating and investing on the European market (Hertig, 2000; Kübler, 2003; Hertig and McCahery, 2004; Enriques, 2005).

Any attempt, therefore, at assessing and evaluating the regulatory goals as well as the prospects of the pursued ECGR and capital market law agendas needs to recognize the degree to which such rules are being developed in, and emerging from, a multilevel process of norm production. With this, a study of European company law necessarily has to take into consideration not only the impact of different localities and the types of norm production emerging in European-wide rules and standards, but also the persisting patterns of political opposition to reform (Hertig and McCahery, 2004, p. 24; Wymeersch, 2004). The German rules governing worker participation in business corporations remain, in this respect, a notorious example of a regime deeply embedded in the country's political economy (Jackson, 2005; Boyer, 2006). To touch upon one part of the legal framework would be likely to result in turmoil which would involve numerous other norms and institutions governing codetermination (see, for example, Pistor, 1999). Likewise, the long and painful struggle over a European takeover regime clearly reflected the complexities of a regulatory, socio-economic minefield, made up of cultural predispositions, institutional traditions (*Volkswagen*) (Adolff, 2002) and established networks – all of which make any capital market law-oriented reformer frown, at the very least (Kirchner and Painter, 2002).

The multifaceted regulatory framework of corporate governance: Polanyi and beyond

The call for a new corporate governance

Where does this leave us? Enriching the classical, formal-functionalist scope of comparative law in the past, scholars in law, economics, sociology and political science have, over the last twenty years, been developing an arguably more interdisciplinary and considerably richer perspective in their efforts to capture the particular dynamics of corporate governance regulation. In light of the space here available, the following list highlights the aspects that such a perspective-building process has been focusing on:

(1) The 'politics' of corporate law-making, meaning the observable policies and programmatic directions of corporate regulation. Corporate regulatory politics have been among the most discussed and contested elements at the heart of the global corporate governance debate. This debate started long before the well-known cases of corporate mismanagement, fraud and accounting manipulation within and around Enron. While this political debate is marked by significant domestic dimensions, a remarkable, comparative perspective has given corporate law scholarship some decisive impulses. The focus has overwhelmingly been on the opposition of the so-called 'insider' versus the 'outsider' model of corporate governance (Hopt, 2002). While the former signifies the role of firms' internal control mechanisms, stakeholders and processes vis-à-vis management, in other words, labour, financial institutions, directors, etc., the latter, the 'outsider' model, labels a structure whereby management is held accountable largely through the presence of independent directors and through the securities markets. The global debate over the last fifteen years has been largely concerned with the discernible trends of either pointing towards a worldwide convergence towards a shareholder-oriented model, or of representing different, resisting

models defended in an argument favouring divergence. Over the
past few years, this debate has differentiated considerably, and
today not only are there legions of comparative corporate law
publications, but also more and more authors are taking the
historical and sociological work explaining the institutional evolution of market structures of different countries into account
(Boltanski and Chiapello, 1999 and 2005). This, in itself, is a
remarkable return to an earlier period in which corporate law
scholarship, much more generally, displayed a great interest in
the political economy of which corporate regulation was a part
(Klein, 1904).

(2) The other focus of transnational corporate governance research[28]
has been on the types of norms that regulate corporate behaviour
today, and on the authors of these norms, the domestic and international, public and private institutions. This part of a faster growing area of regulatory work within corporate and capital market
law,[29] as well as in other very prominent fields, such as standardization, focuses on the interaction of hard, public, official law-
making, on the one hand, and on the private, unofficial, soft
norm-generation, on the other. From this perspective, corporate
law is transformed into an around-the-clock laboratory for the
study of the shift in law-making from public mandate to private
self-regulation, for example, by delegation or appropriation of
'law'-making authority, as illustrated, for example, by the proliferation of codes of conduct. Certainly, an important caveat is already
in order at this point. Only a comparative perspective on different
corporate law-making *cultures* can open our eyes to the differences
of approaches in norm-creation, enactment and enforcement of the
regulatory bodies which govern what corporations do today (Dore
et al., 1999). Comparativists have long established the remarkable
differences in corporate law-making between North America and
Europe to be marked, first and foremost, by the difference between
enabling law in the United States and more mandatory forms of
corporate law rules in Europe. This difference is again echoed in
other much-referenced contrasts, such as that between common
law on one side of the Atlantic, and civil law on the other, with the
UK interestingly sitting on both sides of the fence (Cheffins, 1999
and 2002). In the process of studying the proliferation of corporate
law norms, distinctions between enabling and mandatory law, and

between common law and civil law, matter, but ongoing research questions the stability and, as such, the long-term sustainability and explanatory force of these distinctions (see Shleifer and Vishny, 1997; for an insightful discussion and critique, see Ahlering and Deakin, 2007; Licht *et al.*, 2007; Spamann, 2009).

(3) This has dramatic consequences for the position of corporate law within a larger, highly differentiated, dynamic regulatory environment. Corporate law unfolds in a web of norms, official and unofficial, public and private, from which it receives impulses and to which it sends others – this web is increasingly transnational in both origin and reach.[30] This is certainly true with regard to the evolving private law culture related to product safety, contract regulation, consumer protection, or, to switch to public law, with regard to the environmental law applicable to corporations. But there is clearly another set of regulations, which, only nominally, do not figure as a part of corporate law – whether this is by choice or necessity needs to be discussed. Corporations employ a workforce in a dramatically diversifying global division of labour, no longer merely recognizable by the blue collars of some, and the white collars of others. Both today's workforce and the environment in which it is operating have become a subject of study in and of themselves. Richard Sennett's work on the transformation of work is just one of the more recent illustrations of a far-reaching sociological interest in the fate of workers today (Sennett, 2006 and 2008). Labour lawyers have, for a long time, been struggling to reassert regulatory capacity in the interest of protecting workers' interests in a globalized economy better, where holding a job and working on a project has come to replace long-term employment, without, however, always delivering the accompanying promises of increased control, private autonomy and skills building (Blackett, 2004). In short, 'work', and its changing face, has become something that corporate lawyers increasingly look to more and more – just as Dean Clark told them to in his 1986 textbook (Clark, 1986, p. 5).

The new embeddedness of the firm: transnational corporate governance as transnational legal pluralism

Today, regulatory spaces are opened up and continue to expand as a result of complex interactions of processes and ideas, central to which is the transformation of formal rule creation in politically embedded state legal systems towards a system of specialized transnational law regimes. Such regimes consist of hard and soft laws, which emerge through processes that involve public and private actors, through the experimentation with new rules and their subsequent rejection, transformation and – temporary – solidification. Corporate governance norms provide a telling example of this transformation of traditional state-originating, official norm-setting in favour of increasingly decentralized, specialized processes of norm production (see, in detail, Calliess and Zumbansen, 2010), which can be understood through the concept of 'Rough Consensus and Running Code', originally developed in Internet governance (for more background and application, see Calliess and Zumbansen, 2010). The very nature of these norms themselves has been changing dramatically as a result of this new form of transnational embeddedness. Central to the observation in the particular areas that this chapter has focused on is the particular nature of the regulation of business conduct and corporations in globally interdependent activity spheres (marketization), fundamentally changing national political economies (privatization), and a dramatic expansion of issue-driven, functionalist regulatory regimes (scientization).[31] This constellation, however, suggests nothing less than a fundamental contestation and erosion of boundaries between state and non-state actors, official and unofficial law, and public and private ordering (see, for example, Gessner *et al.*, 2001; Pistor, 2003; Snyder, 2004; Gessner, 2009). Above all, legal theory and doctrine are faced with important methodological challenges. Politics matter still, but they are no longer so easily defined as the politics of 'The Right' or 'The Left', which we learned to distinguish domestically throughout the twentieth century and right up to the recent shock to the financialized global economy. The questions that are raised not only by the commercial and productive, but also the redistributive, sustainable, R&D-related and routine/innovation-related activities of corporations, do not lend themselves to straightforward categorizations of *either* public *or* private, or of domestic *or* international. In response to this situation, it is through the study of transnational regulatory regimes that a revisiting of the political questions and issues that continue to arise around particular regulatory challenges or experiences becomes possible. This study builds on an understanding of *transnational law*, not as a separate field, but as a method and approach to legal reasoning. We must rethink law and regulation without resorting to traditional distinctions in the belief that they will deliver the same explanatory potential that we have grown accustomed to: instead, we must approach emerging institutional regimes from a transnational regulatory perspective. And it is here that comparative corporate law transforms itself into the study of these increasingly deterritorialized corporate governance regimes as an illustration of transnational legal pluralism. Comparative corporate lawyers must search today for the equivalents of, and for compatible, institutional settings and actors that allow a new turn in the long-standing debates about the corporation.

Notes

1 The most explicit contribution was surely Hansmann and Kraakman, 2001; see, also, Hansmann, 2006.

2 Albeit there are exceptions: Dam, 2010.

3 See, for example, the overview at www.ecgi.org, and www.transnationalcorporategovernance.net, last accessed 15 December 2010.

4 With regard to the example of codetermination, see, e.g., Pistor, 1999 and Ziegler, 2001.

5 *The Economist*, 2010. 'Can anything perk up Europe?' 9 July.

6 Polanyi, 1944, p. 43; this passage is later complemented – in the same chapter – by his remarks about 'man as a social being' (*ibid.*, p. 46): 'His natural endowments reappear with a remarkable constancy in societies of all times and places; and the necessary preconditions of the survival of human society appear to be immutably the same.'

7 For this concept, see Sassen, 2006; for earlier elaborations, see Sassen, 1991 and 1998; see, also, Amstutz and Karavas, 2009.

8 Sassen, 2006, p. 349, noting the importance of focusing on financial centres, not 'markets', 'as key nested communities enabling the construction and functioning of such cultures of interpretation'.

9 For a chronology and related documents, see http://ec.europa.eu/internal_market/securities/lamfalussy/index_en.htm, last accessed 15 December 2010.

10 http://ec.europa.eu/internal_market/securities/prospectus/index_en.htm, last accessed 15 December 2010.

11 http://ec.europa.eu/internal_market/securities/abuse/index_en.htm, last accessed 15 December 2010.

12 http://ec.europa.eu/internal_market/company/takeoverbids/index_en.htm, last accessed 15 December 2010.

13 http://ec.europa.eu/internal_market/securities/transparency/index_en.htm, last accessed 15 December 2010.

14 http://ec.europa.eu/internal_market/securities/agencies/index_en.htm, last accessed 15 December 2010.

15 For a conceptual discussion, see Hertig and McCahery, 2004.

16 Möllers, (2010, p. 285) identifies six levels of capital market regulation now in existence (laws, regulation and, in the case of the German BaFin, soft laws, as well as framework directives, implementation directives recommendations/guidelines) within the Lamfalussy process.

17 For an illustration of the latter, see Romano, 1993; for the former, see Buxbaum and Hopt, 1988.

18 'The basic financial innovation on which the pyramid of ever more arcane financial instruments is built is securitization' (Dore, 2008, p. 1099).

19 See, for example, Davidow and Malone, 1992; for the foundations, see Castells, 2000.

20 www.euractiv.com/en/innovation/eu-lisbon-agenda-gets-social-makeover/ article-171013, last accessed 15 December 2010.

21 Kirchner and Painter, 2002; Clarke, 2011; see, also, Armour and Skeel Jr, 2007; for a comprehensive analysis of the Directive in the context of EU corporate governance regulation, see Sjåfjell, 2009. 'The core of corporate governance: implications of the Takeover Directive for corporate governance in Europe', presentation at the 13th Irish European Law Forum, Dublin, 4 December 2009, manuscript on file with author.

22 See the Presidency Conclusions of the Council of the European Union [7652/08] 13–14 March 2008, available at www.consilium.europa.eu/ ueDocs/cms_Data/docs/pressData/en/ec/99410.pdf, p. 4, last accessed 15 December 2010: 'The implementation of the broad-based innovation strategy is key to realising EU ambitions in the area.' See, also, Pestre, 2007.

23 www.ecgi.org.

24 OECD, WCFCG, IVCGN, etc.

25 ECGI, INSEAD, Euroshareholders, etc.

26 O'Sullivan, 2000; that 'culture' matters greatly, has been acknowledged widely; see, only, Buxbaum and Hopt, 1988; Oquendo, 2001; Cheffins, 2002; Hopt, 2002, p. 976.

27 See, for example, the helpful study by Bratton and McCahery, 2002.

28 www.comparativeresearch.net/projects.jsp, last accessed 15 December 2010.

29 www.sustainablefinancialmarkets.net, last accessed 15 December 2010.

30 www.ecgi.org/codes/all_codes.php; www.transnationalcorporategovernance.
net, last accessed 15 December 2010.
31 For an excellent demarcation of these dimensions, see Drori and Meyer,
2006.

References

Adolff, J. 2002. 'Turn of the tide? The "golden share" judgements of the
European Court of Justice and the liberalization of the European capital markets', *German Law Journal* 3, available at www.germanlaw-
journal.com/print.php?id=170, last accessed 15 December 2010.
Aguilera, R., Rupp, D., Williams, C. A. and Ganapathi, J. 2004. 'Putting
the s back in corporate social responsibility: a multi-level theory of
social change in organizations', *Academy of Management Review*
32: 836–63, available at http://papers.ssrn.com/sol833/papers.cfm?
abstract_id=567842, last accessed 15 December 2010.
Ahlering, B. and Deakin, S. 2007. 'Labor regulation, corporate governance,
and legal origin: a case of institutional complementarity?', *Law and
Society Review* 41: 865–903.
Alchian, A. A. and Demsetz, H. 1972. 'Production, information costs, and
economic organization', *American Economic Review* 62: 777–95.
Alford, D. 2006. 'The Lamfalussy process and EU bank regulation: another
step on the road to pan-European regulation?', *Annual Review of
Banking and Financial Law* 25: 389–441.
Amstutz, M. and Karavas, V. 2009. 'Weltrecht: ein Derridasches Monster', in
Calliess, G.-P., Fischer-Lescano, A., Wielsch, D. and Zumbansen, P. (eds.),
*Soziologische Jurisprudenz: Liber Amicorum für Gunther Teubner zum
65. Geburtstag*. Berlin/New York: Walter de Gruyter, pp. 647–74.
Armour, J. and Skeel Jr, D. 2007. 'Who writes the rules for hostile takeovers,
and why? – the peculiar divergence of U.S. and U.K. takeover regula-
tion', *Georgetown Law Journal* 95: 1727–94.
Atleson, J. B., Compa, L. and Rittich, K. 2008. *International Labour Law:
Cases and Materials on Workers' Rights in the Global Economy.*
Thomson West.
Barnard, C. and Deakin, S. 2002. 'Market access and regulatory competi-
tion', in Barnard, C. and Scott, J. (eds.), *The Law of the Single
European Market: Unpacking the Premises*. Oxford/Portland: Hart
Publishing, pp. 197–224.
Basedow, J. 1996. 'A common contract law for the common market',
Common Market Law Review 33: 1169–95.
Baums, T. 2001. 'Interview: reforming German corporate governance: inside
a law making process of a very new nature', *German Law Journal* 2,
available at www.germanlawjournal.com/print.php?id=43.

Bebchuk, L. A. and Fried, J. 2004. *Pay Without Performance: The Unfulfilled Promise of Executive Compensation*. Harvard University Press.

Berman, P. S. 2007. 'Global legal pluralism', *Southern California Law Review* 80: 1155–237.

Black, J. and Rouch, D. 2008. 'The development of global markets as rule-makers: engagement and legitimacy', *Law and Financial Markets Review*: 218–33.

Blackett, 2004. 'Codes of corporate conduct and the labour law regulatory state in developing countries', in Kirton, J. J. and Trebilcock, M. J. (eds.), *Hard Choices, Soft Law: Voluntary Standards in Global Trade, Environment and Social Governance*. Aldershot: Ashgate Publishing, pp. 121–33.

Boltanski, L. and Chiapello, È. 1999. *Le nouvel esprit du capitalisme*. Paris: Gallimard.

2005. 'Die Rolle der Kritik für die Dynamik des Kapitalismus: Sozialkritik versus Künstlerkritik', in Miller M. (ed.), *Welten des Kapitalismus*. Frankfurt aM: Campus, pp. 285–321.

Boyer, R. 2006. 'What is the future for codetermination and corporate governance in Germany?', in Beckert, J., Ebbinghaus, B., Hassel, A. and Manow, P. (eds.), *Transformationen des Kapitalismus: Festschrift für Wolfgang Streeck zum 60. Geburtstag*. Frankfurt aM/New York: Campus, pp. 135–57.

Bratton, W. W. 2002. 'Enron and the dark side of shareholder value', *Tulane Law Review* 76: 1275–361.

Bratton, W. W. and McCahery, J. A. 2002. 'Comparative corporate governance and barriers to global cross reference', in McCahery J. A., Moerland, P., Raaijmakers, T. and Renneborg, L. (eds.), *Corporate Governance Regimes: Convergence and Diversity*. Oxford University Press, pp. 23–55.

Buxbaum, R. and Hopt, K. J. 1988. *Legal Harmonization and the Business Enterprise: Corporate and Capital Market Law Harmonization Policy in Europe and the U.S.A.* Berlin/New York: Walter de Gruyter.

Calliess, G.-P. 2002a. 'Reflexive transnational law: the privatisation of civil law and the civilisation of private law', *Zeitschrift für Rechtssoziologie* 23: 185–216.

2002b. 'The limits of eclecticism in consumer law: national struggles and the hope for a coherent European contract law: a comment on the ECJ's and the FCJ's "Heininger" decisions', *German Law Journal* 3, available at www.germanlawjournal.com/past_issues.php?id=175, last accessed 15 December 2010.

2006. *Grenzüberschreitende Verbraucherverträge: Rechtssicherheit und Gerechtigkeit auf dem elektronischen Weltmarktplatz*. Tübingen: Mohr Siebeck.

Calliess, G.-P. and Zumbansen, P. 2010. *Rough Consensus and Running Code: A Theory of Transnational Private Law*. Oxford: Hart Publishing, pp. 227–47.

Castells, M. 2000. *The Rise of the Network Society: The Information Age: Economy, Society and Culture* (2nd edn) vol. I. Cambridge, MA/ Oxford: Blackwell Publishing.

Cheffins, B. R. 1999. 'Current trends in corporate governance: going from London to Milan via Toronto', *Duke Journal of Comparative and International Law* 10: 5–42.

  2002. 'Putting Britain on the Roe map: the emergence of the Berle-Means corporation in the United Kingdom', in McCahery, J. A., Moerland, P., Raaijmakers, T. and Renneborg, L. (eds.), *Corporate Governance Regimes: Convergence and Diversity*. Oxford University Press, pp. 147–72.

  2009. 'Did corporate governance "fail" during the 2008 stock market meltdown? The case of the S&P 500', *Business Lawyer* 65: 1–62.

Cioffi, J. W. 2000. 'State of the art: a review essay on comparative corporate governance: the state of the art and emerging research', *American Journal of Comparative Law* 48: 501.

  2006. 'Corporate governance reform, regulatory politics, and the foundations of finance capitalism in the United States and Germany', *German Law Journal* 7: 533–62.

Clark, R. C. 1986. *Corporate Law*. Boston, MA: Little, Brown.

Clarke, B. 2011. 'The EU Takeovers Directive: a shareholder or stakeholder model?', in Zumbansen, P. and Williams, C. A. (eds.), *The Embedded Firm: Corporate Governance, Labour and Finance Capitalism*. Cambridge University Press.

Dam, K. W. 2010. 'The subprime crisis and financial regulation: international and comparative perspectives', *Chicago Journal of International Law* 10: 581–638.

Davidow, W. H. and Malone, M. S. 1992. *The Virtual Corporation: Structuring and Revitalizing the Corporation for the 21st Century*. New York: HarperCollins.

Davies, H. and Green, D. 2008. *Global Financial Regulation: The Essential Guide*. Cambridge/Malden: Polity Press.

Deakin, S. 2007. 'Reflexive governance and European company law', *CLPE Research Paper Series*, available at www.comparativeresearch.net/ papers.jsp and Cambridge Centre for Business Research, Working Paper No. 346, available at www.cbr.cam.ac.uk/pdf/wp346.pdf, last accessed 15 December 2010.

  2011. 'Corporate governance and financial crisis in the long run', in Zumbansen, P. and Williams, C. A. (eds.), *The Embedded Firm: Corporate Governance, Labour and Financial Capitalism*. Cambridge University Press.

Derrida, J. 1994. *Specters of Marx: The State of the Debt, the Work of Mourning and the New International*. London: Routledge.

Dhir, A. 2006. 'Realigning the corporate building blocks: shareholder proposals as a vehicle for achieving corporate social and human rights accountability', *American Business Law Journal* 43: 365.

Donald, D. C. 2008. 'Approaching comparative company law', *Fordham Journal of Corporate and Financial Law* 14: 83–178.

Dore, R. 2008. 'Financialization of the Global Economy', *Industrial and Corporate Change* 17: 1097–112.

Dore, R., Lazonick, W. and O'Sullivan, M. 1999. 'Varieties of capitalism in the twentieth century', *Oxford Review of Economic Policy* 15: 102–17.

Drori, G. S. and Meyer, J. W. 2006. 'Scientization: making a world safe for organizing', in Djelic, M.-L. and Sahlin-Andersson, K. (eds.), *Transnational Governance: Institutional Dynamics of Regulation*. Cambridge University Press, pp. 31–52.

Edwards, V. 1999. *EC Company Law*. Oxford University Press.

Ehrlich, E. 1962. *Fundamental Principles of the Sociology of Law* (originally published in German as *Grundlegung der Soziologie des Rechts*, 1913). New York: Russell & Russell, pp. 486–506.

Eidenmüller, H. 2007. 'Forschungsperspektiven im Unternehmensrecht', *Juristenzeitung* 62: 487–94.

Enriques, L. 2005. 'Company law harmonization reconsidered: what role for the EC?', ECGI Law Working Paper No. 53/200, available at http://ssrn.com/abstract=850005, last accessed 15 December 2010.

Enriques, L. and Gatti, M. 2007a. 'EC reforms of corporate governance and capital markets law: do they tackle insiders' opportunism?', *Northwestern Journal of International Law and Business* 28: 1–33.

  2007b. 'Is there a uniform EU securities law after the Financial Services Action Plan?', *Proceedings of the 7th Nordic Company Law Conference*, available at http://ssrn.com/abstract=982282, last accessed 15 December 2010.

Enriques, L. and Volpin, P. 2007. 'Corporate governance reforms in continental Europe', *Journal of Economic Perspectives* 21: 117–40.

Fanto, J. 1998. 'The role of corporate law in French corporate governance', *Cornell International Law Journal* 31: 31–91.

Fleischer, H. 2007. 'Zur Zukunft der gesellschafts- und kapitalmarktrecht lichen Forschung', *Zeitschrift für Unternehmens- und Gesellschaftsrecht*, pp. 500–10.

Galanter, M. 1981. 'Justice in many rooms: courts, private ordering and indigenous law', *Journal of Legal Pluralism* 19: 1–47.

Gessner, V. 2009. 'Theories of change: the governance of business transactions in globalising economies', in Gessner, V. (ed.), *Contractual*

Certainty in International Trade: Empirical Studies and Theoretical Debates on Institutional Support for Global Economic Exchanges. Oxford/Portland: Hart Publishing.

Gessner, V., Appelbaum, R. P. and Felstiner, W. F. 2001. 'Introduction: the legal culture of global business transactions', in Gessner, V., Appelbaum, R. P. and Felstiner, W. F. (eds.), *Rules and Networks: The Legal Culture of Global Business Transactions.* Oxford/Portland: Hart Publishing, pp. 1–36.

Gourevitch, P. A. 2003. 'The politics of corporate governance regulation', *Yale Law Journal* 112: 1829–80.

Gourevitch, P. A. and Shinn, J. 2005. *Political Power and Corporate Control: The New Global Politics of Corporate Governance.* Princeton University Press.

Gurvitch, G. 1947. *Sociology of Law* (originally published in French as *Problèmes de la sociologie du droit*). London: Routledge and Kegan Paul.

Haar, B. 2008. 'Law and finance: Kapitalmarktentwicklung in interdisziplinärer Perspektive', *Juristenzeitung* 63: 964–74.

Hall, P. A. and Soskice, D. (eds.) 2001. *Varieties of Capitalism: The Institutional Foundations of Comparative Advantage.* Oxford University Press.

Hansmann, H. 2006. 'How close is the end of history?' *Journal of Corporate Law* 31: 745–50.

Hansmann, H. and Kraakman, R. 2001. 'The end of history for corporate law', *Georgetown Law Journal* 89: 439–68.

Haunschild, A. 2004. 'Contingent work: the problem of disembeddedness and economic reembeddedness', *Management Review* 1 January, available at www.allbusiness.com/human-resources/careers/1078135-1.html, last accessed 15 December 2010.

Hertig, G. 2000. 'Western Europe's corporate governance dilemma', in Baums, T., Hopt, K. J. and Horn, N. (eds.), *Corporations, Capital Markets and Business in the Law: Liber Amicorum Richard M. Buxbaum.* London: Kluwer Law International, pp. 265–82.

Hertig, G. and McCahery, J. A. 2004. 'An agenda for reform: company and takeover law in Europe', in Ferrarini, G., Hopt, K. J., Winter, J. and Wymeersch, E. (eds.), *Reforming Company and Takeover Law in Europe.* Oxford University Press, pp. 21–49.

2007. 'Optional rather than mandatory EU company law: framework and specific proposals', *European Company and Financial Law Review*: 341–62.

Hill, J. 1989. 'Comparative law, law reform and legal theory', *Oxford Journal of Legal Studies* 9: 101–15.

Hoffmann, J. 2004. 'Co-ordinated continental European market economies under pressure from globalisation: Germany's "Rhineland capitalism"', *German Law Journal* 5: 985–1002.

Hollingsworth, J. R. 1998. 'New perspectives on the spatial dimensions of economic coordination: tensions between globalization and social systems of production', *Review of International Political Economy* (5) 3: 482–507.

Höpner, M. and Jackson, G. 2001. 'Entsteht ein Markt für Unternehmenskontrolle? Der Fall Mannesmann', *Leviathan* pp. 544–63.

Hopt, K. J. 2002. 'Common principles of corporate governance in Europe?', in McCahery, J. A., Moerland, P., Raaijmakers, T. and Renneborg, L. (eds.), *Corporate Governance Regimes: Convergence and Diversity*. Oxford University Press, pp. 175–204.

   2005. 'European company law and corporate governance: where does the action plan of the European Commission lead?', in Hopt, K. J., Wymeersch, E., Kanda, H. and Baum, H. (eds.), *Corporate Governance in Context*. Oxford University Press, pp. 119–42.

   2006. 'Comparative company law', in Reimann, M. and Zimmermann, R. (eds.), *Oxford Handbook of Comparative Law*. Oxford University Press, pp. 1161–91.

Howells, G. and Wilhelmsson, T. 2003. 'EC consumer law: has it come of age?', *European Law Review* 28: 370–88.

Jackson, G. 2005. 'Contested boundaries: ambiguity and creativity in the evolution of German codetermination', in Streeck, W. and Thelen, K. (eds.), *Beyond Continuity: Institutional Change in Advanced Political Economies*. Oxford University Press, pp. 229–54.

Jacoby, S. M. 2004. *The Embedded Corporation: Corporate Governance and Employment Relations in Japan and the United States*. Princeton University Press.

Jensen, M. C. 2000. *A Theory of the Firm: Governance, Residual Claims, and Organizational Forms*. Harvard University Press.

Joerges, Ch. and Neyer, J. 1997. 'From intergovernmental bargaining to deliberative political processes: the constitutionalisation of comitology', *European Law Journal* 3: 273–99.

Kirchner, C. and Painter, R. W. 2002. 'Takeover defenses under Delaware law, the proposed thirteenth EU Directive and the new German takeover law: comparison and recommendations for reform', *American Journal of Comparative Law* 50: 451–76.

Klein, F. 1904. *Die neueren Entwicklungen in Verfassung und Recht der Aktiengesellschaft*. Vienna: Manz.

Klöhn, L. 2006. *Kapitalmarkt, Spekulation und Behavioral Finance: Eine interdisziplinäre und vergleichende Analyse zum Fluch und Segen der Spekulation und ihrer Regulierung durch Markt und Recht*. Berlin: Duncker & Humblot.

Knudsen, J. S. 2005. 'Is the single market an illusion? Obstacles to reform of EU takeover regulation', *European Law Journal* 11: 507–24.

Kolla, P. 2004. 'The Mannesmann trial and the role of the courts', *German Law Journal* 5: 829–47.

Kraakman, R., Davies, P. L., Hansmann, H., Hertig, G., Hopt, K. J., Kanda, H. and Rock, E. B. 2009. *The Anatomy of Corporate Law: A Comparative and Functional Approach* (2nd edn). Oxford University Press.

Kübler, F. 2001. 'The impact of equity markets on business organization: some comparative observations regarding differences in the evolution of corporate structures', *European Business Organization Law Review* 2: 669–83.

2003. 'The rules of capital under pressure of the securities markets', in Hopt, K. J. and Wymeersch, E. (eds.), *Capital Markets and Company Law.* Oxford University Press, pp. 95–114.

Lazonick, W. 1991. *Business Organization and the Myth of the Market Economy.* Cambridge University Press, ch. 3.

Lazonick, W. and O'Sullivan, M. 2002. 'Maximizing shareholder value: a new ideology for corporate governance', in Lazonick, W. and O'Sullivan, M. (eds.), *Corporate Governance and Sustainable Prosperity.* London: Palgrave Macmillan, pp. 11–36.

Licht, A. N., Goldschmidt, C. and Schwartz, S. H. 2007. 'Culture rules: the foundations of the rule of law and other norms of governance', *Journal of Comparative Economics* 35: 659–88.

Luhmann, N. 1988. *Die Wirtschaft der Gesellschaft.* Frankfurt aM: Suhrkamp.

Macaulay, S. 1986. 'Private government', in Lipson, L. and Wheeler, S. (eds.), *Law and the Social Sciences.* Washington, DC: Russell Sage, pp. 445–518.

Maier, S. 2006. 'A close look at the Mannesmann trial', *German Law Journal* 7: 603–10.

Mattei, U. and Nicola, F. 2006. 'A "social dimension" in European private law? The call for setting a progressive agenda', *New England Law Review* 41: 1–66.

Merkt, H. 2003. 'Zum Verhältnis von Kapitalmarktrecht und Gesellschaftsrecht in der Diskussion um die Corporate Governance', *Die Aktiengesellschaft* 48: 126–36.

Merry, S. E. 1988. 'Legal pluralism', *Law and Society Review* 22: 869–901.

Mitchell, L. E. 2007. *The Speculation Economy: How Finance Triumphed over Industry.* San Francisco: Berrett-Koehler Publishers.

2011. 'Financialism: a (very) brief history', in Zumbansen, P. and Williams, C. A. (eds.), *The Embedded Firm: Corporate Governance, Labour and Financial Capitalism.* Cambridge University Press.

Möllers, T. M. J. 2008. 'Europäische Methoden- und Gesetzgebungslehre im Kapitalmarktrecht: Vollharmonisierung, Generalklauseln und Soft Law im Rahmen des Lamfalussy-Verfahrens zur Etablierung von Standards', *Zeitschrift für Europäisches Privatrecht*, pp. 480–505.

   2010. 'Auf dem Weg zu einer neuen europäischen Finanzmarktaufsichts-struktur: ein systematischer Vergleich der Rating-VO (EG) Nr. 1060/ 2009 mit der geplanten ESMA-VO', *Neue Zeitschrift für Gesellschaftsrecht* pp. 285–90.

Moloney, N. 2003. 'New frontiers in EC capital markets law: from market construction to market regulation', *Common Market Law Review* 40: 809–43.

Moore, S. F. 1973. 'Law and social change: the semi-autonomous field as an appropriate subject of study', *Law and Society Review* 7: 719–46.

Oquendo, R. 2001. 'Breaking on through to the other side: understanding European corporate governance', *University of Pennsylvania Journal of International Economic Law* 22: 975–1027.

O'Sullivan, M. 2000. 'Corporate governance and globalization', *The Annals of the American Academy of Political and Social Science [ANNALS]*, 570: 153–72.

   2003. 'The political economy of comparative corporate governance', *Review of International Political Economy* 10: 23–72.

Partnoy, F. and Thomas, R. 2007. 'Gap filling, hedge funds and financial innovation', in Fuchita, Y. and Litan, R. E. (eds.), *New Financial Instruments and Institutions: Opportunities and Policy Challenges*. Washington, DC: Brookings Institution, pp. 101–40.

Pestre, D. 2007. 'Science, society and politics: knowledge societies from historical perspective', *Report to the Science, Economy and Society Directorate at the European Commission*, available at www.ec.europa.eu/research/science-society/document_library/pdf_06/historical-perspectives_en.pdf.

Pistor, K. 1999. 'Codetermination: a sociopolitical model with governance externalities', in Blair, M. and Roe, M. J. (eds.), *Employees and Corporate Governance*. Washington, DC: Brookings Institution, pp. 163–93.

   2003. 'Of legal transplants, legal irritants, and economic development', in Cornelius, P. and Kogut, B. (eds.), *Corporate Governance and Capital Flows in a Global Economy*. Oxford University Press, pp. 347–66.

Polanyi, K. K. 1944. *The Great Transformation: The Political and Economic Origins of Our Time*. Boston: Beacon Press.

Rebérioux, A. 2002. 'European style of corporate governance at the crossroads: the role of worker involvement', *Journal of Common Market Studies* 40: 111–34.

Reich, N. 2005. *Understanding EU Law: Objectives, Principles and Methods of Community Law* (2nd edn). Antwerp/Oxford: Intersentia.

Reich, R. B. 2007. *Supercapitalism: The Transformation of Business, Democracy, and Everyday Life.* New York: Alfred A. Knopf/Random House.

Rheinstein, M. 1941. 'Review: two recent books on sociology of law' (reviewing Timasheff's 'Introduction' and Gurvitch's 'Elements'), *Ethics* 51: 220–31.

Rhodes, M. and van Apeldoorn, B. 1998. 'Capital unbound? The transformation of European corporate governance', *Journal of European Public Policy* 5: 406–27.

Robé, J.-P. 1997. 'Multinational enterprises: the constitution of a pluralistic legal order', in Teubner, G. (ed.), *Global Law without a State.* Aldershot: Ashgate Publishing, pp. 45–77.

Rodrik, D. 2000. 'Governance of economic globalization', in Nye, J. S. and Donahue, J. D. (eds.), *Governance in a Globalizing World.* Washington DC: Brookings Institution, pp. 347–65.

Roe, M. J. 1997. 'Path dependence, political options and governance systems', in Hopt, K. J. and Wymeersch, E. (eds.), *Comparative Corporate Governance: Essays and Materials.* Berlin/New York: Walter de Gruyter, pp. 165–84.

Romano, R. 1993. *The Genius of American Corporate Law.* Washington, DC: The American Enterprise Institute Press.

2005. 'The Sarbanes-Oxley Act and the making of quack corporate governance', *Yale Law Journal* 114: 1521–611.

Rorty, R. 1998. *Das kommunistische Manifest 150 Jahre danach.* Frankfurt aM: Suhrkamp.

Sabel, C. F. and Zeitlin, J. 2008. 'Learning from difference: the new architecture of experimentalist governance in the EU', *European Law Journal* 14: 271–327.

Santos, S. 1987. 'Law: a map of misreading: toward a postmodern conception of law', *Journal of Law and Society* 14: 279–302.

Sassen, S. 1991. *The Global City.* Princeton University Press.

1998. *Globalization and Its Discontents: Essays on the New Mobility of People and Money.* New York: The New Press.

2006. *Territory – Authority – Rights: From Medieval to Global Assemblages.* Princeton University Press.

Schmitthoff, C. M. 1961. 'International business law: a new law merchant', *Current Law and Social Problems* 2: 129–53.

1973. 'The future of the European company law scene', in Schmitthoff, C. M. (ed.), *The Harmonisation of European Company Law.* London: The UK National Committee of Comparative Law, pp. 3–27.

Scott, C. M. 2009. '"Transnational law" as proto-concept: three conceptions', *German Law Journal* 10: 859–76.

Sennett, R. 2006. *The Culture of the New Capitalism*. New Haven: Yale University Press.

2008. *The Craftsman*. London: Allen Lane.

Shleifer, A. and Vishny, R. W. 1997. 'A survey of corporate governance', *The Journal of Finance* 52: 737–83.

Siems, M. M. and Deakin, S. 2009. 'Comparative law and finance: past, present and future research', *Journal of Institutional and Theoretical Economics*, available at http://ssrn.com/abstract=1428247, last accessed 15 December 2010.

Sjåfjell, B. 2009. 'Political path dependency in practice: the Takeover Directive', *Yearbook of European Law* 27: 387–404.

Snyder, F. 2004. 'Economic globalisation and the law in the 21st century', in Sarat, A. (ed.), *The Blackwell Companion to Law and Society*. New York/Oxford: Blackwell, pp. 624–40.

Spamann, H. 2009. 'Contemporary legal transplants – legal families and the diffusion of (corporate) law', *Brigham Young University Law Review*, available at http://ssrn.com/sol3/papers.cfm?abstract_id=1411704, last accessed 15 December 2010.

Supiot, A. 1999. *Au-delà de l'emploi: transformation du travail et devenir du droit du travail en Europe: rapport pour la Commission Européenne*. Paris: Flammarion.

Teubner, G. 1992. 'The two faces of Janus: rethinking legal pluralism', *Cardozo Law Review* 13: 1443–62.

2001. 'Legal irritants: how unifying law ends up in new divergences', in Hall, P. A. and Soskice, D. (eds.), *Varieties of Capitalism: The Institutional Foundations of Comparative Advantage*. Oxford University Press, pp. 417–41.

2004. 'Societal constitutionalism: alternatives to state-centred constitutional theory?' in Joerges, C., Sand, I.-J. and Teubner, G. (eds.), *Constitutionalism and Transnational Governance*. Oxford: Hart Publishing, pp. 3–28.

Trubek, D. and Trubek, L. G. 2005. 'Hard and soft law in the construction of social Europe: the role of the open method of coordination', *European Law Journal* 11: 343–64.

Vitols, S. 2001. 'Varieties of corporate governance: comparing Germany and the UK', in Hall, P. A. and Soskice, D. (eds.), *Varieties of Capitalism: The Institutional Foundations of Comparative Advantage*. Oxford University Press, pp. 337–60.

Wiethölter, R. 1961. *Interessen und Organisation der Aktiengesellschaft im amerikanischen und deutschen Recht*. Karlsruhe: C. F. Müller.

Wouters, J. 2000. 'European company law: quo vadis?', *Common Market Law Review* 37: 257–307.

Wymeersch, E. 2002. 'Convergence or divergence in corporate governance patterns in Western Europe?', in McCahery, J. A., Moerland, P., Raaijmakers, T. and Renneborg, L. (eds.), *Corporate Governance Regimes: Convergence and Diversity*. Oxford University Press, pp. 230–47.

2004. 'About techniques of regulating companies in the European Union', in Ferrarini, G., Hopt, K. J., Winter, J. and Wymeersch, E. (eds.), *Reforming Company and Takeover Law in Europe*. Oxford University Press, pp. 145–82.

Ziegler, J. N. 2001. 'Corporate governance in Germany: toward a new transnational politics?' in Weber, S. (ed.), *Globalization and the European Political Economy*. New York: Columbia University Press, pp. 197–228.

Zumbansen, P. 2006. 'Spaces and places: a systems theory approach to regulatory competition in European company law', *European Law Journal* 12: 534–56.

2009. '"New governance" in European corporate law regulation as transnational legal pluralism', *European Law Journal* 15 (2): 246–76.

2010a. 'The next "great transformation"? The double movement in transnational corporate governance and capital markets regulation', in Joerges, C. and Falke, J. (eds.), *The Social Embeddedness of Transnational Markets*. Oxford: Hart Publishing.

2010b. 'Transnational legal pluralism', *Transnational Legal Theory* 10 (2): 141–89.

2011. 'The new embeddedness of the corporation: corporate social responsibility in the knowledge society', in Zumbansen, P. and Williams, C. A. (eds), *The Embedded Firm: Corporate Governance, Labour and Financial Capitalism*. Cambridge University Press.

13 | The focus of regulatory reforms in Europe after the global financial crisis: from corporate to contract governance

FLORIAN MÖSLEIN

Every crisis offers opportunities to rethink, reform and renew structures and institutions, as well as rules and standards. The market economy will certainly survive the global financial crisis and may even emerge in better shape, but it must be open to scrutinizing or even reinventing itself.[1] This process of regulatory reform started immediately in the midst of the crisis: advisory boards such as the Issing, the Turner and the Larosière Committees soon developed reform proposals at the national and European level (Issing Committee, 2009; Turner Review, 2009; Larosière Group, 2009). Some of them have already been adopted by law-makers or are about to be drafted as legislative proposals (European Commission, 2009a and 2009b). At the international level, a first outline of a global financial architecture came to be identifiable in the aftermath of the London G20 summit (G-20-Summit, 2009a and 2009b). Further actions to assure a sound and sustainable recovery from the global financial and economic crisis were discussed at the summit in Pittsburgh in September 2009.[2]

Reforms in periods of crisis, however, tend to embody overreactions.[3] Hence the financial crisis is a real challenge for governance research as well: scholars have to face difficult questions of legal policy, namely to identify dangers of over-regulation, advise against them in a timely fashion, and develop principles of smart regulation (Kirchner, 2009, p. 14).[4] In order to meet this challenge, governance research might well be forced to rethink its own methods and approaches, specifically to widen its research focus. After all, the financial crunch was not only a crisis of corporations. Contracts and markets played an important role too.

Causes of the global financial crisis

The global financial crisis had many different causes. In any event, it did not only emerge due to specific corporate structures, but was also (and perhaps mainly) rooted in the instability of markets. As is well known, subprime loans in the United States were often approved regardless of financial standing and equity contribution (Grundmann *et al.*, 2009, pp. 3 *et seq.*, with further references). Corresponding risks were collateralized with insufficient security because mortgages were not transparent; or they were transferred by virtue of loan insurances (Richardson, 2009; Taylor, 2009, pp. 61–3). Personal claims against real estate credit users were for legal or practical reasons almost impossible. Low and partly variable mortgage rates and the expectation of rising house prices created further incentives to borrow more money than appropriate with respect to personal solvency (Grundmann *et al.*, 2009, pp. 7 *et seq.*; Zandi, 2009, pp. 45–77; comprehensively, Barth, 2009). On the opposite side of the market, there was no incentive for responsible lending either, because through securitization, transfer and bundling credit risks could be transferred almost at will, and without any real chance for the purchasers to evaluate these risks themselves.[5] Instead, they had to count on the information of rating agencies, who themselves had little incentive to reduce the profitable source of income of the securitization business by poor ratings (Schwintowski, 2009, pp. 45 *et seq.*; Hosp, 2010; see also Levich *et al.*, 2002). More generally, remuneration incentives fostered the dynamics that led to this crisis. These incentives did not only result in remuneration packages of company directors, but also mainly in bonuses of investment bankers and even in commissions of loan and investment advisors: in other words, in compensations that were paid in the operational business.[6]

This short outline demonstrates that the financial crisis had its roots in the allocation of risks and the lack of transparency. However, as opposed to the Asian crisis between 1997 and 1999 or the bankruptcies of Enron and Worldcom, systematic failures of corporate governance were not of key importance (Wymeersch, 2008, p. 1; Mülbert, 2009a and 2009b; see also van den Berghe, 2009). This crisis might have been related to incentives for corporate actors, but incentives for market participants were equally important: 'The relationship between corporate governance and financial stability is an indirect one, as the stability of firms and markets are essential elements for maintaining financial stability. Corporate governance tools do contribute to the intermediate objectives at the firm level, but not directly to financial stability' (Wymeersch, 2008, p. 13). Loans were granted, securitized and rated in a legal and social framework that allocated risks and chances in a manner creating incentives for transactions that destabilized the whole system in the long run. Most of the contracts in question were long-term relationships – loan contracts, bond contracts and loan insurance contracts. Such relationships are, by nature, more likely to provide strong and steady incentives than simple spot contracts.[7] For a thorough understanding of the market instability that was at the heart of the current crisis, it is crucial to analyse the steering effects of all different public, but also social, mechanisms that impacted the autonomous interaction of the various players – central banks, borrowers and private banks, insurance companies and credit rating agencies. It is necessary to understand the entirety of collective, not only hierarchical, influences on a specific social system. This is precisely the task that governance research is all about (Hill and Hupe, 2002, pp. 13 *et seq.*; Köndgen, 2006, p. 514). Yet the social system that was concerned is not only the internal organization of corporations, but also the market.[8] What governance research has to explore and improve in future is the institutional framework of contractual (in addition to intra-organizational) relations.[9]

Therefore, the financial crisis had much to do with governance, but not only with *corporate* governance.[10] Most of the early reports, documents and declarations barely mentioned corporate governance. It was addressed neither in the recommendations of the US President's Working Group on Financial Markets, nor in the reports of the Financial Stability Forum and the International Monetary Fund (President's Working Group on Financial Markets, 2008; Financial Stability Forum, 2009; International Monetary Fund, 2008). There was no mention of corporate governance in the Washington or London Declarations of the G20 (G-20-summit, 2008). In the UK, the above-mentioned Turner Review was a bit more fruitful[11] and was later complemented by the so-called Walker Review, dealing specifically with bank governance arrangements (Walker Review, 2009). Yet the European Larosière Report called corporate governance 'one of the most important failures of the present crisis' (Larosière Group, 2009,

p. 29). Under this heading, however, the report mainly criticized general incentive mechanisms on markets that promote short-term profit orientation. Only the reform proposals on remuneration and risk management are more specifically related to corporate governance as such. The OECD, the world's leading rule-setter in corporate governance issues (OECD, 2004), called for corresponding reforms as a matter of course and launched an ambitious action plan, but its analysis mainly concentrated on the same two aspects (OECD, 2009a).[12] Moreover, the OECD recommended better implementation and enforcement mechanisms, but did not propose any substantive revision of the current corporate governance principles (OECD, 2009b).

Regulatory reforms in response to the financial crisis

Subsequent to these early reactions, a multitude of regulatory reforms and reform proposals have been tackled in order to respond to the causes of the financial crisis. A short survey of the most important developments at the European and national level, particularly in the UK and Germany, will show that some of these reforms relate very well to the corporate governance framework, mainly with respect to financial institutions. However, the main focus of these crisis-related regulatory reforms centres on the architecture of financial markets rather than on the governance of companies.

General framework of corporate governance

With respect to the general corporate governance framework, only minor modifications have taken place since the financial crisis, and most of the respective developments are not directly related to the crisis and its causes.

At the European level, for example, the effectiveness of monitoring and enforcement systems that Member States have put in place with a view to the national corporate governance codes is currently under review. In November 2009, the European Commission published a corresponding external study in order to provide a basis for the European Corporate Governance Forum's work on this subject (Risk-Metrics Group *et al.*, 2009). While this group's further discussions had a certain emphasis on the causes of the financial crisis, most of its statements were related to more general issues such as the transparency of derivative positions and empty voting, the protection of minority shareholder rights and the application of corporate governance codes in cross-border situations (European Corporate Governance Forum, 2010). Similarly, most of the amendments that have recently been proposed by the Commission on the German Corporate Governance Code are not directly linked to the financial crisis, but concerned, inter alia, incentives for sustainable corporate governance, improvements in the professionalism of supervisory boards by continuing education requirements, and sustainable measures for increasing the proportion of women and international representatives on German supervisory boards (German Corporate Governance Commission, 2010). In the UK, the Financial Reporting Council (FRC) published an updated version of the Corporate Governance Code in May 2010, together with a report summarizing the outcome of its recent consultation process (Financial Reporting Council, 2010). Again, the few significant changes in substance do not respond directly to the financial crisis: directors of FTSE 350 companies are expected to put themselves up for re-election annually, the chairman should hold regular development reviews with each director, and there are new provisions relating to boardroom diversity. Further modifications relate to the disclosure of the business model, the leadership responsibility of the chairman, the time commitments of directors and the role of non-executive directors.

One single topic on the reform agenda is more closely related to the financial crisis: remuneration policies. As this issue attracted much public interest in the aftermath of the crisis, many rule-makers felt the need to take a firm stand in this respect. On the European level, the Commission adopted a recommendation on the regime for the remuneration of directors of listed companies in April 2009 (European Commission, 2009c). The recommendation invites Member States to set a limit on severance pay and to ban severance pay in case of failure; to require a balance between fixed and variable pay and link variable pay to predetermined, measurable performance criteria; and to allow companies to reclaim variable pay paid on the basis of data that proved to be manifestly misstated. With respect to the process of determining directors' remuneration, the said recommendation asks Member States, inter alia, to strengthen the role and operation of the remuneration committee through new principles on the composition of such committees, to oblige committee members to be present at the share-holder meeting where the remuneration policy is discussed to provide explanations to shareholders and to avoid conflicts of remuneration consultants. In a communication accompanying this recommendation, the Commission claims that there was 'broad consensus that compensation schemes based on short-term returns, without adequate consideration for the corresponding risks, contributed to the incentives that led to financial institutions' engagement in overly risky business practices' (European Commission, 2009d, p. 2). Even though this argument seems questionable with respect to compensation schemes outside the financial sector, the Commission observes very accurately whether Member States have acted in order to give effect to these recommendations. A recent report states that most recommendations have so far only been implemented by a minority of the Member States, including Germany and the UK (European Commission, 2010a). In the UK, respective principles are now included in the updated version of the Corporate Governance Code, whereas Germany introduced new legislation on the appropriateness of management board compensation, which came into force in August 2009 (VorstAG, 2009).

Corporate governance in financial institutions

When regulatory reforms are specifically targeted to the financial services sector, their link to the financial crisis seems intuitively plausible. Indeed, the elaboration of such sector-specific rules can probably be identified as the single most important trend in European corporate governance since the crisis. This trend recently culminated in a Green Paper on corporate governance in financial institutions and remuneration policies, published by the European Commission on 2 June 2010 and announcing a plethora of legislative and non-legislative proposals to be implemented in the near future (European Commission, 2010b). This approach goes far beyond the developments at the national level, particularly in the UK: whereas the extensive Walker Review of Corporate Governance had a specific focus on the banking industry, it largely refrained from proposing additional provisions and instead advocated amplification and better observance (Walker Review, 2009). Accordingly the revised UK Corporate Governance Code does not include any sector-specific provisions (see Financial Reporting Council, 2009 and 2010).

By contrast, the first European step towards sector-specific governance rules had already been taken in April 2009, with respect to remuneration policies. Along with the general remuneration rules mentioned above, the Commission published a more specific recommendation for the financial services sector (European Commission, 2009f). As opposed to the general scope of application of corporate governance rules, these recommendations apply to all undertakings operating in the financial services industry, regardless of their legal status, and regardless of whether their securities are admitted to trading on a regulated market. Compared to the general recommendation on executive remuneration, the Commission proposes more specific mechanisms of internal transparency, control and review as well as allocation of the responsibility for remuneration policies to the board instead of a remuneration committee (European Commission, 2009f, para. 6 and Section III). Above all, the respective rules are not only recommended for company directors, but for 'those categories of staff whose professional activities have a material impact on the risk profile of the financial undertaking' (European Commission, 2009f, para. 1.2 and Recital 13). A recent report of the Commission states, however, that Member States have responded only very cautiously to this sector-specific recommendation. A relatively high number did not initiate any measures or took unsatisfactory ones; and only seven Member States apply relevant measures across the financial services sector. The Commission concludes disappointedly that 'these substantial differences of national implementation on an element as fundamental as the structure of the remuneration policy are worrying' (European Commission, 2010c, p. 11).

However, this experience did not prevent the Commission from proposing additional corporate governance rules specifically for the financial sector. In its recent Green Paper, the Commission justifies this sector-specific approach by the particularities of financial institutions. On the one hand, their potential systemic risks imply that taxpayers are 'inevitably stakeholders in the running of [such] institutions, with the goal of financial stability and long-term economic growth' (European Commission, 2010b, p. 5). On the other hand, depositors and creditors favour a very low level of risk, so that their expectations are potentially at odds with those of financial institutions' shareholders. While none of these arguments is implausible,[13] the differences to other sectors are arguably in degree rather than in kind. In any event, the question arises whether they justify the wide range of proposals that the Commission set forth. They are aimed not only at changing remuneration policies in companies in order to discourage excessive risk-taking, but also at improving the functioning and the composition of boards of financial institutions in order to enhance their supervision of senior management, at establishing a risk culture at all levels of financial institutions in order to ensure that long-term interests of the business are taken into account, and finally at enhancing the involvement of shareholders, financial supervisors and external auditors in corporate governance matters. Some specific proposals even touch the very concept of private business organizations by considering, for example, giving supervisory authorities 'the power and duty to check the correct functioning of the board of directors and the risk management function' (European Commission, 2010b, p. 15, para. 4.2). Of course, these proposals constitute only the first step of the legislative process; they will be reconsidered in accordance with the input that the Commission receives during the ongoing consultation process. Nonetheless, the radical nature of some Green Paper proposals is quite astonishing, in particular because the European Commission itself acknowledges that 'corporate governance did not directly cause the crisis' (European Commission, 2010b, p. 2).[14]

Governance of financial markets

The Commission's acknowledgement is in accordance with the author's observation that the financial crisis did not primarily emerge due to specific corporate structures, but had its roots in the instability of financial markets. As a consequence, taking stock of respective regulatory reforms must not be confined to corporate governance. Such selective perception would effectively fade out the actual emphasis of European and national rule-makers alike, clearly focusing on ensuring the stability of financial markets. The European Commission explicitly centred its initiatives on the 'governance of international and European financial markets' in order to create responsible and reliable financial markets for the future (European Commission, 2009h, p. 4). The respective legislative and regulatory measures and pending propositions have indeed become so numerous and manifold by now that it is impossible to quote more than some important examples at the national and European level, which are all closely related to the aforementioned causes of the crisis.

With respect to consumer loans, for instance, the European Commission undertook to propose further measures at the EU level regarding responsible lending and borrowing, including a reliable framework on credit intermediation (European Commission, 2009h, p. 7; for the results of the relevant public consultation, see European Commission, 2009j). In order to restore market confidence and provide for sound information about the creditworthiness of companies, governments and sophisticated financial products, the European Parliament and the Council adopted a directly applicable regulation that puts in place a common regulatory regime for the issuance of credit ratings.[15] With respect to banking, insurance and securities markets, various initiatives aim at enhancing competition in order to respond to systemic risks and in particular to the phenomenon that banks become 'too big to fail'. Current proposals include a specific merger control or even a decartelization of banks (Zimmer and Rengier, 2010). Further noteworthy initiatives aimed at reducing this systemic risk effectively propose levies, taxes or capital requirements, the level of which rises with the systemic relevance of an institution (Doluca *et al.*, 2010; Weber, 2010). In a similar vein, the Commission launched an intensive discussion on further possible changes to the Capital Requirements Directive, aimed at strengthening risk coverage, mitigating pro-cyclicality and discouraging leverage, as well as strengthening liquidity risk requirements and forward-looking provisioning for credit losses (European Commission, 2010e). The ultimate goal of the proposal is to prevent market transactions with a potential to jeopardize market stability. The same is true for the proposed Directive on Alternative Investment Fund Managers, considered to be a crucial part of the European Commission's response to the financial crisis. Again, the purpose is to extend regulation and oversight to all actors and activities that embed significant risks for financial market participants and for the stability of the underlying markets (European Commission, 2009k, p. 2 (Explanatory Memorandum)). The same market-oriented focus is even more obvious with respect to the Commission's initiatives on derivatives. Having adopted two different communications on 'Ensuring efficient, safe and sound derivatives markets' in July and October 2009, the Commission launched a public consultation on derivatives and market infrastructures, and is now in the process of finalizing its draft legislative proposals, again with a clear focus on risk mitigation (European Commission, 2009g and 2009i).[16] Various initiatives at national level point in a very similar direction.[17]

Implications for future governance research

'This time is different',[18] at least in one respect: whereas previous crises originated in non-transparent corporate structures, the recent turmoil had its roots also in the instability of markets. Accordingly, most regulatory reforms in response to the financial crisis focused on improving the stability and transparency of markets, not companies. All this should be reflected in future governance research. Oliver Williamson once defined governance as 'an effort to implement the "study of good order and workable arrangements", where good order includes both spontaneous order in the market . . . and intentional order' (Williamson, 2005, p. 1). Henceforward the study of good order and workable arrangements should take markets and contractual relationships into greater consideration, and develop a research area of contract governance.

The nature of contract governance

The notion of contract governance has thus far only been used rather sporadically, usually with a view to worker participation agreements in corporations, that is, in terms of corporate governance on a contractual basis (Windbichler, 2004, pp. 195 *et seq.*; Windbichler, 2005, pp. 529 and 533 *et seq.*; similarly Eidenmüller, 2007, p. 493). Yet contract governance has a wider scope. It aims at improving the proper functioning of markets by providing a research approach that deals with the institutional framework of contractual relations on markets. Contract governance research examines whether their legal, social, cultural or otherwise agreed conditions generate coordinating or steering effects for market participants (in detail, Möslein and Riesenhuber, 2009). For instance, default rules of contract law provide an auxiliary infrastructure with a potential impact on market behaviour (Windbichler, 1998, p. 271; Bachmann, 2003, pp. 20 *et seq.*; Grundmann, 2007b, p. 143; with respect to company law, Fleischer, 2004, p. 707; similarly from the perspective of institutional economics ('facilitative law') Clark, 1985, pp. 60–72; Furubotn and Richter, 2005, pp. 12 *et seq.*). Moreover, information and transparency obligations can serve similar goals as mandatory substantive regulations. Similarly as with respect to corporate structures, the institutional framework of market transactions is therefore by no means restricted to supervisory regulation, but can also be composed of default rules, soft law mechansims or codes of conduct. Such alternative mechanisms might even turn out to function more effectively, for they give guidelines on good conduct, while not prohibiting certain market behaviour. Contract governance research takes these alternative mechanisms into account as well. Such an approach can help to avoid, for instance, counter-reactions and circumventions. As compared with the actual regulatory reforms, contract governance might therefore offer alternative ways to foster long-term market stability, while allowing market players as much contractual freedom as possible (in a similar direction, already prior to the present crisis: Alexander *et al.*, 2006).

As a research perspective, contract governance changes the traditional legal approach in a threefold sense. In the first place, the perspective on contractual and legal rules changes from the usual *ex post* to an *ex ante* perspective: contract governance understands rules not primarily as an instrument of dispute resolution, but as a mechanism for steering and coordinating human behaviour (Möslein and Riesenhuber, 2009, p. 257). Legal scholars have examined the steering effects of private law rules before, but not systematically (in detail, on the legitimacy of preventive and regulatory functions of private law, Wagner, 2006; criticizing, for instance, Honsell, 2008, pp. 626 *et seq.*). Contract governance can help to analyse incentive effects, for example, to better understand the impact of contractual bonus or malus arrangements on individual behaviour. As legal scholarship itself lacks a specific model of human behaviour, such analysis requires a more intensive dialogue with other disciplines – not just economics, but social sciences more generally, in particular sciences of human behaviour, including neurobiology.[19] Experience shows that governance provides a common language which greatly facilitates this dialogue, and may henceforth also do so for contract law (Schuppert, 1999; Hoffmann-Riem, 2004, p. 11). Secondly, contract governance widens the perspective. The contractual relationship between two persons, the bilateral 'privity of contract', represents the focus of classical contract law scholarship (Trebilcock, 1993, pp. 58–77). Contract governance has a wider scope, as it focuses on markets, not only on individual contracts.[20] Individual needs of protection may often appear less relevant once not only the bilateral contractual relationship, but also alternatives on markets, are taken into account (Möslein and

Riesenhuber, 2009, p. 259). Like corporate governance, contract governance therefore includes an internal and an external dimension, thereby linking contract and competition law considerations more closely together (Möslein and Riesenhuber, 2009, pp. 270 and 288). Thirdly, the broader, results-oriented perspective of contract governance can contribute to a contract law theory of rule-making, thus going beyond the mere application of rules (Eidenmüller, 2007, pp. 490 *et seq.*). Strategic advice for legislators, especially with respect to techniques and intensity of regulation, becomes particularly important in times in which uniform statute books are increasingly supplemented and substituted by various regulatory instruments at different regulatory levels (Calliess, 2006; Michaels and Jansen, 2006, pp. 868 *et seq.*; Calliess *et al.*, 2008).

Similarities and differences between contract governance and corporate governance

Contract governance and corporate governance follow very similar patterns. They both help to provide a wider variety of regulatory tools to rule-makers. Moreover, both mechanisms supplement each other. They are indeed closely linked together and interact in a variety of ways. Exchange and cooperation are of course fundamentally different mechanisms, but they are nonetheless often equally suitable to reach specific goals. This idea is the actual starting point of governance research in Williamson's seminal article; it also defines a key decision problem in economic theory (path-breaking, Coase, 1937; cf., furthermore, Williamson, 1985, pp. 32–4, 60–2 and *passim*; for a recent survey, Eidenmüller, 2001, p. 1042). The most important difference between contract and organization is that contracts are typically concluded *pari passu* on markets, whereas business organizations are characterized by a hierarchical order (Möslein and Riesenhuber, 2009, p. 258). Decision-making power and risk-bearing can diverge in instances of majority and management decisions (Behrens, 1986, pp. 110–277). It is mainly because of this divergence that a corporate governance framework is required that makes decision-making procedures transparent and provides incentives for decision-makers to act in the best interest of the corporate organization.[21]

Even in contractual relationships, however, not all relevant questions are decided by mutual consent. Particularly in long-term contracts and contractual networks we can also track 'hierarchical' decision-making mechanisms (in detail Behrens, 1986, pp. 493 *et seq.*). Moreover, the market mechanism does not always provide for equitable solutions (*Richtigkeitsgewähr*).[22] In such cases, alternative governance structures may be required, which are contractual in nature, but feature, depending on their specific design, more or less similarity to corporate governance.[23] This smooth transition between contract and corporate governance corresponds with the insight of business administrations that corporate boundaries are not in every respect fixed. The choice between corporate and contractual structures is rather one of the central challenges for management that has to optimally allocate the various areas of entrepreneurial activity. Due to the advancements of information technologies, outsourcing has gained much importance in recent years so that management experts aptly speak of an 'expansion of corporate boundaries' (Wigand *et al.*, 1997). Corporate boundaries are blurred in many directions, also with respect to financing, where creditors are often granted a similar degree of influence as shareholders by means of contractual covenants (Servatius, 2008; also McCahery and Vermeulen, 2008, pp. 189 *et seq.*). The outsourcing of risks on special-purpose entities or by securitization can be conceptualized as a similar development in the banking business (as a step to banks without boundaries, so to speak; cf. Obay, 2000). Due to this blurring of corporate boundaries the often-cited 'nexus of contracts' is not only a law-and-economics metaphor for the corporate entities,[24] but becomes business reality in a very literal sense. If governance research really wants to take a look at social systems as a whole, it cannot focus exclusively on the single corporate entity but needs to analyse the whole contractual network in which corporations are embedded (similarly, Deffains and Demougin, 2006, p. 7). In other words: 'contracting for control' needs to be taken into account (Baker *et al.*, 2006; in a similar vein Hart and Moore, 2008; Fehr *et al.*, 2009).

Linkages between contract and corporate governance

Not only are corporate governance and contract governance two alternatives with certain similarities, however, but these two mechanisms are closely interwoven. Two major linkages between contract and corporate governance were already indicated in the Larosière Report and the action plan of the OECD, and have subsequently induced intense regulatory activity. The first linkage concerns employment contracts that bind decision-makers to the company. Their incentive structures, especially their remuneration schemes, are of a contractual nature, but they also have an impact on corporate strategy and success (comprehensively, Bebchuk and Fried, 2004). Indeed, there is a general consensus that the design of remuneration schemes had a crucial impact on the financial crisis.[25] Remuneration schemes at the executive level and below are rooted in contractual arrangements between companies and their employees; they often comprise not only a fixed salary, but also variable elements such as annual bonuses, long-term cash incentives or stock options, and possibly even severance payments. Contractual structures therefore create incentives that have an impact on management actions and can, as the Commission states, 'affect the long-term performance and sustainability of the companies and therefore also affect investor confidence, employment, competitiveness and long-term economic growth' (European Commission, 2009e, p. 7). On the other hand, the design of these contractual structures depends on the procedural setting within the corporation, more specifically on the question of which corporate body is competent and accountable to decide on such arrangements (for a comparative survey, see Möslein, 2007, pp. 101 *et seq.*). The importance of appropriate corporate governance structures and adequate disclosure rules for the contract governance of remuneration agreements has triggered corresponding legislative reforms.[26] Given that remuneration incentives in the operational business of investment banks were relevant for the current crisis,[27] remuneration policy is not only a question of corporate governance, but also, and maybe primarily, of contract governance.[28]

A second linkage between contract governance and corporate governance concerns corporate risk management, in other words the systematic identification, assessment and prioritization of risks (Hubbard, 2009, p. 46; comprehensively, Chew, 2008; Merna and Al-Thani, 2008). Since the financial crisis, the focus has been mainly on so-called external risks, on market risks that originate in contractual arrangements (see, for instance, Senior Supervisors Group, 2008, pp. 12 *et seq.*; OECD, 2009a, pp. 8 *et seq.*). Again, the linkage is twofold in nature. On the one hand, contractual risks and incentive structures can have a crucial impact on corporate strategy and corporate success, as the financial crisis has dramatically shown.[29]

On the other hand, the ranking of risk management in the internal corporate governance structure may well have an impact on the structure and design of these contractual relationships, thereby affecting contract governance. Accordingly, the Larosière Report and the Basel Committee on Banking Supervision propose independent risk management at senior management level with direct access to the board (Basel Committee on Banking Supervision 2009; Larosière Group, 2009, pp. 32 *et seq.*). The above-mentioned OECD Paper goes even further and emphasizes the importance of future-oriented stress tests in a very general manner, not only with respect to the financial sector: 'Stress testing must form an integral part of the management culture so that results have a meaningful impact on business decisions' (OECD, 2009b, p. 10; with potential impact on future corporate governance standards: OECD 2009a, pp. 33–40). In other words, contract governance, the forward-looking assessment of long-term contractual relationships, is meant to become a key management responsibility for corporate boards in general.

Future research

Contract governance will only be able to provide new solutions for preventing future systemic crises if such a research approach can indeed offer a useful tool for present challenges. Most governance structures in which we find the causes of the financial crisis were contractual relationships (subprime loans, securitization; the assignment of rating firms and so forth). Problems of credit rating, systemic financial risks, the moral hazard of risk transfer and interlocking contracts therefore need to be tackled from the perspective of contract governance. This observation, however, only adds impetus to a research approach that would be interesting in its own right; research on the stability and constitution of contractually organized mass transactions and on transactions that typically are of a long duration. A governance perspective on these phenomena is important because contract law research, specifically in Europe, has not yet followed the shift from an industrial to a service- and knowledge-based society. The sales contract, in thinking and in codification endeavours, still forms the sole starting point, the paradigm. Reality, however, is different: long-term relationships, contractual relationships of cooperation, relationships of trust with an ongoing and intensive exchange of information and of inputs and with a high amount of cross-decision powers between the parties and mutual positions of influence form largely undiscovered territory, but at the same time one large part of the challenge for today's contract law. Moreover, the multiplicity of contract partners, especially in networks of contracts, but also in the case of parallel behaviour, is a phenomenon which is paramount in real life but still rarely discussed in contract law (see, however, Teubner, 2002; Grundmann, 2007a; Grundmann, 2008; also Cafaggi, 2008). The phenomenon of herd behaviour, in turn, was of utmost importance in the financial crisis. Networks of contracts are dominating all supply relationships, all distribution relationships, thus virtually the whole production chain, but also payment systems as well as many forms of financing. Even less developed – and indeed virtually unexplored – is the theory of herd behaviour in contractual situations. All this points towards a much wider issue: the relationship between contract governance and free market mechanisms.

The concept of 'contract governance' would seem to describe well the panorama of these topics. This term points to other governance discussions, among them most prominently the corporate governance discussion and its breathtaking development. It is of course true that when discussing governance one has to distinguish the original and rather narrow meaning, that is governance of the process of formation of contract and of the phase of performance by the parties (Williamson, 1979), from a governance regime coming from outside, i.e., governance devices in the market order set for mass transactions. However, both the arrangements adopted by the parties and the governance regime set by market organization are interlinked to such an extent that they should not be discussed separately, i.e., governance of a contractual relationship should not be discussed without taking into account market organization. This is particularly evident in situations where parties themselves can change the governance regime set by states, namely in the case of default rules or of 'comply or explain' regimes (Möslein, 2010). In such situations, the governance regime which is finally in place is the result of a combination of both private parties' action and state regime. Governance in contractual relationships, mainly in long-term relationships, in network relationships or in mass transactions that occur in parallel, is the main (although not the exclusive) focus of contract governance research: primarily governance via private arrangement, but also market organization, especially in national or supranational laws, considering as well that the most important players are corporations.

If the research area is called 'contract governance', this obviously implies that research can learn from how the discussion in 'corporate governance' has developed. Corporate governance discussion was also prompted by important crises, and yet it was much more than a mere answer to a crisis. It encompassed the problems raised by these crises but also reached much further. It was all about fundamental research, the need for which had become even more evident against the background of the crises. Moreover, not all problems and concepts that were discussed in a corporate governance perspective concerned fundamentally new questions. Yet that discussion contained a good deal of novelty, at least in style and approach to research, and to a certain extent really new substantive questions were brought up too. The same would seem to be possible for contract governance where similar developments, to a large extent, are yet to happen.

Notes

1 For an extensive account of examples illustrating that good design of a market is crucial to its success, that a market develops over time by trial and error, and that government plays an indispensable role in providing public goods and acting as rule-setter and referee, see MacMillan, 2002.
2 Further information available at www.pittsburghsummit.gov/, last accessed 16 August 2010.
3 For instance, Klaus Hopt warned strongly against 'the danger of over-regulation, a plethora of standards and a new protectionist wave', see Hopt, 2009.
4 The term and concept have been developed in a different area: Gunningham and Grabosky, 1998.
5 Despite early warnings: see, for instance, Center for Responsible Lending, 2006. At a glance on the merits: Grundmann *et al.*, 2009, pp. 8–12.
6 For an extensive account of (non-executive) remuneration practices in the City of London before the crisis, see House of Commons – Treasury Committee, 2009, pp. 10–17.
7 This is one of the central arguments of Williamson, 1979, pp. 247–54; see also Williamson, 1996, pp. 145–70.

8 This fits with the concept of governance as defined, for instance, by Williamson, 2005, pp. 1 *et seq.*

9 For a very similar approach, yet from a purely economic perspective, see the research programme of the Collaborative Research Centre (*Sonderforschungsbereich*) Transregio 15, *Governance and the Efficiency of Economic Systems* (coordinated by Urs Schweizer), available at www.sfbtr15.de, last accessed 16 August 2010.

10 Similarly, Mülbert, 2009a, p. 411: 'After the beginning of the financial turbulences in summer 2007, the issue of banks' corporate governance, with the notable exception of remuneration, went out of focus for some time.' See, however, Isaksson and Kirkpatrick, 2009, p. 11: 'If there is one major lesson to draw from the financial crisis, it is that corporate governance matters.'

11 Turner Review, 2009, p. 78 ('Regulation can and should address issues relating to the proper governance and conduct of rating agencies and the management of conflict of interest'), and p. 93 ('Achieving high standards of risk management and governance in all banks is therefore essential').

12 Two additional, but closely related, aspects are the performance of boards and the exercise of shareholder rights.

13 More extensively, the Walker Review, 2009, pp. 24 *et seq.*

14 In a similar vein, European Commission, 2010f, p. 3: 'Corporate governance weaknesses in financial institutions were not *per se* the main causes of the financial crisis.'

15 European Commission, 2009l. In June 2010, the Commission proposed some amendments in order to improve supervision: European Commission, 2010d.

16 An update on the consultation process is available at http://ec.europa.eu/internal_market/financial-markets/derivatives/index_en.htm, last accessed 16 August 2010.

17 See, for instance, the German proposal for banning certain securities transactions: Deutscher Bundestag, 2010.

18 Reinhart and Rogoff, 2009, drawing sweeping parallels between financial crises, across times and continents.

19 As contract governance concerns the behaviour of market actors, behavioural law and economics appears as an indispensable complementary discipline. Seminally: Kahneman and Tversky, 1979; further, Camerer *et al.*, 2004.

20 Similar to the traditional approach of economic law; very much to the point Hopt, 1972, p. 1019 ('Nicht das einzelne Rädchen, das Räderwerk ist gemeint'). Similarly, for instance, Schwark, 1979, pp. 64–6; and earlier Böhm, 1933, p. 189 (economic law as an aggregate of rules

'serving social order and the steering of the collective economic process', author's translation).

21 On this divergence cf. again Williamson, 1979; on other mechanisms of coordination (such as clans, federations, networks), see the survey of Mayntz, 2006, p. 14 with further references.

22 German legal scholars tend to speak, more cautiously, of *Richtigkeits-chance* instead of *Richtigkeitsgewähr*: a chance rather than a guarantee of just solutions inherent in the contract mechanism; cf. Schmidt-Rimpler, 1941; Schmidt-Rimpler, 1974; recently, Canaris, 1993, p. 883; Singer, 1995, pp. 9–12; Canaris, 1997, pp. 48–51.

23 One example is so-called 'cooperative governance', increasingly studied by economists. See various contributions in Theurl, 2005; Theurl and Schweinsberg, 2004; in a broader framework subject of a recent congress of the prestigious 'Verein für Socialpolitik' (under the heading 'Governance in economic policy').

24 Seminally, Jensen and Meckling, 1976, p. 311 ('The private firm is simply a form of legal fiction which serves as a nexus for contracting relationships'); see also Easterbrook and Fischel, 1989; Eisenberg, 1989.

25 See, for instance, European Commission, 2009e, p. 3: 'badly designed [remuneration] policy and schemes at all levels in the financial services industry contributed to "short-termism" and excessive risk-taking without adequate regard to long-term global performance . . . The problem addressed is not how much directors are paid, but the mismatch between pay and performance.'

26 In Germany, for instance: VorstAG, 2009. For a recent analysis of the regulatory framework and remuneration practices in Europe, see Ferrarini *et al.*, 2009.

27 Larosière Group, 2009, p. 31 (Recommendation 11: '[. . .] the same principles should apply to proprietary traders and asset managers'); OECD, 2009a, p. 14 ('Remuneration problems also exist at the sales and trading function level'). This concern was also shared by the Financial Stability Forum, 2009, p. 20.

28 Quite explicitly OECD, 2009a, p. 17: incentives at lower levels beyond 'the usual focus of corporate governance debates'.

29 While most major banks failed to anticipate the development of the housing market, there was a marked difference in how intensively they were affected, depending on their exposure to certain financial instruments: Senior Supervisors Group, 2008, pp. 3 *et seq.* and *passim*; cf. also OECD, 2009b, p. 7 *et seq.* For an empirical study of the twenty-five largest European banks, see Ladipo and Nestor, 2009.

References

Alexander, K., Dhumale, R. and Eatwell, J. 2006. *Global Governance of Financial Systems: The International Regulation of Systemic Risk.* Oxford University Press.

Bachmann, G. 2003. 'Privatrecht als Organisationsrecht', in Witt, C.-H., *et al.* (eds.), *Jahrbuch Junger Zivilrechtswissenschaftler 2002: Die Privatisierung des Privatrechts.* Stuttgart: Boorberg, pp. 1–29.

Baker, G., Gibbons, R. and Murphy, K. J. 2006. 'Contracting for Control', Working Paper, Stanford University, available at www.stanford.edu/group/SITE/archive/SITE_2006/Web%20Session%206/Gibbons.pdf, last accessed 16 August 2010.

Barth, J. 2009. *The Rise and Fall of the US Mortgage and Credit Markets.* Hoboken, NJ: J. Wiley & Sons.

Basel Committee on Banking Supervision 2009. 'Principles for sound stress testing practices and supervision', available at www.bis.org/publ/bcbs147.pdf, last accessed 16 August 2010.

Bebchuk, L. A. and Fried, J. 2004. *Pay without Performance: The Unfulfilled Promise of Executive Compensation.* Cambridge, MA/London: Harvard University Press.

Behrens, P. 1986. *Die ökonomischen Grundlagen des Rechts.* Tübingen: Mohr-Siebeck.

Böhm, F. 1933. *Wettbewerb und Monopolkampf: Eine Untersuchung zur Frage des wirtschaftlichen Kampfrechts und zur Frage der rechtlichen Struktur der geltenden Wirtschaftsordnung.* Berlin: Heymanns.

Cafaggi, F. 2008. *Contractual Networks and the Small Business Act: Toward European Principles.* Working Paper, European University Institute, No. 2008/15, available at http://cadmus.eui.eu/dspace/handle/1814/8771, last accessed 16 August 2010.

Calliess, G.-P. 2006. *Grenzüberschreitende Verbraucherverträge – Rechtssicherheit und Gerechtigkeit auf dem elektronischen Weltmarktplatz.* Tübingen: Mohr-Siebeck.

Calliess, G.-P., Freiling, J. and Renner, M. 2008. 'Law, the state, and private ordering', *German Law Journal* 9: 397–410.

Camerer, C. F., Lowenstein, G. and Rabin, M. (eds.) 2004. *Advances in Behavioral Economics.* Princeton University Press.

Canaris, C.-W. 1993. 'Verfassungs- und europarechtliche Aspekte der Vertragsfreiheit in der Privatrechtsgesellschaft', in Badura, P. and Scholz, R. (eds.), *Festschrift für Lerche.* Munich: Beck, pp. 873–91.

    1997. *Die Bedeutung der Iustitia Distributiva im deutschen Vertragsrecht.* Munich: Verlag der Bayerischen Akademie der Wissenschaften.

Center for Responsible Lending (ed.) 2006. *Losing Ground: Foreclosures in the Subprime Market and Their Cost to Homeowners*. Working Paper by E. Schloemer, W. Lei, K. Erust and K. Keest, available at www.responsiblelending.org, last accessed 16 August 2010.

Chew, D. H. 2008. *Corporate Risk Management*. New York: Columbia University Press.

Clark, R. C. 1985. 'Agency costs versus fiduciary duties', in Pratt, J. W. and Zeckhauser, R. J. (eds.), *Principals and Agents: The Structure of Business*. Boston, MA: Harvard Business School Press, pp. 55–79.

Coase, R. H. 1937. 'The nature of the firm', *Economica* 4: 386–405.

Deffains, B. and Demougin, D. 2006. 'Governance: who controls matters', *Zeitschrift für Betriebswirtschaft*, Special Issue 5: 1–20.

Deutscher Bundestag 2010. *Entwurf eines Gesetzes zur Vorbeugung gegen missbräuchliche Wertpapier- und Derivategeschäfte*, BT-Drs. 17/1952, 8 June.

Doluca, H., Klüh, U., Wagner, M. and Weder di Mauro, B. 2010. 'Reducing systemic relevance – a proposal'. Working Paper, German Council of Economic Experts, available at www.sachverstaendigenrat-wirtschaft.de/download/publikationen/svrap_04_2010.pdf, last accessed 16 August 2010.

Easterbrook, F. H. and Fischel, D. R. 1989. 'The corporate contract', *Columbia Law Review* 89: 1416–48.

Eidenmüller, H. 2001. 'Kapitalgesellschaftsrecht im Spiegel der ökonomischen Theorie', *Juristenzeitung*: 1041–51.

    2007. 'Forschungsperspektiven im Unternehmensrecht', *Juristenzeitung*: 487–94.

Eisenberg, M. 1989. 'The conception that the corporation is a nexus of contracts, and the dual nature of the firm', *Journal of Corporation Law* 24: 819–36.

European Commission 2009a. *Communication from the Commission for the Spring European Council on Driving European Recovery of 4 March 2009*, COM(2009) 114 final.

    2009b. *Communication from the Commission on European Financial Supervision of 25 May 2009*, COM(2009) 252 final.

    2009c. *Commission Recommendation Complementing Recommendations 2004/913/EC and 2005/162/EC as Regards the Regime for the Remuneration of Directors of Listed Companies*, C(2009) 3177 ('Recommendation on remuneration of directors'), of 30 April 2009.

    2009d. *Communication from the Commission, Accompanying Commission Recommendation Complementing Recommendations 2004/913/EC and 2005/162/EC as Regards the Regime for the Remuneration of Directors of Listed Companies and Commission Recommendation on Remuneration Policies in the Financial Services Sector*, COM(2009) 211 final.

2009e. *Commission Staff Working Document Accompanying the Commission Recommendation Complementing Recommendations 2004/913/EC and 2005/162/EC as regards the Regime for the Remuneration of Directors of Listed Companies and the Commission Recommendation on Remuneration Policies in the Financial Services Sector ('Impact Assessment')*, C(2009) 3159, of 30 April 2009.

2009f. *Commission Recommendation on Remuneration Policies in the Financial Services Sector*, C(2009) 3159, of 30 April 2009.

2009g. *Communication from the Commission to the European Parliament, the Council, the European Economic and Social Committee, the Committee of the Regions and the European Central Bank, Ensuring Efficient, Safe and Sound Derivatives Markets: Future Policy Actions*, COM(2009) 563 final.

2009h. *Communication Driving European Recovery of 4 March 2009*, COM(2009) 114.

2009i. *Communication from the Commission, Ensuring Efficient, Safe and Sound Derivatives Markets*, COM(2009) 332 final.

2009j. *Summary of Responses to the Public Consultation on Responsible Lending and Borrowing in the EU*, 30 November, available at http://ec.europa.eu/internal_market/finservices-retail/docs/credit/resp_lending/feedback_summary_en.pdf, last accessed 16 August 2010.

2009k. *Proposal for a Directive of the European Parliament and of the Council on Alternative Investment Fund Managers and Amending Directives 2004/39/EC and 2009/. . ./EC*, COM(2009) 207 final.

2009l. *Regulation (EC) No. 1060/2009 of the European Parliament and of the Council on Credit Rating Agencies*, 16 September, OJ EC 2009 L 302/1.

2010a. *Report from the Commission to the European Parliament, the Council, the European Economic and Social Committee and the Committee of the Regions on the Application by Member States of the EU of the Commission 2009/385/EC Recommendation (2009 Recommendation on Directors' Remuneration) Complementing Recommendations 2004/913/EC and 2005/162/EC as Regards the Regime for the Remuneration of Directors of Listed Companies*, COM(2010) 285 final.

2010b. *Green Paper on Corporate Governance in Financial Institutions and Remuneration Policies*, COM(2010) 284 final.

2010c. *Report from the Commission to the European Parliament, the Council, the European Economic and Social Committee and the Committee of the Regions on the Application by Member States of the EU of the Commission 2009/384/EC Recommendation on Remuneration Policies in the Financial Services Sector (2009 Recommendation on Remuneration Policies in the Financial Services Sector)*, COM(2010) 286 final.

2010d. *Proposal for a Regulation of the European Parliament and of the Council on Amending Regulation (EC) No. 1060/2009 on Credit Rating Agencies*, COM(2010) 289 final.

2010e. *Commission Services Staff Working Document, Possible Further Changes to the Capital Requirements Directive (2009/111/EC)*, available at http://ec.europa.eu/internal_market/consultations/2010/crd4_en. htm, last accessed 16 August 2010.

2010f. *Commission Staff Working Document, Corporate Governance in Financial Institutions: Lessons to be Drawn from the Current Financial Crisis, Best Practices*, SEC(2010) 669.

European Corporate Governance Forum 2010. *Annual Report 2009*.

Fehr, E., Hart, O. and Zehnder, C. 2009. 'Contracts, reference points, and competition: behavioral effects of the fundamental transformation', *Journal of the European Economic Association* 7: 561–72.

Ferrarini, G., Moloney, N. and Ungureanu, M.-C. 2009. 'Understanding directors' pay in Europe: a comparative and empirical analysis', Law Working Paper No. 126, European Corporate Governance Institute, available at www.ssrn.com, last accessed 16 August 2010.

Financial Reporting Council 2009. 'Statement welcoming the Walker Report' (26 November), available at www.frc.org.uk/press/pub2174. html, last accessed 16 August 2010.

2010. *The UK Corporate Governance Code* (28 May), available (together with details on the consultation process) at www.frc.org.uk/corporate/ reviewCombined.cfm, last accessed 16 August 2010.

Financial Stability Forum 2009. 'Report of the Financial Stability Forum on Enhancing Market and Institutional Resilience', available at www. financialstabilityboard.org/publications/r_0804.pdf, last accessed on 16 August 2010.

Fleischer, H. 2004. 'Gesetz und Vertrag als alternative Problemlösungsmodelle im Gesellschaftsrecht', *Zeitschrift für das gesamte Handelsrecht und Wirtschaftsrecht* 168: 673–707.

Furubotn, E. G. and Richter, R. 2005 (2nd edn). *Institutions and Economic Theory: The Contribution of New Institutional Economics*. Ann Arbor: University of Michigan Press.

G-20-Summit 2008. 'Declaration of the Summit in Financial Markets and the World Economy, Action Plan to implement Principles for Reform' (November), available at www.g20.utoronto.ca/2009/2009communique0402.pdf, last accessed 16 August 2010.

2009a. *The Global Plan for Recovery and Reform*, Final communiqué (2 April), available at www.g20.org/Documents/final-communique. pdf, last accessed 16 August 2010.

2009b. *Communiqué of the Meeting of Finance Ministers and Central Bank Governors* of 14 March, available at www.londonsummit.gov. uk/en/summit-aims/key-documents/, last accessed 16 August 2010.

German Corporate Governance Commission 2010. *Draft of the German Corporate Governance Code*, as amended 26 May 2010, available at www.corporate-governance-code.de/index-e.html, last accessed 16 August 2010.

Grundmann, S. 2007a. 'Die Dogmatik der Vertragsnetze', *Archiv für die civilistische Praxis* 207: 718–67.

2007b. 'Regulating breach of contract: the right to reject performance by the party in breach', *European Review of Contract Law* 3: 121–49.

2008. 'Vertragsnetz und Wegfall der Geschäftsgrundlage', in Aderhold, L., Grunewald, B., Klingberg, D. and Paefgen, W. G. (eds.), *Festschrift für H.P. Westermann.* Cologne: Schmidt, pp. 227–44.

Grundmann, S. and Möslein, F. 2007. *European Company Law.* Antwerp: Intersentia.

Grundmann, S., Hofmann, C. and Möslein, F. (eds.) 2009. *Finanzkrise und Wirtschaftsordnung.* Berlin: de Gruyter.

Grundmann, S., Hofmann, C. and Möslein, F. 2009. 'Finanzkrise und Wirtschaftsordnung: Krisenursachen, Finanzmarktstabilisierung, Finanzmarktstabilität', in Grundmann, S., Hofmann, C. and Möslein, F. (eds.), *Finanzkrise und Wirtschaftsordnung.* Berlin: de Gruyter, pp. 1–40.

Gunningham, N. and Grabosky, P. 1998. *Smart Regulation: Designing Environmental Policy.* Oxford: Clarendon Press.

Hart, O. and Moore, J. 2008. 'Contracts as reference points', *Quarterly Journal of Economics* 123: 1–48.

Hill, M. and Hupe, P. 2002. *Implementing Public Policy: Governance in Theory and in Practice.* London: Sage.

Hoffmann-Riem, W. 2004. 'Methoden einer anwendungsorientierten Verwaltungsrechtswissenschaft', in Hoffmann-Riem, W. and Schmidt-Aßmann, E. (eds.), *Methoden der Verwaltungsrechtswissenschaft.* Baden-Baden: Nomos, pp. 9–72.

Honsell, H. 2008. 'Die Erosion des Privatrechts durch das Europarecht', *Zeitschrift für Wirtschaftsrecht*: 621–30.

Hopt, K. J. 1972. 'Rechtssoziologische und rechtsinformatorische Aspekte im Wirtschaftsrecht', *Betriebs-Berater*: 1017–24.

2000. 'Common principles of corporate governance in Europe?', in Markesinis, B. S. (ed.), *The Clifford Chance Millennium Lectures: The Coming Together of the Common Law and the Civil Law.* Oxford: Hart, pp. 105–32.

2009. 'Gefahr einer Überregulierung', *Handelsblatt*, 2 January, p. 12.

Hosp, P. 2010. 'Problematic practices of credit rating agencies: the neglected risks of mortgage-backed securities', in Kolb, E. (ed.), *Lessons from the Financial Crisis: Insights and Analysis from Today's Leading Minds.* Hoboken, NJ: J. Wiley & Sons, pp. 247–57.

House of Commons – Treasury Committee (ed.) 2009. *Banking Crisis: Reforming Corporate Governance and Pay in the City,* Ninth Report of Session 2008–2009, pp. 10–17.

Hubbard, D. W. 2009. *The Failure of Risk Management.* Hoboken, NJ: J. Wiley & Sons.

International Monetary Fund 2008. 'The recent financial turmoil – initial assessment, policy lessons, and implications for fund surveillance', available at www.imf.org/external/np/pp/eng/2008/040908.pdf, last accessed on 16 August 2010.

Isaksson, M. and Kirkpatrick, G. 2009. 'Corporate governance: lessons from the financial crisis', *OECD Observer* No. 273, June 2009, p. 11.

Issing Committee 2009. *New Financial Order: Recommendations* (February), available at www.bundesregierung.de/Content/DE/__Anlagen/2009/02/2009-02-09-finanzexpertengruppe,property=publicationFile.pdf, last accessed 16 August 2010.

Jensen, M. C. and Meckling, W. H. 1976. 'Theory of the firm, managerial behaviour, agency costs and ownership structure', *Journal of Financial Economics* 5: 305–60.

Kahneman, D. and Tversky, A. 1979. 'Prospect theory: an analysis of decision under risk', *Econometrica* 47: 263–91.

Kirchner, C. 2009. 'Prinzipien für eine kluge Regulierung', *Frankfurter Allgemeine Zeitung,* 26 March, p. 14.

Köndgen, J. 2006. 'Privatisierung des Rechts', *Archiv für die civilistische Praxis* 206: 477–525.

Ladipo, D. and Nestor, S. 2009. *Bank Boards and the Financial Crisis.* London: Nestor Advisors Ltd.

Larosière Group. 2009. *Report of the High-Level Group on Financial Supervision in the EU* (February), chaired by Jacques de Larosière, available at http://ec.europa.eu/internal_market/finances/docs/de_larosiere_report_en.pdf, last accessed 16 August 2010.

Levich, R. M., Majnoni, G. and Reinhart, C. (eds.) 2002. *Ratings, Rating Agencies and the Global Financial System.* Boston: Kluwer Academic Publishers.

MacMillan, J. 2002. *Reinventing the Bazaar: A Natural History of Markets.* New York: Norton.

Mayntz, R. 2006. 'Governance-Theorie als fortentwickelte Steuerungstheorie?', in Schuppert, G. F. (ed.), *Governance-Forschung: Vergewisserung über Stand und Entwicklungslinien* (2nd edn). Baden-Baden: Nomos, pp. 11–20.

McCahery, J. A. and Vermeulen, E. 2008. *Corporate Governance of Non-Listed Companies*. Oxford University Press.

Merna, T. and Al-Thani, F. 2008 (2nd edn). *Corporate Risk Management*. Hoboken, NJ: J. Wiley & Sons.

Michaels, R. and Jansen, N. 2006. 'Private law beyond the state? Europeanization, globalization, privatization', *American Journal of Company Law* 54: 843–90.

Möslein, F. 2007. *Grenzen unternehmerischer Leitungsmacht im marktoffenen Verband*. Berlin: de Gruyter.

2010. 'Governance by default: Dispositives Recht als Entdeckungs- und Koordinationsverfahren', in Grundmann, S., Merkt, H. and Mülbert, P. O. (eds.), *Festschrift für K. J. Hopt*. Berlin: de Gruyter pp. 2861–80.

Möslein, F. and Riesenhuber, K. 2009. 'Contract governance: a draft research agenda', *European Contract Law Review* 5: 248–89.

Mülbert, P. O. 2009a. 'Corporate governance of banks', *European Business Organization Law Review* 10: 411–36.

2009b. 'Corporate Governance von Banken', *Zeitschrift für das gesamte Handelsrecht und Wirtschaftsrecht* 173: 1–11.

Obay, L. 2000. *Financial Innovation in the Banking Industry: The Case of Asset Securitization*. New York: Garland.

OECD 2004. *Principles of Corporate Governance* (revised edn). Paris.

2009a. 'The corporate governance lessons from the financial crisis'. Working Paper by Grant Kirkpatrick, available at www.oecd.org, last accessed 16 August 2010.

2009b. 'Corporate governance and the financial crisis: key findings and main messages', available at www.oecd.org/dataoecd/3/10/43056196.pdf, last accessed 16 August 2010.

President's Working Group on Financial Markets 2008. *Policy Statement on Financial Markets* (March), available at www.ustreas.gov/press/releases/reports/pwgpolicystatemktturmoil_03122008.pdf, last accessed 16 August 2010.

Reinhart, C. M. and Rogoff, K. 2009. *This Time is Different: Eight Centuries of Financial Folly*. Princeton University Press.

Richardson, M. 2009. 'Causes of the financial crisis of 2007–2009', in Acharya, V. and Richardson, M. (eds.), *Restoring Financial Stability: How to Repair a Failed System*. Hoboken, NJ: J. Wiley & Sons, pp. 57–60.

RiskMetrics Group *et al.* (eds.) 2009. 'Study on monitoring and enforcement practices in corporate governance in the Member States', available at http://ec.europa.eu/internal_market/company/ecgforum/studies_en.htm, last accessed 16 August 2010.

Schmidt-Rimpler, W. 1941. 'Grundfragen einer Erneuerung des Vertragsrechts', *Archiv für die civilistische Praxis* 147: 130–97.

1974. 'Zum Vertragsproblem', in Baur, F., Esser, J., Kübler, F. and Steindorff, E. (eds.), *Festschrift für Raiser*. Tübingen: Mohr, pp. 3–26.

Schuppert, G. F. 1999. 'Schlüsselbegriffe der Perspektivenverklammerung von Verwaltungsrecht und Verwaltungswissenschaft', *Die Verwaltung* supplement 2 (Werkstattgespräch aus Anlass des 60. Geburtstags von Eberhard Schmidt-Aßmann), pp. 103–25.

Schwark, E. 1979. *Anlegerschutz durch Wirtschaftsrecht*. Munich: Beck.

Schwintowski, H.-P. 2009. 'Finanzmarktkrise: Ursachen, Grundsatzfragen, institutionelle Konsequenzen', in Grundmann, S., Hofmann, C. and Möslein, F. (eds.), *Finanzkrise und Wirtschaftsordnung*. Berlin: de Gruyter, pp. 41–53.

Senior Supervisors Group 2008. 'Observations on risk management practices during the recent market turbulence', available at www.newyorkfed. org/newsevents/news/banking/2008/SSG_Risk_Mgt_doc_final.pdf, last accessed 16 August 2010.

Servatius, W. 2008. *Gläubigereinfluss durch Covenants*. Tübingen: Mohr Siebeck.

Singer, R. 1995. *Selbstbestimmung und Verkehrsschutz im Recht der Willenserklärungen*. Munich: Beck.

Taylor, J. 2009. *Getting Off Track: How Government Actions and Interventions Caused, Prolonged, and Worsened the Financial Crisis*. Stanford: Hoover Institution Press.

Teubner, G. 2002. 'Hybrid laws: constitutionalizing private governance networks', in Kagan, R. A. and Winston, K. (eds.), *Legality and Community*. Lanham, MD: Rowman & Littlefield, pp. 311–31.

Theurl, T. (ed.) 2005. *Economics of Interfirm Networks*. Tübingen: Mohr Siebeck.

Theurl, T. and Schweinsberg, A. 2004. *Neue kooperative Ökonomie: moderne genossenschaftliche Goverancestrukturen*. Tübingen: Mohr Siebeck.

Trebilcock, M. 1993. *The Limits of Freedom of Contract*. Cambridge, MA: Harvard University Press.

Turner Review 2009. *A Regulatory Response to the Global Banking Crisis* (March), available at http://www.fsa.gov.uk/pages/Library/Corporate/ turner/index.shtml, last accessed 16 August 2010.

van den Berghe, L. 2009. *To What Extent is the Financial Crisis a Governance Crisis? From Diagnosis to Possible Remedies*. Working Paper, available at www.ssrn.com,abstract_id=1410455, last accessed 16 August 2010.

VorstAG. 2009. Gesetz zur Angemessenheit der Vorstandsvergütung (VorstAG) of 31 July 2009, *Bundesgesetzblatt* I: 2509.

Wagner, G. 2006. 'Prävention und Verhaltenssteuerung durch Privatrecht – Anmaßung oder legitime Aufgabe?', *Archiv für die civilistische Praxis* 206: 352–476.

Walker Review 2009. 'A review of corporate governance in UK banks and other financial industry entities: final recommendations', available at www.hm-treasury.gov.uk/walker_review_information.htm, last accessed 16 August 2010.

Weber, A. 2010. 'Making the financial system more resilient: the role of capital requirements', Speech at Financial Services Ireland, available at www.bundesbank.de/download/presse/reden/2010/20100310. weber_fsi.en.pdf, last accessed 16 August 2010.

Wigand, R., Picot, A. and Reichwald, R. (eds.) 1997. *Information, Organization and Management: Expanding Markets and Corporate Boundaries*. Chichester: Wiley.

Williamson, O. E. 1979. 'Transaction-cost economics: the governance of contractual relations', *Journal of Law and Economics* 22: 233–61.

1985. *The Economic Institutions of Capitalism*. New York: Free Press.

1996. *The Mechanisms of Governance*. Oxford University Press.

2005. 'The Economics of Governance', *American Economic Review* 95 (2): 1–18.

Windbichler, C. 1998. 'Neue Vertriebsformen und ihr Einfluss auf das Kaufrecht', *Archiv für die civilistische Praxis* 198: 261–86.

2004. 'Arbeitnehmerinteressen im Unternehmen und gegenüber dem Unternehmen: eine Zwischenbilanz', *Die Aktiengesellschaft*: 190–6.

2005. 'Cheers and boos for employee involvement: co-determination as corporate governance conundrum', *European Business Organization Law Review* 6: 507–37.

Wymeersch, E. 2008. 'Corporate governance and financial stability'. Financial Law Institute Working Paper No. 11 (2008), 1, available at www. ssrn.com,abstract_id =1288631, last accessed 16 August 2010.

Zandi, M. 2009. *Financial Shock: A 360 Degree Look at the Subprime Mortgage Implosion, and How to Avoid the Next Financial Crisis*. Upper Saddle River, NJ: Financial Times Press.

Zimmer, D. and Rengier, L. 2010. 'Entflechtung, Fusionskontrolle oder Sonderregulierung für systemrelevante Banken? Ansätze zur Lösung des "Too-big-to-fail" Problems', *Zeitschrift für Wettbewerbsrecht* 8: 105–38.

14 | The Great Recession's impact on global corporate governance

JAMES SHINN

'Recessions reveal what the auditors missed.'
John Kenneth Galbraith[1]

The Great Recession of 2008–9 is not a story of wholesale corporate governance failure. On the contrary, the evidence suggests that corporate governance for listed firms in most developed country markets has continued on a slope of gradual improvement of minority shareholder protections over the past decade, maintaining the momentum that it sustained during the 1990s.

It is true that the meltdown of a handful of large financial firms was the proximate trigger for the Great Recession, and that this meltdown, in turn, was the result of (among other sins) poor risk management supervision by the boards and perverse compensation structures for the managers of these firms. These cataclysmic failures of governance were an anomaly, however, and one limited to a small number of firms within the financial sector. In fact, indices of corporate governance for listed firms improved across the board during the 1990s, and this improvement continued right through the deep trough of the recession in 2008–9, although this pattern showed some divergence between developed and emerging markets.

What were the effects, if any, of the Great Recession on the trajectory of improved corporate governance? To answer this question, I will revisit an earlier analysis of the forces that caused improved minority shareholder protections based on data from the 1990s (Gourevitch and Shinn, 2005); test two models of change – the Investor model and the Pension Preferences model – against more recent data; and finally examine the effects of the Great Recession on the mechanisms of change in corporate governance suggested by these two models.

Two models of corporate governance change

What is the underlying cause of corporate governance practices, and what causes these practices to change over time? In *Political Power and Corporate Control* Peter Gourevitch and I argued that:

. . . the choice of corporate governance practices in any country expresses the interaction of economic preferences and political institutions . . . [C]orporate governance arises from incentives created by rules and regulations that emerge from a public policy process, reflecting the power of alternative political coalitions. (Gourevitch and Shinn, 2005, p. 5)

As for the actual mechanism of change, we argued that:

Corporate governance changes occur within any particular country when preferences or institutions change. If the policy preferences of one or more groups of intrafirm actors – owners, managers or workers – shift enough to upset the *ex ante* coalition balance, a new alignment ensues. Or political institutions can change, though this is far less common than a change in preferences. (Gourevitch and Shinn, 2005, p. 5)

We went on to explain that there are two broad hypotheses about this 'interaction of economic preferences and political institutions' that purport to explain improved minority shareholder protections, models that we termed the 'Investor model' and the 'Pension Preferences model'. Both models focus on changes in economic preferences rather than on changes in political institutions. Both models are also regularly invoked in press and policy commentaries on corporate governance, although not necessarily by name, and the two models, along with their underlying mechanisms of change, are often conflated.

Although their observed effects are similar, the underlying causal mechanisms of the two models are quite different. In the Investor model, firms respond to positive incentives proffered by global investors to improve their corporate governance practices. In contrast, in the Pension Preferences model firms respond to rules imposed on them by regulatory changes that are in turn rooted in political pressures generated by the preferences that citizen-voters express regarding corporate governance. The Investor model is an example of 'private ordering' through the good governance bargains struck between firms and investors, while the Pension Preference model is an example of 'public ordering' through regulatory change, which in turn is rooted in public politics.

Investor model

The first model proposes that listed firms improve their corporate governance practices because outside investors, particularly minority investors, pay a premium for the shares of firms that practise good governance. For example, a recent *Financial Times* article argued the following:

In a shift that represents perhaps the single most important change in European capitalism in the past decade, domestic owners of companies are being replaced by foreigners. That in turn is having a profound impact on how European companies are run and how they behave – pushing continental groups to adopt practices more common in the UK or US. The role of foreign investors agitating for change is likely to come in for renewed attention as the annual meeting season kicks off in Europe in earnest this month [March 2010], with confrontation particularly likely over executive pay . . . Foreign investors own 37 percent of listed European companies . . . whereas they held only 29 percent in 2003. (Milne, 2010)

We call this the Investor model, for it is often associated with the arguments made by the Organisation for Economic Co-operation and Development (OECD) in the discourse of its corporate governance Code of Conduct and by the International Corporate Governance Network (ICGN) that firms will improve their governance practices in response to financial globalization.[2] The driving force that underlies this model is the spread of institutional investors around the world and the increased penetration of these investors into most domestic capital markets, which – before the influx of large foreign investors – typically had high levels of ownership concentration in the hands of founders or families, the so-called 'blockholders' of many listed firms in Europe and Asia as well as in emerging markets. In the Investor model, moreover,

. . . the owners of firms and external providers of capital work out a 'good governance' bargain through a combination of private ordering and public regulations, thus providing protections for minority shareholders . . . Outside investors and insider owners are presumed to have the power to have their respective corporate governance preferences adopted by democratic countries with market economies. (Gourevitch and Shinn, 2005, p. 96)

There are various estimates of the premium that outside investors will pay as their part of this 'good governance' bargain, but there is empirical evidence that good governance is associated with higher returns for outside minority investors, although there is considerable disagreement about which aspects of corporate governance account for this premium.[3]

For example, in a recent carefully structured statistical study of revealed preferences for governance, Ammann *et al.* test the relationship between corporate governance and firm value on a global sample of 6,663 firms in twenty-two countries from 2003 to 2007 compiled by GovernanceMetrics. The authors use Tobin's Q as a proxy for firm value and conclude that their '. . . results indicate that better corporate governance practices are reflected in statistically significant and economically significantly higher market values' (Ammann *et al.*, 2009, p. 20).

How can we test the Investor model? According to this model, corporate governance quality in any given market should be positively correlated with foreign investor penetration (FIP) into that country's capital markets, specifically the equity markets for listed firms, which is evidence that an underlying 'good governance bargain' is taking place through private ordering between investors and blockholders. The higher the percentage of market capitalization held by foreign investors, the higher the corporate governance index should be, *ceteris paribus*. The Investor model predicts that corporate governance should improve over time as a function of capital market globalization.

Pension Preferences model

A second model that purports to explain the broad trend of corporate governance improvement suggests that listed firms improve their corporate governance because they are required to do so by regulatory changes and that these changes are imposed on firms by investors working through the political process. These investors believe that they have a financial stake in improved corporate governance and that they can count on reasonably broad political support for such measures.

For example, in the spring of 2009 as accountants were sifting through the debris of the 2008 equity market collapse in the United States, the giant California Public Employees Retirement System (CalPERS) vowed to pursue public ordering reforms instead of private consultations with firms:

The nation's biggest public pension fund, which has lost more than a quarter of its value in the last seven months, is planning to rally big investors nationwide to demand changes in the way Wall Street operates. The new chief executive of the California Public Employees Retirement System said the fund would work with other state pension funds and retirement systems to insist on greater openness in the way companies are run, tougher regulation by federal agencies, stricter rules on investment-rating groups and better international financial oversight. CalPERS, an acknowledged pioneer in pushing companies it invests in to improve their internal governance, is ready to take the tactic 'to a new level,' said lawyer Anne Stausboll, a 10-year fund veteran, who took over Jan. 12. Such moves, she said, will be a vital part of CalPERS' efforts this year to boost its financial performance. The $174.1-billion fund has lost $65 billion across its investment portfolio since July 1. (Lifsher, 2009)

We call this the Pension Preferences model because preferences shift when economic conditions change in substantial ways as a result of changes in competition, terms of trade or technology or in response to events such as depression or inflation:[4]

. . . we have called special attention to one of these underlying economic situations: pension systems and the onward effects of these systemic choices on the accumulation of pension assets. If the citizen-workers have a strong stake in good governance by means of funded pension plans, then 'lock in' effects can take place to sustain the new equilibrium, as in Chile. If citizen-voters do not have this stake, as in a country heavily weighted towards a pillar 1, unfunded, government-run pension plan, these effects will not lock in. (Gourevitch and Shinn, 2005, p. 279)

According to Perotti and Schwienbacher, this bifurcation of states into those with higher and lower minority investor protections is rooted in historical experience that '. . . pension funding choices after the Second World War reflected national political preferences on financial markets shaped by the experience of the middle class during the tumultuous interwar period. Moreover, this historical choice had a self-reinforcing effect, as voters support investor protection only to the extent that they hold security claims on the private sector' (Perotti and Schwienbacher, 2007, pp. 1–2).

   The Great Recession of 2008–9 was not as tumultuous a financial period as the one that Europe experienced in the interwar years, as Perotti and Schwienbacher described in their model (Perotti and Schwienbacher, 2007), but it certainly changed the global economic situation in substantial ways. These changes included, notably, massive losses in pillar 2 and pillar 3 pension assets. These losses raised the ire of both the individual beneficiaries of these pension plans and their agents, the pension funds, and prompted them to seek publicly imposed corporate governance reforms.

How can we test the Pension Preferences model? According to this model, corporate governance quality should be correlated with the exposure of citizens' pension savings to equity holdings in listed firms in their home country. The higher this exposure, measured in terms of the ratio of pension assets to GDP, the higher the corporate governance index should be, *ceteris paribus*.

A long trend of corporate governance reform

The preponderance of the evidence shows that corporate governance has been improving steadily – though with some fits and starts, as well as occasional backsliding in various countries – for the past two decades. This is a brave assertion, as indices of corporate governance are notoriously rife with measurement ambiguities, limited sample sizes and inconvenient gaps in the time series. Academics and market makers alike have vapourized gallons of laser printer ink over the past decade in fierce debates over the index question.

There are two methods of measuring minority shareholder protections: by assessing so-called 'black letter' legal governance at the country level and by evaluating 'revealed' governance at the firm level.

Black letter governance

One way to assess corporate governance is based on a careful reading of country-level rules and regulations, which are sometimes referred to as black letter governance.

One of the most influential data sets on black letter governance was developed in a series of six papers between 1997 and 2000 by Rafael La Porta, Florencio Lopez-de-Silanes and Andrei Shleifer – a group of authors now widely known by the initials LLSV.[5] Their original data set was based on a careful review of corporate governance laws and regulations in twenty-seven countries in the mid 1990s, a review that emphasized legal protections for minority shareholders and that is sometimes known as the 'anti-director rights index'.

We based our 2000 index of corporate governance on LLSV's original index but added indicators on accounting quality and managerial compensation that are important to institutional investors (Gourevitch and Shinn, 2005).[6] We cobbled together data on accounting and compensation from disparate sources, including Big Four accounting firms, investment banking buy-side analysts and compensation consultants. Taking into account these additional measures, the correlation between our country rankings and the original LLSV index was still high, at .90. As in the case of LLSV's original data set, this was a static indicator, a snapshot of corporate governance of firms in a sample of thirty-nine countries circa 1999–2000, that gave us little basis from which to estimate change – either sign or slope – over time.[7]

Since that time, there has been much revision of the LLSV approach in the academic literature, including arguments that LLSV's measurements of legal protections for many countries in their sample were incorrectly scored (Spamann, 2010), that their methods introduced statistical distortions of both omitted variables (notably, intra-country variation in firms) and aggregation (different countries had widely varying sample sizes for firms) (Holderness, 2008) or that LLSV's anti-director rights approach missed key differences between firms with dispersed shareholdings and those with concentrated blockholders (Bebchuk and Hamdani, 2009).

Martynova and Renneboog addressed some of these criticisms by modifying the LLSV approach in ways that are similar to the method that we used (Martynova and Renneboog, 2010). These authors also extended the LLSV model backward and forward in time, taking into account data from 1990 to 2005 for a sample of more than twenty European countries. They used a scoring approach for governance rules that was similar to that of LLSV, but cast a somewhat wider net, developing 'three new corporate governance indices that reflect the quality of national laws aimed at protecting (i) corporate shareholders from being expropriated by the firm's management, (ii) minority shareholders from being expropriated by the large blockholder, and (iii) creditors from being expropriated by the firm's shareholders' (Martynova and Renneboog, 2010, p. 3). Their index of corporate governance also showed a steady improvement over the fifteen-year period that they studied, rising from a mean value of 13.2 in 1990 to a mean value of 17.6 in 2005, as shown in Table 14.1 below.

Table 14.1 *Modified LLSV Index (Martynova and Renneboog, 2009)*

	1990	1995	2000	2005	Growth 1990–2005
Ireland	16	16	18	21	0.31
UK	19	22	24	24	0.26
USA	15	15	15	17	0.13
Belgium	15	17	18	18	0.20
France	11	11	11	16	0.45
Greece	12	12	15	20	0.67
Italy	15	15	22	26	0.73
Luxembourg	11	11	11	12	0.09
Netherlands	15	15	15	19	0.27
Portugal	15	15	17	20	0.33
Spain	15	15	15	19	0.27
Austria	9	10	14	14	0.56
Germany	12	14	16	18	0.50
Switzerland	10	10	13	17	0.70
Denmark	9	9	9	11	0.22
Finland	15	15	17	19	0.27
Iceland	20	18	18	22	0.10
Norway	14	14	16	16	0.14
Sweden	9	12	12	12	0.33
Czech Republic	14	15	15	18	0.29
Hungary	6	6	10	15	1.50
Poland	13	18	14	15	0.15
Mean	13.17	14.04	15.17	17.57	0.38
Std Dev	3.30	3.56	3.54	3.73	
Min	6.00	6.00	9.00	11.00	
Max	20.00	22.00	24.00	26.00	

Revealed governance

Black letter governance rankings of country-level corporate governance are now being complemented by rankings based on firm-level practices. This change is possible because, as institutional investors have become convinced of the causal relationship between corporate governance quality and firm value, they have invested time and money in assessing governance at the firm level. Responding to this demand, companies such as RiskMetrics Group and GovernanceMetrics International offer firm-level governance assessments on a growing sample of listed firms, across a growing sample of country markets.[8] The samples are now large enough to calculate country-level rankings as well. These data provide us with a new window onto corporate governance, as it is actually practised by firms, rather than as the country-level rulebook says it should be – providing, in effect, a revealed preference for governance.

Rulebook governance and revealed governance are unlikely to match up closely for several reasons. One reason is the gap between what the rulebooks say and how these rules are enforced, which can be quite wide in some countries. A second reason is the lag between changes in rules and the adoption of the modified practices by firms, which can be several years in duration.

In theory, firms may have the option of adopting corporate governance practices that are more progressive in protecting minority shareholders than the country-level rulebooks require, if the firms are sufficiently motivated to do so by a prospective 'good governance bargain' premium. However, as Doidge *et al.* point out:

Countries matter because they influence the costs that firms incur to bond themselves to good governance and the benefits they receive from doing so. Better governance reduces a firm's cost of funds only to the extent that investors expect the firm to be governed well after the funds have been raised. It is, therefore, important for the firm to find ways to commit itself credibly to higher quality governance. However, mechanisms to do so may be unavailable or prohibitively expensive in countries with poor investor protection from the state. (Doidge *et al.*, 2007, p. 3)[9]

Table 14.2. shows the values of corporate governance on a country basis between 2004–8 from the RiskMetrics Group database of firm-level scores, summed and averaged by country of listing (Aggarwal *et al.*, 2009, p. 36). The mean score rose from 39.7 in 2004 to 48.6 in 2008. The sample showed increased variation in 2008, but all country values increased, some quite substantially.

It is interesting that these 'revealed preferences' in the mean values of firms on a country basis are positively correlated with the LLSV and Gourevitch-Shinn values of 'black letter' governance, but only moderately so, and have almost no correlation with the Martynova-Renneboog estimates. The RiskMetrics values for 2005 have a correlation of .62 with the original LLSV 2000 values, a correlation of .49 with the Gourevitch-Shinn 2000 values and a correlation of almost zero (.06) with the Martynova-Renneboog 2005 values.

Table 14.2 *RiskMetrics Group corporate governance scores by country (2004–8)*

		2004	2005	2006	2007	2008	Change 2004–8
Australia	AUS	46.60	47	47.2	47.3	48.00	0.03
Austria	AUT	42.20	41.3	42	40	45.10	0.07
Belgium	BEL	31.20	33.8	36.8	36.7	37.80	0.21
Canada	CAN	62.40	65.4	67.4	68.5	72.80	0.17
Denmark	DNK	37.00	41	44.3	48.2	39.40	0.06
Finland	FIN	39.60	52.8	53.7	52.7	52.50	0.33
France	FRA	40.60	43.7	42.8	44.8	44.90	0.11
Germany	DEU	38.40	44.9	48.7	45.8	48.20	0.26
Greece	GRC	35.50	38.4	32.1	27.3	35.90	0.01
Hong Kong	HKG	39.30	39.8	43.9	44.2	47.70	0.21
Ireland	IRL	40.80	48.9	48.8	47	55.00	0.35
Italy	ITA	33.60	39.1	41.8	41.4	46.40	0.38
Japan	JPN	35.20	37	37.4	37.7	40.90	0.16
Netherlands	NLD	37.70	46.5	49	49	55.70	0.48
New Zealand	NZL	45.60	45.2	45.7	45.7	45.40	0.00
Norway	NOR	33.00	38.8	43.4	44.4	37.30	0.13
Portugal	PRT	31.10	36.2	35.9	36.2	36.20	0.16
Singapore	SNG	38.50	42.5	45.2	45.4	51.80	0.35
Spain	ESP	34.20	42.8	45.1	47	46.80	0.37
Sweden	SWE	31.60	40.4	46.2	44.9	51.90	0.64
Switzerland	CHE	40.70	51	52.1	52.2	56.60	0.39
UK	GBR	45.20	51	54.1	50.8	59.30	0.31
USA	USA	53.80	58.1	59.9	60.9	62.20	0.16
Mean		39.73	44.59	46.24	46.00	48.60	0.23
Max		62.4	65.4	67.4	68.5	72.80	0.64
Min		31.1	33.8	32.1	27.3	35.90	0.00
Std Dev		7.42	7.42	7.84	8.31	9.11	

Source: Aggarwal *et al.*, 2009, Table 2, p. 36.

Table 14.3 shows similar values for GovernanceMetrics International for the period 2005–9, further divided by data for developed and emerging markets. The mean score for the developed markets increased from 5.3 to 5.7 at the end of the five-year period. One-third of the sample countries showed a slight downward trend over the period. This may be an artefact of the growing firm sample size each year, since GovernanceMetrics began by scoring the largest, most

Table 14.3 *GovernanceMetrics International corporate governance rankings (2005–9)*

		2005	2006	2007	2008	2009	Change 2005–9
Developed Markets							
Australia	AUS	6.98	7.24	7.5	7.25	7.32	0.01
Austria	AUT	4.59	4.94	5.61	5.26	5.63	0.14
Belgium	BEL	3.80	4.71	5.11	4.81	4.54	−0.04
Canada	CAN	7.29	7.33	7.31	7.38	7.35	0.00
Denmark	DNK	4.43	4.63	4.98	4.48	4.42	−0.04
Finland	FIN	5.88	6	6.4	6.22	6.41	0.07
France	FRA	4.00	4.47	4.62	4.43	4.53	0.01
Germany	DEU	5.12	5.66	6.15	5.73	5.73	0.01
Greece	GRC	2.40	2.52	3.8	4.4	4.11	0.63
Ireland	IRL	6.71	7.13	7.39	7.55	7.44	0.04
Italy	ITA	5.23	5.64	5.95	5.32	5.60	−0.01
Japan	JPN	3.55	4.01	4.26	3.34	3.32	−0.17
Netherlands	NLD	6.35	6.51	6.69	6.41	6.60	0.01
New Zealand	NZL	6.46	6.67	6.79	6.5	6.42	−0.04
Norway	NOR	5.00	5.58	5.85	5.52	5.59	0.00
Portugal	PRT	4.25	4.36	4.64	4.33	4.38	0.00
Spain	ESP	4.42	4.91	4.73	4	3.77	−0.23
Sweden	SWE	5.11	5.45	5.87	5.46	5.61	0.03
Switzerland	CHE	5.40	5.61	5.61	6.21	5.96	0.06
UK	GBR	7.32	7.3	7.4	7.28	7.36	0.01
USA	USA	7.06	7.22	7.25	7.25	7.18	−0.01
Mean		5.30	5.61	5.9	5.67	5.68	
Max		7.32	7.33	7.5	7.55	7.44	
Min		2.4	2.52	3.8	3.34	3.32	
Std Dev		1.37	1.29	1.14	1.26	1.29	

		2006	2007	2008	2009	Change 2006–9
Emerging Markets						
Brazil	BRA	3.23	4.08	4.18	4.01	0.24
Chile	CHL	3.95	3	2.54	1.96	−0.50
China	CHN	2.94	3.34	3.18	3.01	0.02
Hong Kong	HGK	5.08	4.72	4.29	4.02	−0.21
India	IND	4.67	5.08	4.91	4.61	−0.01
Malaysia	MYS	4.72	4.74	4.24	4.40	−0.07
Mexico	MEX	5.1	4.74	3.04	2.48	−0.51
Russia	RUS	4.9	4.4	3.88	4.17	−0.15

Table **14.3** (*cont.*)

		2006	2007	2008	2009	Change 2006–9
Singapore	SGP	5.65	5.77	5.03	5.07	−0.10
South Africa	ZAF	6.26	6.34	6.35	6.49	0.04
South Korea	KOR	2.31	4.05	3.7	3.84	0.66
Taiwan	TAI	4.53	4.71	4.41	4.45	−0.02
Turkey	TUR	5.15	5.04	4.25	3.87	−0.25
Mean		4.50	4.62	4.15	4.03	
Max		6.26	6.34	6.35	6.49	
Min		2.31	3.00	2.54	1.96	
Std Dev		1.12	0.90	0.97	1.14	
Total Sample						
Mean		5.19	5.41	5.09	5.05	
Min		2.30	3.00	2.54	1.96	
Max		7.5	7.5	7.6	7.44	
Std Dev		7.33	7.50	7.60	7.40	

widely traded firms in each market and then began scoring progressively smaller firms by market cap. The larger the firm, the more positive its governance features, *ceteris paribus*, and so the growth of the firm sample size in markets over time would tend to bring down the average governance score over time. The mean value for governance for emerging markets reduced somewhat over the period, from 4.50 to 4.03. Scores for nine of the thirteen sample countries were slightly down over the same period; the sample bias imposed by the growing firm sample may be at work here or we may be observing a divergence in the trend of corporate governance change between developed and emerging markets.

Testing the two models of change

This is a difficult test, with a long list of caveats up front, so any claims about its results must be modest. In addition to the usual problems facing country-level comparisons, with their small sample size, we are here confronted with two alternative explanations (the Investor model and the Pension Preferences model) for variance in a single dependent variable (the corporate governance index), so the dependent variable is causally over-determined. We also have to deal with an unknown degree of endogeneity between the dependent variable and the two alternative independent variables, some correlation between the two independent variables and the fact that both independent variables tend to move the dependent variable in the same direction. As in the case of the data series on corporate governance quality, the data available to test both the Investor model and the Pensions Preference model are rife with measurement ambiguities and with missing values.

The Investor model driver test

In Gourevitch and Shinn, 2005, we tested the Investor model by examining the relationship between foreign investor penetration and our index of corporate governance for a sample of thirty-nine countries based on data from 1990 to 2000, and the correlation between the two indices for the set of common country rankings was found to be .89. Our test showed no significant correlation between foreign investor penetration and our corporate governance index – indeed, the correlation we found was marginally negative, at −.08. We were initially surprised by this result, as it falsified what was then our leading hypothesis (the first of the two 'Millstein models') about what causes corporate governance change around the world.

The penetration data covering the decade from 1990 to 2000 were drawn from a hotchpotch of sources, including the Federation Internationale des Bourses de Valeurs (FIBV), the International Monetary Fund (IMF) and a variety of national stock exchanges (see Gourevitch and Shinn, 2005, Table 5.1, p. 105). Strikingly, the mean value of foreign investor penetration in this sample doubled over this period, from 12.6 per cent of the weighted market capitalization in 1990 to 25.1 per cent in 2000, while the standard deviation increased from 13 to 17.6. The mean penetration value in developed markets more than doubled, from 12 per cent in 1990 to 28.6 per cent in 2000; the same value for emerging markets quintupled over the same period, rising from 2.3 per cent to 13 per cent.

Using the Conference Board's annual Survey of Institutional Investors and other sources, we traced this tsunami of foreign investment to Anglo-American institutional investors, who accounted for more than three-quarters of the foreign investors' equity holdings in this country sample. Fund managers for these investors made two broad portfolio allocation decisions in the 1990s that drove this wave of money. First, they increased the weight of equities vs. fixed-income assets in their portfolios and, secondly, they moved away from the home-country bias to take advantage of foreign equity markets, which in those days had a low correlation to the equity markets in the United States and the UK.

What happens when we repeat this test with more current data? Table 14.4 shows the FIP estimates and the RiskMetrics scores for the test sample of twenty countries for which we have complete (and internally consistent) data sets for the limited snapshot of three years from 2005 to 2007. The FIP estimates are drawn largely from Federation of European Securities Exchanges, 2008, with additional estimates drawn from the IMF and from various country-level stock exchange sources.

In this sample, the mean value of FIP increased gradually, from 36.5 to 38.7, presumably continuing the same trend that we saw in the 1990s with a long-term 1 to 2 per cent yearly rate of increase in financial globalization, while the mean value of the RiskMetrics index for these countries increased from 44.9 to 46.1.

Here again, however, as found in our 2000 test – and contrary to the predictions of the Investor model – we found no positive correlation between FIP and RiskMetrics for this sample of countries during this three-year period. The correlation is moderately negative: $-.14$ in 2005, $-.23$ in 2006 and $-.27$ in 2007.

What might explain the failure of the data to support the Investor model? To help us understand this phenomenon, let us look back at the country cases that we examined in 2005.

In *Political Power and Corporate Control*, we supplemented the statistical tests with a 'deep dive' into the historical narrative of corporate governance changes in thirteen country cases from our sample during the period 1990–2000. In these detailed case studies, we found little or no anecdotal evidence of a 'good governance' bargain being struck between firms and international investors in countries where most listed firms had high ownership concentration in the hands of one or more blockholders. As we put it then: ' . . . there is ample evidence that pressures for enhanced minority shareholder protections are growing on the demand side; money flows towards firms and countries that provide such protections. And yet there was little evidence on the supply side that blockholders worked to change the system to provide these enhanced protections' (Gourevitch and Shinn, 2005, p. 120).

Contrary to the predictions of the Investor model, we found that in countries where most listed firms had large blockholder concentration:

> . . . there is more evidence of blockholders resisting these reforms . . . For example, employer federations in countries with high blockholder ratios tended to oppose corporate governance reforms in many cases, as the Korean Federation of Industry adopted public positions on corporate governance reforms closely aligned with those of the individual *chaebol* firms, which were largely family-controlled. (Gourevitch and Shinn, 2005, p. 121)

Nor did labour unions rally to demand improved corporate governance by their employers in order to reap the notional good governance premium from foreign institutional investors. On the contrary, organized labour unions in many markets viewed foreign investors as a threat to employment stability and labour rents. Labour insiders presumably believed that blockholders who reaped a good governance premium by 'going public' to outside minority shareholders would simply pocket the premium. Having forked over a control premium to the previous blockholder, foreign investors would then be motivated to squeeze labour rents (through professional managers and an independent board of directors) in order to help recoup this expense, hardly a recipe for labour peace.

A superficial anecdotal survey of these same country examples in the decade since 2000 reveals little evidence of a reinvigorated rush by private firms to a 'good governance bargain' with global investors. This may be the result of the persistence of the structural problems that we suggested had impeded such a bargain (at least from the firms' side) in the previous decade.

In 2005, we argued that blockholders might find it difficult to protect or realize private benefits of control in a transaction that hands control to a widely dispersed group of outside shareholders. For example, Stulz formally modelled this blockholder's problem of protecting the benefits of control when presented with the opportunity to win a good governance premium, and his results showed that the gains from the premium were neutralized by the blockholder's need to re-invest capital as the firm grows in order to maintain control levels (Stulz, 2005). Moreover, we also speculated that incumbent managers and/or employees impeded such a transfer out of the similar motives of protecting their own labour rents from profit-maximizing external shareholders (Gourevitch and Shinn, 2005).

There are, however, several other private ordering mechanisms that could provide a way around such obstacles. The first alternative is private equity transactions between a blockholder and a (usually) foreign private equity firm. In such a transaction, the private equity firm pays some of the control premium to the blockholder, restructures the firm, adopts good governance 'best practices' (including standard accounting and disclosure rules, an independent board of directors and appropriate executive incentive compensation practices), arranges some side-payments to incumbent managers and employees and ultimately takes all or part of the restructured firm public on an international exchange.

The second alternative is early-stage bargains between new start-ups and foreign investors. These entrepreneurs need immediate capital, and they have as yet few private benefits of control to protect, so they are inclined to bind themselves to good governance practices in exchange for funds. In this regard, Stulz offers the following:

. . . consider the case in which the cost of capital drops because of financial globalization. Insiders in existing firms receive a benefit from improvements in investor protections when a reduction in the cost of capital enables them to profitably increase the scale of the firm or to take advantage of growth opportunities that would not otherwise have been profitable. In this case, the firm must raise new capital and does so on better terms with better investor protection. However, the insiders have to trade off the benefit of raising capital more cheaply against the loss resulting from their decreased ability to extract private benefits of control. But insiders who raise funds for the first time instead benefit from the ex ante reduction in private benefits. (Stulz, 2005, p. 1631)

If country-level 'black letter' governance rules make binding firms to good governance practices too expensive to offer credibly (or too expensive to monitor from the investor's standpoint), then the entrepreneur has the option of issuing securities in a foreign capital market, such as American Depository Receipts (ADRs) in the United States or, in the case of many Chinese firms, using the Hong Kong stock market.

A third alternative emerges when government blockholders sell off all or part of a state-controlled entity (a state-owned enterprise or SOE) to foreign investors, naturally seeking in the process to reap as high a price as possible from the outside investors. These SOE privatizations are usually accompanied by extensive political negotiations with the firm's unions, after which a portion of the proceeds of the sale is paid to the unions, with the money usually going to fund their pension plans (just as many state-controlled pension plans are thinly funded, so too are the pension plans of many state-controlled enterprises).

All three of these mechanisms continued to function throughout the decade from 2001–2010, although attenuated in various ways. The pace of SOE privatizations slackened from that which we saw in the 1990s and the increase in the rate of entrepreneurial start-ups was interrupted by the abrupt end of the 'dot-com' boom. All three mechanisms were further blunted by the Great Recession, as will be explained further below under 'Impact of the Great Recession on the two models of change'. In any case, all three mechanisms are examples of private ordering and, with the partial exception of SOE 'privatizations' and ADR issuance, are conducted largely behind closed doors and with only limited statistical footprints.

Let us turn now to an updated test of our alternative hypothesis for the forces underlying corporate governance changes, the Pensions Preference model.

The Pensions Preference model driver test

Our 2005 book predicted that minority shareholder protections (or corporate governance quality) would be positively correlated with the ratio of pension assets to GDP. We compiled data on the ratio of private pension assets to GDP from a variety of sources, principally the World Bank, for twenty-five of the countries in our sample as of 1999–2000 (Gourevitch and Shinn, 2005, Table 7.2, p. 217). These values included all assets in so-called 'pillars 1 and 2' pension plans but excluded pillar 1 assets in national social security systems (which were only partially funded or sometimes zero funded).

The correlation between country scores of private pension assets to GDP with our corporate governance index was positive, at .56. An OLS linear regression of these data suggested that each one-unit increase in private pension assets to GDP resulted in a .29 unit increase in the corporate governance index score (which ran from zero minimum to 100 maximum), significant at the .005 level with an r2 of .31.

Table 14.4 *RiskMetrics Group (RMG) corporate governance index and foreign investment penetration (2005–7)*

Market		RMG	FIP	RMG	FIP	RMG	FIP
		2005		2006		2007	
Australia	AUS	47	38	47.2	39	47.3	40
Austria	AUT	41.3	39.6	42	44.9	40	30.96
Belgium	BEL	33.8	36.2	36.8	37.8	36.7	38.7
Canada	CAN	65.4	6.2	67.4	5.8	68.5	4.4
Denmark	DNK	41	24.1	44.3	27	48.2	30.2
Finland	FIN	52.8	50.9	53.7	50.1	52.7	61.6
France	FRA	43.7	40.5	42.8	40.7	44.8	41.1
Germany	DEU	44.9	18.4	48.7	19.7	45.8	21.3
Greece	GRC	38.4	40.3	32.1	46.6	27.3	51.8
Ireland	IRL	48.9	65	48.8	67	47	70
Italy	ITA	39.1	16.3	41.8	13.2	41.4	13.9
Japan	JPN	37	26.7	37.4	28	37.7	27.6
Netherlands	NLD	46.5	80	49	79	49	71
Norway	NOR	38.8	37.1	43.4	39.7	44.4	40.8
Portugal	PRT	36.2	39.8	35.9	42.8	36.2	44.8
Spain	ESP	42.8	34.2	45.1	32.6	47	36.8
Sweden	SWE	40.4	35.3	46.2	37.2	44.9	38
Switzerland	CHE	51	56	52.1	59.3	52.2	60
UK	GBR	51	36.1	54.1	40	50.8	40
USA	USA	58.1	9	59.9	9.2	60.9	10
Mean		44.91	36.49	46.44	37.98	46.14	38.65
Max		65.4	80	67.4	79	68.5	71
Min		33.8	6.2	32.1	5.8	27.3	4.4
Std Dev		7.89	17.79	8.41	18.28	8.93	18.35

In the current study, this test was repeated for the set of countries for which we could obtain more recent data on both pension assets and the RiskMetrics corporate governance values.[10] The data are shown in Table 14.5 and include twenty countries for the years 2005 to 2007. The OECD's Pension Statistics Project provides data on both the ratio of private pension assets to GDP (which corresponds to pillar 1 and 2 assets) and the portfolio allocation of these assets. To obtain the equity exposure value for each country, we summed the percentage allocated to shares with the sum in mutual funds, assuming that the bulk of the mutual funds is also ultimately held in shares and that

Table 14.5 *Pension assets to GDP and equity exposure to GDP (2005–7)*

	2005			2006			2007		
	Assets	Equity (%)	Exp	Assets	Equity (%)	Exp	Assets	Equity (%)	Exp
AUS	80.38	0.80	64.30	90.40	0.84	75.94	110.36	0.80	88.29
AUT	4.78	0.37	1.77	4.94	0.36	1.78	4.82	0.35	1.69
BEL	4.41	0.84	3.70	4.22	0.88	3.71	4.47	0.84	3.76
CAN	50.26	0.64	32.17	53.88	0.66	35.56	62.33	0.64	39.89
DNK	33.71	0.38	12.81	32.43	0.42	13.62	32.36	0.41	13.27
FIN	68.61	0.38	26.07	71.33	0.44	31.38	71.05	0.47	33.39
FRA	1.16	0.00	0.00	1.11	0.00	0.00	1.06	0.00	0.00
DEU	4.04	0.35	1.41	4.21	0.34	1.43	4.65	0.39	1.81
GRC	0.00	0.00	0.00	0.00	0.00	0.00	0.01	0.05	0.00
IRL	48.26	0.65	31.37	50.22	0.63	31.64	46.62	0.66	30.77
ITA	2.79	0.20	0.56	3.01	0.22	0.66	3.27	0.19	0.62
JPN	6.63	0.00	0.00	0.00	0.00	0.00	0.00	0.00	0.00
NLD	121.73	0.46	55.99	125.74	0.47	59.10	138.05	0.40	55.22
NOR	6.71	0.29	1.95	6.79	0.33	2.24	7.05	0.36	2.54
PRT	12.73	0.41	5.22	13.64	0.51	6.96	13.74	0.50	6.87
ESP	7.22	0.30	2.17	7.52	0.30	2.26	7.54	0.30	2.26
SWE	9.07	0.35	3.18	9.26	0.39	3.61	8.68	0.40	3.47
CHE	117.03	0.45	52.66	119.97	0.48	57.59	119.18	0.48	57.21
GBR	78.63	0.60	47.18	83.43	0.57	47.56	78.90	0.53	41.82
USA	74.15	0.68	50.42	78.92	0.58	45.77	79.40	0.66	52.40
Mean	36.61	0.41	19.65	38.05	0.42	21.04	39.68	0.42	21.76
Max	121.73	0.84	64.30	125.74	0.88	75.94	138.05	0.84	88.29
Min	0.00	0.00	0.00	0.00	0.00	0.00	0.00	0.00	0.00
Std Dev	40.39	0.25	22.96	42.68	0.25	24.71	45.36	0.24	26.22

the individual beneficiary has some insight into the share allocation of his or her mutual fund. The product of private pension assets to GDP and the percentage of equity allocation gives us the equity exposure value, also expressed as a percentage of GDP.

When we run the test of the RiskMetrics Index and both the total pension assets and net equity exposure values for the twenty countries, the correlation is strongly positive for both independent variables in this test: overall pension assets (PGDP) and the more refined measure of equity exposure of those assets (Equity), as shown in Table 14.6.

Table 14.6 *Correlation of overall pension assets and equity exposure with RiskMetrics and GovernanceMetrics International indices for 20 countries, 2005–7*

	2005	2006	2007
RMG/PGDP	0.63	0.62	0.59
RMG/Equity	0.67	0.61	0.59
GMI/PGDP	0.68	0.62	0.6
GMI/Equity	0.75	0.69	0.59

The same test with the GovernanceMetrics International (GMI) Index shows a slightly stronger correlation than the RiskMetrics Group (RMG), but generally the same relationship.

Repeating the methods of our 2000 test, an OLS linear regression of these data using the RiskMetrics Index suggests that each one-unit increase in private pension assets to GDP results in a .12 unit increase in the corporate governance index score (which ran from zero minimum to 50 maximum for this data set), significant at the .005 level with an r2 of .40.

In our 2005 book, we examined in detail the public ordering politics of minority shareholder protections in the UK, the United States and France during the 1990s, a phenomenon that we explained by the emergence (or lack of emergence, as the case may be) of a 'transparency coalition' and by the active push of institutional investors such as Hermes in the UK and CalPERS in the United States for enhanced shareholder protections – along with the active push-back by both corporate managers and some reputational intermediaries. As we observed:

The reputational intermediaries [such as accounting firms and investment banks] and the sometimes mixed motives of money managers matter greatly in connecting worker-voters' interests as investors to policy preferences. In some countries their interests are shut out, fragmented and blocked by the conflicted interests of the fund managers. In this respect, workers as pension beneficiaries face the same collective action problem towards the governance of investment firms that they face as fragmented shareholders in other public firms. (Gourevitch and Shinn, 2005, p. 44)

This to-and-fro contest within the realm of public ordering featured the emergence of the Sarbanes-Oxley Act in the United States and a host of corporate governance codes around the world, along with increased activism by big institutional investors, particularly civil-service employee investors, in the 1990s. Large institutional investors in high pension fund countries, working through collective bodies such as Australia's Council of Superannuation Investors and the Netherlands' Eumedion, pressed their case through a combination of voluntary codes, regulatory modifications and legislative reforms in corporate governance. We can observe this contest continuing through the last decade, with listed firms increasingly put in the position of 'comply or explain' by corporate governance codes.

Of course, blockholders remained indifferent or hostile to these pressures, in some firms and in some countries, for reasons noted earlier, and both managers and unions actively opposed them in several countries as well. For example:

- Japan's *Keidanren* Federation of Business Organizations waged a continuous rear-action battle against shareholder protections, vociferously objecting to proposals for independent directors and compensation disclosure, while painting activist investors and other proponents of a market in corporate control with the brush of *yakuza* gangsters and 'greenmailers'.
- In the United States, a group of managers invoked the 'excessive costs' of compliance with Section 404 of Sarbanes-Oxley as the reason why firms were 'deserting New York for London' as part of a lobbying campaign to roll back some of the corporate governance provisions of SarBox in 2005–2007, although this effort was rudely terminated by the onset of the Great Recession.

Summary of the tests of the Investor and Pension Preferences models

Table 14.7 below shows the results of our first-order tests.

If these data tests are indicative of an underlying phenomenon, then we should expect the effects of the Great Recession on global corporate governance to be stronger to the degree that they encourage the dynamics of the Pension Preferences model rather than those of the Investor model, although both mechanisms may come into play to some degree.

Table 14.7 *Results of first-order tests for Investor model and Pension Preferences model*

	1990s	2006–8
Investor model	No correlation	Weak negative correlation
Pensions Preferences model	Strong correlation	Strong correlation

Impact of the Great Recession on the two models of change

In assessing the impact of the financial meltdown on our models, we need to examine three main features of the Great Recession: the financial sector trigger, global asset repricing and monetary and fiscal policy response.

The financial sector trigger

The Great Recession started in the financial sector, as losses on securities in financial firms' inventories (particularly securitized real estate) undermined the solvency of several firms as counterparties. This process snowballed until it paralysed several financial asset markets, and ultimately caused the insolvency of several investment and commercial banks, prompting a series of bailouts and de facto nationalizations of financial institutions, especially in the United States and the UK.

Global asset repricing

Risk premia for a wide range of financial assets quickly returned to historic levels (and, indeed, went higher in some cases) and the prices of many asset categories were sharply marked down to reflect these higher risk premia. Equity markets tanked around the world. Institutional and personal investors alike sustained dramatic losses on a mark-to-market basis.

Monetary and fiscal policy response

The financial sector meltdowns and asset repricing quickly spread to the real economy in a reverse wealth effect. Consumption dropped sharply as households began the long process of financial de-leveraging, even as banks also began to de-leverage, thereby closing off credit to firms (and households). Governments around the world responded with low interest rates and, to varying degrees, deep fiscal deficits to 'pump prime' aggregate demand.

How did these three features of the Great Recession affect the forces driving corporate governance reform according to the Investor and Pension Preferences models? The Great Recession could shape the causal mechanisms of the Investor model by altering the incentives for firms and outside investors to enter into the private ordering 'good governance' bargain in either direction. At the same time, the Great Recession could shape the causal mechanisms of the Pension Preferences model by altering the incentives and the ability of investors to alter the regulations of corporate governance through the political process. As we observed in our 2005 book, recourse to public ordering involves more players than just the firm and outside investors: in the public process, employees within the firm and citizen-voters outside the firm get a voice in the process. In this sense, public ordering involves more players and thus is more complex than most forms of private ordering.

The financial sector trigger

When the financial institutions collapsed spectacularly and the tax-payers in effect bailed them out, this process established a direct route for citizens to express their corporate governance preferences through public ordering rather than private ordering. Since the taxpayers were the new owners, in effect the new blockholders of key banks (given the majority ownership of the US Department of the Treasury and the UK Exchequer in several banks), they imposed new rules for disclosure, executive compensation and risk management on those financial firms that were bailed out.[11]

This was clearly not a private-ordering 'good governance' bargain; rather, it was imposed by political *fiat*. '[W]e can', for example, 'safely characterize Kenneth Feinberg, the "Special Master" for executive compensation and better known as the pay czar, as an *ex officio* member of the compensation committees of the companies he is required to oversee' (Bennett, 2009, p. 40).

In the United States, at least, the intensity of the popular sentiment favouring public reordering of corporate governance was reflected in the fact that the new rules were not left to the discretion of bureaucratic rule-makers in the Treasury Department, the Federal Reserve and the Securities and Exchange Commission (SEC), but were back-stopped by several laws proposed or passed by the US Congress. Indeed, a barrage of legislation was passed or proposed to tighten corporate governance rules in order to improve minority shareholder protections. Examples include the Troubled Assets Relief Program (TARP), the American Recovery and Reinvestment Act (ARRA) and the Emergency Economic Stabilization Act (EESA), all of which targeted financial services companies in an effort to reform terms of information disclosure, board supervision of risk manage-ment and executive compensation. Although banks were the primary target of these reforms, their impact will ultimately be felt much more widely:

These provisions, and the specific terms of the Treasury's investments in financial institutions and the automotive industry, effectively raise the expectations, and hence the bar, for all public companies – regardless of the industries they are in and whether or not they are receiving TARP or related funding from the U.S. government. Several provisions of EESA echo long-held sentiments of institutional investors and proxy advisors. (Weil Gotshal, 2009, p. 7)

The Dodd-Frank Wall Street Reform and Consumer Protection Act (Public Law 111–203), which became law in July 2010, enshrined in law a host of reforms on issues such as majority voting for directors, enhanced disclosure, compensation structure, claw back and nullification of golden parachutes, independent compensation advisors and split CEO/chairman roles. Compliance with these new rules on these issues will be a requirement for public companies, a reform that brings the SEC into the surveillance and enforcement game. Even state-level politicians competed with federal politicians in riding the wave of public anger, a dynamic apparent in the prosecutions that the State of New York pursued against both securities and insurance firms, most notably the American Inter-national Group (AIG).

The simultaneous repricing of the same asset classes around the world uncomfortably demonstrated to institutional investors that national capital markets, including stock markets, were more closely correlated than many investors had previously assumed – at least during the big run-up of foreign and emerging market equities in the

1990s. These highly correlated market losses reduced one of the appeals of international investment diversification; thus, many investors became more sensitive to the relative returns of foreign portfolio investments (the so-called alpha value) than to the presumed reduction in overall portfolio volatility (the so-called beta value). On balance, this effect served to make these investors more attentive to the good governance premium, which promised both to contribute to the potential alpha return of their international portfolios and to reduce the probability of wholesale write-offs caused by insolvency or collapse by their investment targets.

The Great Recession also gave financial globalization a politically bad name around the world. Even the IMF has recently publicly questioned its long-treasured assumption of the benefits of capital mobility, adding its voice to a long string of academic critiques of financial globalization. Indeed:

> . . . following the crisis, policymakers are again reconsidering the view that unfettered capital flows are a fundamentally benign phenomenon and that all financial flows are the result of rational investing/borrowing/lending decisions. Concerns that foreign investors may be subject to herd behavior, and suffer from excessive optimism, have grown stronger; and even when flows are fundamentally sound, it is recognized that they may contribute to collateral damage, including bubbles and asset booms and busts. (Ostry *et al.*, 2010, p. 5)

Ironically, this renewed critique of international capital mobility and of the role of 'speculators' has served to tar, by extension, financial firms pressing for better governance, including big institutional investors (such as CalPERS), activist funds (such as Knight Vinik) and hedge funds generally.

In many countries, 'foreign speculators' were blamed for the market upheavals in 2008–9. For example, in 2005 the former head of the Frankfurt stock exchange accused hedge funds of 'ripping the heart out' of Germany:

> The shareholder revolt at Deutsche Börse 'rips into the heart of the German economy,' Rolf Breuer, the outgoing chairman of the Frankfurt stock exchange operator said yesterday. He also said Germany should look at new laws to curb hedge fund activity. Mr Breuer was ousted as chairman of Deutsche Börse on Monday along with the chief executive, Werner Seifert,

after a shareholder revolt led by hedge funds including The Children's Investment Fund (TCI) over the German company's controversial plans for a £1.3bn bid for the London Stock Exchange (LSE). The hedge funds also objected to Deutsche Börse's corporate governance standards. In an interview with the German magazine *Capital*, Mr Breuer said: 'It is dangerous when hedge funds take over and impose their view on stability oriented shareholders. I fear it can happen to anyone now. It heralds a new world for company boards in Germany and rips into the heart of the German economy.' (Kollewe and Reece, 2005)

With support from both the employers' association (BDI) and several large unions, the German government then unsuccessfully pressed the European Commission in 2007 – before the Great Recession – to adopt new rules that would constrain the ability of hedge funds to put market pressure on firms or to use voting power to interfere with managers' (and employees') prerogatives.

Apparently, the effects of the Great Recession in Europe presented a window of opportunity to resurrect this effort via the European Commission. In 2007, Euro Intelligence noted that according to the *Frankfurter Allgemeine* '. . . the German government is planning to introduce a law to force hedge funds to reveal their strategic intentions if their stake in a company rise [*sic*] above 10%. [The journal] quotes Jorg Asmussen, head of the German finance ministry's international department as saying the German government planned this law in order to strengthen the position of companies (managers!) against hedge funds' (Euro Intelligence, 2007). In 2009, the European Commission proposed a Directive on Alternative Investment Fund Managers (AIFM), which sought to impose a host of regulations on the performance, disclosure and governance of hedge funds across the European Union (EU). The Commission went on to observe that:

While AIFM were not the cause of the crisis, recent events have placed severe stress on the sector. The risks associated with their activities have manifested themselves throughout the AIFM industry over recent months and may in some cases have contributed to market turbulence. For example, hedge funds have contributed to asset price inflation and the rapid growth of structured credit markets. The abrupt unwinding of large, leveraged positions in response to tightening credit conditions and investor redemption requests has had a procyclical impact on declining markets and may have impaired market liquidity. (European Commission, 2009)

The long liquidity boomlet that preceded the Great Recession featured a consistent de-leveraging of many non-financial corporations in many markets, as many firms engaged in a broad pay-down of debt, substituted relatively low-interest long-term debt for short-term bor-rowings and accumulated a striking amount of cash. The net effect was to reduce the dependence of these firms on financial markets, including both equity and debt markets. This trend reduced the appeal of the good governance premium, at least from the standpoint of the firms (blockholders and incumbent managers alike), and thus likely attenuated the mechanism that prompts the Investor model's private reordering of governance bargains.

There were some notable exceptions to this liquidity *richesse*. Some non-financial firms (and quite a few banks) in emerging markets with mismatched foreign currency and maturity positions were caught out by the rapid exit from those markets by foreign investors as well as by the wholesale 'flight to quality' in 2008.

Global asset repricing

The dramatic losses incurred by institutional investors in their foreign and domestic portfolios, including the huge amounts lost in financial firms' equity value, proved to be the most powerful galvanizing influence on these investors' views of corporate governance. These losses directed investors' attention – and that of their beneficiaries, especially whenever they received their quarterly statements – towards public ordering via imposed regulations instead of the more indirect methods of 'consulta-tive engagement' via private ordering of corporate governance.

The losses of private pension funds in the 2008 repricing were impressive, as shown by the contrast between the 2007 and 2008 columns in Table 14.8 below. The mean value of the ratio of pension assets to GDP plunged by six percentage points of GDP in the single twelve-month period from 2007 to 2008 for the whole sample, includ-ing both developed and emerging markets. This figure understates, however, the impact of pension fund losses on those countries with both high private assets and high equity exposure ratios.

For example, for those countries with both high private pension assets to GDP ratios and relatively high levels of exposure to equities within these portfolios, the contraction was much sharper. Table 14.8 breaks out the country sample into Set A, countries with private

Table 14.8 *Developed (Set A) and emerging (Set B) markets, pension assets and equity exposure to GDP (2005–8)*

	CY05			CY06			CY07			CY08		
	PGDP	Eq	Exp	PGDP	Eq	Exp	PGDP	Eq	Exp	PGDP	Eq	Exp
Set A												
AUS	80.4	0.8	64.3	90.4	0.8	75.9	110.4	0.8	88.3	91.8	0.8	72.5
CAN	50.3	0.6	32.2	53.9	0.7	35.6	62.3	0.6	39.9	50.6	0.6	29.3
DNK	33.7	0.4	12.8	32.4	0.4	13.6	32.4	0.4	13.3	47.5	0.2	8.6
FIN	68.6	0.4	26.1	71.3	0.4	31.4	71.0	0.5	33.4	58.7	0.3	19.4
IRL	48.3	0.7	31.4	50.2	0.6	31.6	46.6	0.7	30.8	34.1	0.3	9.6
NLD	121.7	0.5	56.0	125.7	0.5	59.1	138.1	0.4	55.2	113.7	0.4	42.1
CHE	117.0	0.5	52.7	120.0	0.5	57.6	119.2	0.5	57.2	101.1	0.4	43.5
UK	78.6	0.6	47.2	83.4	0.6	47.6	78.9	0.5	41.8	59.2	0.6	32.6
USA	74.1	0.7	50.4	78.9	0.6	45.8	79.4	0.7	52.4	58.4	0.6	32.1
Mean	74.8	0.6	41.4	78.5	0.6	44.2	82.0	0.6	45.8	68.3	0.5	32.2
Std Dev	29.7	0.1	16.6	31.0	0.1	18.6	34.6	0.1	21.1	27.1	0.2	19.7
Min	33.7	0.4	12.8	32.4	0.4	13.6	32.4	0.4	13.3	34.1	0.2	8.6
Max	121.7	0.8	64.3	125.7	0.8	75.9	138.1	0.8	88.3	113.7	0.8	72.5
Set B												
AUT	4.8	0.4	1.8	4.9	0.4	1.8	4.8	0.4	1.7	4.4	0.2	0.9
BEL	4.4	0.8	3.7	4.2	0.9	3.7	4.5	0.8	3.8	3.3	0.8	2.6
FRA	1.2	0.0	0.0	1.1	0.0	0.0	1.1	0.0	0.0	0.0	0.0	0.0
DEU	4.0	0.4	1.4	4.2	0.3	1.4	4.7	0.4	1.8	4.7	0.4	1.7
GRC	0.0	0.0	0.0	0.0	0.0	0.0	0.0	0.1	0.0	0.0	0.1	0.0

Table 14.8 (*cont.*)

	CY05			CY06			CY07			CY08		
	PGDP	Eq	Exp	PGDP	Eq	Exp	PGDP	Eq	Exp	PGDP	Eq	Exp
ITA	2.8	0.2	0.6	3.0	0.2	0.7	3.3	0.2	0.6	3.4	0.2	0.6
JPN	6.6	0.0	0.0	0.0	0.0	0.0	0.0	0.0	0.0	0.0	0.0	0.0
KOR	1.9	0.0	0.0	3.0	0.1	0.2	3.1	0.1	0.2	3.0	0.3	0.7
MEX	10.0	0.1	1.1	11.5	0.1	1.6	11.5	0.1	1.5	10.4	0.1	1.1
NOR	6.7	0.3	1.9	6.8	0.3	2.2	7.0	0.4	2.5	6.0	0.3	1.8
PRT	12.7	0.4	5.2	13.6	0.5	7.0	13.7	0.5	6.9	12.2	0.3	4.1
ESP	7.2	0.3	2.2	7.5	0.3	2.3	7.5	0.3	2.3	7.1	0.2	1.1
SWE	9.1	0.4	3.2	9.3	0.4	3.6	8.7	0.4	3.5	7.4	0.3	2.2
Mean	5.5	0.2	1.6	5.3	0.3	1.9	5.4	0.3	1.9	4.8	0.2	1.3
Std Dev	3.7	0.2	1.6	4.3	0.2	2.0	4.2	0.2	2.0	3.8	0.2	1.2
Min	0.0	0.0	0.0	0.0	0.0	0.0	0.0	0.0	0.0	0.0	0.0	0.0
Max	12.7	0.8	5.2	13.6	0.9	7.0	13.7	0.8	6.9	12.2	0.8	4.1

pension assets to GDP ratios greater than 25 per cent, and Set B, which consists of countries with a lower ratio. The mean percentage of pension assets to GDP for Set A (nine countries) is 74 per cent. When compared to the mean for Set B (thirteen countries) of 5.5 percent, the figures reveal a fifteenfold difference. The mean exposure to equities of these private pension assets in Set A countries grew from 42 per cent in 2005 to 46 per cent in 2007, but then fell promptly off a cliff in 2008; in that year, they lost, on average, the asset equivalent of 14 points of GDP.

By contrast, although equity markets in emerging markets plunged even more steeply than in developed markets, the combination of lower private pension assets to GDP ratios and a lower equity exposure meant that Set B countries experienced a modest loss of 3.7 points of GDP in asset valuation in the 2008 repricing.

The Great Recession's liquidity drought and sharp stock market repricing thus attenuated the private equity mechanism for improved corporate governance. In better times, private equity firms provide a channel through which outside investors can purchase a controlling interest in firms from their previous blockholders (usually founders or families), restructure the firm in a variety of ways – including adopting more attractive corporate governance practices of accounting, disclosure, executive compensation and board oversight – and then float the firm with a public offering. In this process, outside investors can reap the 'good governance premium' from institutional investors that the firm's previous blockholders had not exploited. In 2008–9, however, any number of private equity deals were stopped dead in their tracks at various points in the pipeline, from acquisition right on through to stock flotation.

Monetary and fiscal policy response

All OECD countries responded to the 2008–9 downturn with both monetary loosening and fiscal expansion and experienced a broad deepening of government deficits as a result. For example, as reported earlier this year, 'Amidst continued uncertainty about the pace of recovery as well as the timing and sequencing of the steps of the exit strategy, gross borrowing needs of OECD governments are expected to reach almost USD 16 trillion in 2009, up from an earlier estimate of around USD 12 trillion. The tentative outlook for 2010 shows a stabilizing borrowing picture at around the level of USD 16 trillion' (Blommestein and Gok, 2009, p. 2). This cyclic dip accentuated stubborn structural deficits for almost all OECD countries, including, notably, the United States. The additional claims on limited government revenues that emerged just as the tax take declined (precipitously, in some countries) and as the recession deepened posed a significant risk to the beneficiaries of government-sponsored pension plans, both partially funded and conventional pay-as-you-go (PAYGO) plans.

Other things being equal, this risk is higher for countries in which PAYGO plans (so-called pillar 1 pension assets) constitute a higher percentage of expected retirement benefits than for countries in which private pension assets (pillars 2 and 3) constitute a higher percentage of retirement benefits. As noted earlier, the developed countries in our sample fall into two groups, with the countries in Set A showing relatively low levels of reliance on pillar 1 PAYGO plans and higher rates of pillar 2 and pillar 3 plans and the countries in Set B showing high reliance on pillar 1 PAYGO plans.

All OECD countries are headed towards a fiscal crunch for their national social security systems. This problem is driven primarily by demographics, although the crunch will be worse for nations with relatively smaller pillar 2 and pillar 3 pensions assets – namely, the Set B countries. Indeed, in our 2005 book we compiled World Bank estimates of the 'implicit pension debt' of twenty-six countries in our sample, circa 2000. The mean value was −115 per cent of GDP, with a wide variance: standard deviation of 75, minimum negative value of −330 and maximum value of 6 (Gourevitch and Shinn, 2005, p. 214). The estimate of implicit pension debt (IPD) was inversely correlated both with the ratio of private pension assets to GDP and with our index of corporate governance.

It would follow logically that efforts to reform corporate governance by means of public ordering, efforts that are often based on a political appeal to citizen-voters whose retirement assets have been reduced and put at risk by corporate governance failures, could collide with efforts to protect PAYGO pensions, efforts that are based on a political appeal to citizen-voters whose retirement claims have been put at risk by shrinking government revenues and towering fiscal deficits. Indeed, the beneficiaries of PAYGO plans are usually aware that they face some combination of reduced benefits, later vesting or much higher taxes unless state social security system claims are given fiscal priority in government budget-making.

This collision would be sharper in Set B countries than in Set A countries, *ceteris paribus*, since Set B states' citizen-voters' pensions are more at risk from steep fiscal deficits than are those of Set A states' citizen-voters, whose pension assets are fully or partially funded (in contrast to PAYGO systems, which are partially funded or zero-funded) and are essentially in private hands. This contrast suggests that we can predict a gradual divergence in the tone and terms of the political debate over public ordering of corporate governance between Set A and Set B countries. Set A countries will have a debate over the size and sustainability of pensions that involves a set of fiscal constraints but also involves a direct link between the viability of pensions and the quality of corporate governance. In contrast, Set B countries will experience a debate over the size and sustainability of pensions that is largely disconnected from corporate governance issues but that features an intense contest between pension claims and other fiscal claims on government budgets.

Conclusion

The central question of this chapter has been as follows: What will the net effect of the three main features of the Great Recession be on pressures for change in corporate governance through the private ordering mechanisms of the Investor model and the public ordering mechanisms of the Pension Preferences model? To summarize the evidence and arguments presented towards a response to this question, the Great Recession appears to have had the following effects:

- The financial bailouts and other liquidity injections made by governments on both sides of the Atlantic appear to have strengthened the ability of investors to use public ordering to press their corporate governance agenda directly, not only with respect to financial firms but also more broadly.
- At the same time, the speed and intensity of the panic in 2008 gave financial globalization a bad name in many countries, thereby undermining the credibility and political leverage of institutional investors and hedge funds to press for governance improvements via public ordering.

- Asset repricing, especially with respect to the substantial losses incurred by pension funds in many countries, has engendered widespread public support for corporate governance reforms. This pressure is likely to be proportional to the equity exposure of the pension assets in each country.
- Asset repricing and awareness of higher international market correlation have increased the incentive for outside investors to press firms in their portfolio for increased alpha performance by means of private ordering engagement (as the Investor model suggests).
- At the same time, the conservative funding strategy adopted by many non-financial firms, at least in developed markets, may have attenuated this private ordering leverage.
- The fiscal crunch stemming from structural deficits and counter-cyclical stimulus packages is likely to have a differential impact depending (again) on the relative exposure of pensioners to equity markets. Nations in which pensioners face substantial equity exposure are likely to see amplified and sustained support for corporate governance reforms via public ordering. Conversely, countries with largely state-centric PAYGO systems will see bitter contests over state revenues, a debate that will be largely disconnected from a corporate governance reform agenda.

On balance, it appears that the net effects of the Great Recession are attenuating some of the mechanisms of the Investor model and amplifying some of the mechanisms of the Pension Preferences model. These tentative conclusions are qualified by the caveats noted earlier, most prominently by the fact that it is still too soon to test these propositions statistically for a Great Recession whose trough we have probably passed but whose duration and ultimate impact are still to be calculated and assessed. In the meantime, we eagerly anticipate more current and detailed data sets on corporate governance, foreign investor penetration and pension asset exposure.

Notes

1 From an interview conducted in Cambridge, Massachusetts and printed in *The Independent*, 10 July 2002.
2 We also referred informally to this approach as the 'Millstein model', in reference to Yale Professor Ira Millstein's eloquent and precisely argued invocation of the power of global capital markets as an engine for reforms

in minority shareholder protections in his contributions to the OECD Corporate Governance Principles and to organizations such as ICGN.

3 Gourevitch and Shinn, 2005, pp. 101–3. For a sophisticated discussion of the empirical literature see Becht *et al.*, 2007.

4 In Gourevitch and Shinn, 2005, we sometimes refer to this nexus as the 'Transparency and Voice' coalition. In a sense, the Pension Preferences mechanism is another 'Millstein model', since Professor Millstein originally suggested it to the author in conversations in the late 1990s, based on Millstein's recollections of his involvement with the early corporate governance reform efforts of the New York State Employees Pension Fund.

5 These papers are summarized in La Porta *et al.*, 2002.

6 We made these additions based on an extensive set of interviews with institutional investors in New York, London, Paris, Tokyo, Hong Kong and Singapore between 1998 and 2002. These investors consistently weighed accounting and managerial compensation as important indicators of firm-level corporate governance and believed that changes in these two areas in particular were an essential ingredient of a viable 'good governance' bargain. Their argument, in a nutshell, was that as minority investors they were unlikely to gain board seats or to be able to observe the way in which the board monitored the firm, since such oversight was in the hands of the controlling blockholders, but that they could evaluate the financial situation themselves with good accounting data and disclosure along with insight into how the managers were compensated. In this sense, our index anticipated some of the objections to LLSV raised in Bebchuck and Hamdani, 2009, and in Martynova and Renneboog, 2010.

7 We found significant variation in our sample: a mean of 46.9, a standard deviation of 19.4, a minimum value of 4.1 and a maximum value of 90 (on a scale from 1 to 100). Developed countries on average had higher values than emerging markets and the index revealed a negative correlation of $-.33$ between the corporate governance ranking of a country and the mean ownership concentration ('blockholding') of listed firms in that country. Gourevitch and Shinn, 2005, pp. 48–9.

8 Firms are rated on a list of governance attributes, which are usually divided into those that apply to the board of directors, auditing practices, executive compensation and shareholder rights. These values are adjusted for certain country-level factors, normalized and presented in numerical form. For more details see RiskMetrics Group and GovernanceMetrics International 2010.

9 In their empirical tests, the authors found that 'Strikingly, for the S&P scores and the FTSE ISS index [an earlier version of the RiskMetrics data series], country characteristics have greater explanatory power than the observed and unobserved firm characteristics' (Doidge *et al.*, 2006, p. 3).

They also found that the country characteristics, even when just a dummy for the country variable, explain much more of the variation in firm-level governance scores (from 39 per cent to 73 per cent) than do other observable firm-level features such as size, ownership concentration, sales growth and so forth, which explain from 4 to 22 per cent of the variation.

10 The fact that the OECD private pension assets data for 2005 have a correlation of .90 with the data that we used in the 2000 test is no surprise since these assets grew in relative terms over the ensuing five years.

11 Curiously, similar changes in corporate governance were not imposed on Japanese banks in the wake of widespread bailouts and de facto nationalization of the Japanese banks in the mid 1990s.

References

Aggarwal, R., Erel, I., Ferreira, M. and Matos, P. 2009. 'Does governance travel around the world? Evidence from institutional investors', available at http://fisher.osu.edu/supplements/10/9860/20098.pdf, last accessed 10 December 2010.

Ammann, A., Oesch, D. and Schmid, M. 2009. 'Corporate governance and firm value: international evidence', available at www.phitrust.com/data/file/Documents_site_Internet/Corporate_Governance_and_Firm_Value_International_Evidence_Ammann_Oesch_and_Schmid_3_25_09.pdf, last accessed 15 January 2010.

Bebchuk, L. and Hamdani, A. 2009. 'The elusive quest for global governance standards', *University of Pennsylvania Law Review* 157: 1263–317.

Becht, M., Bolton, P. and Roell, A. 2007. 'Corporate law and governance', in Polinsky, M. and Shavell, S. (eds.), *Handbook of Law and Economics, Volume 2*. Amsterdam: Elsevier.

Bennett, R. 2009. 'The US: the government as shareholder', *International Corporate Governance Network 2009 Yearbook*.

Blommestein, H. and Gok, A. 2009. 'The surge in borrowing needs of OECD governments: revised estimates for 2009 and 2010 outlook', *OECD Journal: Financial Market Trend* 97: 177–89.

Doidge, C., Karolyi, G. and Stulz, R. 2007. 'Why do countries matter so much for corporate governance?', *Journal of Financial Economics* 86 (1): 1–39.

Euro Intelligence 2007. 'Germany plans hedge fund law', available at www.eurointelligence.com, last accessed 15 January 2010.

European Commission 2009. 'Proposal for a directive of the European Parliament on alternative investment fund managers and amending Directives 2004/39/EC and 2009/.../EC', available at http://ec.europa.eu/internal_

market/investmentdoes/alternative_investments/fund_managers_proposal_ en.pdf, last accessed 10 December 2010.

Federation of European Securities Exchanges 2008. *Share Ownership Structure in Europe*. Brussels: Federation of European Securities Exchanges.

Gourevitch, P. and Shinn, J. 2005. *Political Power and Corporate Control: The New Global Politics of Corporate Governance*. Princeton University Press.

GovernanceMetrics International. 'Pioneering accountability ratings', available at www.gmiratings.com/Products.aspx#basic, last accessed 15 January 2010.

Holderness, C. 2008. 'Do differences in legal protections explain differences in ownership concentration?', available at http://ssrn.com/abstract= 1104678, last accessed 10 December 2010.

Kollewe, J. and Reece, D. 2005. 'Hedge funds accused of "ripping heart out of German economy"', *The Independent*, 11 May.

La Porta, R., Lopez-de-Silances, F., Shleifer, A. and Vishny, R. 2002. 'Investor protection and corporate valuation', *Journal of Finance* 57 (3): 1147–70.

Lifsher, M. 2009. 'CalPERS to seek improved corporate governance, stricter Wall Street rules: the huge state pension fund also plans a thorough review of its investments in May', *Sacramento Bee*, 9 February.

Martynova, M. and Renneboog, L. 2010. 'A corporate governance index: convergence and diversity of national corporate governance regulations', CentER Discussion Paper Series No. 2010–17.

Milne, R. 2010. 'A meeting of minds', *Financial Times*, 1 March.

Ostry, J. D., Ghosh, A. R., Habermeier, K. F., Chamon, M. Q., Mahvash, S. and Reinhardt, D. B. S. 2010. 'Capital inflows: the role of controls', IMF Staff Position Note.

Perotti, E. and Schwienbacher, A. 2007. 'The political origin of pension funding', CEPR Discussion Paper No. 6100.

RiskMetrics Group 2010. 'Governance risk indicators: a new measure of governance-related risk', available at www.riskmetrics.com/sites/ default/files/GRId_Tech_Doc.pdf, last accessed 10 December 2010.

Spamann, H. 2010. 'The "antidirector rights index" revisited', *Review of Financial Studies* 23 (2): 467–86.

Stulz, R. 2005. 'The limits of financial globalization', *The Journal of Finance* 60 (4): 1595–638.

Weil Gotshal. 2009. 'SEC disclosure and corporate governance: challenges of the 2009 10-K and proxy season', available at www.weil.com/files/ upload/Briefing_SEC_CG_December_9.pdf, last accessed 10 December 2010.

15 | Corporate governance in the Islamic finance industry and mitigation of risks post the global financial crises

NASSER SAIDI

The ongoing financial crisis poses a series of challenges to policy-makers and regulators as they attempt to stabilize financial markets and prevent a meltdown.

The political and popular backlash is eliciting and promising deep banking and financial sector reform, including in the Bretton Woods international financial architecture and a wave of regulations, encompassing corporate governance.

At the most basic level, the current crisis stemmed from excessive risk-taking for short-term profit by senior managements in highly leveraged banking and financial institutions. Boards were not fulfilling their obligations in ensuring the sustainability of their operations. Regulators were failing to provide satisfactory oversight of a system that provided incentive to leverage through securitization and sent the wrong prudential signals through the pro-cyclicality of capital adequacy and value-at-risk measures.

In other words, the crisis originated from failures on three principal levels:

(1) the senior management level,
(2) the board level and
(3) at the regulatory level.

The underlying theme, whether at the level of senior management, board of directors or at the regulatory level, is the lack of understanding of the risks being taken.

In these testing times, we need to rethink the overall system, its architecture and incentive schemes; but we must also bear in mind that many of the technical solutions exist, and, arguably, by proper implementation of corporate governance best practices, the crisis could have been avoided or its consequences mitigated.

Based on Saidi, 2009a.

As the financial crisis spread across the globe, a number of commentators were quick to point out that Islamic finance would be more resilient to the crisis owing to the stricter rules imposed on lending by Islamic law, which bans some of the subprime mortgages backed by collateralized debt packages that subsequently precipitated a global credit crunch.

Corporate governance in Islamic finance[1]

Corporate governance (CG) in Islamic finance necessitates that Islamic financial institutions (IFIs) abide by a set of rules called the Islamic law or Shari'a. The Shari'a governs the banks' operations and transactions in accordance with Islamic principles derived from the Quran and Hadith. However, the framework for ensuring compliance with Shari'a, the Islamic law, within financial institutions brings into focus a number of interesting corporate governance issues. First, Islamic banking is subject to an additional layer of governance in the form of Shari'a Supervisory Boards (SSBs) and internal Shari'a audits. In addition, financial arrangements based on equity participation and risk and profit-and-loss sharing imply different stakeholder relationships, and by corollary, governance structures, from the conventional model since depositors have a direct financial stake in the banks' investment and equity participations.

Table 15.1 suggests the build-up of a corporate governance framework for IFIs. To ensure that a national or sector-specific CG framework is consistent with international best practice, the framework should incorporate the OECD principles of Corporate Governance and the Guidance by the Basel Committee on Banking Supervision on Enhancing Corporate Governance for Banking Organizations 2006.

The Islamic Financial Services Board (IFSB) in its guiding principles places the focus on Investment Account Holders (IAHs) and protecting their rights. Conceptually, under the principle of Modaraba, IAHs as Rabb al-Māl bear the risk of losing their capital invested by the institutions offering Islamic Financial Services (IIFS) as Mudarib. Effectively, this means the IAH's investment risk is similar to that of the shareholders of IIFS who bear the risk of losing their capital as investors in the IIFS.

Under a Modaraba contract, whether the investment mandate is restricted or unrestricted, the IIFS has a fiduciary duty to the IAHs

Table 15.1 *Regulatory and corporate governance (CG) framework for IFIs*

Regulatory and corporate governance (CG) framework of banks
  I. National CG framework
      – Banking sector-specific laws/codes/guidelines
      – Stock exchanges listing rules and regulations
      – Listed companies regulatory authorities' laws, rules and regulations
  II. Islamic finance and Shari'a-specific codes and standards
      – IFSB Guiding Principles on Corporate Governance for Institutions
        Offering Islamic Financial Services 2006
      – Accounting and Auditing Organization for Islamic Financial Institutions
        (AAOIFI) accounting, auditing and governance standards (for Islamic
        financial institutions)
      – Islamic Financial Services Board (IFSB) published standards including
        guidance on key elements in the supervisory review process of insti-
        tutions offering Islamic financial services (excluding Islamic insurance
        (Takaful) institutions and Islamic mutual funds)
  III. International standards and codes
      – The OECD Principles of Corporate Governance
      – Guidance by the Basel Committee on Banking Supervision on Enhancing
        Corporate Governance for Banking Organizations 2006

to uphold its interests no less than those of the IIFS's own shareholders. In other words, although as investors in the IIFS' assets the shareholders would rank *pari passu* with the IAHs, the IIFS as a party in the Mudarib side of the Modaraba contract also owes a fiduciary duty to the IAHs and would have to ensure the protection of the IAH's interests.

Hence, it is appropriate that IIFS put IAHs on an equal footing with the IIFS' own shareholders by duly acknowledging the IAHs' right to access all relevant information in relation to their investment accounts. This would assist the IAHs in making an informed decision on their selection or choice of the investment accounts in which to place their funds with the IIFS. In a situation where the local legal framework is not yet capable of facilitating the exercise of these rights by the IAHs, the supervisory authorities should play a role in protect-ing the interests of the IAH vis-à-vis the shareholders of IIFS with regard to their rights, provided that they are in compliance with Shari'a rules and principles.

The IAHs' right to monitor the performance of their investment should not be misconstrued as a right to intervene in the management of the investments by the IIFS. It should be noted that shareholders of IIFS who are entitled to vote in general meetings, to pass resolutions on the appointment of directors and auditors, and to access the documents of the IIFS are also not considered as intervening in the management of the IIFS. Therefore, it is only appropriate that IIFS discloses to the IAHs their policies and practices in respect of the investment accounts which they offer.

The Accounting and Auditing Organization for Islamic Financial Institutions (AAOIFI) has also issued standards on accounting, auditing, governance, codes of ethics and Shari'a. The AAOIFI explains the role of the Audit and Governance Committee as being responsible for overall monitoring of business covering internal control, compliance with Shari'a laws and principles and adherence to code of ethics. In 2008, AAOIFI revised the Accounting, Auditing and Governance Standards (for Islamic Financial Institutions) to take account of changes in international accounting and auditing standards and their impact for IIFS.

Internal and external Shari'a compliance for IFIs

To ensure Shari'a compliance, Islamic banks employ an individual Shari'a advisor and/or board. Central to such a framework is the Shari'a Supervisory Board (SSB) and the internal controls which support it. In some countries the SSB is established at central banks while in others Shari'a advisors are established at commercial banks. In the latter case, their independence from bank management is an issue. On occasions a number of banks might use the advice of the same Shari'a advisor (SA), which could raise an issue of conflict of interest. Establishing guidelines for, and coordinating the advice of an SA, appears to be an issue of concern that has drawn the attention of regulators. Similarly, cross-country coordination among SSBs' interventions/guidance is also an issue that has led the authorities in a number of countries to call for harmonization.

In principle, the role of the SSB covers five main areas: ensuring compliance with overall Islamic banking fundamentals, certifying permissible financial instruments through Fatwas and verifying that transactions comply with issued Fatwas, calculating and paying Zakat, disposing of non-Shari'a-compliant earnings, and advising on the distribution of income or expenses among share-holders and investment account holders. The SSB issues a report to certify that all financial transactions (including investments) comply with the above-mentioned principles. This report is often an integral part of the Annual Report of the Islamic financial institution. In practice an SSB's tasks may vary according to provisions stipulated in the articles of association of the financial institution or those stipulated by national regulators.

The SSB can also issue recommendations on how the institution could best fulfil its social role as well as promote Islamic finance. In addition to internal corporate arrangements, national regulators and international standard-setters have developed guidelines for SSBs. These often refer to the SSBs' general duty to ensure Shari'a compliance of transactions and, less frequently, indicate areas of competence, composition and decision-making.

There are external arrangements in place as well; such arrangements, including mechanisms of market discipline, can provide complementary channels inducing compliance with rulings and their harmonization. Indeed these are similar to the Basel II pillars, where the second and third pillars focus, respectively, on supervisory/regulatory review and market discipline.

Table 15.2 illustrates the different roles and competencies of the internal Shari'a review unit as compared with the external Shari'a review and audit.

Corporate governance in Takaful and Retakaful industry

The underdevelopment and low penetration rates of the insurance industry, both conventional and Shari'a-compliant, in the Middle East North Africa (MENA) region and countries with an important Islamic finance industry are attributable to a number of factors, including poor corporate governance, barriers to entry, restricted market access and protection of local insurers. The near absence of competition, restrictions on entry of foreign insurers and the dominance of government-owned insurers and regulatory control of insurance pricing and products has led to expensive insurance and an absence of new products and innovation.

The guidelines laid down by the OECD and the International Association of Insurance Supervisors (IAIS) for corporate governance in the

Table 15.2 *Comparison between internal and external Shari'a arrangements*

	Internal Shari'a review unit	External Shari'a review and audit
Focus	Provides exhaustive internal review, and trains employees on Shari'a-related matters. It responds to managerial concerns over upholding Shari'a conformity of all transactions.	Primarily provides an independent certification as to the reasonableness of financial information provided to shareholders and stakeholders. It responds to regulators' and stakeholders' desire for an independent appraisal of Shari'a compliance.
Activities	Assesses compliance of *all* transactions with the Fatwas issued by the SSB. To this effect, it creates systems of control and assessment.	Assesses the information provided by the managers and presents statements according to relevant Shari'a accounting standards. It uses *samples* of transactions to evaluate truthfulness of compliance and expresses an opinion on financial statements.
Management	Reports to management administratively. Builds relationships throughout the organization to ensure concerns are identified and resolved in a timely manner.	Primarily reports to the board/audit committee on financials and internal control.
Board of directors/ committee	Reports directly to the audit committee. Provides opinions on the organization's business risks, financial statements, system of internal control and level of compliance with laws, regulations and policies.	Attests to the audit committee the accuracy of the financial reports and attests on management's assessment of internal controls over financial reporting. Provides updates on pending accounting pronouncements and their potential impact on the organization.

Table 15.2 (*cont.*)

	Internal Shari'a review unit	External Shari'a review and audit
Independence	Should demonstrate organizational independence and objectivity in work approach, but is managerially dependent on the organization.	It is organizationally and managerially independent of the organization.
Results	Identifies problems, makes recommendations and helps facilitate resolutions.	Meets statutory requirements and provides necessary adjustments to meet financial accuracy.
Risk	Identifies and qualifies key business risks to estimate probability of occurrence and impact on business. Makes appropriate recommendations as a result of the risk assessment.	Identifies key transactions and exposures for financial statements.
Fraud	Includes fraud detection steps in audit programmes. Investigates allegations of fraud. Reviews fraud prevention controls and detection processes put in place by management and makes recommendations for improvement.	Includes fraud detection steps in audit plan. Gathers information necessary to identify risks of material misstatement due to fraud, by inquiring of management and others within the entity about the risks of fraud. Considers the results of the analytical procedures performed in planning the audit and fraud risk factors.
Recommendations	Communicates to management in the audit reports recommendations for corrective action.	Communicates recommendations for corrective action to the board audit committee.

insurance sector serve as an industry benchmark for standard-setting. These guidelines emphasize the importance of sound risk management and decision-making processes. They also include setting out the role and responsibilities of directors and ensuring that the rights of policy-holders and shareholders are protected. Transparency, disclosure and regular reviews are also key requirements to facilitate good decision-making as well as protecting stakeholder rights.

The IAIS has also developed insurance core principles (ICP) and methodology stating the essential principles that need to be in place for a supervisory system to be effective. In particular, ICP 9 deals with corporate governance and emphasizes that the corporate governance framework should recognize and protect rights of all interested parties. The board is the focal point of the corporate governance systems and is ultimately accountable and responsible for the performance and conduct of the insurer. The delegation of authority to board committees, Shari'a committees or executive management does not in any way mitigate or dissipate the discharge by the board of directors of its duties and responsibilities.

In August 2006, the IFSB and IAIS published an informative 'Issues in Regulation and Supervision of Takaful' which touched on corporate governance, noting that international corporate governance principles extend to the Shari'a board/committee. The latter should be an integral part of the internal governance structure of the insurer and ensure compliance with the Shari'a.

Consideration also needs to be given to the relationship between the Shari'a committee and other governance structures of the company to ensure that responsibilities are clearly and appropriately allocated.

The corporate governance framework should ensure the independence, confidentiality and competence of Shari'a scholars, as well as the consistency of Shari'a scholars' Fatwas (rulings).

There are additional specific challenges faced by the Takaful industry in terms of corporate governance. Governance issues to be addressed include the protection of minority shareholders, improved disclosure of risks, commingling of resources, balancing Unrestricted Investment Account (UIA) holders' risks and rights, and the rules for the utilization of reserve funds. More generally, regulators need to impose mandatory, uniform financial reporting standards and disclosure requirements.

Increasingly, good corporate governance practices are integral to creating and sustaining the long-term value of firms, whether or not

Shari'a-compliant. Empirical evidence suggests that more than 84 per cent of global institutional investors are willing to pay a premium for the shares of a well-governed company over one considered poorly governed but with a comparable financial record. Similarly, a study of S&P 500 firms by Deutsche Bank showed that companies with strong or improving corporate governance outperformed those with poor or deteriorating governance practices by about 19 per cent over a two-year period.

Transparency and disclosure is a key element of corporate governance. Good CG practices not only impact a company's performance in terms of its equity, but better corporate governance standards lead to banks and rating agencies giving improved credit ratings, thereby reducing the cost of borrowing of well-governed companies. It also improves an institution's market perception and rating and positively affects its market value.

Islamic finance and the global financial crisis[2]

Despite the global economic crisis the MENA region continued to grow in 2008 and 2009. An economic and financial renaissance during 2003–8 was accompanied by a surge in Islamic finance. Islamic finance grew by about 15–20 per cent up to the year 2008.

Since the inception of modern Islamic banking, the number and reach of Islamic financial institutions worldwide has risen from one institution in one country in 1975, to more than 300 institutions operating in more than seventy-five countries.

Although Islamic banks are concentrated in the Middle East and South-East Asia, they are also niche players in Europe and the United States.

As mentioned earlier, IFIs have displayed strong resilience amid the current global financial crises, though they have not been immune. One obvious reason for their proven ability to weather the storm is embedded within the core principles of Islamic banking. Both speculation (maysir) and interest rates (riba) are prohibited. However, it is not because IFIs' risk management architecture and culture were more robust that they avoided carrying toxic products on their books; structurally, they have simply been banned from investing in such asset classes, as per the core principles they abide by. IFIs are not risk-immune, but their current capacity to resist this crisis has been bolstered by the lack of investment in such securities. However, they remain exposed in their investments to the weaknesses of the real estate market in the Gulf countries.

The Dubai World case study[3]

The Gulf Cooperation Council (GCC) region weathered the global economic crisis better than other regions. But pressures on highly leveraged corporate entities in Dubai culminated in November 2009 when Dubai World, a state-controlled company, announced that it would seek a debt standstill on debt service relating to some $26 billion, mainly linked to its two property firms, Nakheel and Limitless World – in other words, negotiate an agreement with its creditors to modify the original credit terms and avoid foreclosure proceedings.

Dubai World's request for a six-month moratorium on debt service was an unexpected event that led to a re-evaluation of the economic and financial prospects of the Emirate. It followed the $22 billion debt-restructuring involving the Saudi family-owned groups Saad and Algosaibi. The two events – for different reasons – raised global investor concern over issues of transparency, disclosure, creditor rights, accountability and corporate governance practices in the region. Although the Dubai World amount in question was trivial (compared to e.g. Lehman Brothers which owed in excess of $600 billion when it went into bankruptcy protection), it acted as a signal of potential widespread financial distress, which undermined international confidence in the ability of financially vulnerable Gulf businesses to restructure their debts. It caused observers to re-evaluate the extent of the effects of the global economic and financial crisis and contagion effects on the region's financial institutions and investment companies. Dubai and its companies were seen as a litmus test for the Gulf countries and other emerging economies.

Gulf policymakers needed to take steps to address this international concern and demonstrate the need to embed global best practices and implement the principles of good corporate governance at all political and economic levels.

Driven by promising regional growth prospects, positive demographics, strong foreign direct investment, a liberalization of property laws allowing foreign ownership of real estate and a rapid influx of expatriate labour and professionals, Dubai real estate developers, including government-related entities, had borrowed extensively in 2004–8 to fund a major push into commercial and residential property and its related infrastructure. The first opening-up of real estate investment in a GCC country, and the accompanying significant increase in domestic credit growth, led to a real estate bubble, which burst in mid 2008, its effects compounded by a global financial crisis and sudden stop of foreign capital. To deal with the resulting domestic liquidity crunch, the government of Abu Dhabi provided Dubai a loan of $10 billion to cover some of Dubai World's maturing debt obligations, including about $4.2[4] billion in Islamic bonds (Sukuk) of its real estate subsidiary Nakheel, which matured on 14 December 2009. The cost of insuring Dubai's debt against default (CDS rates) fell sharply on the news, and the stock market in the Emirate rose 10.4 per cent, its biggest one-day gain in fourteen months. The intervention helped calm markets, but uncertainties remained as the government of Dubai developed a strategy to put its corporate sector on a viable path.

Government intervention

Despite the fact that the liabilities of Dubai World and Nakheel were neither sovereign liabilities nor sovereign-guaranteed liabilities, the government of Dubai decided to intervene to prevent contagion effects and Dubai World becoming an element of systemic risk for Dubai.

In March 2010, the government of Dubai, along with Dubai World and Nakheel, announced proposals for the restructuring of the two companies' liabilities. The government would provide up to US $9.5 billion in new funding to Dubai World and Nakheel via the Dubai Financial Support Fund (DFSF). Some $5.7 billion of this would come from the balance of the loan from the government of Abu Dhabi and the remaining $3.8 billion would come from existing resources. The $9.5 billion cash injection would allocate $1.5 billion to Dubai World and $8 billion to Nakheel.

Dubai World: The statement noted that $23.5 billion in Dubai World financial liabilities under restructuring (as of end December 2009) included $14.2 billion owed to non-DFSF creditors, and $9.3 billion in claims by the DFSF. The government of Dubai will convert $8.9 billion of the remaining $9.3 billion remaining claims into equity, thereby subordinating itself to other creditors. The conversion by the Dubai government of $8.9 billion of debt and claims – representing

38 per cent of the total amount of standalone debt and guarantees of Dubai World – into equity, effectively answers questions on ownership.

Significantly, it was the government of Dubai that absorbed the burden of the debt-equity conversion, and not the private sector, unlike the case with many recent restructurings around the world. The move clearly demonstrates Dubai's commitment to supporting its state-owned enterprises, a mainstay of its economic development strategy.

The $14.2 billion in non-DFSF claims would be restructured into two tranches of new debt with five- and eight-year maturities with no haircut. In addition, the government of Dubai committed $1.5 billion in new funds to Dubai World from the DFSF to fund working capital and interest payments that will arise from the new debt obligations.

Nakheel: The Nakheel statement noted that the DFSF will provide Nakheel with up to $8 billion in additional funds, as required. This would be converted into equity on completion of the two restructurings. In addition, DFSF will convert its existing $1.2 billion claim on Nakheel into equity. All creditors would receive 100 per cent principal repayment over time but, as described below, the terms vary considerably depending on the creditor type. Significantly, Sukuk holders are repaid in full as scheduled, but banks and trade creditors face a maturity extension (being finalized at the time of writing).

Lessons

The debt-equity conversion gives Dubai World and Nakheel a stronger equity base and sound financial footings which allow them to proceed with organizational (initiated with the set-up of a new Nakheel board) and operational restructuring. One of the more important lessons from this episode is the need to avoid maturity mismatches arising from long-gestation projects (such as the Palm) being financed with short-term money and subsequently facing rollover risk. The other major lesson is the need for strengthened corporate governance, better financial controls and risk management to avoid a resurgence of excessive credit leverage. Improving corporate governance and transparency is now paramount in view of heightened lender risk aversion, which now impels GCC conglomerates and government-related entities to focus more on disclosure and transparency. Clear communication of policy by the authorities would help implementation, ease investor uncertainty, and reduce speculation and market volatility.

Financial structural reforms are also required to build market infrastructure. The region's authorities should prioritize the development of local currency debt and Sukuk markets to diversify financing channels away from banks and from dependence on foreign capital.[5] The development of local currency markets would also facilitate the longer-term goal of diversifying GCC economies away from oil, by providing an alternative and new source of finance for the private sector. The related issue is reform and modernization of the region's insolvency and creditor rights frameworks, in particular in relation to dealing with the Sukuk market and creditor rights.

Challenges faced by the Islamic finance industry

Islamic finance has transcended borders and regions but many challenges lie ahead before it can make that crucial leap from being an interesting but niche market to being an integral part of the global financial markets.

Lack of standardization in the Islamic finance industry results in higher costs and lengthier time faced by financial institutions offering Shari'a-compliant products.

The absence of a single global regulatory regime results in less innovation and passportability barriers in cross-border transactions. Generally, when products transcend the boundaries of the country of origination the regulations and legal requirements of the recipient jurisdiction must be adhered to. In the context of Islamic finance, the added component of Shari'a adds a further consideration, that of seeking to ensure that the Shari'a-compliant product remains Shari'a-compliant in the recipient jurisdictions.

There is a need for risk and liquidity management due to prohibition on investing in hedging instruments in most jurisdictions and the lack of instruments with short-term maturities.

Lack of reliable statistical data and shortage of professionals and expert talent is also one of the challenges being faced by the Islamic finance industry.

For IFIs in particular, there needs to be standardization in the accounting treatment of Islamic finance transactions between AAOIFI standards and the International Financial Reporting Standards. The roles and responsibilities of the SSB members need to be defined and their relationship with the board of directors and accountability towards the shareholders need to be addressed.

The regulation of Islamic finance should be aligned with the regulation of conventional finance to the maximum extent consistent with Shari'a requirements.

These actions should be viewed as a step in the direction of streamlining and harmonizing laws and regulations relating to Islamic finance. The ultimate objective should be an Islamic Financial Passport, an IFP, to facilitate cross-border trade in Islamic Finance Securities (IFSs) and the mutual recognition and establishment of IFIs.

Post-global financial crisis: what needs to be done

In light of the near meltdown of markets, the key objective is restoring market and investor confidence in the banking and finance sector whether it is conventional or Islamic.

The way out of the crisis is through intelligent regulation, one that does not pre-empt or hinder market driven adjustments, but supports and strengthens financial innovation and the market, and does so through creating and maintaining a culture of transparency and accountability.

From the perspective of regulators, this means three things. The regulators need to ensure that they themselves are both transparent and accountable, that their responsibilities are well defined and not conflicted, that they are not subject to political intervention or 'regulatory capture' and that they are staffed with competent and experienced personnel. Regulators should develop and implement governance guidelines on good practices for regulators as promoted by the Bank for International Settlements and International Organization of Securities Commissions. Juvenal's *Quis custodiet ipsos custodes?* or 'Who will guard the guards themselves?' requires an urgent answer.

Secondly, a major lesson is the need to extend the regulatory powers of the Central Bank to investment banking and related non-bank financial intermediation, in coordination with capital market regulators. The high volume of financial product engineering that preceded the current financial crises led to a dramatic increase in financial intermediation outside the core banking system – in the so-called grey banking sector, which was subject to little or no regulation. The financial turmoil has highlighted the interconnectedness of financial institutions. The complexity of markets, instruments and financial institutions and balance-sheet interconnectedness requires a corresponding supervisory net. Regulatory gaps need to be filled to prevent regulatory arbitrage and abuse.

Thirdly, regulators need to impose, and ensure compliance with, mandatory corporate governance principles in the banking sector, for both conventional and Shari'a-compliant banks and financial institutions. Governance principles for the banking sector should also be stricter and reflect a higher level of standard from a sector that is regulated, leveraged and benefits from deposit guarantee schemes and other publicly provided financial safety net provisions. Banks dominate the financial systems in the MENA region and play a key role in the credit and investment process that is so vital to economic development. Good governance can play a critical role in the process of building strong domestic financial markets. It increases public confidence in the securities markets, improving liquidity and enhancing bank, corporate and sovereign ratings.

Strengthening corporate governance in the financial sector will also extend better corporate governance to the firms the banks lend to.[6]

Financial institutions need to address their board structures, and pay special attention to any concentration of power. The roles of chairman and chief executive should be separate and the boards need to comprise sufficient, if not majority, independent non-executive representation to protect shareholder interests. In particular, critical board committees, such as the audit, risk management and remuneration committees, should be composed of independent non-executive directors.

The competency of board members should also be addressed. Directors should be appointed through formal and rigorous appointment processes based on merit and against objective criteria, having regard to succession plans. Directors need to have relevant experience and know-how to enable them to address the current and, in particular, future challenges of the business. Critically, they also have to be able to say 'No'!

Boards should see that conflicts of interest are avoided and if avoidance cannot be achieved in specific circumstances, conflicts should be identified, managed and, depending on their materiality, disclosed to the supervisor and, where appropriate, to shareholders in the annual report. Material related-party transactions should also be disclosed, and there should be an outright prohibition on certain specific types of related-party transactions, such as personal loans to board members and controlling shareholders.

Rigorous internal control processes should be developed and enforced. Sound risk management is built on a robust system of checks and balances, following clearly documented procedures and reporting lines. Professionally competent and independent internal and external audit functions are required to monitor and test the efficiency of the control system. Demonstrably, risk management failures are life threatening for the enterprise and are a major source of systemic risk. It is appropriate that regulators and boards are responsible for ensuring compliance.

Wholly independent remuneration committees should develop policies on executive pay and the total remuneration packages should be disclosed to, and approved by, shareholders. The financial crisis has made it evident how damaging remuneration practices can be if the wrong incentives are provided, and investors are increasingly pushing for remuneration packages that are risk-based, linked to long-term performance, relevant to the individual company's strategic goals, and consistent with sound corporate risk management.

Boards need to be given incentives to provide more transparency and public disclosure, and more specifically provide meaningful statements of their activities, not as a compliance activity, but to demonstrate awareness of risks and their skill in managing them.

Corporate governance should not be seen as a compliance exercise, but as a tool building competitive advantage to be exploited in that it helps boost and maintain shareholder confidence, but also provides the appropriate framework for preserving market integrity and the proper execution of compliance activities such as anti-money laundering throughout institutions. Good governance, through improved transparency and accountability, facilitates the early detection of shortcomings and prompts adequate responses, and thereby not only helps prevent crises but also ensures that companies following best practices are more adaptable to any future regulations.

Corporate governance improvements do not occur in a vacuum, but are often supported, incentivized and facilitated by the regulator. It is likely that in the post-credit quake world, markets which will fare the best are those in which fundamental investor concerns are identified and addressed by the regulators and companies alike.

Notes

1 Based on Saidi, 2008, reproduced with permission of Euromoney Books from *Islamic Wealth Management: A Catalyst for Global Change and Innovation.*
2 Based on Saidi, 2009b.
3 Sources from www.nakheel.com/en/news/nakheel-launches-comprehensive-recapitalisation-plan; http://blogs.ft.com/maverecon/2009/11/the-intrinsic-unimportance-of-dubai-world-and-the-important-wider-message-it-conveys, last accessed 10 April 2010.
4 $4.1 billion reported by Reuters.
5 See 'Developing local currency bond markets as a cornerstone of development policy', DIFC Economic Note No. 7, available at www.difc.ae/index.php/press-centre/publications/research-reports-white-papers, last accessed 10 April 2010.
6 See the Dubai World case study discussed earlier in this chapter.

References

Khamis, M. and Senhadji, A. 2010. 'Learning from the past: IMF Survey March 2010', available at www.reuters.com/article/idUST RE5BD0D720091214; Deutsche Bank report, 25 March 2010, available at www.lse.ac.uk/collections/LSEKP/documents/WakeUpCall.pdf, last accessed 10 April 2010.
Saidi, N. 2008. 'Corporate governance in Islamic finance', in Jaffer, S. (ed.), *Islamic Wealth Management: A Catalyst for Global Change and Innovation.* London: Euromoney Institutional Investor.
    2009a. 'Financial crises and the corporate governance solution: moving forward on remedies', keynote address at SAMA Institute of Banking, 24 March 2009, Riyadh, KSA.
    2009b. 'Islamic finance is coming of age', *Formiche*, June 2009.

16 A holistic approach to corporate governance: lessons from the financial crisis and the way forward

SUZANNE YOUNG AND VIJAYA THYIL

The heightened focus on corporate governance and, in particular, the failure of boards to protect corporations in the aftermath of the global financial crisis (GFC) underline the timeliness of this chapter. The current events, which include failures of monitoring and oversight and fraudulent behaviour by board members and their excessive remuneration levels, have all contributed to make the recent crisis one of the worst international financial collapses since the early part of the twentieth century. Improved decision-making is thus called for in moving corporations to better performance levels (Useem, 2006). However, boards are facing challenges in trying to balance their function as compliance officers with their function as shapers of the corporation's future (Lorsch and Clark, 2008). Simultaneously, a broader issue has emerged where society is redefining deviant behaviour, so that lower levels of conduct that were previously stigmatized are now considered acceptable (O'Brien, 2004). Thus, even though researchers and commentators have usually linked corporate governance to control and compliance with a focus on regulatory solutions, increasingly, we are seeing new approaches that call for behavioural and leadership change and the development of a holistic paradigm that is more suitable for the complexities of the twenty-first century (see *Corporate Governance: An International Review*, Vol. 17, Issue 4). This chapter picks up these developments and argues for a holistic perspective of governance and moves the debate from a narrow regulatory approach that excludes crucial variables, to highlight the importance of viewing governance problems and solutions from a wider and more inclusive multi-disciplinary paradigm.

In pointing to the impact of the current financial crisis, the chapter reviews the current research, and draws on various approaches to dealing with it – including the need for effective and enforceable regulation, a greater focus on ethics and leadership, a strengthening of governance codes, the enhancement of shareholder voice and the

365

strengthening of disclosure and transparency (Young, 2009). Other drivers of governance are originating from corporate responsibility and socially responsible investment themes (Brennan and Solomon, 2008; Solomon, 2009). Learning from relationship-based systems may also assist and provide another path – where key stakeholders have greater influence and decision-making rights, and more input into the strategies of corporations (Clarke, 2009). In exploring these themes and using a holistic model of governance (Young and Thyil, 2008b), longitudinal interview data were collected in 2007 and again in 2009, from institutional investors, corporate governance executives and fund managers. The data are used to illustrate changes in focus in governance, their drivers and key features over time. Moreover, the 2009 data are used to highlight the antecedents and features of Australian governance, their impact on the financial crisis and how Australian corporations have reacted.

The importance of incorporating a multidisciplinary perspective in governance research appears to be the key to understanding governance failures. Governance research has often been left to accounting and legal academics and it is increasingly evident that this approach is far too narrow. Drawing on a more holistic approach to governance will provide a wider lens through which to view the antecedents and impact of the GFC. In addition, it will provide executives and directors with a range of variables that influence good governance and highlight where the focus should be in introducing good governance practices.

Literature

Anglo governance systems rely on a number of controls to align shareholders' and boards of directors' interests. Agency theory (Fama and Jensen, 1983; Eisenhardt, 1989) proposes that control mechanisms are necessary as human nature is such that directors and managers act with self-interest and bounded rationality, which can result in sub-optimal decision-making.

One form of control is regulation which varies across Anglo systems. The US governance system relies on prescriptive legislation whereas the Australian and UK systems rely on what is referred to as a 'comply-or-explain' or principles-based system, where publicly listed companies either comply with certain principles or explain why not. This system, therefore, provides somewhat more flexibility than the US system.

Criticisms of reliance on regulation have been noted. For instance, Clarke (2007, p. 162) argued that minimum *standards* of practice become minimum *acceptable* practice, as new and imaginative ways are created to get around the rules, although, Clarke added (p. 130), regulation is a necessary component of governance to ensure disclosure and transparency and to reduce information asymmetry, explaining that the introduction of tougher rules in the United States has improved reporting and governance behaviour (p. 155). Similarly, Francis and Armstrong (2003) contended that ethical self-regulation complements the law and can be considered an aspirational standard, in contrast to legal or what are referred to as 'minimal standards'. Dallas (2004, p. 23) also argued that reliance on rules and compliance is fraught with danger, although adding that objective standards are required to facilitate meaningful comparative analysis, to bring about discipline and to ensure shareholders receive a fair share of rewards.

Ongoing debate has centred on the benefits of the regulatory or the principles-based system and, alongside the US origin of the GFC, questions continue to be raised as to whether more regulation is the answer. Moreover, as the crisis spread to the UK and Europe, UK executives were making statements reflecting that the full implications of their own practices and behaviours were not fully recognized, with fault being seen to reside solely in US practices (Young and Thyil, 2009). As Clarke (2009, p. 221) has recently argued, it is often only at times of crisis that governance is examined, and when times are booming excesses are ignored.

The business environment of the 1990s and 2000s has displayed evidence that, at board level, the questioning of decisions that focus on short-term decisions, greedy capitalism and over-exuberant remuneration has neither been accepted nor encouraged. But, in academic circles, board decision-making has increasingly been explored by behaviouralist researchers with Adams and Ferreira (2007) and Zhang *et al.* (2009) contending that it is understanding the board's information-generation and -sharing capacity that is important to exploring decision-making. Many others also point to the importance of a change of approach which examines cognition and decision-making to illuminate our understanding of what happens inside the boardroom (or black box) (Sundaramurthy and Lewis, 2003; Huse, 2007; van Ees *et al.*, 2009). Moreover Gillan (2006, p. 396) argued for more empirical research that focuses on board responses to changes in the environment, while Brennan and Solomon (2008, pp. 890, 893) argued that there is growing interest in a more stakeholder-based approach, with consideration of broader theoretical frameworks and methodologies.

As Young and Thyil (2008b) have previously argued, many types of theoretical frameworks have been used to analyse the governance system, including regulation, both internal and external (Jensen and Meckling, 1976), behavioural (Leung and Cooper, 2003), decision-making (Cutting and Kouzmin, 2000; Kaufman and Englander, 2005), leadership (Gabrielsson *et al.*, 2007), power (Handy, 1978; Pfeffer, 1992; Cutting and Kouzmin, 2000, 2001, 2002), class (Murray, 2006) and ethics (Wood, 2002, 2005; Francis and Armstrong, 2003; Wood and Callaghan, 2003; Lagan, 2006). Others have examined governance with the aim of addressing the needs of different groups of stakeholders such as shareholders (Lynall *et al.*, 2003), employees (Deakin *et al.*, 2002), customers (Lines, 2004) or society (Jensen, 2001). Others have presented contrasting perspectives such as the shareholder versus stakeholder models, and market versus control models (Sharma, 1997; Jensen, 2001).

In addition, drawing from international governance frameworks may provide a broadening of perspective. Historically, relationship-based governance systems have been predisposed to the stakeholder approach and the incorporation of corporate responsibility into strategy and operations. Relationships between board members are common with insider representation including family members, banks and other providers of capital, employees or unions, and strong links within business groups (Franks and Mayer, 2005; Zattoni *et al.*, 2009). A longer-term focus is the norm (Zattoni *et al.*, 2009). Such relationships, according to institutional theory, provide structural and cultural control of behaviour and resource-sharing and are particularly important for countries with weak market control (Khanna and Palepu, 1999, 2000; North, 1990). Cultural norms act as a guide to corporate behaviour and impact on what is seen as 'responsible'. Boards and managers (often with family ties) view responsibilities to employees and community as inherently linked to organizational purpose – and often as the primary focus (Bertrand *et al.*, 2002). Conversely, the Anglo system, despite its market controls, often looks to legislation for guidance in defining responsibility and where the responsibility lies. Convergence between the Anglo and relationship-based governance systems is often discussed (Clarke, 2009, for a full discussion of convergence; Moerland, 1995; Mayer, 1997; Coffee, 1998; Cernat, 2004) although generally as a one-way approach with Asian and European governance systems converging with 'best practice' Anglo systems primarily in order to attract foreign investment and credit ratings (Aras and Crowther, 2008, p. 440; Jackling and Johl, 2009).

It is evident, however, that exemplary practice has not been demonstrated recently in Anglo systems. Palmer (2009, p. 7) in *The Economist* wrote that a result of the GFC is that regulation has been imposed on Western banking institutions in the United States and UK to increase liquidity and, more generally, as a quid pro quo for the government providing financial support. The risk appetite of countries such as the United States has been blamed and a governance review has been called for (Palmer, 2009, p. 17), with examples of private capital exhibiting more patience and a longer-term focus than publicly listed companies.

The review of the literature highlights the crucial point that a multidisciplinary framework is needed to grasp the various nuances of corporate governance. The framework needs to incorporate both firm-specific, internal perspectives and the broader, market-related macro perspectives, spanning legal, regulatory, sociological, ethical, human resource management, behavioural and strategic aspects. This will extend the analysis from a prescriptive regulatory approach that limits actions, to one that is more descriptive and explains the context of actions and decision-making approaches. This is vital for achieving an in-depth understanding of corporate governance.

Using Young and Thyil's (2008b) model of holistic governance as a framework (see Figure 16.1), this research will investigate views of key actors within the Australian governance system to ascertain what factors they believe affect governance. Comparing the interview data over two time periods will highlight the antecedents and impact of the GFC on governance.

Methodology

In exploring these themes, the chapter uses data from interviews with institutional investors, corporate governance executives and fund managers, conducted in Australia prior to the GFC in 2007, and again in November 2009. The data are used to illustrate any changes in the

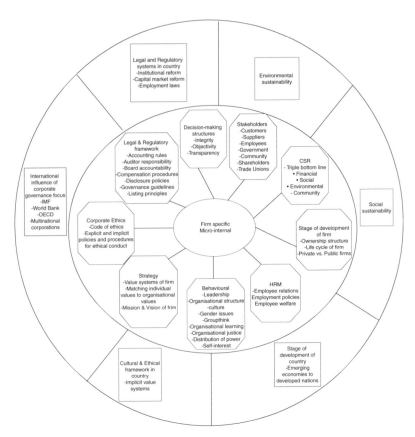

Figure 16.1 Holistic model of governance

focus of the respondents in discussing governance, the drivers and the key features over that time.

The sample for this study consists of two rounds of interviews. In round one, seven interviews were conducted in six Australian corporations in public, private and government enterprises, operating in the brewing, mining, accounting and superannuation industries in 2007. Round two consisted of five interviews, conducted in November 2009, in five Australian organizations, in public and private enterprises and institutional investors operating in banking, financial services and superannuation industries. The choice of the companies was based on convenience sampling. Senior key executives in the organizations were interviewed using a semi-structured interview schedule. Interviewees were first contacted by telephone to explain the research. A plain language information statement and consent form, as approved by the Ethics Committee of La Trobe University and accepted by Deakin University, were then forwarded to them. Each interview lasted for approximately one-and-a-half hours and was audio-taped. The transcriptions were sent to the interviewees for verification. Table 16.1 presents the sample used.

Content analysis was used to identify, code and categorize its primary patterns. The data were coded according to the major themes, namely, the micro and macro factors that impact on governance, as presented in the model (Figure 16.1). Secondary coding was then conducted on the second round of interviews on the basis of the impact of the GFC.

Data Description[1]

Interview data: round one – 2007

Micro factors

Laws and regulation

In Australia, laws and regulation are important but differ in scope from the US system. 'The ASX [Australian Securities Exchange] rules are not as prescriptive as those in the US, which works for the size of the corporate community. The US system really is "box ticking"' (BCS). Company Secretary (MINCS) argued that America is 'not as mature' and agreed that they have become very prescriptive. While GCS spoke of Australia's principles-based approach compared to the US system: 'The flexibility is there as long as you can transparently report as to how or why you have not done what the principles recommend that you should.' And ACG: 'The level of work required to follow the Sarbanes-Oxley (SOX) regime is far greater than would be required in alternative systems. Does it get a better result? I doubt it. An American company will fail again and SOX is not a guarantee that it won't.'

In relation to the effect of laws and regulation on enhanced disclosure, criticisms as to size and scope were made. 'In relation to disclosure, it has got to the stage where board reporting to shareholders is a

Table 16.1 *Sample background*

Schedule	Category of organization	Respondent	Nomenclature	Selected details
Round one	Mining company	Principal Advisor on Environment	MINE	Revenues of US$58,065 million. 20,346 employees in Australia and New Zealand (2008)
Round one	Mining company	Company Secretary	MINCS	Revenues of US$51,918 million. 41,000 employees (2008)
Round one	Superannuation fund	Executive Manager – Investments and Governance	SFI	National industry superannuation fund. Manages over AUD13 billion. Over 650,000 members and 60,000 employees.
Round one	Australian government enterprise	Corporate Secretary	GCS	Revenues of AUD4,959.2 million. 25,042 employees (2008)
Round one	Brewery	Director of Communications	BC	Revenues of AUD4,372.7 million. 7,000 employees (2008)
Round one	Brewery	Company Secretary	BCS	As above
Round one	Accounting and consulting firm	Executive Director AABS – RCIP	ACG	Global consulting company. Offers services in assurance, tax, transactions and advisory services. Reported revenues of US$24.5 billion in 2008. 135,730 employees (2008)
Round two	Bank	Company Secretary	BACS	Banking and financial services. Reported revenues of AUD22.2 billion. 32,000 employees (2008)

Round two	Superannuation fund	Chief Governance Officer	CGO	Superannuation services. Manages over AUD7 billion. Over 208,000 members and over 2,400 employees.
Round two	Bank	Corporate Secretary and Head of Corporate Affairs	HCA	Financial products and services. Reported revenues of AUD212.2 million. 800 employees (2008)
Round two	Research and advisory council	Chief Executive Officer	CEO	Research and advisory services. Over 40 members who represent more than AUD250 billion in superannuation funds under management.
Round two	Financial services	General Counsel and Managing Director	LMD	Financial services. Reported revenues of AUD472.9 million. 1,250 employees (2008)

Source: Annual reports and websites.

joke and annual reports are unreadable' (BCS). Other comments were more favourable, arguing that the 'comply or explain' approach is 'absolutely the way to go with continuous disclosure' (MINCS). BC supported this, and added: 'there is more of a willingness to communicate . . . for instance, we put out a press release to announce that our head of marketing was resigning after thirty-nine years. Do we need to do that? Probably not.'

Behaviour and organizational culture

Behaviour and culture were inextricably linked. Interviewees were unanimous that regulations will not stop bad behaviour; only culture can do that. 'Basically the fault of HIH was that they had a board of *dorks* . . . and no amount of corporate governance rules, regulations and checks and balances could have prevented these problems' (BCS). 'You cannot regulate people's behaviour. You can only put in place structures, and people have to buy into them from a cultural point of view' (MINCS; BC). BC emphasized that 'it is actually living by the rules, or not, and it is not a question of needing more rules. There is often a tendency to generate more rules because that is easier than actually enforcing behaviour.'

Ethics and codes

The necessity for ethical behaviour was stressed by all respondents. 'I have noticed over the years in corporate governance it is just corporate ethics . . . ' (MINCS). 'It all goes back to ethical behaviour. People know what is right and what is wrong' (GCS).

Codes, an important component of governance, still rely on self-regulation and behavioural change. 'You can have codes of conduct, policies and procedures beautifully typed up by the greatest legal minds . . . but, if people won't follow them, or behave differently, then that's not going to keep you out of trouble' (ACG).

Human resource management

Good governance 'comes back to people. If you have the right sort of people in place you are not going to have a problem', and, linking it to ethics and values, the interviewee went on to say, 'if they have the right moral fibre you are just not going to have a problem' (BCS). 'To get the best access to people we need to be doing something different. So, human capital is part of it and increasingly now, with this boom, we can't even get enough people to work for us' (MINE).

Leadership and strategy

Leadership was vital for good governance. 'It comes from the board down, and if the board's not signed-on and doesn't understand it, then you have some issues' (MINCS). 'If the CEO and directors don't believe in the importance of the environment, why would you expect them to say to their staff that it is important?' (SFI).

Decision-making structures

Clearly, decision-making structures are seen as important in governance practices. The key is, who actually 'makes the decisions and who you delegate to . . . It is all about the limits given to the CEO and how the CEO has to behave, make decisions, and [whether] the board gets regular reporting' (MINCS). However, challenges were highlighted, 'openness, honesty and transparency being a key goal [but] it is quite hard for companies to do that. At what level are you open and transparent enough?' (MINE).

Shareholders and stakeholders

'I think the big governance question is you've got to re-look at the relationship between investors in the company and those running the company and make that more meaningful' (BCS). 'And it is not like the institutions are the passive investors that they used to be. There has been a shift of power' (MINCS). Support comes from the superfund interviewee, who states that the 'Principles of Responsible Investing are a driver of change impacting on the role of investors and communicating to companies there is a broader issue than just shareholders' (SFI). Similarly, 'The landscape has actually changed in that companies can no longer act solely for their shareholders with complete disregard for other stakeholders, because of what we now term the social licence to operate' (ACG). But even so, the superfund interviewee argues that 'most members don't even read the financial section of *The Age*[2] and, as long as they are getting their dividends, the vast majority will be happy' (SFI).

Corporate social responsibility

Corporate social responsibility was spoken about in relation to governance. For instance, 'Breaching the social licence to operate in areas such as the use of child labour introduces risks with consumers choosing not to buy products, and fund managers and brokers questioning a company about its supply chain. In managing risk, companies need to understand the changing nature of what is socially acceptable and how it changes' (SFI). Another talked about their 'Governance framework being based on their risk management framework which was expanded eighteen months ago to include non-market risks' (BC).

Stage of development of the firm

Governance has evolved as part of the 'normal evolution of companies and the corporate structure . . . it is just the way corporations and societies develop over time' (BCS). Another added, more holistically, that the major factor impacting on the governance framework is 'company maturity, the size of the company, whether it is global, what it actually does, trust between board and senior management and whether you are regulated' (MINCS). Moreover 'the comply-or-explain is more realistic and more flexible for the different needs of different organizations at different stages of their development such as start-up or mature industry, those looking for takeovers or to be a dominant player' (ACG).

Macro factors

Governance shifts also come from the macro-environment, 'from governments, from shareholders, from country initiatives, from corporate collapses . . . We are part of a global economy' (MINCS). BC confirmed, 'We are part of a global economy' (BC).

Laws and regulation and international governance frameworks

Companies viewed themselves as part of a broad international environment. 'We have lots of US and European and other investors, and we use their global standards in terms of how we report and approach our dealings with them' (BC).

International listings

'Governance has been influenced by what happens globally with multi-national companies with dual or multiple listings' (ACG). SFI adds that the influence has come from companies that have parent companies in the United States because of the SOX compliance regime.

National culture

Linked to societal evolution 'in the early parts of the last century what was regarded as sensible business practices would be regarded now as corruption' (BCS). 'It is looking broader than regulation, and seeing what society is actually allowing' (SFI). 'In the US, people think if it is not in the law then they think they can do it . . . And this is a critical issue in the mindset of people, of how people operate . . . In a culture where it is more principles-based, you will have more people mindful of that, versus a culture where the law is the law' (SFI).

In conclusion in thinking about the holistic framework and its use for organizations one respondent stated that 'it would be better to look at it as a layering approach. When companies begin and start small what are the core elements; then as they grow and become international you think of international issues and then sustainability issues which differ between places' (BCS). Another stated that 'what was interesting is that a lot of companies spend an enormous amount of time worrying about their balance sheet as opposed to other things, like behaviours. It will collapse again' (MINCS).

Thus, even prior to the financial crisis, interviewees were highlighting flaws in the system in areas of behaviours, cultures, transparency and decision-making. It was generally felt that regulation is necessary, especially in maintaining disclosure and transparency and in providing principles against which companies can set up their own policies and procedures and internal structures. However, it was cautioned that, in relation to disclosure, a focus on quantity is problematic, while quality and timeliness were seen to be key. Many spoke of pervasive behaviours setting the climate within which organizations operate. Interestingly, several interviewees actually stated that corporations will still fail and that regulation would not prevent this occurring. The data also highlight that the governance system should reflect the organization's situation, including the society and the company's stage of development, and that too structured a system does not provide the flexibility to adapt to the international,

national and inter-organizational environment. We now turn to the 2009 interviews focusing on the antecedents and effects of the crisis.

Interview data: round two – 2009

Micro factors

Laws and regulation

In the 2009 interviews there was complete agreement on the anticipated increase in regulations due to the GFC. 'More regulation will be introduced' (BAC; CGO). However, there is a significant concern that a lack of enforcement of the regulations that existed pre-GFC is set to continue. As CGO elaborated, 'Although there is a lot of regulation and legislation, there's probably been a lack of enforcement activity as opposed to supervision. It seems to me that, on occasions, they could be more rigorous in enforcing the law and make an example of wrongdoers.'

The view of the respondents was that this lack of enforcement would mean that, despite the additional regulations, such crises would occur again. 'It's just been fortunate, I think, that the vast majority of corporate trustees in Australia have been keen to obey the law and to do the right thing by their members and fund. But that doesn't mean to say that will always be the case, and you'll always have rogue elements and I think that it's only been fortuitous to date that there hasn't been a large number of rogue actions' (CGO).

Behaviour, ethics, codes, people, HRM, leadership, decision-making structures, organizational culture and stakeholders

Interestingly, the data point to the need for a holistic perspective that links behaviour, ethics, codes, people and HRM policies, leadership, decision-making structures, organizational culture and stakeholders. LMD sets out the issue: 'How do you regulate for culturally good behaviour? You can be as prescriptive as you like, but I don't know what that'll necessarily do to make people less dodgy.' Thus, the interview data, in discussing the influences and impact of the GFC, have been presented in a combined format, as opposed to their separate presentation in round one.

The 2009 data clearly underscore the root of the crisis. CGO explained the problem succinctly: 'When there is a clear breach of corporate governance in Australia it is not a case of misinformation or lack of knowledge. It's a conscious decision on the part of an experienced, well-educated, knowledgeable individual who's decided to push the boundaries. It's because there's been a strong one or two individuals who have decided that they were more interested in themselves than meeting their fiduciary obligations to their company and their shareholders.' HCA concurred, stating, 'the cause (of the crisis) just seems to have been greed . . . self-interest and corruption. It wasn't accidental. It was deliberate behaviour.'

Codes and governance structures are useless if they exist only on paper. As CGO observed: 'Superficially it will appear that you've got good corporate governance but the reality might be quite different.' LMD agreed, and added that the Australian listed companies' corporate governance reports look fabulous, but the key is implementation. 'Every listed company will have these fabulous governance principles and all those sorts of things. But, come in and talk to the people and see whether they really know what it means to be a director.' BACS concurred: 'At the end of the day, it is always about people. Governance is not going to stop fraud. Governance is only a system, rules, processes, but it depends on people and the culture within the organization' (BACS).

When respondents were asked if the Productivity Commission's recommendation on shareholder voting on executive remuneration will alter board behaviour, they thought it would certainly have an impact but not necessarily in a positive direction. For instance, BACS felt that 'it would make us think but not necessarily change'. CGO thought it would go a bit further than that. 'It will shake boards up to either be more transparent or be more devious. It depends on the make-up of the boards.'

The data emphasize the requirement of a duty of care in decision-making processes.

'If you're a shareholder in a company and that CEO triples the value of your shares and he walks away with triple his initial salary but everybody comes out a winner – it is okay. But when he diminishes your value by 40 or 30 per cent and then walks away with a $28 million bonus, well, how does that work? He might say, "Well, three years ago that was agreed with directors." Well, I'd be saying, "How did those directors come to that decision? How is that in my best interest?"' (CGO).

More inclusive decision-making processes were also highlighted. HCA explained how his organization managed through the crisis. 'We're the only bank that didn't retrench staff during the GFC. The debate around the board was not to do that because it is not the right thing to do. We will continue to maintain our staff engagement score in the top quartile. They [the staff] will reward that commitment.' He articulates the bond in his company: 'the very strong bond that binds the board, the shareholders, the executive team and the stakeholder. I mean, an incredibly strong bond.'

Macro factors

Laws and regulation

'I don't think corporate Australia said that "we want to be leaders in this, we want to improve corporate governance". I think they've been forced to do it through shareholder activism, through unions and funds' (HCA). LMD was quite critical in stating: 'I think their [ASIC and other regulators'] motivation is "Let's do it and try and shut up the constituencies and media and everyone who thinks we've been asleep on the job." It is very politically driven. The regulations tend to be scatter-gun. The factors that have influenced change over the last twenty years have been problem-based rather than "I just want to make it better because I just want to make it better."' Another spoke of over-emphasis on compliance and explained: 'I think we need to bring our risk management compliance system back a bit. We've gone from four years ago having nothing to the other extreme where it's almost impossible to make a decision because of all these compliance rules, regulations, practices' (CGO).

National culture and stage of development of the country

National culture was seen as being linked to the reforms and systems of the country and its development. 'What's saved Australia [from the GFC] is the fact there's not the same degree of corruption in the Australian business system that there is in many Asian countries. There's not the extreme poverty where people fear they'll become destitute' (CGO).

Australia also seems to have no problems with accepting what they believe to be fundamental governance practices. 'The independence between the Chair and the CEO is clearly understood in Australia.

In the US they grimly hang on to that dual notion. Shareholders are much more empowered in the Australian environment' (HCA).

More generally, respondents had mixed feelings about the nature of proposed changes to executive remuneration and the power of shareholders as a result of the GFC. 'There might just be more talk about it now but I don't think there's been any real change, other than the fact that it's more for PR spin, about the remuneration of directors, and rightly so. So there needs to be more transparency there' (CGO). Others felt no radical governance changes would result although there had been effects at the operational or management level. 'Nothing happened [in Australia] to expose the flaws in governance. The board structures stay the same; independence stays the same. No radical changes to the system. But, at the business level, focus changed, day-to-day; operations changed. There is more focus on liquidity now' (BACS). In contrast, others thought some flaws had indeed been exposed.

'Conflicts of interest in terms of business strategy have been exposed by the crisis; that if you pay somebody for volume turnover, rather than value, there is going to be a problem. Also, regarding the private equity takeover that occurred in Australia before the crisis . . . The financial crisis exposed that most of them were, in fact, ways to load up companies with debt' (CEO).

The 2009 data emphasize the importance of individual behaviours, greed, self-dealing, conflict of interest and lack of honesty as causes of the GFC. In doing so, the interviews point to the importance of transparency, decision-making and organizational culture in ensuring that processes lead to better practices. The crisis appears to have overshadowed the CSR agenda of firms, with none of the interviewees mentioning this aspect. It seems that when the very survival of the firm is at stake, CSR can certainly be expected to take a back seat to financial aspects such as balance sheet reorganizations and structural or board issues. There also appears to be enhanced scrutiny of the 'debt profile and funding' (BACS), in comparison to the focus on profits, while fears were expressed that the GFC will lead to more regulation which, generally, was seen as problematic.

Implications and conclusions

The chapter has highlighted the importance of key variables that impact upon effective governance, namely, laws and regulation, behaviour and organizational culture, ethics and codes of conduct, human resource management and leadership, decision-making structures, and shareholders and stakeholders. While every variable in the governance system should be considered to ensure effectiveness, some variables are more important than others depending on the situation and environment, thus pointing to a contingency approach. The data highlight that the root causes of the GFC are greedy and unethical individuals in senior positions. And even though, pre-crisis, many spoke of governance's links to CSR and sustainability agendas, after the crisis the focus was on behaviours, leadership and decision-making.

Pointing to the importance of cultural, class, power and behavioural considerations, Sonnenfeld (2002, p. 109) asked, if following good governance regulatory recipes doesn't produce good boards, what does? He added: 'The key isn't structural, it's social. What distinguishes exemplary boards is that they are robust, effective social systems' with members who have mutual respect, which leads to a virtuous cycle of respect, trust and candour. Nadler (2004, p. 104) concurred, observing that better governance lies in the working relationships between boards and managers, and in the social dynamics of board interaction. The comments of HCA regarding the bond between his company's board members, and the respect mentioned by LMD regarding her board, are examples of this.

Calls for enhanced shareholder voting rights and limits to executive remuneration were spoken of and seen as a way of controlling behaviours. Indeed, the relatively good position of Australia during the GFC was seen to be due to the use of shareholder power in making board decision-making more transparent. In understanding that the board may often act as an agent in its own right, it is important to emphasize cognition and decision-making and illuminate our understanding of what happens inside the boardroom. Martin (2006, p. 21) observed that 'the only good reason for joining a board is to serve the public by protecting capital providers from the worst motives of managers'. He continued: 'Only directors who view themselves primarily as public servants, and are seen by the public that way, are free of the self-interest that feeds the problem.' As Eliot Spitzer, the New York State Attorney-General, observed in his interview with O'Brien (2004, p. 74), '[in the United States] we are yet to see boards going back to the managers and firing them for not managing costs aggressively'. Too often we witness boards acting in their own interests – as agents not of shareholders but of themselves. A reliance on agency theory and its propositions around internal structures, the use of options to align interests, and market controls have all been found to be inadequate in the current financial crisis. Indeed it is evident that the overemphasis on executive compensation schemes and the use of options has actually exacerbated the problems.

The 2007 data correctly predicted that regulations would not prevent companies from failing yet again, while the 2009 data conveyed that the companies now foresee (although negatively) more stringent regulations. Calls for the enforcement of regulation, rather than more regulation, were emphasized here. Similarly, flaws in governance processes have also been exposed. This may mean drawing on relationship-based systems and their focus on stakeholder priorities and inclusion, which may again bring CSR activities to the fore. Responsible business practices are even more important now, and both the 2007 and 2009 data reveal that ethical behaviour is seen as vital despite the extent of regulations.

The data also point out that there is a solution. Among the variables examined, the ethical behaviour of the board appears to have the strongest impact in pre-empting a crisis. By setting a culture of ethics, and ensuring a top-down percolation of that culture, it is possible to have a self-managed, self-regulated system which can act as a 'system of barriers' for individual wrongdoing. LMD summed up the crucial points with reference to her organization: 'no matter how much money you write for this organization, if you behave badly you will be sacked. As a group [the board] it is enforced.' The question then arises as to how such behaviour can be inculcated into the board. LMD explained: 'This organization is owned by staff members and I am an owner too. It means we don't think about the share price in an instantaneous way; we don't think about our next bonus; my vision for the success of the company is absolutely long-term. During the crisis when other companies were fretful, we [the board] met daily with the CFO who owns a big slab of the company as well and went through our capital adequacy, our liquidity and all those things.'

This can require radical steps, such as Home Depot's Chairman Bernie Marcus' decision not to serve on a board where dissent was discouraged. Only after passionate disagreements had been voiced would a decision be taken together as a group (Sonnenfeld, 2002). In regard to decision-making and access to information, Klapmeier (2007, p. 23) contended: 'You can't ask a question of somebody who doesn't understand the question and make a decision based upon their answer.' Sonnenfeld (2002) argued that it is the responsibility of the board to insist that it receives adequate information, but adds that it is amazing how often this does not happen. As Lorsch and Clark (2008, p. 108) argued: 'The directors must not only be intelligent, well-informed and highly interactive, but must also push management to address the company's future.' Considering the additional regulations anticipated as a result of the GFC, the fact that interview data affirm that this sort of apathy continues to exist raises concerns. Too often investors, including institutional investors, do not use the power and legislative capabilities already vested in them to bring about more discussion, force explanations of deviations and vote against directors' and managers' motions. Murray (2006) and Nicholson *et al.* (2004), in explaining board connections and influences on decision-making, use a political analysis of the influence wielded by the corporate elite to discuss how members of the ruling classes maintain power in the corporate sector. In this vein, institutional investors being required to divulge their voting patterns could bring about improvements and transparency in decision-making. Greater consideration of power, leadership, culture, decision-making and information-use in the board room, alongside the acceptance, or even encouragement, of greater investor involvement, would then produce better results than simply more regulation.

The data unequivocally point to the need for a holistic, multi-disciplinary approach, integrating multiple lenses and perspectives in understanding corporate governance practices. This would enable corporations and the economy to mitigate and to better manage a crisis. In this way, a balance between compliance and behavioural approaches is important – regulation to ensure timely and valid disclosure and good structures, alongside a focus on ethics, culture, leadership, power and human resource practices to ensure organizational objectives are met in an ethical manner. The use of a purely structural approach is limited, and the inclusion of processes to ensure there is a fit between the internal and external environment, shareholder and stakeholder needs and organizational purpose would bring about more effective governance. A better understanding of the influences on decision-making, of the culture of the boardroom, of the networks and structures of the decision-makers and elites, would all contribute to a deeper and richer model of governance.

Notes

1 A report of some of the 2007 Australian data was published in Young and Thyil (2008a), and the UK data (Young and Thyil, 2009) in 2009. For this chapter, the data were recoded in terms of the model (see Young and Thyil, 2008b).
2 A broadsheet national newspaper.

References

Adams, R. and Ferreira, D. 2007. 'A theory of friendly boards', *Journal of Finance* 62 (1): 217–49.
Aras, G. and Crowther, D. 2008. 'Governance and sustainability: an investigation into the relationship between corporate governance and corporate sustainability', *Governance and Sustainability* 46 (3): 433–48.
Bertrand, M., Mehta, P. and Mullainathan, S. 2002. 'Ferreting out tunnelling: an application to Indian business groups', *Quarterly Journal of Economics* 117: 121–48.
Brennan, N. B. and Solomon, J. 2008. 'Corporate governance, accountability and mechanisms of accountability: an overview', *Accounting, Auditing & Accountability Journal* 2 (7): 885–906.
Cernat, L. 2004. 'The emerging European corporate governance model: Anglo-Saxon, continental, or still the century of diversity?', *Journal of European Public Policy* 11 (1): 147–66.
Clarke, T. 2007. *International Corporate Governance: A Comparative Approach*. London: Routledge.
    2009. 'Globalisation of governance', in Young, S. (ed.), *Contemporary Issues in International Corporate Governance*. Melbourne: Tilde University Press, pp. 207–24.
Coffee, J. C. 1998. *'The future as history: prospects for global convergence in corporate governance and its implications'*, Working Paper No. 144. The Centre for Law and Economics Studies: Columbia University School of Law.
Cutting, B. A. and Kouzmin, A. 2000. 'The emerging patterns of power in corporate governance: back to the future in improving corporate decision-making', *Journal of Managerial Psychology* 15 (6): 477–507.
    2001. 'Formulating metaphysics of governance: explaining the dynamics of governance using a new JEWAL synthesis framework', *Journal of Management Development* 20 (6): 526–64.
    2002. 'Evaluating corporate board culture and decision-making', *Corporate Governance* 2 (2): 27–45.
Dallas, G. 2004. *Governance and Risk: An Analytical Handbook for Investors, Managers, Directors and Stakeholders*. New York: McGraw-Hill.

Deakin, S., Hobbs, R., Konzelmann, S. and Wilkinson, F. 2002. 'Partnership, ownership and control: the impact of governance on employment relations', *Employee Relations* 24 (3): 355–82.

Eisenhardt, K. 1989. 'Agency theory: an assessment and review', *Academy of Management Review* 14 (1): 57–74.

Fama, E. and Jensen, M. 1983. 'Separation of ownership and control', *Journal of Law and Economics* 26: 301–25.

Francis, R. and Armstrong, A. 2003. 'Ethics as a risk management strategy: the Australian experience', *Journal of Business Ethics* 45 (4): 375.

Franks, J. and Mayer, C. 2005. 'Corporate ownership and control in the U.K., Germany, and France', in Chew, D. and Gillan, S. (eds.), *Corporate Governance at the Crossroads: A Book of Readings*. New York: McGraw-Hill/Irwin, pp. 360–75.

Gabrielsson, J., Huse, M. and Minchilli, A. 2007. 'Understanding the leadership role of the board chairperson through a team production approach', *International Journal of Leadership Studies* 3 (1): 21–39.

Gillan, S. L. 2006. 'Recent developments in corporate governance: an overview', *Journal of Corporate Finance* 12: 381–402.

Handy, C. 1978. *Gods of Management*. Sydney: Random House.

Huse, M. 2007. *Boards, Governance and Value Creation: The Human Side of Corporate Governance*. Cambridge University Press.

Jackling, B. and Johl, S. 2009. 'Board structure and firm performance: evidence from India's top companies', *Corporate Governance: An International Review* 14 (4): 492–509.

Jensen, M. 2001. 'Value maximization, stakeholder theory and the corporate objective function', in Chew, D. and Gillan, S. (eds.), *Corporate Governance at the Crossroads: A Book of Readings*. New York: McGraw-Hill/Irwin, pp. 7–20.

Jensen, M. and Meckling, W. 1976. 'Theory of the firm: managerial behaviour, agency costs and ownership structure', *Journal of Financial Economics* 3: 305–60.

Kaufman, A. and Englander, E. 2005. 'A team production model of corporate governance', *Academy of Management Executive* 19 (3): 9–22.

Khanna, T. and Palepu, K. 1999. 'Emerging market business groups, foreign investors, and corporate governance', *NBER Working Paper No. 6955*. Cambridge, MA: National Bureau of Economic Research, Inc.

    2000. 'Is group affiliation profitable in emerging markets? An analysis of diversified Indian business groups', *Journal of Finance* 55: 867–91.

Klapmeier, A. 2007. 'Passion', *Harvard Business Review* 85 (1): 22–3.

Lagan, A. 2006. 'Ethics at work', *Intheblack*, March, 76 (2): 72–4.

Leung, P. and Cooper, B. 2003. 'The mad hatter's corporate tea party', *Managerial Auditing Journal* 18 (6/7): 505–16.

Lines, V. L. 2004. 'Corporate reputation in Asia: looking beyond bottom-line performance', *Journal of Communication Management* 8 (3): 233–45.

Lorsch, J. W. and Clark, R. C. 2008. 'Leading from the boardroom', *Harvard Business Review* 86 (4): 104–11.

Lynall, M. D., Golden, B. R. and Hillman, A. J. 2003. 'Board composition from adolescence to maturity: a multi-theoretic view', *Academy of Management Review* 28 (3): 416–21.

Martin, R. 2006. 'Directing for all the wrong reasons', *Harvard Business Review* 84 (6): 20–1.

Mayer, C. 1997. 'Corporate governance, competition and performance', *Journal of Law and Society* 24: 152–76.

Moerland, P. W. 1995. 'Alternative disciplinary mechanisms in different corporate systems', *Journal of Economic Behaviour and Organization* 26 (1): 17–34.

Murray, G. 2006. *Capitalist Networks and Social Power in Australia and New Zealand*. Aldershot: Ashgate.

Nadler, D. A. 2004. 'Building better boards', *Harvard Business Review* 82 (5): 102–11.

Nicholson, G. J., Alexander, M. and Kiel, G. C. 2004. 'Defining the social capital of the board of directors: an exploratory study', *Journal of the Australian and New Zealand Academy of Management* 10 (1): 54–72.

North, D. 1990. *Institutions, Institutional Change, and Economic Performance*. Cambridge University Press.

O'Brien, L. 2004. 'How to restore the fiduciary relationship: an interview with Eliot Spitzer', *Harvard Business Review* 82 (5): 70–7.

Palmer, A. 2009. 'A special report on international banking', *The Economist*, 16–22 May, pp. 3–20.

Pfeffer, J. 1992. *Managing with Power*. Boston: Harvard Business School Press.

Sharma, A. 1997. 'Professional as agent: knowledge asymmetry in agency exchange', *Academy of Management Review* 22 (3): 758–98.

Solomon, J. 2009. 'The transformation of socially responsible investment', in Young, S. (ed.), *Contemporary Issues in International Corporate Governance*. Melbourne: Tilde University Press, pp. 131–40.

Sonnenfeld, J. 2002. 'What makes great boards great', *Harvard Business Review* 80 (9): 106–13.

Sundaramurthy, C. and Lewis, M. 2003. 'Controls and collaboration: paradoxes of governance', *Academy of Management Review* 28 (3): 397–415.

Useem, M. 2006. 'How well-run boards make decisions', *Harvard Business Review* 84 (11): 130–8.

van Ees, H., Gabrielsson, J. and Huse, M. 2009. 'Toward a behavioural theory of boards and corporate governance', *Corporate Governance: An International Review* 17 (3): 307–19.

Wood, G. 2002. 'A partnership model of corporate ethics', *Journal of Business Ethics* 40 (1): 61–73.

2005. 'The relevance to international mergers of the ethical perspectives of participants', *Corporate Governance* 5 (5): 39–50.

Wood, G. and Callaghan, M. 2003. 'Communicating the ethos of codes of ethics in corporate Australia, 1995–2001: whose rights, whose responsibilities?', *Employee Responsibilities and Rights Journal* December, 15 (4): 209–21.

Young, S. (ed.) 2009. *Contemporary Issues in International Corporate Governance*. Melbourne: Tilde University Press.

Young, S. and Thyil, V. 2008a. 'Principles-based Anglo governance system is not a science but an art', *Corporate Ownership and Control* 6 (1) Fall: 127–37.

2008b. 'A holistic model of corporate governance: a new research framework', *Corporate Governance* 8 (1): 94–108.

2009. 'UK governance at the time of the financial crisis: calls for change', *Corporate Ownership and Control* 6 (4) Summer: 568–74.

Zattoni, A., Pedersen, T. and Kumar, V. 2009. 'The performance of group-affiliated firms during institutional transition: a longitudinal study of Indian firms', *Corporate Governance: An International Review* 17 (4): 510–23.

Zhang, P., Voordeckers, W., Gabrielsson, J. and Huse, M. 2009. 'From boards as value assemblers to value creators', in Young, S. (ed.), *Contemporary Issues in International Corporate Governance*. Melbourne: Tilde University Press, ch. 3.

Index

Note: the following abbreviations have been used: *n* – note; *f* – figure. The index has been arranged in word-by-word order.